THE BOOK AROUND IMMANUEL:
STYLE AND STRUCTURE IN ISAIAH 2–12

BIBLICAL AND JUDAIC STUDIES FROM THE UNIVERSITY OF CALIFORNIA, SAN DIEGO

Volume 4

edited by
William Henry Propp

Previously published in the series:

1. *The Hebrew Bible and Its Interpreters*, edited by William Henry Propp, Baruch Halpern, and David Noel Freedman (1990).

2. *Studies in Hebrew and Aramaic Orthography*, by David Noel Freedman, A. Dean Forbes, and Francis I. Andersen (1992).

3. *Isaiah 46, 47, and 48: A New Literary-Critical Reading*, by Chris Franke (1994).

THE BOOK AROUND IMMANUEL:
STYLE AND STRUCTURE IN ISAIAH 2–12

by
Andrew H. Bartelt

EISENBRAUNS
Winona Lake, Indiana
1996

Published for Biblical and Judaic Studies
The University of California, San Diego

by

Eisenbrauns
Winona Lake, Indiana

Library of Congress Cataloging in Publication Data

Bartelt, Andrew H., 1949–
    The book around Immanuel : style and structure in Isaiah 2–12 / by
Andrew H. Bartelt.
        p.   cm. — (Biblical and Judaic studies ; v. 4)
    Includes bibliographical references and index.
    ISBN 1-57506-006-X (alk. paper)
    1. Bible. O.T. Isaiah II–XII—Criticism, interpretation, etc.
2. Bible. O.T. Isaiah II–XII—Language, style.   3. Rhetoric in the
Bible.   I. Title.   II. Series.
BS1515.2.B36   1996
224′.106—dc20
                                                              96-8275
                                                              CIP

The paper used in this publication meets the minimum requirements of the American
National Standard for Information Sciences—Permanence of Paper for Printed Library
Materials, ANSI Z39.48-1984.♾™

CONTENTS

Preface

The origin of this work lies at the intersection of two lines of current research. A resurgence of interest in biblical Hebrew poetry has advanced the understanding of the very definition of poetry, its style and structure, and the way it functions in literature and rhetoric. Second, a new wave of literary criticism has fueled fresh thinking and fostered some rethinking concerning the difficult questions of the composition of prophetic books, especially the book of Isaiah. The formation of a consultation within the program of the annual meeting of the Society of Biblical Literature and its maturing into a seminar dealing with the "Formation of the Book of Isaiah" reflects this renewed interest, and I am grateful for the insights gained through my association with this group. Likewise, those involved with the Biblical Hebrew Poetry section have encouraged and generated fresh approaches to ancient problems. The previous volume (Franke 1994) in this series by the current chair of that section represents a significant contribution toward understanding a part of the book of Isaiah by employing helpful insights gained from poetic and literary analysis. The present study follows in a similar vein.

It is essentially toward the methodological issues of literary criticism, especially in the areas of structural analysis, poetic stylistics, and what is generally called "rhetorical criticism" that this research seeks to make a contribution. While various contemporary and contiguous issues are addressed, the primary thesis is simple and straightforward. It asserts that the *length* of poetic units—at levels both small and large—is a factor to be taken seriously in stylistic and structural analysis.

The influence of David Noel Freedman will be immediately apparent in tables of syllable, stress, and word counts, and a major focus of this research is the methodology of measuring length. The issues are complex, and the danger of manipulating the data to conform to one's method is ever present. In recognition of this concern and in response to this potential abuse, the method that is here developed and tested is multifaceted and deliberate, with the explicit purpose of being careful and reasonable. Above all, I have sought by this method, simply to be forthright in demonstrating and discussing a rationale for every decision that has been made.

After establishing a method that is, I hope, neither arbitrary nor manipulative, I have proceeded to apply this method of measuring to a corpus that is both small enough to be manageable and large enough to be used to test the theory against an extended literary section. The method has proven to be helpful at all levels of literary analysis, from bicolon to strophe and stanza to larger literary pieces. While the results for the entire corpus are striking, it must be remembered that the process of discovering a scheme for the whole was conducted at the level of each individual part, without imposing a structural plan upon the overall data. The conclusions were developed piece by piece, with careful and cautious decisions reached independently for each smaller unit along the way.

Having demonstrated that the length of literary units is, indeed, a factor that is helpful in understanding the composition of a text, I attempt to show that this method can also aid in the interpretation of a text. The striking correspondences in length between small subunits and even between large blocks of material suggest the deliberate work of the author or redactor who probably intended to communicate meaning through the connections among different parts of a text. For example, at the levels of colon, verse, stanza, and strophe, countless instances of relationships in poetic structure give new appreciation for both the art of the poetry and the meaning conveyed.

On a larger level, the correspondence between Isa 5:8–25 and 9:7[1]–10:4 has provided new insight not only into the compositional integrity of these difficult texts but also into their meaning as commentary on the narrative enclosed between them. The connection between the Song of the Vineyard designated as a song of my 'friend' (דוד) in Isa 5:1–7 and the oracle of the Davidic (דוד) child in 8:23b–9:6 is another example of a fresh interpretation derived from a consideration of length. The isolation of the smaller unit 8:19–23a and its relation to 5:26–30 have shed new light on the boundaries of units and defined the "Book of Immanuel" more precisely as 6:1–8:18. The final conclusion, that this "Book of Immanuel" lies in the center of a grand inclusio, demonstrates a massive but meticulous sense of symmetry, even turning upon the very name of the child. This gives striking testimony to the sophistication built into the composition of even larger literary pieces.

In addition to this major premise, another goal of mine has been to clarify various methodological issues in Hebrew poetry and to advance the state of the art in poetic analysis. For example, I have proposed a method that addresses the difficult problems of lineation and versification. Atten-

---

1. English = 9:8. Verse numbers throughout this volume refer to the Hebrew Text. The major difference in versification between the two texts occurs in 8:23 (= 9:1 in English translations). All references to Isaiah 9 will be one verse higher in the English versions.

tion has been given to the careful crafting of intricate verse structures. Other related theories have been tested, such as the helpfulness of prose particle counts as an aid in distinguishing poetry from prose and the nature and definition of what has been dubbed "prophetic rhetoric" as a *tertium quid* along that continuum.

While modified slightly for inclusion in this series, this work is essentially that of my dissertation, defended in 1990, under David Noel Freedman at the University of Michigan. Readers should understand that the gap between completion and publication has not been filled with an extensive updated bibliography or a hurried attempt to interact comprehensively with more recent literature, although occasional references are made in the introductory chapter.

It is a pleasurable custom to take this opportunity to express personal appreciation to some of the many without whose encouragement and support this project would not have seen completion: to those who first encouraged me in the study of the Hebrew Scriptures: Greg K. Smith, John Ribar, Henry St. John Hart, and Ronald Clements, with whom I first read much of Isaiah; to those, especially at the University of Michigan, who broadened my horizons to include the larger Semitic world of languages and literature: Drs. George Mendenhall, Charles Krahmalkov, Piotr Michalowski, and David Noel Freedman.

Special appreciation is due Drs. Peter Machinist, Gernot Windfuhr, and Ralph Williams for their kind support and helpful expertise in serving as readers of the original thesis. To my advisor, Dr. David Noel Freedman, I express my sincere gratitude for his tireless energy, constantly flowing wellspring of creative ideas, meticulous care and attention to detail, and his generous and gracious gifts of time and concern. Always seasoned with good humor, his criticism and guidance have been profound, and his wisdom is well-woven into the fabric of this work.

I would also thank Concordia Seminary for supporting this project through study and sabbatical leaves as well as financial assistance. My colleagues have all been most encouraging, and I would especially acknowledge Horace D. Hummel, Paul R. Raabe, Paul L. Schrieber, and James W. Voelz. Special thanks are due to Charles M. Henrickson and Paul G. Wenz for their keen sight and insight in editorial assistance.

Those responsible for the publication of this work deserve special appreciation. As editor of this series, William H. C. Propp has been generous with his counsel and patient in his encouragement. James Eisenbraun and his staff have been extremely cordial and helpful in applying their expertise in dealing with some very difficult and technical material.

Above all, I would thank my family for patience and longsuffering that could rival that of the biblical saints: my father, who modeled for me a love for the study of Scripture; my mother, who instilled a love and appreciation for the art and beauty of language; and, more than one can ever say, my dear wife, Lucy, who, along with Marybeth, Allison, and Amy, has had to share far too much time with this project but who has always been a reminder of the joy of the bridegroom and the bride.

Abbreviations

BDB   F. Brown, S. R. Driver, and C. A. Briggs, *Hebrew and English Lexicon of the Old Testament*

BHS   *Biblia Hebraica Stuttgartensia*

CA   *Codex Aleppo*

CL   *Codex Leningradensis*

LXX   Septuagint

MT   Masoretic Text

Chapter 1

Introduction:
Focus and Method

Background Studies and Issues

This study is borne by the confluence of two streams of recent research: the study of Hebrew poetry, especially studies of poetic stylistics, and the type of literary investigation that has come to be called rhetorical criticism.

The watershed for the latter can be traced to James Muilenburg's challenge in 1969, although he was building on and rallying forces already on the rise. The resurgence of studies in Hebrew poetry finds upstream markers in the works of F. M. Cross and D. N. Freedman (1950), but the high-water mark remains the work of Robert Lowth, whose "Lectures on the Sacred Poetry of the Hebrews" in 1753 set forth the basic principles and definitions that would dominate the study of poetry in the Hebrew Bible until the contemporary era.

That these rising waters should converge on the study of the Hebrew prophets seems only natural. Prophetic oracles, however one may wish to define and determine poetry, are generally considered to be poetic. And thus the literary repositories of individual oracles that have come to us in the Hebrew Bible as the Latter Prophets are likely to display poetic features. Contemporary studies and even major commentaries (for example, Andersen and Freedman on Hosea [1980] and Amos [1989]) have begun to apply insights gained from both fields to prophetic literature, which has been designated both prophetic poetry and prophetic rhetoric.

Many of Muilenburg's own examples come from the prophetic corpus; his work on Isaiah 40–66 (1956) antedated and, to a great degree, led to his watershed challenge in 1969. Lowth's own work (1753: lectures 18–21) included far-ranging discussion of the prophetic materials, and he followed his landmark lectures by applying theory to practice in his "new translation" with notes and commentary specifically on the book of Isaiah (1778).

Studies in Hebrew Poetry

The influence of Lowth on studies in Hebrew poetry today may seem to lie more in the ways his thesis has met with challenge and change than

1

in the affirmation of his theories. Nevertheless, his twofold description of Hebrew poetry based on *parallelismus membrorum* and meter remains fundamental to the discussion. Major works of current importance have taken issue with one or the other of Lowth's categories, affirming, denying, or refining them.

In a major challenge to traditional thinking, for example, J. Kugel (1981) rejects Lowth's twofold description by removing meter from consideration and focusing on parallelism, which he defines broadly[1]—but in his opinion more precisely—as simply "A, and what's more, B." Although he admits that this basic binary relationship of poetic lines "can work in a way comparable to meter" (p. 200) through the shaping and regularity of bicola, his thesis asserts that parallelism, and only parallelism, forms the "idea"[2] of biblical poetry.

The recent work of S. Geller (1979), E. Greenstein (1982), and especially A. Berlin (1979, 1985) has also focused on the category of parallelism. Their contribution to Lowth's description is a more helpful one; parallelism is not redefined too broadly but instead refined beyond the oversimplified system that Lowth devised. To be sure, Lowth's threefold classification of synonymous, antithetical, and synthetic parallelism has not stood up well to contemporary criticism. All three categories have been challenged, and the last has been virtually dismissed as being far too vague and general.

However, these recent studies have expanded and enhanced the understanding of parallelism to include not only semantic relationships but also grammatical, lexical, and even morphological linkages. Semantic parallelism has also been observed beneath the level of surface structure to a correspondence between constituents at a deeper structural level as well.

Concerning Lowth's other major categories, theories about meter continue to play a significant role in discussions of Hebrew poetry, although approaches cover a wide spectrum of methodological issues. In his study of early Hebrew metrics, for example, D. Stuart (1976) not only affirms the existence of meter but also accents the importance of careful metrical analysis in the study of Hebrew poetry.

As he surveys previous research into Hebrew metrics, however, Stuart (1976: 1) astutely notes the limitations imposed by the data, namely, that we have little knowledge of actual Hebrew phonetics and that we are simply dependent on the accentual systems of the Masoretes. Thus he criti-

---

1. Geller's criticism (1982) is apt, namely, that Kugel's definition is simply too broad to be helpful.

2. His terminology is careful and deliberate, since he rejects the category of "poetry" as a distinct term (see below, p. 3).

cizes the various "traditional approaches" in noting Gottwald's comment, "meter may be reduced to nothing more than a tallying of accents provided by the Masoretes" (Gottwald 1962: 835, cited by Stuart 1976: 41 n. 6). Nevertheless, the importance of meter to a definition of poetry continues to form the basis of further study (for example, the work of J. Kurylowicz [1972], D. Christensen [1984, 1985a], and the continuing work of Cross and Freedman).

While the debate has often focused on which of Lowth's two factors, parallelism or meter, is the more significant (even to the exclusion of the other, for example, Kugel), some have rejected both in favor of new categories entirely. T. Collins (1978) has developed a grammatical approach, based on a typology of line-forms, in which he simply catalogs poetic lines according to syntactical relationships (for example, whether the line [= bicolon] contains one or two sentences and if two, to what degree the second matches the constituents of the first).

M. O'Connor (1980: 29ff.) carefully and severely criticizes what he has dubbed the "Standard Description" of Hebrew poetry inherited from Lowth, and instead of either meter or parallelism, he has suggested a system of syntactic constraints that governs the poetic line. Based on his description of a selected corpus of Hebrew poetry, he has observed that the shape of the line (= colon) is bound by a limited number of "clause predicators" (0–3), grammatical "constituents" (1–4), and individual word "units" (2–5).

At the heart of the issue is the very definition of poetry. If the traditional categories and definitions are to be found wanting, how is poetry to be described, not to mention defined? And those who operate with and affirm either meter or parallelism do not necessarily confirm the distinctive application of these categories to poetry. The system of metric scansion employed by D. Christensen (see, for example, 1985a, 1991), for example, is applied to poetry and prose alike. In his study of parallelism, Kugel (1981: 94) has noted that this phenomenon is also a feature of prose, and since meter has been rejected as a component of poetry, he has suggested that the clear distinction between poetry and prose is artificial: "No great service is rendered here by the concept of biblical poetry."

Some have appealed to other formal and stylistic factors that define poetry. Cross (for example, Cross 1983) continues to work with the basic distinctions of a "short" (*breve*) and "long" (*longum*) colon. L. Alonso-Schökel (1963, 1988) and W. G. E. Watson (1986) have produced virtual catalogs of stylistic features. R. Alter (1981, 1985) has discussed with great insight into literary style the "art" of both biblical narrative and poetry. Through analysis of the so-called prose particle counts, Freedman (1977 = 1980: 2ff.)

has suggested a quantitative, "mechanical test" based on the percentage of such particles (see also Andersen and Forbes 1983). In a careful critique and detailed study, W. T. W. Cloete (1989a) proposes, as a starting point, that "the proper opposite of prose is *verse*, for which unfortunately the word *poetry* is often used as a synonym" (p. 2), and he calls attention to the basic issues of versification and lineation.

All of these concerns and their concomitant conclusions have important elements of validity. In fact, the major flaw in much previous discussion is that both definition and description of poetry are often limited to and focused on only the one factor that each scholar deems essential. For example, in restricting the essence of "poetry" (if one dare use the term) to parallelism, Kugel is destined to blur any further distinctions between poetry and prose. As Berlin (1985: 5) has pointed out, "it is not parallelism *per se*, but the predominance of parallelism, combined with terseness, which marks poetic expression of the Bible."

"Terseness," of course, begs for clear definition, but Berlin is certainly right that some measurement of length is an important factor. Although Kugel, O'Connor, and Pardee (1981) adamantly reject meter as a feature of Hebrew poetry, they have not provided a satisfactory replacement. Although it hardly seems appropriate to describe O'Connor's system as an "over-simplification" (Cloete 1989a: 208, and hinted at by Geller 1982), the fact remains that his system of syntactic constraints, though not incorrect as a description of the poetic line, is, in the end, simply another way of describing one of the components of poetry. And as Geller (1982: 70) has pointed out, "O'Connor's 'constriction' is, despite his protests, a kind of simple meter." Thus Cloete (1989a: 222), who agrees that O'Connor's numerical levels of measurement are a kind of meter, has refined O'Connor's method by the addition of stress accents.

The issue of metrics is difficult, and there is no doubt that early attempts left much to be desired. In his now classic work, G. B. Gray (1915) expanded the two basic categories of Lowth but presented no new theory of Hebrew meter:

> His views throughout are characterized by a cautious pragmatism: he affirms the existence of metrical principles in Hebrew poetry, but questions whether enough is yet known to substantiate the "regular symmetrical forms" which other scholars claim to have identified in the poetry of the Old Testament (Freedman 1972c: viii).

Part of the basic problem of metrical analysis is determining what to count and how to count it. The so-called "traditional" approach, developed by J. Ley (1875, 1886), K. Budde (1882, 1922), and further refined by

E. Sievers (1901, 1904), counts every accented word, or "content word," although differences occur in the handling of monosyllabics. H. Kosmala (1964, 1966) suggested simply counting word units. More recently, J. Kurylowicz (1972, 1975, followed by Cooper 1976) has devised a system of "syntactic-accentual" units, rather than individual words, based on the distinction within the Masoretic system between *accentus dominus* and *accentus servus*. The difficulty, however, is that this method results in a very small number of accents, which may not allow for larger differences in line length. Christensen has also worked on the basis of the Masoretic disjunctive accents and, in addition, he has revived the system of counting "morae," which recognize the distinction between long and short vowels. This method, however, has been criticized because it "depends entirely upon the Masoretic vocalization of the text" and therefore "hardly reflects the realities of vowel quantity in classical Biblical Hebrew" (Freedman 1986: 413–14).

Stuart's work on Hebrew metrics (1976) takes into consideration the problems of textual criticism and admits that "textual emendation may be required, sometimes on a major scale" (p. 21). Building on the work of Cross and Freedman, his work includes a careful study of historical grammar and phonetics on the basis of which he defends a certain amount of reconstruction of the Masoretic vocalization. Although Stuart is careful and cautious about indiscriminate emendation, large amounts of reconstruction of the text itself have opened his method to the criticism that he no longer describes the text but rather what he wishes to describe. "In conclusion, it is clearly dangerous to found a metrical theory upon an emended-restored text, and unfortunately, this is precisely the pitfall in which the Cross-Stuart approach to meter falls. It has taken the text and made it fit their theory" (Longman 1982: 236).

Building on the same historical study of Hebrew poetry as Cross and Stuart, Freedman (1977) has suggested and practiced a system of syllable counting, although "he is open to virtually any approach to Hebrew meter" (Longman 1982: 236).[3] His method should be distinguished from Cross and Stuart's in that he takes a much more conservative approach to the text and eschews emendation *metri causa* (for example, Freedman 1987a: 21).

---

3. Freedman's own comments (1987a: 20) are quite to the point: "How to count . . . is almost immaterial. . . . I steer a middle course between counting words, which will work but may be a little too crude, and counting morae, which may be more precise but seems overly fussy and produces more detailed information than is necessary or desirable. But so long as a system is applied consistently, it should work reasonably well and tell us what we want to know—namely, how long a line, a stanza, or a poem is."

Cloete (1989a) has called for more careful terminology, distinguishing meter, which is defined as an abstract, theoretical scheme, from rhythm, which describes the actual patterns of verse (1989a: 10–11; 1989b: 44–45). He concludes (1989a: 223) that Hebrew verse is, indeed, rhythmically structured, and his addition of the constraint of 1–4 stresses per colon to the syntactic measurements of O'Connor provides a "colometric system" that "could be regarded as a *component* of metre" (emphasis his). Unfortunately, by his own admission, the rest of a versification system lies beyond the scope of his study, and "the question whether the whole of that system is metrical cannot be answered here" (1989a: 223).

Assuming that Cloete's technical distinction between meter and rhythm is useful, he has, in my opinion, focused on the wrong term. Rhythm, as measured by stress accents, is certainly a more helpful measurement of line length than O'Connor's syntactic constraints or, as Kugel would assert, no meter at all. But the difficulties and imprecision in counting stresses have already been noted, especially if the goal is the description of the "actual patterns of verse." In view of the lack of knowledge in the areas of phonetics and actual pronunciation of a rhythmical accentual system, a more abstract, theoretical (but demonstrably functional and normative) scheme would prove more helpful still.

Nevertheless, Cloete (1989a: 47) has confirmed the need for some numerical measurement of length that counts something other than syntactic units. But because such units can range from one short word to several long words, measurements can disguise significant differences in the number of accents or syllables or simply in the time needed to speak or read the syntactic units. However, Cloete has also rejected all systems of measurement (including stress accents) as secondary to (that is, based on) a system of lineation already determined according to syntax, which he affirms as the primary factor in versification.[4] In the end, therefore, he has simply added another element to a system of describing lines already lineated, either arbitrarily or by means of the descriptive system itself.

Cloete has, however, raised the important issue of lineation, even if he stops short of breaking out of the circularity of the need both to define and to describe the line somewhat at the same time. Thus, in spite of his own

---

4. "The conclusion is reached, then, that all the non-syntactical systems presently applied to Hebrew verse are unable to provide a valid and reliable delimitation of cola. With the partial exception of the approach through parallelism, this is so because the systems are all descriptions of the colometric system itself" (Cloete 1989a: 47). He clearly sees the circularity involved. However, the same circle can be applied to a system that declares syntax as the control on lineation, based on lines that have been syntactically lineated.

objective to develop a system of lineation (colometry), he leaves the fundamental issues of versification unresolved. The need remains for some more objective methodology helpful in the determination of colon boundaries.

Another problem in the discussion of Hebrew metrics moves beyond these largely unsettled issues of versification and lineation to the question of the regularity of meter, or rhythm, over longer stretches of lines. While some have questioned the "repetitiveness" of the metrical patterns proposed, for example, by Stuart and Freedman (compare Longman's criticism 1982: 250[5]), Freedman has argued affirmatively, showing that much of Hebrew poetry displays a metric regularity, as measured by syllables and stresses, throughout the course of a longer poetic unit.

In his work on the acrostic poetry of Lamentations, Psalms, and Proverbs 31, Freedman (1972a) observed two distinct patterns of line length: (a) bicola of 13–14 syllables, exemplified by Lamentations 1–4; and (b) bicola that average "around $16\frac{1}{2}$ syllables,"[6] exemplified by Lamentations 5 and the other passages. Later he identified these as a 3:2 and a 3:3 stress pattern (1986: 430). Further study of so-called nonalphabetic acrostics showed a dominance of this second pattern and led him to affirm a "standard meter of Hebrew poetry, which we may define in the words of the 4th-century Church Father Eusebius of Caesarea as an hexameter of sixteen syllables" (1986: 430).

In addition to this regularity of syllable and stress counts, and equally significant, Freedman (1986: 430) also discovered "many modifications, deviations, and departures from the norm," so that the regularity must be observed within the larger context of an entire piece, which may reveal a system of balancing shorter lines against longer lines. Cloete agrees, although without the evidence marshalled by Freedman: "the inequality of cola is no argument against the classification of literature as verse, nor against the possible metricality of that verse" (Cloete 1989b: 46). This tension between regularity and irregularity aptly describes the tension between opposing schools of thought concerning meter:

> Scholars have gone in two directions. One group began by assuming that Hebrew poetry was severely metrical; but when they discovered that lines and stanzas do not conform to any strictly metrical system, they either gave up, or went ahead to reconstruct the poem so as to conform to the meter they had already established for the

---

5. Cloete (1989b: 46), however, argues that Longman *wrongly* focuses on the need for regularity.

6. Both figures were based on counting the longer second-person suffixes and therefore indicate maximum counts. My method (see below, p. 24) generally seeks minimal counts.

poem. The other group decided that lines and stanzas are irregular, and hence that there is no meter in Hebrew poetry. Both sides are right in their way, and wrong in another. The specifically Hebrew phenomenon has not been recognized for what it is: it is quantitative, but with a degree of freedom rarely seen in metrical poetry. The result is that we should recognize the phenomenon for what it is, and we should also recognize our limitations in dealing with Hebrew poetry (Freedman 1987a: 20).

The affirmation of a quantitative feature of line length, regular even amidst its own "irregularities," has not only confirmed that metric considerations are a factor in Hebrew poetry but has also led to the suggestion that some measurements need to be applied and observed on structural levels larger than individual bicola or verses. Thus, in discussing the implications of his observations, Freedman suggests "that we should look more closely at large structures, expecting to find rigid constraints and nearly equal counts of length for major parts and complete poems" (Freedman 1987a: 26).

In his study of psalm structures, P. Raabe (1990) has confirmed just this expected phenomenon in the controlled corpus of psalms with refrains. By dealing with psalms in which refrains offer a clear demarcation of stanzas, he has extended Freedman's work, in which colon boundaries were clearly marked by the acrostic patterns, to a larger level of structural analysis. Raabe discovered that these psalms demonstrate an overall structure based on stanzas of equal size, or with combinations of full- and half-stanzas. In either case, a measurement of length seems to have served as a control on structure and also to have produced a sense of balance and symmetry operative on the stanza level.

In summary, despite extensive research, both ancient and contemporary, the basic definition of poetry as verse remains only somewhat clarified. Most attempts to define the "essence" of Hebrew verse falter on being simply descriptive of a set of lines arbitrarily lineated ("We *must* describe"; O'Connor 1980: 149, emphasis his). Collins, who works more deductively from a grammatically generated typology to a catalog of examples, fails to describe fully any specific corpus.

All agree that parallelism of various sorts and kinds is a factor that contributes to the relationship between lines, predominantly couplets, or bicola. Many of the stylistic features noted by Watson and Alonzo-Schökel are characteristics of parallelism, and Berlin, Geller, and Greenstein have greatly enlarged the categories.

Meter, broadly defined as a numerically measured factor of line length ("terseness"), appears to be operative even when not recognized (contra

Kugel, O'Connor), and the failure of any system to deal adequately with metrics does not necessarily lead to the conclusion that "the only surviving indisputable phonetic limitation of biblical verse is the relative brevity of the poetic line in relation to prose" (Geller 1982: 66) or, "what's more," no meter at all (Kugel).

Therefore Lowth's two categories remain: attacked, altered, augmented, but affirmed. Parallelism, whether semantic or syntactic, is recognized as a factor in versification, although it is not present in every instance. Line length, by anyone's system of measurement, is limited. Syntax, usually following the boundaries of parallelism, does fall within certain constraints, although the possibilities may just as well be bounded by metrical considerations as by a limited number of syntactic restraints (that is, O'Connor has described the *effect* of "terseness" rather than the cause). In the end, there has not yet emerged a clear method for defining colon boundaries. Indeed, enjambment remains a debated issue (Watson 1986: 332–33; Cloete 1989a: 14–15) that lies at the heart of the methodology of lineation (see below, p. 26).

Thus, many problems remain unanswered. Unfortunately, much recent research has approached these two broad categories of parallelism and meter as though they were to function on the same level. Parallelism, which usually relates to semantic features, even on the syntactic level,[7] has to do with the meaning of words. Meter, even the specific pattern of rhythm, has to do with the number and pronunciation of the actual letters (signs), which can be measured quite apart from meaning.[8] Therefore it is not only possible but also quite likely that both parallelism and meter can function at the same time, even in occasional tension with one another, because they are dealing with two distinct, though related, levels of control on the poetic line. Simply observing this distinction may also prove helpful in the question of lineation, especially where clear colon boundaries are not apparent, for example, where metric considerations appear incompatible with the "sense" or the syntax of individual versification.

As a further problem, the means of metric measurement continues to elude consensus. Although Cloete rejects all methods of nonsyntactical systems of measurement, he has felt the need to add the constraint of 1–4

---

7. That is to say, syntax and grammar serve the meaning of a sentence. It is theoretically possible for two sentences, for example, to be syntactically parallel either on the surface or in the deep structure without any semantic relationship, but this is highly unlikely even within the detailed categories and examples demonstrated by Berlin (1985).

8. Thus metric notation or scansion employs its own system of "signs" or symbols (-/-/-/) in the place of morphemes or lexemes.

stresses to O'Connor's syntactic system. Various scholars measure line length in various ways. Indeed, the fact that different methods of measurement all work, to a greater or lesser degree, indicates that line length is indeed a factor in Hebrew poetry. The insight that metric considerations of line length function both as a regularity and as a norm to control irregularities (Freedman 1986) needs to be tested beyond the controlled situation of acrostic poetry, where lineation is not in doubt.

Finally, the observation that line lengths balance out over a larger unit suggests that balance and a sense of symmetry are important features of Hebrew poetry that should be taken into consideration on levels larger than the individual line or verse.

It would seem that the reason no one system seems to function adequately is due to the fact that any one system inevitably deals with only certain components of poetry. My analysis will attempt to take into consideration as many of these features as present themselves. While Lowth hardly resolved the problems of the definition of Hebrew poetry, he may prove to have been basically correct all along. Although his categories have benefited greatly from clarification and expansion, they still lie at the heart of both the description and the definition of Hebrew poetry.

Rhetorical Criticism

Interestingly, it was the growing field of stylistic studies in Hebrew poetics that played a major role in Muilenburg's challenge to "go beyond" form criticism. He cited (1969: 7–8) specifically the work of Alonzo-Schökel as the foremost representative of "aesthetic criticism," although other studies are noted as well. In outlining his program of "rhetorical criticism," he discussed several methodological concerns.

First, Muilenburg sought better methods of delimiting the literary unit through stylistic devices such as inclusio, climactic lines, and word repetitions. By using such literary and rhetorical markers, he sought to overcome the arbitrary and atomistic abuses of *Gattungsforschung* and paved the way for a more holistic approach to literary units, including the distinctive peculiarities of a given text that may differ from the form of a particular (and often hypothetical) pattern.

Second, he suggested that such stylistic markers are helpful also in determining the internal structure of a composition. Beginning with the basic poetic feature of parallelism, he noted that the "bicola and tricola appear in well-defined clusters or groups, which possess their own identity, integrity, and structure" (Muilenburg 1969: 11), which he then called strophes and/or stanzas. By observing the use and position of particles, vocatives, rhetorical questions, repetitions, and refrains, he demonstrated that larger compositions may reflect a structural integrity and unity that had not been appreciated by the attention to the hypothetical definition and history of small and separate units so typical of the form-critical approach.

Due perhaps to the tenor of the times as much as the force of Muilenburg's own arguments, the major problem resulting from his clarion call is the fact that research has moved so quickly and in so many ways "beyond" form criticism that "rhetorical criticism" has become an almost undefinably broad category. Numerous studies on the structural analysis of individual passages have appeared as well as attempts to describe larger units and whole books by means of a unifying structure (for example, inter alia, Holladay 1976, Polzin 1977, Parunak 1978, Gileadi 1981, Watts 1985, Ball 1987, Hagstrom 1988), not to exclude the previous work by Muilenburg himself (1956) on Isaiah 40–66.

Indeed much exploratory work concerning Hebrew poetry, such as the studies of Kosmala (1964, 1966), has focused on an argument for a symmetrical composition of larger units and whole poems, a style that Kosmala (1964: 445) claims is thoroughly Semitic. Likewise Freedman (1987a, 1987c), also working from a focus on poetry, has suggested implications for better understanding of the unity and structure of poetic literature.

The agenda of a more holistic reading of texts has also been supported by the influence of structuralism on the interpretation of the Hebrew Bible (for example, Polzin 1977), although this methodology operates at a level beyond the stylistic structural features more common to the rhetorical-critical school. R. Lack, for example (1973), who presents a structuralist approach to the unity of Isaiah, is sympathetic to the concerns of more traditional rhetorical criticism, but he feels (1973: 253) that it simply does not go far enough beyond the surface structures.

Although redaction criticism functions as a quite different discipline, a concern for the text as a whole (at least in its final form) has generated a search for a purposeful rationale for the ordering and structuring of smaller units into larger ones (for example, H. Barth 1977, Vermeylen 1977, Clements 1980b, Sweeney 1988, Seitz 1993, all on Isaiah 1–39, in whole or in part; and Melugin 1976; Rendtorff 1984, 1989, 1991; Carr 1993, as examples of insights concerning the composition of the whole book of Isaiah).

Attention to "rhetorical" features of the text has been expanded to include a host of issues far beyond Muilenberg's original program. Rhetorical criticism as understood and practiced today bears only a partial resemblance to the stylistic and structural concerns on which this work will focus. The contemporary discipline signified by "rhetorical criticism" has encompassed a holistic approach not just to the text itself but to the entire hermeneutical enterprise, including text production and reception (compare Wuellner 1987, 1989). Much of what Wuellner surveys, however, has not affected recent studies of Hebrew poetry or the more traditional understanding of rhetorical criticism.[9]

Nevertheless, the work of Y. Gitay, for example (1980, 1981, 1983, 1991), seeks to take seriously the orality and rhetorical effect of prophetic proclamation as persuasion.[10] B. Wiklander (1984: 248) has modeled a "text-linguistic and rhetorical approach" influenced by modern communicative theory in demonstrating that Isaiah 2–4 is a "structural and functional unit of discourse" that must be understood holistically.

Isaianic Studies

Certainly attention to and concern for literary structure is not new. Muilenburg's contribution lay in the combination of the advances in stylistic features from the study of Hebrew poetics with the more general needs of literary criticism and in the timely appreciation of aesthetic concerns within the precise and even unique formulation of a writer's thought.

Thus the prophetic material, which has long been the subject of form-critical study, has become also a fertile field for the so-called rhetorical approach.[11] On the one hand, since they are to be understood as oral proclamation uttered for the purpose of persuasion, prophetic oracles are rhetoric, poetic rhetoric. On the other hand, they have been formulated into larger units that have long challenged structural description and holistic analysis. This study focuses attention on the prophet Isaiah, to whom is ascribed a literary work, which has long been the subject of form-, redaction-, and more recently, rhetorical-critical study.

---

9. This is precisely the point of Wuellner's criticism: "Reduced to concerns of style, with the artistry of textual disposition and textual structure, rhetorical criticism [*a la* the 'Muilenburg School'] has become indistinguishable from literary criticism . . ." (1987: 451–52).

10. See the helpful discussion of method, which is then modeled in his thorough study of the truly rhetorical features of Isaiah 1–12 (Gitay 1991: 1–13). Gitay takes seriously the oral nature of rhetoric as well as its essential purpose—and power—to pursuade.

11. I intend to use both the term and the method in the more traditional sense in which Muilenburg intended, *pace* Wuellner, although I am quite aware of the developments and concerns that he has noted.

However, due in large part, no doubt, to the very broad strokes that outline the rhetorical-critical discipline, a very diverse spectrum of method has ensued, much of it in search of a rationale for the whole of a text. For example, in his commentary on Isaiah 1–33, J. Watts (1985: xxiii) states a very holistic objective, and he cites the work of H. Wildberger, to whom "it was clear from the beginning of his work on Isaiah that what was finally paramount was the interpretation of the book as it now exists."[12] Watts suggests a unity of form to the entire book, but his rather esoteric theory of literary drama has won him few followers. His work on individual sections is characterized by attention to poetics, recurrent word themes, and he includes stress counts for all lines, although he rarely refers to them in the commentary.

Building on the "bifid" theory of W. Brownlee (1964: 247ff.), who argued that the whole book consists of two roughly equal and parallel halves, A. Gileadi (1981) has proposed "a holistic view of the book of Isaiah," arguing for a large double outline in which chaps. 1–33 are carefully matched by the structure of chaps. 34–66. He notes repetition of subject matter and vocabulary, but he pays little attention to poetic details and the structuring of the individual parts and deals with structure predominantly at the level of a linear outline of themes and motifs. Although he remains tentative, if not somewhat unclear, on the questions of historical context, he does suggest a sense of editorial coherence and balance to the book as a whole.

Another "holistic" approach to at least the first half of the book of Isaiah is taken by Hayes and Irvine (1987: 13), who argue that the whole of Isaiah 1–39 (apart from chaps. 34–35) "derives from the eighth-century B.C.E. prophet." They accent the role of rhetoric in both the spoken and the written word and deal with larger units of material (for example, chaps. 24–27) as "the result of deliberate composition, . . . intended as a written text for public use in a complex national celebration" (Hayes and Irvine 1987: 60–61). But although they note items of structural interest, for example, a proposed "structural symmetry" to Isa 5:8–24a (1987: 103), little attention is given to matters of stylistic and poetical detail.

Rémi Lack (1973) represents the work of a French structuralist applied to the whole of the prophet Isaiah, especially in seeking out the deep structures, "les schèmes imaginaires" (based on the work of G. Durand), which

---

12. "Daß letzlich da jetzt vorliegende Buch als Ganzes zu werten ist, stand mir von Anfang an fest" (Wildberger 1982: vii) may not necessarily imply "paramount" importance, but Wildberger does claim to want to take seriously "das Buch" ("ich sage bewußt 'das Buch'") as a whole.

underlie the surface markers. "La structure d'un texte consiste dans l'ordonnance effective de ses parties. Sa structuration . . . englobe les eléments qui ont déterminé sa structure" (Lack 1973: 19 n. 31). He studies especially the use of imagery and symbols in examining both parts and whole and suggests a sense of unity on the basis of word and theme repetitions. While he remains sensitive to historical issues (1973: 13), he focuses not on any *Sitz im Leben* but on a more fundamental "*Sitz im Mensch*" (1973: 252), and he claims a structural unity that goes beyond the intentionality of the writers and editors of the text.

Although R. Clements's commentary on Isaiah 1–39 (1980b) is in the mainstream of redaction criticism, he builds on the work of H. Barth (1977) (and, to a lesser degree, of Vermeylen 1977) in considering the literary stages of the book, beginning with a Josianic redaction that incorporated the original *Denkschrift* (6:1–8:18) into a larger, integrated whole from 5:1–14:27.[13] Although Barth, Vermeylen, and Clements attempt to determine a sense of deliberate redactional structuring, the insights of poetic and rhetorical stylistics are rarely noted or examined; their analyses of structure are based predominantly on thematic issues.

In a study of a smaller section of Isaiah, M. Sweeney (1988: 7–8) presents a detailed analysis of Isaiah 1–4 based on structure, intent, and setting. While his method is, like that of Clements, basically redaction-critical, he raises important methodological issues in terms of a holistic reading of the final form, that is, that the parts are to be understood, in their present setting, in relationship to the whole.

Recent years have witnessed even more energy devoted to compositional and thematic issues related to the "unity" of Isaiah (for example, Gitay 1991; Conrad 1991; Rendtorff 1991; Seitz 1991, 1993; Carr 1993; Darr 1994), including the development of a seminar within the annual meeting of the Society of Biblical Literature devoted to the "Formation of the Book of Isaiah." Recent research utilizing insights of a rhetorical-critical approach have raised new methodological issues. How, for example, shall structural unity and integrity be measured or determined? How does a sense of "unity" of composition relate to the historical questions of a text within its context? Is there common ground between so-called diachronic approaches (historical, form- and redaction-critical, with emphasis on the stages of the text before its final form) and synchronic approaches (literary, rhetorical-critical, with emphasis on the final form of the text). The shift from *Sitz im Leben* to *Sitz im Text* is an important move "beyond" form criticism, but it has raised difficult problems of historical setting, which

---

13. Actually Barth (1977: 311ff.) included much of chaps. 2–32 in this so-called *Assur-Redaktion.*

are then often resolved along the lines of redaction *history* (so Barth, Vermeylen, Clements, Sweeney) or simply avoided by ahistorical categories, such as structuralism (for example, Lack) or reader-response criticism (for example, Conrad).

Attention to the "final form" of the text should seek to combine the concerns of both historical and literary methods, but they need to be allowed to inform and complement each other. Indeed, one insight of rhetorical criticism (sometimes forgotten) is the function of the text within its "rhetorical situation," that is, the historical setting in which it functioned as rhetoric. "The prophetic language is a reflection of both the rhetorical situation and the prophet's goal, and has to be studied accordingly" (Gitay 1983: 221). Thus, the synchronic, holistic approach should not—and cannot—be separated from the historical.

Nevertheless, the quest for the historical moment has never been an easy task. For example, to cite only a few studies on one text, Isaiah 2–4, Wiklander (1984: 24) argues not only that Isaiah 2–4 must be approached as a whole, recommending a "*primary* orientation toward the final shape of the text" (emphasis his), but also that the historical setting of these chapters can be dated between 734–620 B.C.E., contra Sweeney or Clements, who believe chaps. 2–4 could only have reached their present form in the exilic (Clements) or early restoration (Sweeney) period. Others have argued for an eighth-century date (Oswalt 1986, Hayes and Irvine 1987, Gitay 1991). Seitz (1993: 30) suggests "evidence of a later (Babylonian) redaction," but he has, helpfully in my opinion, tried to find some common ground between a purely historical approach and one that emphasizes a message that looks beyond any one historical moment. In fact, the "original" message of the text certainly looked beyond its own time in a proclamation of both judgment and salvation.

But perhaps a more fundamental question concerns the very nature of a text, for example, a section of prophetic discourse such as Isaiah 2–4, or even Isaiah 2–12. Is it to be assumed that such blocks of material are collections of loosely connected sections, each of which can be understood as a relatively self-contained unit? This has served as a basic assumption of form- and source-criticism. Or is there a sense of organization and order inherent in both the various stages and the final form of a text, so that a literary history can be tracked through a process of deliberate reworkings of textual material? This seems to be the current focus of redaction-critical work, in which the final form is understood as a consciously-shaped last stage. Or are even large blocks of text so clearly and so tightly knit together that they suggest a sense of unity and integrity original to their composition? If this is the case, texts cannot be understood except as a whole, with each part playing a role toward a unified message. This calls into question both the assumption of a lengthy redactional process and the attempt to understand any part of a text as an independent and isolated unit. But what criteria or controls are appropriate for finding a deliberately organized unity in a text?

Thus, attention to questions of structure and composition on the level of both individual and larger units calls for greater methodological precision and consistency, and it is in this area that the present work seeks to focus attention. Many studies of structure proceed on the basis of content or theme without concern for the rhetorical or stylistic features (for example, Marshall 1962, Sweeney 1988). On the other hand, structural hypotheses supported by attention to stylistic features often follow a somewhat random approach. The use of chiasm, for example, explored as a structuring and emphatic device by Ceresko (1978; see also Kselman 1977), has become a fashionable way of suggesting larger structures (for example, Watts 1985: 15 and passim); unfortunately, this has been done without much further attention to poetics and stylistics on the smaller levels of composition, attention to which is the strength of the examples cited by Ceresko. The study of Isaiah 5–10(11) by B. Anderson (1988), for example, attempts to make use of rhetorical markers, but does not go far enough, in my opinion, in appreciating the balanced structuring of these chapters. In the end, he has used stylistic features only to confirm an outline drawn from thematic concerns.

Further, the very relationship of form to content needs increased attention. At times, rhetorical and stylistic studies stop short of relating what become simply "interesting" observations of features of literary style to the meaning and understanding of the text as communicative discourse. However, studies that take seriously the overall structure of both parts and whole should not only relate the structure to the meaning of a text; they should also use the structure as a helpful basis for understanding the meaning of a text, as, for example, P. Raabe (1990) has shown in suggesting that a psalm should be "read" in accordance with its stanzaic structure. Most recently, C. Franke (1994) has shown how a literary-critical reading of Isaiah 46–48 can enhance the understanding of that text as a unified whole.

Current Issues and Objectives of This Study

Methodological Considerations

The previous discussion has surveyed the advances and current issues in studies of Hebrew poetry and in what has come to be included in the rather loosely defined discipline of rhetorical criticism. Interestingly, the problems highlighted as concerns relative to Hebrew poetry have resulted from methods that have been described as too narrow, while the concerns raised about rhetorical criticism result from a method that has become too broad.

The study that follows suggests a method that seeks to till middle ground, not only between the broad and narrow within each field but also between the fields themselves. On the one hand, it will utilize many of the insights gained in recent studies in Hebrew poetry and in so doing address some of the issues still left unresolved (see below on specific issues of method, pp. 23ff.). On the other hand, it borrows from rhetorical criticism[14] a concern for delimitation of individual sections and for a structuring of both parts and whole, believing that it is necessary to relate carefully the smaller units to the larger units and vice versa. It is hoped that the insights of poetic analysis can provide some helpful resources for the methodological issues of a holistic approach.

Most significantly, this method argues and seeks to demonstrate that the length of literary units is a helpful factor in determining the structural plan and compositional integrity of literary units. Within the context of poetic analysis, length has proven to be a useful criterion toward resolving questions of lineation, structure, symmetry, and even the very nature of poetry as defined by "terseness." But these insights have not been systematically and rigorously applied both to poetic structures and to larger structures within the broader concerns of rhetorical approaches.

As this method seeks to bring together the goals of poetic study and rhetorical criticism, so the object of this research is the type of literature in which the concerns of these disciplines have already overlapped, namely, prophetic discourse. Freedman (1983: 142) has described prophetic literature as something of a *tertium quid*, which shares features of both poetry and prose, and it is important to test the helpfulness of detailed poetic analysis of such material, and in so doing to consider the relationship of prophetic discourse to poetry through its use of poetic features.

Further, a large enough corpus has been selected to test Freedman's suggestion that the quantitative feature of Hebrew poetry, which operates on the level of line and bicolon, should likely function as a control for larger units and complete poems. The most detailed part of this study focuses on two major poetic units in Isa 5:8–25 and Isa 9:7–10:4, which have been selected for several reasons: (1) they are long enough to serve

---

14. Again it should be noted that I am using this term in the conventional sense, much in line with the stylistic concerns outlined by Muilenburg, in other words, precisely what Wuellner (1989: 33) calls "Muilenburg's distorted, albeit conventional, use of 'rhetorical'."

as a test case; (2) they appear to be interrelated in some way; (3) the nature of their relationship to each other as well as to the material around and between them within the greater context of Isaiah 2–12 has been the subject of much detailed discussion, toward which this study seeks to make a contribution.

Thus these poems offer the further opportunity to test whether this type of literary analysis will prove helpful in dealing with questions of compositional unity and integrity on the larger structural levels. The whole of Isaiah 2–12 will be considered in light of the larger literary relationships that are part of the holistic concerns of rhetorical criticism.

Finally, this method has as its goal the relationship of form to content: namely, the way that poetic and structural analysis relate to the meaning and historical occasion of the text. Indeed, it is hoped that the method employed and evaluated here will enhance the understanding of the text. The structure of both the parts and the whole of a given unit as well as the relationship of parts to whole and whole to parts will be shown to affect the meaning and therefore to serve the understanding of the text.

Isaiah 2–12: State of the Research

The study of Isaiah as a prophet of exemplary poetic skill goes back at least as far as Bishop Lowth, who offered the following appraisal (1753: 228):

> Isaiah, the first of the prophets, both in order and dignity, abounds in such transcendent excellencies, that he may be properly said to afford the most perfect model of the prophetic poetry. He is at once elegant and sublime, forcible and ornamented; he unites energy with copiousness, and dignity with variety. In his sentiments there is uncommon elevation and majesty; in his imagery, the utmost propriety, elegance, dignity, and diversity; in his language, uncommon beauty and energy; and, notwithstanding the obscurity of his subject, a surprising degree of clearness and simplicity.

As indicated, I will focus on the unit of Isaiah 2–12, which is short enough to allow for detailed analysis yet long enough to address the questions of larger structural features and to test the hypothesis of structural unity and integrity.

The question of literary boundaries is important, and I recognize the problem of setting arbitrary ones. Indeed, the issue of demarcation of units was a major concern addressed by Muilenburg, and I hope to demonstrate that this method will prove helpful in determining where literary units begin and end.

For example, should chap. 1 be included in this study of Isaiah 2–12? Most commentators view 2:1 as a new superscription. Ackroyd (1963: 1978) and more recently Gitay (1991) assert that the unit 2:1–4(5) belongs to chap. 1, but the evidence will show that chaps. 2–12 clearly form a large literary block. Another question is the range of 2:1: does it govern 2:2–4(5) (Ackroyd 1978, Kaiser 1979, Scott 1957, Watts 1985); 2:2–4:6 (Lowth 1778, Duhm 1922, Clements 1980b, Wiklander 1984, Sweeney 1988); or 2:1–12:6 (Gray 1912, Kaiser 1963)?

At the other end of Isaiah 2–12, both the change in theme and the introduction of the term מַשָּׂא suggest that the superscription in 13:1 begins a new section. Here Ackroyd reflects the majority view in suggesting that chap. 12 forms a concluding colophon to the whole piece, which in its present form is the result of a process of reflection upon the message of the prophet (Ackroyd 1978).

Although there is general agreement concerning the major units of Isaiah 2–12 (chaps. 2–4; chap. 5; 6:1–8:18; 8:19–9:6; 9:7–10:4; 10:5–34, 11:1–16; 12:1–6), there is considerable disagreement over details of structure and outline. For example, does chap. 5 continue chaps. 2–4, or does it begin a new unit? Why is the "call" of Isaiah in chap. 6? Do chaps. 2–12 present a chronological order, with the material in chaps. 2–5 antedating the "year in which King Uzziah died" in 6:1? Or does chap. 5 begin a new section that continues into 10 or 11? What is the relationship of 5:8–30 to the material in 9:7–10:4? Is chap. 11 a later insertion? Is chap. 12 an independent, concluding doxology or an integral part of a larger unit?

While several focused studies have addressed the question of the form and structure of individual oracles (Scott 1957; Kosmala 1964, 1966) or smaller units (Sweeney 1988, Wiklander 1984) within Isaiah 2–12, others have attempted to deal with the larger structural issues, often using the so-called Isaianic *Denkschrift* of Isaiah 6–8 as a starting point.

The study by R. Marshall (1962), for example, proposes a literary unity to Isaiah 1–12, based on a meaningful organization of materials and a thematic outline that is arranged in a climactic order and linear progression. He also suggests that oracles of hope were balanced on either side of the biographical material (chaps. 6–8), but that the early announcements of hope were expressed in more eschatological terms (2:2–5, 4:2–6) and the latter (10:9ff.) in more historical terms.

The major works by J. Vermeylen (1977) and H. Barth (1977) are fully developed redactional-critical studies that attempt to reconstruct the literary history of Isaiah 1–35 (Vermeylen) and Isaiah 2–32 (Barth), based on their analyses of the various redactional levels reflective of the use and application of the text in different historical situations. In striking contrast, Gitay has argued that the whole of Isaiah 1–12 should be understood as a series of speeches focused on the Syro-Ephraimite threat (Gitay 1991). On a smaller scale, several recent studies (L'Heureux 1984, Sheppard 1985, Anderson 1988, Brown 1990) have focused on the composition of the material around the *Denkschrift,* especially the series of woes in 5:8ff. and the poem of refrained stanzas in 9:7–10:4. I will begin by turning my attention to these texts.

Isaiah 5 and 9:7–10:4: State of the Research

As my conclusions will confirm, the *Denkschrift* in Isaiah 6–8 does turn out to be a very good starting point (also see below, pp. 131ff.), but for my purposes it serves not as the focus of detailed analysis but as the center around which the material in chaps. 5 and 9 is organized and as the core of the whole of Isaiah 2–12. Marshall notes, for example, the "darkness and distress" motif broken between 5:30 and 8:22, and he views the narratives in chaps. 6–8 as an insertion into earlier collections of oracles, now displaced.

On the other hand, L'Heureux (1984) focuses specifically on 5:8–10:4 as intentionally structured *around* the material in chaps. 6:1–9:6 by means of a double inclusio: "woe sayings" in 5:8–24 and in 10:5ff. and parts of the "outstretched hand poem" in 5:25–29 and 9:7–20[15] + 10:1–4, which form an outer and inner circle around the "Emmanuel Booklet" in 6:1–9:6. While interacting predominantly with Vermeylen's reconstruction, he nevertheless views the whole of 5:1–10:4 (as well as 10:5ff.) as part of H. Barth's *Assur-Redaktion,* and he argues (contra Vermeylen) that the whole of this section can be dated between the time of Hezekiah (post-701) and the fall of Assyria toward the end of the reign of Josiah.

Although L'Heureux connects the "woe sayings" of 5:8ff. with 10:5ff., rather than with 10:1–4, his proposal of a carefully crafted "double inclusio" as the work of a single hand offers a much simpler explanation of the mechanics of the literary structure of this unit than the redactional displacement proposed by Vermeylen and Barth. L'Heureux further asserts, again contra Vermeylen, that the intervening materials in the "Emmanuel Booklet" were not later insertions but rather a core around which a unified whole was structured.

With similar insight, G. Sheppard (1985) builds on Barth's work and, without reference to L'Heureux's article, also suggests a double inclusio around the "Testimony of Isaiah," although he calls 10:1–4 the seventh

---

15. His summary on p. 113 cites "9.7–10," which surely must be a mistake for 9:7–*20.*

"woe" to complement 5:8–24 and therefore does not reach into 10:5ff. for the outer circle of the inclusio.

Furthermore, Sheppard considers the function of chap. 12, which was eliminated and ignored by Barth, as a summarizing conclusion to Isaiah 2–11, possibly added sometime after the Assur-Redaktion. He notes the use of the phrase "your anger turned away" in 12:1 as distinctive of the refrains in 9:7ff. and the occurrence of the verbal root שׁוּב (in a *Niphal* form only in 12:4 and 2:11, 17) as a concluding echo of chap. 2 in chap. 12.

B. Anderson (1988) approaches the editorial structure of Isaiah 5–10 (11) with the objective both to take seriously the present shape of the text and to explain the position of the "call" of Isaiah at chap. 6. He considers chaps. 2–4 a separate redactional unit, although he believes that chap. 12 forms a doxological conclusion to the whole of Isaiah 2–12 (1988: 244 n. 2). Although he does not pursue the "double inclusio" mechanism, he proposes a detailed outline of 5:1–30 as an integral whole, which is continued in 9:7ff. Into this structure, the "Memoirs of Isaiah" (originally chaps. 7–8 but already augmented by chap. 6 and 9:1–6) were inserted in order to locate Yahweh's summoning of Assyria at the beginning of Isaiah's career (5:26–30). Immediately following the "Memoirs," the example of the arrogance and fate of Ephraim (9:7ff.) forms an object lesson for Judah consistent with Isaiah's message to Ahaz.

The strength of Anderson's approach is his attempt to deal with the text in its present state rather than propose a hypothetical reconstruction, although he is careful to avoid saying that his outlines reflect "the original layout of the Isaianic text." He notes, however, that while "perhaps a better, and conceivably more original, text can be reconstructed, . . . commentators have not reached a consensus on the matter" (1988: 238).

Clearly there is also little consensus on the matter of the text as it now stands. Questions remain concerning the boundaries of the units, especially at the end of chap. 5 (see below, p. 33). It is disputed whether the connection between 5:8ff. and 9:7ff. is accidental or intentional, or, as argued by W. Brown (1990), even real. Brown contends, contra Barth, L'Heureux, and Anderson, that 5:25–30 and 9:7ff. are, in fact, quite independent pieces. Based on the integral relationship of 5:25 to its own context, which he shows to be part of a piece from v. 24 through v. 30, all of which follows from 5:8ff., Brown concludes that the function of 5:25 is quite different from the *true* refrains, which stand apart from their context, in 9:7ff. Further, 10:4 lies within a unit that extends to 10:19, so that 9:7–10:19 must be considered independently from chap. 5.

Thus Brown (1990: 443) asserts that previous attempts to explain the location of 5:25 as due to either accidental displacement or intentional redactional activity are all "marred by their assumption that 5:25–30 and 9:7–20 are inextricably linked together by the refrain." I believe, however, and intend to demonstrate, that 5:25 is, in fact, related not only to its present context but also to the complementary poem in 9:7ff, in which is found an additional "woe" formula (10:4), which Brown does not connect at all with chap. 5.

Nevertheless, the question of the position and structuring of these poems around the so-called *Denkschrift* material remains difficult and un-settled. While it is generally assumed (contra L'Heureux) that the *Denk-schrift* was *inserted* into an originally connected piece, causing displacement of some sort, one should at least consider, with L'Heureux, the opposite possibility: that 5:8–25 and 9:7–10:4 were constructed *around* the *Denk-schrift*. Finally, whatever the process, it remains to be asked whether it was the result of ongoing redactional activity or the intentional structuring of an original author/editor.

Objectives of This Study

In focusing this research on a specific unit of prophetic literature (Isaiah 2–12), and in narrowing the starting point to the two poems in 5:8–25 and 9:7–10:4, I have surveyed a number of issues toward which this study will seek to make a contribution. In line with the methodological con-siderations discussed above (pp. 16ff.), my poetic analysis will attempt to demonstrate a relationship between these two poems based on poetic and rhetorical stylistic features, including the suggestion that a quantita-tive feature of length plays an important role in the structuring of this material.

By approaching this prophetic literature as poetry, I shall deal with current issues in the study of Hebrew poetry, testing the method and helpfulness of syllable and stress counting as a means of determining a quan-titative feature. Likewise, prose particles will be counted to see if this "mechanical test" does indeed establish this prophetic material as a *tertium quid* between poetry and prose. A method will be suggested that attempts to deal with the troublesome problem of lineation. Poetic and rhetorical structural features will be observed and analyzed at the various levels of bicolon, verse, strophe, and stanza, and to see if they might suggest a unifying structure for each poem.

Further, I shall extend this structural analysis beyond the levels within each poem to see if the same poetic and rhetorical stylistic features might play a role in the structure of the larger unit. If poetry does exhibit a quan-titative feature of length that produces a sense of balance over a larger unit, then one might expect to find and to utilize this factor of length in seeking a sense of structural unity on the level of what can be called macrostructure. This will allow for a more detailed hypothesis concerning the unity and structure of Isaiah 2–12.

Finally, I shall attempt to remember that this literary analysis should serve the meaning of the text within its historical context or "rhetorical situation." Thus it is my hope to contribute to a better understanding not only of Isa 5:8–25 and 9:7–10:4 within their literary context but also of the structure and meaning of Isaiah 2–12 as a whole.

Method

Turning to the specific details of poetic and rhetorical analysis, I first deal with Isa 5:8–25 and 9:7–10:4 as individual units (chaps. 2 and 3 below). Then I shall discuss their interrelationship as well as the structural relationship to the intervening and surrounding material (chap. 4 below). Finally, I shall propose, in slightly broader strokes and without as much detailed analysis, that the relationship of these two central units suggests a structuring of the larger unit of Isaiah 2–12 (chaps. 5 and 6 below).

Chapters 2 and 3, which demonstrate in detail the method of analysis, are organized as follows. Each section will be set forth as lineated text, with syllable and stress counts noted. This is followed by an original, annotated translation. The demarcation of the particular unit will be explained and defended. Questions of lineation, of the results of the syllable and stress counts, and of verse structure will be discussed in light of current theory concerning the nature of Hebrew poetry. Larger issues of structure dealing with the composition of each section will be approached with an eye (and an ear) to the relationship of structure to meaning. Thus I shall consider how this analysis of structure affects the understanding of the thought progression of the text. This same procedure will be followed in lesser detail in the discussion of the remaining materials.

It remains now to continue and conclude this preliminary discussion by dealing with specific methodological concerns and definition of terms.

Syllable Counting

Though often criticized and even maligned, syllable counting offers one of the most helpful and objective means of quantitative measurement. In fact, one of the most thorough and helpful critiques of syllable counting summarizes only the following concerns (Cloete 1989a: 44):

1. A measure of uncertainty as to the number of syllables cannot be avoided, and the counts are therefore only approximate.

2. It is unlikely that the poets as a rule counted syllables and, if they did not, the number of syllables does not directly relate to the versification system.

3. Syllable counting can only be undertaken after cola have been delimited by other means, namely in accordance with parallelism and syntactic boundaries.

With the sentiment of Cloete's first statement, I agree. However, syllable counting is certainly no less precise than any other system. The wide range of opinion on *what* to count has already been surveyed (see pp. 4ff. above); indeed, I will count stresses and words as well. But simply because there are more syllables to count, the margin for error becomes less significant.[16] The difference between 15 and 17 syllables in a bicolon is statistically less distracting ($\pm \frac{1}{16} = .0625$) than the variance between 5 and 7 stresses ($\pm \frac{1}{6} = .1667$).

As will be described below, I follow a "reconstructed" syllabification in line with commonly accepted theory concerning the phonetics of Biblical Hebrew of the classical period (see Stuart 1976: 26ff.), but I will track the Masoretic counts as well, for the sake of comparison. On the whole, an analysis of the MT results in slightly higher counts, but the differences do not affect the general patterns (see Andersen and Freedman 1980: 77). While the somewhat arbitrary nature of certain principles is recognized, I would maintain that even with certain variables and uncertainties, the overall patterns are clear (see Freedman 1986: 411–12).

In brief, segolate formations are counted as monosyllabic, and auxiliary vowels associated with laryngeals (unless substituting for vocal shewa) are not counted, nor do I count furtive *patah*. There is uncertainty concerning second-person-masculine-singular suffixes and verbal affixes; where there is doubt, I will show a long and a short count. In general, the option is for a short, or minimal count throughout in my analysis, but the differences overall are themselves minimal.

The handling of syllabic prefixes is difficult, specifically when the so-called "rule of *shewa*" contracts two syllables into one. Again, a minimum count is generally preferred for the sake of consistency. However, in the case of the prefixed conjunction before shewa, I show a double count. Certainly the Masoretic vocalization of the conjunction as *šureq* does not reflect biblical pronunciation (*wĕ-*), but whether a short vowel or vocal

---

16. Note Freedman's comment (1987a: 20), "I have opted for syllables because there are a lot of them, and hence a disagreement about a few of them will not make much difference."

shewa was given the length of a full syllable is not clear. In any case, the possibility of occasional elision must be taken seriously, and the prefixed conjunction before shewa is the most likely to have been compressed for the sake of metric considerations.

While the counts may appear to be "approximate," this is due to an admitted range in the possible number of syllables. But the variables will be discussed and I will provide a rationale toward a reasonable and defensible figure within that range, leading to very specific counts. As a result of this careful method, I would propose that syllable counting becomes a very accurate method of measuring length. Thus Cloete's first criticism is hardly a reason to eschew syllable counting.

The second of Cloete's criticisms is that it is unlikely that the poets counted syllables. To be sure, we do not know *whether* they counted syllables (or anything else!), and, if they did count something, we do not know for certain *what* the poets actually may have counted. Thus any attempt to find numerical regularity by counting anything or everything (including syntactical constraints or even stress accents) could suffer equally well from this superficial criticism. While it cannot be proven that the ancient Hebrew poets necessarily counted syllables, I shall attempt to demonstrate that syllable counts are a helpful factor in determining a sense of balance in both the smaller levels of line and verse as well as at the larger levels of strophe, stanza, and even in the determination of macrostructure. In fact, the data that this method seeks to produce may actually strengthen the assumption that the poets possibly did count syllables. Further, against the second part of Cloete's statement, I believe that as *a* measure of line length, the number of syllables does relate to the versification system.

Thus I disagree with Cloete's third criticism, not because parallelism and syntactic boundaries do not function in "cola delimitation," but because I believe that line length *also* functions in lineation, as I will discuss and attempt to show below (pp. 26ff.). Which of the controls is primary is not easy, or necessary, to say, but the question of line length and balance is certainly a factor, and syllable counting is one method—and I believe, the most accurate method—of measuring length.

Stress Counting

Apart from those who argue against the usefulness of meter as a concept (O'Connor, Kugel, Pardee), most scholars practice some system of stress counting. Here Cloete's summary (1989a: 32) is not critical but only cautious: stress counting is not the only factor in cola delimitation. I have already noted the spectrum of various approaches, along with certain specific difficulties (see above, pp. 4ff.). Freedman (1986) has advocated and practiced a combination of stress and syllable counting, and since each complements the other as a further measurement of length, I shall include stress counts.

In general, I follow the so-called "Ley-Sievers-Budde" system (for history and description: see Stuart 1976: 1ff.), which counts major word units. Each nomen and verb receives one stress; construct chains may thus receive multiple stresses. Monosyllables are problematic, although monosyllabic prepositions and the so-called nota accusativi are treated as proclitic, even when not so marked by Masoretic *maqqep*. A bound form of a monosyllabic word is most difficult to decide; at times both possibilities are shown. Two monosyllabic particles in the same line suggest at least one stress. When counts are debatable, I will show more than one possibility and again create a range within which a reasonable and defensible number will be fixed.

As with syllable counting, my figures conflict at times with those indicated by the Masoretic Text. Although the amount of variation is less, I shall include the accents marked in the MT alongside my own figures for the sake of comparison.

Prose Particles

The massive tables of statistics offered by Andersen and Forbes (1983) indicate the helpful attention given to the so-called prose particles: the prefixed article with *he* (when the consonant ה itself is present and therefore not included when the article is indicated only by the Masoretic vocalization with an inseparable preposition), the so-called object marker (אֶת), and the relative pronoun (אֲשֶׁר). I offer prose particle counts, that is, the percentage figure that results from dividing the number of prose particles by the total number of words, in accordance with the principles upon which Andersen and Forbes have compiled their work.

According to the statistical data and hypothesis of Freedman (1987a), classic poetry exhibits counts of less than 5%; narrative prose of over 15%. If prophetic rhetoric is indeed a *tertium quid,* the counts should fall in between these figures (see Freedman 1987a: 15–16).

Lineation

The problem of lineation is basic, yet no clear method has emerged from the morass of methodological issues that strike at the heart of the very definitions of poetry. If Cloete (1989a: 2) is correct in emphasizing the *formal* distinction of prose vs. *verse*, the issue of colon boundaries is of fundamental importance. His study (1989a: 13) is properly focused on Hebrew colometry, or more technically, colography.

I agree with Cloete that the basic unit is the line, or colon (although it rarely stands alone), and that the determination of lineation is by no means clear. As a case in point, analysis of Exod 15:1b-18 has shown a poem of 78 cola (Freedman 1974), 64 cola (Stuart 1976: 79–91), or 53 cola (O'Connor 1980: 178–85). BHS divides it into 70 cola.

However, before the poetic line may be described it must first be defined. But since the definition of the line is often dependent on one's understanding of the nature of the line, it is little wonder that no clear method for lineation has been articulated. In fact, it has generally been avoided. Even in an undertaking as massive as O'Connor's, the end result is simply a description of a corpus of lines delineated as the describer saw fit, subject to being criticized as "arbitrary" (discussed by Cloete 1989a: 91). And even Cloete, despite his lament over the lack of a clear measure of lineation, fails to develop a method and falls prey to making arbitrary judgments.

This is not to say that such judgments are without good reason. For the most part, lineation is clear and follows a broad definition of parallelism. Both O'Connor and Cloete have shown the role of syntax as a control and reject enjambment as rare (Cloete 1989a: 14, 216). But the fact remains that even Cloete's fine-tuning of O'Connor's system leaves certain questions unanswered.

For example, already in the fourth verse that he has analyzed, (Jer 2:5c), Cloete (1989a: 142) determines that the second verb (וַיֶּהְבָּלוּ) cannot exist as a separate colon "because that would produce a fourth colon of only one unit." But neither he nor O'Connor allows for such a one-unit colon, simply because they have not found any. Collins's examples (1978: 253) of one-word (a single verb form) lines are deemed by Cloete (1989a: 142) "not convincing, because they are either delimited incorrectly or must be regarded as cola of two units." Collins (1978: 253) argues, however, that "this truncation of the line produces an abruptness in rhythm which focuses attention on the isolated verb," and one should not dismiss this stylistic argument too quickly.

This is not an isolated instance, as Collins's examples illustrate. In fact, his most striking example of an intentionally variable rhythm is Jer 14:18c, which Collins (1978: 253) lineates as follows:

כִּי־גַם־נָבִיא גַם־כֹּהֵן
סָחֲרוּ אֶל־אֶרֶץ
וְלֹא יָדָעוּ

Cloete (1989a: 176), however, lineates the same unit as only two lines,
combining the second and third cola into his v. 18f. He asserts that the final unit, from which he has dropped the initial *waw* based on text-critical
evidence (in my opinion, nonconclusive), is an "asyndetic relative clause."
To his credit, Cloete provides his rationale for each decision, arguing on the
basis of syntax and parallelism and similar examples. Further, he (1989:
148–49) notes other possibilities, though often dismissing them without
cause (for example, inter alia, on 4:12bc or 4:17a).

My point is not to argue these individual cases but simply to note the
existence of questionable and difficult instances of lineation and the fact
that the various "systems" of analyzing the poetic line do not solve the problems. As an example from my corpus, I note Isa 9:9:

לְבֵנִים נָפָלוּ וְגָזִית נִבְנֶה
שִׁקְמִים גֻּדָּעוּ וַאֲרָזִים נַחֲלִיף׃

Is this one bicolon, or is it two, formed by subdividing each colon, so
that there are four lines? Syntax and parallelism provide neither problem
nor solution. Either lineation falls within O'Connor's or Cloete's system.
Collins's typology does not show a line (= bicolon) that consists of four
clauses; in his system one must assume this is a double bicolon (that is,
four lines) of line-type II A $(NP^1 + V - NP^1 + V)$. BHS, on the other hand,
lineates as a single bicolon, as do the commentaries.

What is needed is another controlling factor, as well as some objective
data upon which to base analysis. Although he is cautious about the atypi-
cal form of the acrostic poems providing a "suitable base on which to for-
mulate principles governing the nature of the metrical systems employed
by the biblical poets," Freedman (1972a) has at least based his work on a
corpus in which lineation is already provided by the poet. As noted previously Freedman (1972a: 392) has found two quite regular structures for
such poems, one (represented by Lamentations 1–4) having bicola of 13–
14 syllables, and a larger group (Lamentations 5, Proverbs 31, Psalms 25,
34, 37, 111, 112, 119, 145) having bicola averaging ca. $16\frac{1}{2}$ syllables (actually from 15.4 in Psalms 111–112 to 18.2 in Psalms 145, with all others
ranging between 16.3 and 16.7 syllables) (see above, p. 7 and n. 6).

Freedman's work was expanded in depth as well as breadth (1986)
through the inclusion of stress counts and a study of "nonalphabetic" acrostic poetry. What is most helpful to the discussion at this point is the inclusion of the feature of line length, whether measured by syllables or
stresses, as a factor in the question of lineation. To be sure, the question of
"meter" is difficult in itself, and I recognize various approaches (see above,
pp. 4ff.). But the two conclusions that Freedman reached (1986: 430–31)

are significant: (1) that the 16-syllable, 6-stress line (bicolon) was the standard or common meter of extant Hebrew poetry, and (2) that this basic meter occurs with many "modifications, deviations, and departures from the norm, also deliberate alterations and adjustments."

If this is true not only for the books of Proverbs, Job, and much of the Psalter but also "throughout the prophetic literature" (Freedman 1986: 431), then it is both helpful and valid to consider the normative function of the 16-syllable bicolon and, further, to use this standard as an aid for lineation.

However, in returning to the example from Isa 9:9, it is clear that help is not immediately available. As four cola, the lines have 6 + 5 + 5 + 5/6 syllables, depending on whether the conjunction in the final clause receives a full syllable or not. Stresses are 2 + 2 + 2 + 2. Either there are four short cola of 5–6 syllables and 2 stresses each or two longer cola of 11 syllables and 4 stresses each. Either solution fits within the ranges of syllable and stress patterns that have been found in poetry generally. How has the consideration of the 16-syllable bicolon helped in this problem of lineation?

The answer lies not in the individual case but in the overall pattern of the poem. First, one needs to establish that the prophet/poet is, in fact, using this 16-syllable, 6–stress pattern as a metrical guide of some sort. To begin with, one should therefore take into account only those lines where lineation is clear and undisputed, considering also syntax and parallelism. If one discovers that the dominant line length is, in fact, the 8-syllable colon or the 16-syllable bicolon, it is reasonable to assume that this pattern lies behind the poet's composition.

In fact, it is at least theoretically possible that the poet worked with a metric lineation that was based solely on the 8-syllable line, as I have shown in the hypothetical lineation of Isa 5:8–25 and 9:7–10:4 in appendixes 1C and 2C (see also below, pp. 264ff. and 273ff.). Such a lineation, however, ignores syntactic boundaries where necessary, and one must seek a system that allows for both factors.

Turning then to the difficult lines, I take up the second of Freedman's conclusions, namely, that the norm is operative also in its variations. Clearly there are modifications from the norm, but are they changes toward a longer or shorter line? Appendixes 1A and 1B, and 2A and 2B show the result of lineation based on deciding each uncertain case as consistently short (appendixes 1A and 2A) or long (appendixes 1B and 2B), which set the outside limits on the total number of lines and which give a range in the number of syllables per line from well below 8 per colon to well above 8 per colon.

If the 8-syllable colon / 16-syllable bicolon norm were operative, one should expect the number of lines to produce an average of very nearly 8 per colon, and that figure is reached simply by dividing the number of syllables in the whole by 8. This produces a "target" number of lines that falls between the outside limits previously noted and that can now be used as a basis for deciding individual cases that deviate either above or below the norm. This number of lines is consistent with what was determined by the purely metric lineation shown in appendixes 1C and 2C.

Thus, while either "shorter" or "longer" cola may work for Isa 9:9, the decision is based on whether the poet perceived these lines as a unit of 2 or 4 cola in relation to the total number of cola in the entire poem. If, for example, there are lines elsewhere that vary upward from the norm but cannot be divided, then one may well decide for shorter lines in the case in question. Indeed, Freedman (1972a: 387) has suggested a poetic technique of "balancing" that can function at the level of bicolon as well as at the level of the larger lineation and structure of a whole poetic piece, and it is likely that the poet/prophet intentionally balanced long lines against short lines, both of which were measured against the standard of 8 syllables per colon.

This methodology is not without its problems, to be sure. For one, it may be argued that the poet simply did not operate this way, that the total number of lines was not relevant to his purposes. But surely this is simply a surrender to ignorance and returns us helpless to the original problem.

More significantly, this may seem a somewhat circular process, that to "divide by 8 and lineate" produces the right number of lines because one has already predetermined the right number of lines of the right length. However, it must be remembered that the 8/16 syllable pattern has already been documented as normative elsewhere and confirmed as dominant in this particular case. It is not being created from within the handling of the data but has been determined by both external and internal data themselves.

A valid criticism is that, in the end, individual situations may have more than one solution, especially when multiple decisions are made in relationship to each other. For example, two sets of the kind of problem illustrated in Isa 9:9 could allow for one to be solved on the basis of short lines and the other in favor of longer lines, or vice versa. I recognize this difficulty and thus allow for other combinations of short and long lines that will nevertheless produce an overall balance.

The method I have described at least has confronted the basic issues and problems that have not previously been solved or even addressed. This methodology takes into consideration the various factors of Hebrew poetry and poetics, including not only syntax and parallelism but also metrics and line length, using them to complement and control each other. If it is correct that parallelism and meter operate concurrently but at two different levels (see above, p. 9), then lineation must deal with both of these factors even when they appear to be in tension with each other.

Verse, Strophe, Gross Structure: Definitions and Method

Due to some inconsistency in the use of terminology, I note the following definitions, used in this study, as building blocks of poetic structure.

Line. By *line* I mean a colon,[17] the basic unit of verse. Other terms employed elsewhere include *stich, hemistich, stichos,* and *verset.*

Verse. I consider a verse a structurally bound series or grouping of lines, the most common of which is the bicolon, usually bound together by parallelism of semantics, grammar, and/or phonology (see Berlin 1985). While a monocolon would not qualify as a "series of lines," it is possible for a single colon to be considered a verse. Often a monocolon is combined with a bicolon into a tricolon. Other groupings are possible. I shall pay attention to the use of poetic devices, such as the ones analyzed and cataloged by Alonso-Schökel (1988) and Watson (1986), as structural devices that may indicate the unity and integrity of individual verses.

Strophe. A subunit of a poem consisting of one, but generally two or more verses, that are bound by semantic/syntactic structural unity.

Stanza. A major subunit of a poem, a stanza consists of one or more strophes and contributes to the gross structure of an individual poem.

Beyond the stanza level, designation of parts becomes somewhat arbitrary. I have employed the term *panel* for the next larger unit, the first subunit of a major section.

At these levels, I shall begin to count words as well. While this is a less precise measurement, since words are obviously of varying length, it is, at least, one objective datum that the ancient scribes clearly noted and distinguished. All extant Biblical Hebrew manuscripts, regardless of questions of vocalization, accentuation, or lineation, show divisions between words. The inclusion of word counts will simply test whether this procedure is a helpful measurement of length at these larger levels of structure.

---

17. The term is used in the traditional sense of verse or single line relative to the study of poetry and not in the technical linguistic sense "as essentially a 'thought unit'" (for example, see J. Louw 1982: 114).

As a related issue, I shall also consider the usefulness of the paragraph markers in the Masoretic Text (*petuchah* and *setumah*), as well as the divisions indicated in the Qumran scrolls, to determine whether these ancient traditions preserve a legitimate and helpful guide to structural concerns.

Macrostructure. I use the term to describe the structure that extends beyond and between the individual poetic units (poems) and, it may be argued, gives a unity and integrity to the whole of Isaiah 2–12. Again, I shall argue from the bottom up, from the smaller to the greater, and suggest that the same stylistic features, rhetorical devices, and poetic concerns for length and balance operate even on this larger level.

Chapter 2
Isaiah 5:8–25

Boundaries of This Unit

Discussions of this literary unit, usually defined as 5:8–30, regularly take into consideration the related material in Isa 9:7ff. Although the nature and extent of that relationship is much debated, one thing is clear: 5:25 contains the words of the refrain found four times in 9:7–10:4. Various attempts to explain this fact have assumed some sort of textual dislocation and have sought to reconstruct the original form of the text and to trace the redactional process that has resulted in the current state of the text.

The interdependence between the material in Isaiah 5 and 9:7ff. will be taken up later (see pp. 96ff.). The focus at this point is the material in Isa 5:8ff., and my objective is to attempt to deal with the text as it stands. It will be shown that the unit 5:8–25 displays a unity and integrity that allow it to be considered an independently constructed and carefully composed poem in itself.

Muilenburg's first concern is apt: one needs to establish the boundaries of the unit. That 5:8 begins a new section is universally attested, although attempts to place it into the larger context are helpful (for example, Anderson [1988] links it thematically with 5:1–7). The Masoretic Text indicates a break between 5:7 and 5:8; BHS (CL) has a *setumah* marker, and CA has a *petuchah*.

The conclusion of the unit is not nearly as clear, however. The MT indicates several subdivisions through v. 23 (although CL and CA do not always agree), but neither indicates any break from v. 24 through v. 30. Yet surely, as all commentators agree, v. 24 expresses a conclusion to the series of "woes," at least to the second set of them (vv. 18–23), in a way similar to the way which the "therefore" of v. 14 follows the first two "woes" in vv. 8–12.

The greater question concerns v. 25. Commentators disagree about whether it concludes the previous section or begins a new unit running through v. 30. Duhm, Kaiser, Wildberger, and Hayes and Irvine deal with vv. 25–30 as a unit, as do Barth (1977), Sheppard (1985), Sweeney

(1988), and Brown (1990). Lack (1973) suggests a major break in the structure of Isaiah 1–39 between v. 24 and v. 25. Gray divides v. 25 itself into v. 25a–c (transitional) and vv. 25d–29, which belong with 9:7ff. Clements,[1] Watts, and Oswalt divide between v. 25 and v. 26, as does Anderson (1988).

To be sure, v. 25 appears to be distinct from vv. 8–24. As noted, this verse forms an apparent link to the material in Isa 9:7ff. (either intentionally or accidentally) with its use of the vocabulary of the refrain found in 9:7–10:4.[2] Further, the word used for 'therefore' is עַל־כֵּן (also used in 9:16), while לָכֵן has been used previously in chap. 5 (vv. 13, 14, 24). Thus v. 25 seems to be an intrusion into chap. 5, a redundant conclusion without appropriate antecedent.

Nevertheless, v. 25 now follows vv. 8–24 within the current text of chap. 5, a fact that, though obvious, needs to be taken seriously. Those who would see the present position of 5:25 as due to intentional redactional displacement support the probability that v. 25 now belongs in some purposeful way to what precedes it in chap. 5. Further, in light of the fact that 10:1 contains a "woe" oracle that offers another possible link to chap. 5, even those who argue for accidental displacement of 5:25 admit that these two larger units are somehow mixed and interrelated, and the pres-

---

1. Clements (1980b: 69) goes so far as to suggest that vv. 26–30 "at one time formed a quite separate prophecy."

2. But see Brown (1990), who claims no connection with the refrain (see above, pp. 21–22 and the following note here, n. 3).

Text

| | | Syllable Count[4] | | Stress Count | |
			MT		MT
5:8a	הוֹי מַגִּיעֵי בַיִת בְּבַיִת	7	9	4	4
b	שָׂדֶה בְשָׂדֶה יַקְרִיבוּ	8	8	3	3
c	עַד אֶפֶס מָקוֹם	4	5	2	3
d	וְהוּשַׁבְתֶּם לְבַדְּכֶם	12	14	4	4
	בְּקֶרֶב הָאָרֶץ׃				

---

4. A word of explanation concerning the numbers: the first column for both the syllable count and stress count provides a figure based on the methods discussed above (pp. 23ff. and 25ff.). Where more than one possibility exists, a slash (/) indicates

ence of an additional connection should suggest a search for a rationale behind the present order of the text.

The issue is not simply whether v. 25 is to be understood as linked to the thought of v. 24, but also whether the section of 5:8–25 continues into and beyond v. 26. Manuscript evidence is not conclusive, as noted, although 1QIsa[a] has a space equivalent to a *setumah* (Oesch 1979) after v. 25. Commentators disagree, although Anderson (1988) makes a case for the inclusion of v. 25 with vv. 8–24, which then conclude with a "double 'therefore'" in vv. 24–25 to match the "double 'therefore'" of vv. 13–14. He also observes the thematic change in vv. 26–30, suggesting it is a separate unit that deals with Yahweh's summoning of Assyria. Further, it is to be noted that vv. 26–30 have few, if any, links of vocabulary or theme with 5:8–25, or with 9:7–10:4, for that matter.

One factor often overlooked is the simple observation that the refrain is used in 9:7ff. as a *conclusion* to each stanza,[3] and that therefore it is likely to serve as a conclusion also in chap. 5. Furthermore, no previous work has seriously considered the structural integrity of this material based on considerations of length, as this study intends to do (see especially pp. 58ff.).

Beginning, then, with the hypothesis that the boundaries of this unit are 5:8–25, my detailed analysis will serve to confirm or reject this assumption.

---

3. Clements notes this but concludes that "evidently something [preceding] has been lost" (1980b: 69). On the other hand, Brown (1990) rejects the argument that something has dropped out, since, in his opinion, 5:25ff. has nothing to do with the similar refrained stanzas in 9:7ff. He argues that it is linked to what follows in 5:26–30. He does not recognize that 5:25 actually *concludes* the poem begun in 5:8.

Translation

5:8a   **Hey!** Ones who join house to house!
  b   Field they bring to field,
  c   until there is no place,
  d   and you are forced to live all alone in the midst of the land.

---

alternatives. Parentheses exclude the numbers determined (and discussed on, for example, pp. 45ff.) to be less likely. The second column provides counts based simply on the Masoretic vocalization.

9a	בְּאָזְנָי יְהוָה צְבָאוֹת	8	8	3	3
b	אִם־לֹא בָּתִּים רַבִּים	6	6	3	3
c	לְשַׁמָּה יִהְיוּ	5	5	2	2
d	גְּדֹלִים וְטוֹבִים	6	6	2	2
e	מֵאֵין יוֹשֵׁב׃	4	4	2	2
10a	כִּי עֲשֶׂרֶת צִמְדֵּי־כֶרֶם	11	14	4/(5)	6
	יַעֲשׂוּ בַּת אֶחָת				
b	וְזֶרַע חֹמֶר יַעֲשֶׂה אֵיפָה׃	7	10	4	4
Verses 8–10		**78**	**89**	**33/(34)**	**36**

11a	הוֹי מַשְׁכִּימֵי בַבֹּקֶר	6	7	3	3
b	שֵׁכָר יִרְדֹּפוּ	5	5	2	2
c	מְאַחֲרֵי בַנֶּשֶׁף	6	7	2	2
d	יַיִן יַדְלִיקֵם׃	4	5	2	2
12a	וְהָיָה כִנּוֹר וָנֶבֶל	7	8	3	3
b	תֹּף וְחָלִיל וָיַיִן מִשְׁתֵּיהֶם	9	10	4	4
c	וְאֵת פֹּעַל יְהוָה לֹא יַבִּיטוּ	9	10	3/(4)	5
d	וּמַעֲשֵׂה יָדָיו לֹא רָאוּ׃	8	9	3/(4)	4
Verses 11–12		**54**	**61**	**22/(24)**	**25**

13a	לָכֵן גָּלָה עַמִּי מִבְּלִי־דָעַת	10	11	4	4
b	וּכְבוֹדוֹ מְתֵי רָעָב	(7)/8	8	3	3
c	וַהֲמוֹנוֹ צִחֵה צָמָא׃	7/(8)	8	3	3
14a	לָכֵן הִרְחִיבָה שְׁאוֹל נַפְשָׁהּ	9	9	4	4
b	וּפָעֲרָה פִיהָ לִבְלִי־חֹק	8/(9)	9	3	3
c	וְיָרַד הֲדָרָהּ וַהֲמוֹנָהּ	9/(10)	10	3	3
d	וּשְׁאוֹנָהּ וְעָלֵז בָּהּ׃	(7)/8	8	3	3
Verses 13–14		**57/62 =59**	**63**	**23**	**23**

15a	וַיִּשַּׁח אָדָם וַיִּשְׁפַּל־אִישׁ	9	9	3	3
b	וְעֵינֵי גְבֹהִים תִּשְׁפַּלְנָה׃	9	9	3	3
16a	וַיִּגְבַּהּ יְהוָה צְבָאוֹת בַּמִּשְׁפָּט	11	11	4	4
b	וְהָאֵל הַקָּדוֹשׁ נִקְדָּשׁ בִּצְדָקָה׃	11	11	4	4
17a	וְרָעוּ כְבָשִׂים כְּדָבְרָם	9	9	3	3
b	וְחָרְבוֹת מֵחִים גָּרִים יֹאכֵלוּ׃	10	10	4	4
Verses 15–17		**59**	**59**	**21**	**21**

9a In my ears Yahweh Seba^ɔoth [has sworn]

b "Surely many houses

c will become a waste,

d large, good (ones)

e (will be) without resident.

10a For ten 'acres' of vineyard will yield
  one bath,

b And (ten) homers of seed will yield one ephah."

11a **Hey!** Ones (you) who rise early in the morning!

b Strong drink they pursue.

c Ones who tarry into the twilight!

d Wine makes them burn.

12a There are lyre and lute

b timbrel and flute and wine [at] their feasts.

c But the work of Yahweh they do not observe;

d the action of his hands they do not see.

13a **Therefore** my people go into exile without knowledge

b and their "glory" [has become] famished men,

c and their multitude is parched with thirst.

14a **Therefore** Sheol has opened wide its throat,

b and opened its mouth without limit.

c And her pomp and her mob will go down;

d her revelry, and the jubilation within her.

15a Mankind will be sunk; man will be stooped.

b The eyes of the haughty ones will be stooped.

16a And Yahweh Seba^ɔoth will be exalted in justice.

b The Holy God will show himself holy in righteousness.

17a Lambs will graze as in their pasture,

b and [in the] waste places of the fat ones sojourners will eat.

18a	הוֹי מֹשְׁכֵי הֶעָוֺן בְּחַבְלֵי הַשָּׁוְא	12	12	5	5
b	וְכַעֲבוֹת הָעֲגָלָה חַטָּאָה:	10	11	3	3
19a	הָאֹמְרִים יְמַהֵר ׀ יָחִישָׁה מַעֲשֵׂהוּ	13	14	4	4
b	לְמַעַן נִרְאֶה	4	5	2	2
c	וְתִקְרַב וְתָבוֹאָה: עֲצַת קְדוֹשׁ יִשְׂרָאֵל	14	14	5	5
d	וְנֵדָעָה:	4	4	1	1
Verses 18–19		57	60	20	20
20a	הוֹי הָאֹמְרִים לָרַע טוֹב	8	8	4	4
b	וְלַטּוֹב רָע	4	4	2	2
c	שָׂמִים חֹשֶׁךְ לְאוֹר	5	6	3	3
d	וְאוֹר לְחֹשֶׁךְ	4	5	2	2
e	שָׂמִים מַר לְמָתוֹק	6	6	3	3
f	וּמָתוֹק לְמָר:	5	5	2	2
Verse 20		32	34	16	16
21a	הוֹי חֲכָמִים בְּעֵינֵיהֶם	8	8	3	3
b	וְנֶגֶד פְּנֵיהֶם נְבֹנִים:	8	9	3	3
Verse 21		16	17	6	6
22a	הוֹי גִּבּוֹרִים לִשְׁתּוֹת יָיִן	7	8	4	4
b	וְאַנְשֵׁי־חַיִל לִמְסֹךְ שֵׁכָר:	8	9	4	3
23a	מַצְדִּיקֵי רָשָׁע עֵקֶב שֹׁחַד	7	9	4	4
b	וְצִדְקַת צַדִּיקִים יָסִירוּ מִמֶּנּוּ:	12	12	4	4
Verses 22–23		34	38	16	15
24a	לָכֵן כֶּאֱכֹל קַשׁ לְשׁוֹן אֵשׁ	8	9	5	5
b	וַחֲשַׁשׁ לֶהָבָה יִרְפֶּה	7/(8)	8	3	3
c	שָׁרְשָׁם כַּמָּק יִהְיֶה	6	6	3	3
d	וּפִרְחָם כָּאָבָק יַעֲלֶה	8	9	3	3
e	כִּי מָאֲסוּ אֵת תּוֹרַת יְהוָה צְבָאוֹת	12	12	4	6
f	וְאֵת אִמְרַת קְדוֹשׁ־יִשְׂרָאֵל נִאֵצוּ:	12	12	4	4
Verse 24		53/(54)	56	22	24
25a	עַל־כֵּן חָרָה אַף־יְהוָה בְּעַמּוֹ	10	10	4	4
b	וַיֵּט יָדוֹ עָלָיו וַיַּכֵּהוּ	10	10	4	4
c	וַיִּרְגְּזוּ הֶהָרִים	7	7	2	2
d	וַתְּהִי נִבְלָתָם כַּסּוּחָה בְּקֶרֶב חוּצוֹת	13	14	5	5

18a **Hey!** Ones (you) who drag out iniquity with ropes of vanity,
  b   as (with) cart bindings (they drag out) sin.
19a Those who say, "Let him hasten, let him hurry his work,
  b   so that we may see [it].
  c   Let the counsel of the Holy One of Israel draw near and come
        to pass,
  d   so that we may know [it]."

20a **Hey!** Ones (you) who call evil good
  b   and good evil,
  c   exchanging darkness for light
  d   and light for darkness,
  e   exchanging bitter for sweet
  f   and sweet for bitter.

21a **Hey!** Ones (you) wise in their [own] eyes
  b   and in front of their [own] faces (they are) smart.

22a **Hey!** Heroes at drinking wine!
  b   Men valiant at mixing drinks!
23a Justifying the wicked because of a bribe,
  b   the justice of the just they remove from him.

24a **Therefore**, as a tongue of fire consumes stubble,
  b   so chaff sinks down [because of] the flame.
  c   Their root like rot will be,
  d   and their sprout like dust will come up,
  e   for they have rejected the *torah* of Yahweh Seba'oth;
  f   and the speech of the Holy One of Israel they have spurned.

25a **Therefore**, the anger of Yahweh has burned against his people,
  b   and he has extended his hand against them, and he struck them.
  c   The mountains shook,
  d   and their corpse(s) were like refuse in the middle of the streets.

		Syllables	MT	Stresses	MT
e	בְּכָל־זֹאת לֹא־שָׁב אַפֹּו	7	7	3	3
f	וְעֹוד יָדֹו נְטוּיָה:	7	7	3	3
Verse 25		54	55	21	21
Totals		494/500 = 496	532	200/(203)	207

Notes on Translation and Text

5:8a. "Hey!" The function and translation of הוי are a matter of some debate. Form-critically, the interjection has been linked to the Ge-richtsankündigung (Westermann 1960), popular wisdom (Gerstenberger 1962; criticized by Wanke 1966), funeral lament (Clifford 1966; elaborated and refined by Janzen 1972; further refined by Hillers 1983). Clifford summarizes three uses and traces a chronological development, concluding that the eighth-century use (for example, Amos and Isaiah) regularly employs a substantive participle as a vocative (see also Hillers). He translates, 'alas . . .'. I agree that the "curse formula" is least likely, especially in light of the careful and, I think, distinctive use of אוי elsewhere (6:5). However, I am not convinced that the "cry to get attention" is as limited as Clifford suggests, nor is that sense necessarily distinct from overtones of lament. My translation attempts to reproduce both sound and substance in English, although Clifford's 'alas' is a worthy alternative. Perhaps 'look out!' is possible. In all discussion that follows, the more traditional terminology found in commentaries will be used, and the formula will be called a "woe."

5:10b. "ten" It is likely that עשרת does double duty into line c, especially in view of the unequal length between lines 10a and 10b.

5:13b. "glory" Quotation marks are used to contrast with the "glory" of Yahweh (compare 6:3). See also 10:3, where vain human "glory" is meant sarcastically. Here, the combination with המונו in the following line could well be rendered 'glorious multitude'.

"famished men" The phrase is literally 'men of hunger', which makes reasonable sense. BHS suggests following the versions (for example, the LXX reads νεκρῶν) and repointing to מֵתֵי, which anticipates v. 14. On the other hand, death is not the point of v. 13: the men are still starving. Watts follows BDB (607) and emends to מְזֵי, citing Deut 32:24

> e In all this, his anger has not returned;
> f his hand is still outstretched.

---

as a better parallel to צחה צמא in the following line, despite no textual evidence. Poetically, it is possible to take צחה צמא as being parallel solely to רעב, the second line showing expansion (compare with "ballast variant"). Thus מתי is as much a parallel to המונו as כבודו is: "men // multitude" vs. "honor // abundance," and likely כבודו does double duty. The poetic artistry allows כבודו to be heard but not really paralleled in the second line.

5:14c. "her" The nearest feminine antecedent of in the immediate context is "Sheol," but this makes little sense. The reference is most likely to "Jerusalem," which appears in 5:3. Nevertheless, it is possible that "Sheol" is also in mind; perhaps some tension and confusion is intended between Jerusalem and Sheol: the revelry of Jerusalem is actually that of Sheol.

5:17b. "fat ones" Read מחים from the root מחח, although there may be wordplay on the root מחה (BDB: 562 I 'wipe out' or(!) II 'strike'). The word is used only once elsewhere (Ps 66:15), where it refers to the fatling sacrificial animals. Here the reference may be to humans (so Oswalt), whose arrogant life-style has resulted in "waste places." Possibly the preposition *kap* does double duty from the previous line: "as in their pasture" // "as in waste places." The "fat ones" should then parallel "lambs," and מחים could be read as a construct form with enclitic *mem*: 'as in wastelands the fatlings of sojourners eat'.

"sojourners" The chiastic structure of the bicolon (see below, p. 55) suggests that גרים is parallel to the כבשים, who are grazing in waste places "as" in their pasture and are therefore quite "out of place." Thus emendation to גדים 'kids' (Wildberger, Oswalt), is unnecessary.

5:21b. "and in front of their [own] faces" Translation is literal. Better would be 'as far as they are concerned'.

5:23b. "him" The antecedent is undoubtedly the "just one(s)." צדקים could be read as singular (compare the versions, possibly the *mem* is enclitic), or the singular pronoun is simply collective. The line is better paraphrased, 'and they deny justice to the just'.

5:24b. **"chaff"** 1QIsaᵃ reads אש לוהבת which seems to reflect scribal error. Possibly וחשש was lost due to haplography (homoioteleuton with אש), then a second אש inserted, either as dittography or deliberately to provide the full expression אש להבה.

"flame" The translation is difficult. The bicolon is matched by pairs of terms: קש // חשש and אש לשון // להבה. The verbs match cause to effect, and a paraphrase would combine the subjects and objects as follows: 'as a tongue of fire and flame consume stubble and chaff, the (stubble and chaff) are reduced [to ashes]'.

Lineation

The methodological problems surveyed in the preliminary discussion (see pp. 26ff.) are exemplified by the lines at hand. Decided on the basis of syntax and parallelism, there is a range from 72 lines (appendix 1A, in which every uncertain division is decided in favor of short lines) to 58 lines (appendix 1B, in which every difficulty is decided in favor of long lines).

In either lineation, however, the most common line length is the 8-syllable colon, of which there are 13 (out of 72 = 18.1%) in appendix 1A, and 12 (out of 58 = 20.7%) in appendix 1B. Approximately half of the lines have 7–9 syllables, and approximately two-thirds have 6–10 syllables:

Appendix 1A (shortest possible lines):
lines with 8 syllables:	13	(18.1%)
lines with 7–9 syllables:	32	(44.4%)
lines with 6–10 syllables:	45	(62.5%)

Appendix 1B (longest possible lines):
lines with 8 syllables:	12	(20.7%)
lines with 7–9 syllables:	30	(51.7%)
lines with 6–10 syllables:	39	(67.2%)

Furthermore, if all difficult or questionable lines are eliminated from consideration and one analyzes only the lines that can be clearly lineated, the 8-syllable line again appears dominant:

v.	8ab:	7 + 8	v.	17:	9 + 10
v.	9a:	8	v.	21:	8 + 8
v.	12ab:	7 + 9	v.	22:	7 + 8
v.	12cd:	9 + 8	v.	23:	7 + 12

v. 13bc:	8 + 7		v. 24ab:	8 + 7
v. 14ab:	9 + 8		v. 24cd:	6 + 8
v. 14cd:	9 + 8		v. 25abc:	10 + 10 + 7
v. 15:	9 + 9		v. 25ef:	7 + 7
v. 16:	11 + 11			

Of these 34 lines, the most common line length is 8 syllables (11 lines):

6-syllable lines:	1	10-syllable lines:	3
7-syllable lines:	9	11-syllable lines:	2
8-syllable lines:	11	12-syllable lines:	1
9-syllable lines:	7		

32.4% (11) of these lines have 8 syllables.
79.4% (27) of these lines have 7–9 syllables.
91.2% (31) of these lines have 6–10 syllables.

On the basis of the lines that can be clearly lineated, lines of 7–9 syllables account for over 79% of the cola.

With these data as a foundation, a lineation based simply on the 8-syllable, 3-stress line has produced a poem of exactly 62 lines (appendix 1C). Obviously this method ignores considerations of syntax and parallelism and allows for enjambment in favor of more balanced line lengths. Nevertheless, it has used the factor of line length to produce a number of lines within the limits of the 58–72 lines set by considerations of syntax and parallelism alone.

Using this figure as a target for the overall total number of lines, one can now return to the difficult questions of lineation and deal with them on a case-by-case basis in relationship to the overall pattern.

Verse 8cd. As a bicolon, there are 16 syllables and 6 stresses, and perfect metrical balance could be shown by moving הושבתם to line 8c, as in appendix 1C. I show the lines unbalanced, even though this represents a decision "away" from the norm (and so better to test the norm, see below, p. 45). In either case, this example demonstrates the tension between syntax and meter; either "system" works.

Verse 9bcde. Line 9a is elliptical, but it forms an independent line. Lines 9bcde could be read as one bicolon (11 + 10 syllables, 5 + 4 stresses; see appendix 1B). The syllable and stress count is actually that of a tricolon (see appendix 1C), but syntactically one should read as either 2 or 4 lines. Based on the longer lines found later in the poem that will balance shorter lines, I opt for the shorter lines here.

Verse 11. As with lines 9bcde, these lines could be read as one bicolon (11 + 10 syllables, 4 + 4 stresses; so appendix 1B). Consistent with the decision regarding v. 9, I read this as 4 lines. This is confirmed by the parallelism with lines 8ab, where the הוֹי is followed by a participle and matched by a finite verb at the end of the second line.

Verse 12. While v. 12 presents no difficulties, one should note at least the possibility of producing a balanced bicolon (8 + 8 syllables) in 12ab by moving תֹף to line 12a, against the syntax (appendix 1C).

It is theoretically possible, based on syntax alone, to divide 12cd into 4 lines (appendix 1A), but there is no reason to break up lines of this length.

Verse 13. 13a could be divided (so appendix 1A), but the line is not unreasonably long. By analogy to לִבְלִי־חֹק in line 14b, the phrase מִבְּלִי־דָעַת should remain part of line 13a.

Verse 18. Two lines yield a long bicolon, but the syntax does not allow easy division. The total length is that of a tricolon (so appendix 1C).

Verse 19. Meter and syntax are in tension and the lines could be arranged in a more balanced way (appendix 1C). Total length indicates 4 lines, which can be achieved by either a metrical or syntactical lineation. I leave the syntactic units intact and am forced by the parallelism between 19b and 19d to suggest a one-word, one-unit line in 19d (contra O'Connor 1980: 307 and Cloete 1989a: 209).

Verse 20. Line lengths are short, but the parallelism demands either one tricolon or three bicola. Total length indicates a 4-line unit (32 syllables), as shown in appendix 1C. The number of stresses (16), however, argues for a greater number of lines.

Verse 23. The verse presents no major difficulty; 23b is somewhat long but cannot be divided.

Verse 24. Lines 24ef are long, but the parallelism demands a bicolon. The total length is better shown as a tricolon (appendix 1C), but I leave it as a long bicolon to balance the shorter lines earlier (for example, lines 9bcde, 11abcd).

Verse 25. There are no great problems, although the lengths of 25abc are somewhat long. The lines could be evened out (as in appendix 1C), with enjambment. The total length is slightly long for 6 lines (54 syllables and 21 stresses), but the division of 25d (as appendix 1A) is awkward. Again, one should note the presence of longer lines that balance shorter lines earlier in the composition.

In summary, this method of lineation has allowed various factors to play a role: parallelism and syntax as well as the dominant pattern of line length measured by syllables and stresses. Based on instances in which lineation was clear, the dominance of the 8-syllable (or 7–9-syllable) colon was established and then used to produce a target figure for the total number of lines. This overall target, in turn, then aided in making decisions on individual cases.

In fact, in a majority of cases (34 of 62 lines) the factors of grammar, parallelism, and line length overlapped so that there was no difficulty in lineation. This suggests that these factors complement one another and are all operative in the formation of Hebrew verse.

Nevertheless, in a number of instances, the "metric" consideration of line length stands in tension with the grammatical divisions of lines, although this tension is generally limited to the internal divisions within a bicolon. In fact, I have shown an alternative presentation of the versification of this composition, based entirely on the function of line length (appendix 1C). This indicates again that both grammar and "meter" function concurrently—at times in harmony, at times in disharmony, but the dissonance is often balanced out within the bicolon or verse level.

Syllable Counts

There are five instances where a prefixed conjunction may have been elided into the following syllable, followed by shewa, and these have been indicated by a double syllable count (lines 13b, 13c, 14c, 14d, and 24b). One 3d feminine-singular pronominal suffix (line 14b) is also uncertain. Thus the total number of syllables falls between a minimum of 494 and a maximum of 500 (the MT count is 532). Sixty-two 8-syllable lines would yield 496 syllables, which is undoubtedly the correct number, however they might be counted. Thus I shall use the short count for line 14b and consider the three prefixed conjunctions in lines 13c, 14c, and 24b to be elided. Those lines are tabulated also according to the shorter syllable count, with the alternatives shown in the text (pp. 34ff.) placed in parentheses.

Individual line lengths, of course, display a wide diversity. Nevertheless, the data suggest that a consideration of length forms a control on the poem as a whole. Based on the lineation that is shown and described, the line lengths are tabulated as follows:

4-syllable lines:	7	10-syllable lines:	5
5-syllable lines:	4	11-syllable lines:	3
6-syllable lines:	6	12-syllable lines:	5
7-syllable lines:	10	13-syllable lines:	2
8-syllable lines:	12	14-syllable lines:	1
9-syllable lines:	7		

Of the 62 lines,
   19.4% (12 lines) have 8 syllables,
   46.8% (29 lines) have 7–9 syllables,
   64.5% (40 lines) have 6–10 syllables.

The most common line length is 8 syllables.
The median line length is 8 syllables.
The average line length is 8.00 syllables per line (496/62).

Represented graphically, the distribution of line length appears as a roughly bell-shaped curve, with the peak at 8 syllables per line:

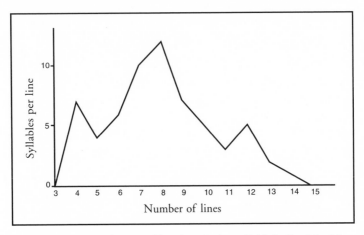

Fig. 2.1.   Distribution of line lengths (in syllables): Isa 5:8–25

On the level of bicola (including also one monocolon and one tri-colon) these figures are confirmed. In fact, the percentages are slightly higher, since long and short lines can be balanced within a bicolon, for example, lines19ab, cd. To summarize:

v. 8ab:	7 + 8 = 15	v. 18:	12 + 10 = 22
v. 8cd:	4 + 12 = 16	v. 19ab:	13 + 4 = 17
v. 9a:	8	v. 19cd:	14 + 4 = 18
v. 9bc:	6 + 5 = 11	v. 20ab:	8 + 4 = 12
v. 9de:	6 + 4 = 10	v. 20cd:	5 + 4 = 9
v. 10:	11 + 7 = 18	v. 20ef:	6 + 5 = 11
v. 11ab:	6 + 5 = 11	v. 21:	8 + 8 = 16
v. 11cd:	6 + 4 = 10	v. 22:	7 + 8 = 15
v. 12ab:	7 + 9 = 16	v. 23:	7 + 12 = 19
v. 12cd:	9 + 8 = 17	v. 24ab:	8 + 7 = 15
v. 3abc:	10+8+7 = 25	v. 24cd:	6 + 8 = 14
v. 14ab:	9 + 8 = 17	v. 24ef:	12 + 12 = 24
v. 14cd:	9 + 8 = 17	v. 25ab:	10 + 10 = 20
v. 15:	9 + 9 = 18	v. 25cd:	7 + 13 = 20
v. 16:	11 + 11 = 22	v. 25ef:	7 + 7 = 14
v. 17:	9 + 10 = 19		

Eliminating the monocolon (line 9a) and the tricolon (lines 13abc), the range of syllable length for the 29 bicola is as follows:

9-syllable bicola:	1	17-syllable bicola:	4
10-syllable bicola:	2	18-syllable bicola:	3
11-syllable bicola:	3	19-syllable bicola:	2
12-syllable bicola:	1	20-syllable bicola:	2
13-syllable bicola:	0	21-syllable bicola:	0
14-syllable bicola:	2	22-syllable bicola:	2
15-syllable bicola:	3	23-syllable bicola:	0
16-syllable bicola:	3	24-syllable bicola:	1

10.3% (3) of the bicola have exactly 16 syllables.
34.5% (10) of the bicola have 15–17 syllables.
51.7% (15) of the bicola have 14–18 syllables (7–9 per line).
69.0% (20) of the bicola have 12–20 syllables (6–10 per line).

The median length of the bicola is 16 syllables.
The average length of a bicolon is 15.97 syllables.

Represented graphically, the number of syllables per bicolon appears as in fig. 2.2.

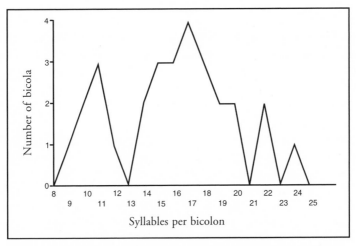

Fig. 2.2.   Distribution of bicola lengths (in syllables): Isa 5:8–25

It is of further interest to observe how the individual lines within each bicolon relate in length. For example, in 15 of the 29 bicola, the first (or A) line is longer; in 8 bicola, the second (or B) line is longer; in 6 cases the cola are exactly the same length. This would indicate a sense of greater weight in the A lines. However, in direct reference to the stress accents (see below, pp. 49ff.), several of these lines seem to carry an "extra" accent, because of the use of the הוי and of the לכן or על־כן formulae, all of which would fall into the first lines of their respective bicola.

Furthermore, if a one-syllable difference between lines is considered to be insignificant, that is, if we count as longer only the lines that are at least two syllables longer, the figures for the 29 bicola are much more balanced:

> bicola in which the A line is longer: 7
> bicola in which the B line is longer: 5
> bicola in which both lines are within one syllable: 17

This suggests that, in spite of bicola in which the two lines are as different as 14 + 4 syllables (lines 19cd) or 13 + 4 syllables (lines 19ab) or 4 + 12 syllables (lines 8cd), the overall tendency is toward a balancing of the two lines. In fact, if one adds up all of the A lines plus all of the B lines, and includes the monocolon as an A line and the tricolon as an A plus two B lines, there are a total of 257 syllables (A lines) + 239 syllables (B lines). In light of the "extra" stresses and syllables in at least ten of the A lines, these totals are quite close

In summary, there is a wide diversity of individual line (colon) lengths, ranging from 4 to 14 syllables per line. In fact, this diversity was widened by the fact that within a bicolon, I often lineated along boundaries of syntax and parallelism, against the 8-syllable norm. For example, lines 8cd, which could be shown as an 8 + 8 bicolon (see appendix 1C) were lineated as a 4 + 12 unit.

Nevertheless, the most common line length, as well as the median line length, proved to be 8 syllables. The average line length is 8.00 syllables per line. The figures were similar on the level of bicola, where, in spite of a range of 9–24 syllables, both the greatest number of bicola as well as the average length fell at and around 16 syllables per bicola.

This suggests several tentative conclusions. First, the 8-syllable colon / 16-syllable bicolon plays a dominant role in the lineation of this poetry. But secondly, any normative function is to be associated with a wide diversity of variation from the norm. However, the deviations produce a strong sense of balance, especially on the outer edges of the spectrum. There are 11 lines under 6 syllables per line and 11 lines over 10 syllables per line.

It was observed in conclusion to the discussion of lineation (p. 45) that a sense of both harmony and tension existed between grammar and line length, which was often resolved by balancing at the level of the verse or bicolon (for example, lines 8cd, 19ab, and 19cd). Based on the spectrum of lengths for both cola and bicola spread over the entire poem, a sense of balancing extends beyond individual verses or bicola. For example, the short bicola in v. 9 and v. 11 are balanced out by longer bicola elsewhere (for example, v. 18 and v. 24). It would seem that the poet/prophet worked with a clear sense of compensation in mind, so that short lines would be balanced by longer lines within the structure of the whole composition.

Stress Counts

My figures show a total of 200/203 stresses for these 62 lines (the MT count is 207). Following the minimum count, individual lines have 1–5 stresses:

1-stress cola:	1	(1.6%)
2-stress cola:	12	(19.4%)
3-stress cola:	25	(40.3%)
4-stress cola:	20	(32.3%)
5-stress cola:	4	(6.5%)

Thus 57 lines (91.9%) have 2–4 stresses.
The average number of stresses per colon is 3.22.

Several individual lines appear "heavy": for example, line 8a has 7 syllables and 4 stresses, and likewise line 10b. Line 11a has 6 syllables and 3 stresses. Lines 13a, 14a, 18a, 20a, 22a, 24a, 25a are also noteworthy. In fact, these lines include all but one (21a) of the "woes" and the four uses of a "therefore" formula. It seems safe to assume that such features were used intentionally to overweight a line (marked in the translation by boldface type). If one subtracts the six uses of "woe" and four "therefores," the total number of stresses becomes 190, summarized as follows:

1-stress cola:	1	(1.6%)
2-stress cola:	14	(22.6%)
3-stress cola:	29	(46.8%)
4-stress cola:	16	(25.8%)
5-stress cola:	2	(3.2%)

Thus 59 (95.2%) of the cola have 2–4 stresses.
The average number of stresses per colon is 3.06.

If 3 stresses per colon were mutliplied by the 62 lines, one should expect to have 186 stressess, which is very close to the reduced figure I have counted. In spite of the greater imprecision with which stresses can be counted (as compared to syllables), my calculations are very close to what is likely the exact number of stresses. Even without further adjustment, these figures show that the pattern being followed is an 8-syllable, 3-stress line.

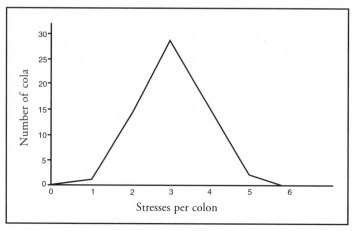

Fig. 2.3. Distribution of stresses per colon: Isa 5:8–25

When the evidence is represented graphically (fig. 2.3), the dominance of 3-stress cola is clear.

Likewise, the number of stresses per bicolon is summarized as follows, eliminating the one monocolon and the one tricolon:

4-stress bicola:	3	(10.3%)
5-stress bicola:	5	(17.2%)
6-stress bicola:	10	(43.5%)
7-stress bicola:	8	(27.6%)
8-stress bicola:	3	(10.3%)

Thus 100% of the bicola have 4–8 stresses (2–4 per colon).

The average number of stresses per bicolon is 6.14.

When these statistics are represented graphically (fig. 2.4), a similar configuration appears.

Other uses of extra stresses for emphasis appear in lines 10ab, where two "heavy" lines conclude a subsection and match the "heavy" line with which it began (8a). Interestingly, the MT overloads this bicolon even more severely, giving it 10 accents. One might include also 12cd, which the MT accents as a 9-stress bicolon.

A similar technique appears in 24ef, where the MT accents both object markers as well as the particle כי, creating a 6-stress colon in 24e. My counts leave the particles unaccented and suggest a number of stresses consistent with the (long) length of these lines, which are themselves emphatic by their unusual length.

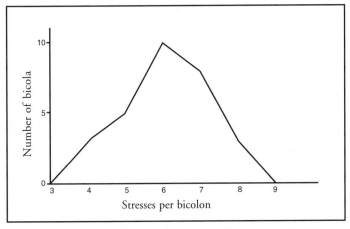

Fig. 2.4. Distribution of stresses per bicolon: Isa 5:8–25

Finally, one should notice also the balancing of the stresses between the lines of the bicola. Excluding the extra stresses, the stress patterns are tabulated as follows:

Balanced Bicola		*Unbalanced Bicola*		
2:2	3 bicola	A dominant:	3:2	4 bicola
3:3	7 bicola		4:2	1 bicolon
4:4	4 bicola		4:3	2 bicola
			5:1	1 bicolon
		B dominant:	2:3	1 bicolon
			2:4	1 bicolon
monocolon:	3		2:5	1 bicolon
tricolon:	3:3:3		3:4	4 bicola

Of the 29 bicola, 14 are perfectly balanced (2:2, 3:3, or 4:4), and 2 are variants of the 3:3 pattern (2:4 or 4:2). In addition, the monocolon and the tricolon all have 3 stresses. It is clear that the most common stress pattern is 3:3.

Among the unbalanced bicola, no dominant single pattern emerges. There are 8 bicola in which the A line has more stresses and 7 bicola in which the B line is dominant. The total ratio of lines A:B in bicola in which the A line is dominant is 16:8. The total ratio of A:B lines in the B dominant bicola is 9:16. The total ratio of A:B lines of all the unbalanced bicola is 25:24. Thus while there are both balanced and unbalanced bicola, the unbalanced lines tend to equal out, producing an overall sense of balance and symmetry.

In summary, I note the dominance of the 3–stress colon and the 6-stress bicolon, which correspond to the 8/16-syllable counts for the same units. For a composition of 62 lines, one should therefore expect 186 stresses. However, a total of 200/202 stresses was found. Yet at least 10 of these were discovered to be rhetorically significant in "overloading" lines and can be considered analogous to "accidental" or non-structural accents. Reduced by 10, and with allowance for other occasional emphatic uses of an "extra" stress, the total of 190/192 is very close to the figure expected were the poem composed on the basis of a 3-stress line.

This suggests that stress accents were a factor in poetic composition. Like the feature of line length as measured by syllable counts, accents seem to have formed a part of a metrical grid on which the poem was constructed. And as with line length, there appear both a sense of a normative pattern and a frequent deviation from that norm that is nevertheless controlled and balanced across the norm.

Prose Particles

Within these lines are 7 uses of the article and 3 object markers for a total of 10 prose particles, or 4.59% of the 218 words. The object markers appear in line 12c, where extra, emphatic accents have already been noted, and in 24ef, where an excessively long bicolon concludes a subunit. In spite of its length, 24ef forms a perfectly balanced and chiastic bicolon that cannot be divided, and it seems that the prose particles contribute to the overall rhetorical effect.

While very near the outside limit of 5% for classical poetry proposed by Freedman (1987a; see above, p. 26), this prose particle count is nevertheless within the boundaries of poetry.

Verse and Strophe Structure

It has already been shown that factors of grammar and syntax, parallelism, and metric considerations of length, measured by syllables and accents, all contribute to the composition of the poem. Here I shall discuss in greater detail the careful crafting involved in the integral structure of the verses, and in so doing note how such poetic and rhetorical features aid in the understanding of the meaning of the text.

Strophe A: Verses 8–10

Verse 8 presents the first הוי, followed by a plural participle, a pattern to be followed in five of the "seven" woes (10:1–4, I shall argue, is the seventh).

The verse is a quatrain of 31 syllables and 13 stresses. More significantly, the lines develop a tension between third and second person. The initial participle is ambiguous: "those who . . ." or "you who. . . ." The second line clarifies by using a third-person verb. Lines a and b form an ABBA chiasm: the inner terms match; therefore the verb and participle should match.

But line c continues the syntax, running the thought on, as though the action portrayed in lines a + b has not stopped; clearly the behavior has gone too far. Finally, the last line unambiguously uses the second person, making clear that the third-person reference applies to the intended audience. Thus the "woe," which may first have been perceived as directed to others, is forcefully driven home to the hearers.[5]

Further, lines 8cd convey irony. "Until there is no place" suggests overcrowded conditions. However, the meaning is related to the previous lines and is quite different: "there is no more place to take for oneself." Thus the last line contrasts "no more place" with "live all alone" and adds the ironic sense of the *Hophal*: 'you are (lit.) "caused to live" all alone in the midst of the land'. What was intended as a great achievement is reduced to the passive/causative: they have lost control of the very thing they had succeeded in doing, and their quest for space has resulted in loneliness.

Verses 9–10 expand the thought of v. 8ab: "house" of v. 8a becomes "many houses" in 9bc; "field" of 8b becomes "ten 'acres' of vineyard" in 10a. After the introductory monocolon (v. 9a), two short bicola are followed by one longer bicolon; together they are roughly equivalent: 9bcde = 21 syllables and 9 stresses; 10ab = 18 syllables and 8/9 stresses. The longer lines, heavy with accents, in the final bicolon bring the first strophe to conclusion and echo the fact that the initial line also has an extra accent (הוי).

Strophe B: Verses 11–12

Verse 11 introduces the second strophe with the second "woe," followed by a participle in a bound construction, as in v. 8. I note again the tension between the ambiguous participle and the third-person verb form at the end of the second line. Unlike v. 8, however, the following bicolon (as well as the one beyond it) continues the use of the third person. In light of the use of both third and second person in v. 8, my translation includes the

---

5. Hillers (1983: 186) notes the interplay between third and second person, suggesting "that a vocative element comes right after the *hoy* and pronouns referring back to this are for a time in third person in keeping with ancient usage; explicitly second-person forms reassert themselves later."

second-person pronoun with the initial participle in this and in the following "woes" to indicate that the "they" was to be perceived as "you."
Although this is speculative, it could be that in the original rhetorical setting, eye contact and gestures were used both to clarify and to heighten
the tension within the audience addressed.

Unlike v. 8, which has an AABC pattern, the quatrain of v. 11 is
marked by ABAB parallelism. The A lines each contain an interrupted or
"broken" construct chain, and the B lines pun on a noun pair and two
verbs within the same semantic field (compare Lam 4:19, the only other
place in the Hebrew Bible where the verbs רדף and דלק occur together),
but with subject and objects reversed. In line 11b, "they" *pursue* alcoholic
drink. The result, in 11d is that wine *pursues* them.

Verse 12 consists of two bicola, continuing the thought of v. 11. Lines
12ab are chiastic in that the inside terms form the subject of the predicate "there are . . . at their feasts." Two pairs of terms in the pattern
"x + y" are concluded by an additional single item: ויין. Line 12c begins
with the prose particle object marker in an initial, emphatic position,
and it does double duty with the following line, where inverse word order
(O–V) parallels the previous line (thus an ABAB structure for 12cd in
contrast to the chiasm of 12ab). Again one notices the use of a bicolon
with possible extra stresses, especially in the MT accentuation, to close
the strophe. The use of the noun מעשׂה in the final line echoes the
double occurrence of the verb עשׂה with which the first strophe concluded in v. 10.

Strophes C–D: Verses 13–14

Each verse is best understood as a separate strophe with unifying features.
Verse 13 is left as a tricolon (see above, p. 44), but v. 14 is a quatrain or
double bicolon. While of uneven length (25 + 34 syllables), each strophe
begins with לכן as an indication of Yahweh's judgment and as a result
of the actions previously described. The two are further linked by the
use of similar negatives, מבלי // לבלי, both translated 'without'. The first
speaks of "my people, 'without' knowledge"; the second of Sheol's appetite, "without" limit.

Indeed, both strophes play on the theme of the first two "woes": the
desire for space and for food and drink. Famine and thirst will be the result in the land; Sheol has both appetite and space to consume everyone.
The strophes are further held together by the fact that v. 14 clarifies what
is meant by גלה in 13a. Exile is here perceived as more than captivity in
another country; it is described as a descent to Sheol.

Strophe E: Verses 15–17

Verses 15–17 form a unit of three bicola, the first of which is a variant of the refrain that appears in 2:9, 11, 17. The fuller versions in 2:11 and 17 show an initial bicolon based on the interplay of the verbs שחח and שפל, which is compressed in 5:15a. On the other hand, 5:15b expands the use of עיני גבהים into the second colon. What was the third line in 2:11, 17 has been altered by replacing the verb שׂגב with a synonym, גבה, linking 5:16a with 5:15b.

Yet 5:16a is also the first colon of a new bicolon, 16ab, which has an AB:C :: BA:C structure: the first three words of each line form a chiasm, with two verbs on the outside and divine names on the inside, but at the end of each line are the parallels בצדקה // במשפט.

Verse 17 concludes this strophe with another chiastic bicolon, the second line forming the reverse order of the first (ABC:CBA) with חרבות מחים a ballast variant of כדברם. Possibly the preposition *kap* does double duty with גרים, and a paraphrase would be something like, "sheep will graze and eat like strangers (in) the waste places of the fat ones as their pasture." Thus the content of this bicolon returns to the theme of desolate and deserted fields and forms a thematic inclusio with v. 8 (see below on larger structures). It also rounds out a strophe of near perfect balance, although the final line adds both a syllable and an accent: the three bicola are $(9 + 9) + (11 + 11) + (9 + 10)$ syllables and $(3 + 3) + (4 + 4) + (3 + 4)$ stresses.

Strophe F: Verses 18–19

With vv. 18–19, the "woe" formula reappears, followed by another participle in the construct state. Here, however, the construction is determined; the use of the article may well be vocative, again implying, though still somewhat ambiguously, a second-person address, as the translation indicates.

The first bicolon is chiastic, based on the pairing of חטאה // עון, both of which bind the construct משכי, which serves double duty at the beginning and end of the verse. Line 19a begins with the articulated participle, parallel to משכי העון, and it links the quotation that follows with the actions just described. The lineation problem of lines 19ab and cd has been noted previously; here I suggest, speculatively and thus cautiously, that the unevenness of the lines from long to short might serve the rhetorical function of quickening the pace of presentation and of creating a sense of urgency. This would be consistent, at least, with the fact that the next two strophes, v. 20 and v. 21, become increasingly shorter. The impression is given that the "woes" are coming more quickly.[6]

Strophes G–H: Verses 20–21

Verse 20 continues the alternation of longer and shorter lines; here even the longer lines become shorter and the stress pattern becomes 4:2 :: 3:2 :: 3:2. If, as shall be argued below, vv. 18–23 form a stanza containing the majority of the "woes," then lines 20ab lie at the midpoint of this stanza (as the fourth "woe" lies at the midpoint of a list of seven). The pace quickens. The rhetoric reaches the heart of the matter: confusion of good and evil (compare Amos 5:14 at the heart of that whole book!). The vocative האמרים links to the previous strophe (see line 19a); the short lines hurry on to the next "woe."

As anticipated, v. 21 is the shortest "woe," which, unlike all the other strophes, does not elaborate beyond a single bicolon. Yet the line lengths suddenly even out to an 8 + 8 syllable pattern and a 3 + 3 stress pattern. Again, chiasm binds the bicolon together, the second line adding a syllable in ונגד פניהם as a ballast variant to בעיניהם in lieu of the initial הוי.

Strophe I: Verses 22–23

The final "woe" is a double bicolon (vv. 22–23), roughly equal in length to the fourth "woe" in v. 20. Here the expected participle is replaced by a plural noun, followed by the infinitive, paralleled in v. 22b in an ABAB pattern. The content echoes v. 11.

The vocabulary of righteousness and evil in v. 23, however, picks up not only the theme of v. 20 but also the one introduced in v. 8. The sixth and last "woe," therefore, reiterates the themes of both the second and first, as well as the fourth, or middle of a list of seven. This tension between a list of six or seven items is an important indication of the larger structure of 5:8–25 and of its relationship to 9:7–10:4 (see below, pp. 64 and 96ff.).

---

6. Contrast this explanation and this approach to that of, for example, Gray (1912: 88), who argues in his introductory remarks to 5:8–24 that "rhythmical differences, as well as these differences of structures, suggest that the following sections are sayings uttered at different times . . . and then ultimately brought together by an editor on account of their beginning with the same interjection." I do not reject the possibility of an editor's hand, unless his method of compilation is considered to be haphazard. However, the argument for intentional differences in length and structure based on a rhetorical function and objective suggests that such differences may just as well have been part and parcel of the original piece.

The structure of v. 23 offers a further link to the first two "woes." At first sound and sight, צדקת צדיקים seems to parallel מצדיקי רשע; the lines seem to read ABAB (better, ABAC). However, the syntactic parallel to the participle מצדיקי is the finite third plural verb יסירו in the second half of line 23b, a verse structure similar to the participle—preformative verb chiasm noted in lines 8ab and 11ab and cd, that is, in the first two "woe" sections and not elsewhere in vv. 18–23.

Moreover, the participle form at the beginning of v. 23a is exactly what should be expected after the הוי in v. 22a, where the exceptional noun form has already been observed. This strophe has carefully delayed the anticipated participle until the second bicolon, binding the two bicola together into one strophe, which again indicates that v. 23 is intended to be a part of the sixth "woe" and not a "lost" seventh. The rhetorical effect, however, is that it may have formed a "false" seventh (see discussion below, pp. 101–2).

Strophes J–K: Verses 24–25

Verses 24–25 introduce two concluding strophes, each of which begins with a different form of the particle translated 'therefore'. Verse 24 begins with a quatrain of different bicola patterns: ABBA :: ABAB, introduced by the same לכן heard twice previously, at the beginning of the quatrains of v. 13 and v. 14. However, v. 24 continues with a final bicolon, which, were it not for the very tight chiastic parallelism, could qualify as prose. The double use of the object marker is found elsewhere in 5:8–25 only in 12cd, the bicolon immediately preceding the other two לכן quatrains. Like its use in line 12c, it is no doubt emphatic here as well, and it brings a strophe and appears to bring a stanza to conclusion.

Verse 25, however, adds a final unit, introduced by על־כן. Like v. 24, the strophe has 6 lines that can be divided 4 + 2, and the concluding bicolon in v. 25 consists of the refrain that is also to be found four times in 9:7–10:4. However, in 5:25 the first bicolon anticipates the third. The structure is not simply 4 + 2 lines; it is 2 + (2) + 2. The first bicolon introduces the "anger of Yahweh" and the "stretching out" of "his hand" against his people. These motifs are then reiterated in the refrain in the last bicolon in this poem and then also in chaps. 9–10 (and alluded to in 12:1c). In fact, the finite verb forms used in 5:25ab indicate the initiation of the action that is reported in each refrain as being unresolved (until 12:1c!).[7]

---

7. Kaiser (1963 = 1972: 133; 1979 = 1983: 221) and Clements (1980b: 69) represent an opposite and, I acknowledge, majority view in seeing 5:25 as the *conclusion* to

On the other hand, 25ab has in common with 25cd the fact that the two bicola are the same length (20 syllables), although the individual cola of 25cd are uneven (7 + 13). This middle bicolon expands the sphere of Yahweh's anger to the realm of nature, and the reference to the "corpses" of the people recalls the deathly appetite of Sheol in v. 14. The use of בקרב חוצות provides an echo of בקרב הארץ from the initial verse (line 8d) and suggests that, while man's quest for new acquisitions moves from house to field to land, the result will be not only loneliness "*in the midst of* the land" but also dead bodies like corpses "*in the midst of* the streets."

Gross Structure

Having discussed the detailed structuring of the verses and strophes, I shall now consider the structure of the entire composition. The following observations serve as a starting point:

1. The first "woe" is followed (in vv. 9–10) by a direct quotation of Yahweh's words to the prophet, likely overheard in the divine council.
2. The second "woe" is longer than the first (two quatrains vs. one), and it adds a concluding bicolon with an object marker and inverted sentence structure for emphasis.
3. Following the second "woe," there are two "therefore" strophes (vv. 13–14), each introduced by לכן.
4. Verses 15–17 form a strophe introduced by the refrain found in 2:9, 11, 17 and concluded by thematic allusions to the content of the first "woe."
5. Verses 18–23 contain four more woes (##3–6), the first of which includes a direct quotation of the people's words against Yahweh's counsel (compare with 1, above).
6. The second and third of this second series of "woes" (overall ##4–5) grow increasingly shorter and therefore would have been spoken/ read in more rapid succession.
7. The fourth "woe" within this second series (v. 22, #6 overall) is really only a single bicolon, as is the third (v. 21, overall #5). But instead of a final or seventh "woe," an additional bicolon is added (v. 23), the content of which echoes the very first "woe" in v. 8.

---

the poem in 9:7ff., based both upon content and the use of the עלֿכן formula. My argument is that 5:25 is neither the first nor the last stanza of the poem in 9:7ff.; it simply anticipates it and introduces the theme.

8. The total length of the four "woes" in vv. 18–23 is 139 syllables, 58 stresses, and 58 words, which is roughly equivalent to the length of the first two "woes" in vv. 8–12: 132 syllables, 55 stresses, and 63 words.

9. This series of four "woes" in vv. 18–23 is followed by a "therefore" strophe (v. 24), introduced by לכן, and concluded with a long bicolon that contains two object markers and a perfect chiastic structure for emphasis (2, above).

10. This single לכן strophe (v. 24) is roughly equivalent in length to the double "therefore" strophe in vv. 13–14. Verse 24 contains 53 syllables, 22 stresses, and 25 words. Verses 13–14 contain 59 syllables, 23 stresses, and 25 words.

11. Verse 25 forms a strophe that concludes with the refrain found in 9:11, 17, 20, and 10:4. The first bicolon introduces the vocabulary of Yahweh's "anger" and the "stretching out of his hand."

12. The length of v. 25 (54 syllables, 21 stresses, and 25 words) is roughly equivalent to that of vv. 15–17 (59 syllables, 21 stresses, and 22 words).

The whole of 5:8–25, therefore, divides into two halves or "panels": vv. 8–17 and vv. 18–25. Each follows the same general order: a series of woes; the impending result, based on the actions condemned and introduced by "therefore"; and a concluding strophe (or stanza), which contains a refrain to be found elsewhere in Isaiah 2–12, the first echoing what is to be found previously, the second anticipating words yet to come.

These two panels are equivalent in length:

vv. 8–17:	250 syllables	99 stresses	110 words
vv. 18–25:	246 syllables	101 stresses	108 words

The individual strophes and stanzas fall into the following outline:

Panel I: Stanza 1: Strophe A: vv. 8–10 (woe #1 and quotation)
78 syllables, 33 stresses, 38 words
Strophe B: vv. 11–12 (woe #2)
54 syllables, 22 stresses, 25 words
Stanza 2: Strophe A: v. 13 (לכן #1)
25 syllables, 10 stresses, 11 words
Strophe B: v. 14 (לכן #2)
34 syllables, 13 stresses, 14 words
Stanza 3: Refrain: vv. 15–17 (contains refrain found in chap. 2)
59 syllables, 21 stresses, 22 words

Panel II: Stanza 1: Strophe A: vv. 18–19 (woe #3 and quotation)
57 syllables, 20 stresses, 20 words
Strophe B: v. 20 (woe #4)
32 syllables, 16 stresses,16 words
Strophe C: v. 21 (woe #5)
16 syllables, 6 stresses, 6 words
Strophe D: vv. 22–23 (woe #6 and
"false" seventh)
34 syllables, 16 stresses, 16 words
Stanza 2: v. 24 (לָכֵן #3)
53 syllables, 22 stresses, 25 words
Stanza 3: Refrain: v. 25 (contains refrain found in
chaps. 9–10)
54 syllables, 21 stresses, 25 words

Significantly, one should note that length equivalencies do not occur at the level of verse and strophes, but that the larger structures, which I have labelled stanzas and panels, present a sense of overall balance.[8] Indeed, I admit other possible groupings; for example, stanzas two and three of each panel could be combined into one larger second stanza, or stanzas one and two of each panel could be combined, leaving only the final stanza (which consists of a single strophe) as a refrain. In all three options, the length equivalencies between the corresponding stanzas of each panel are striking:

Option A (stanzas outlined as shown above):
I. Stanza 1: 132 syllables, 55 stresses, 63 words
Stanza 2: 59 syllables, 23 stresses, 25 words
Stanza 3: 59 syllables, 21 stresses, 22 words
II. Stanza 1: 139 syllables, 58 stresses, 58 words
Stanza 2: 53 syllables, 22 stresses, 25 words
Stanza 3: 54 syllables, 21 stresses, 25 words

Dividing between stanzas two and three of each panel shows that their individual lengths are equivalent. Combining them according to the second option only demonstrates more clearly that their totals are also similar:

Option B (combining stanzas two and three):
I. Stanza 1: (as shown)
Stanzas 2–3: (combine vv. 13–17): 118 syllables,
44 stresses, 47 words

8. See the conclusion of P. Raabe (1990: 175), in reference to his study of psalms with refrains, ". . . symmetry in length operates on the stanza level rather than the strophe level."

II. Stanza 1:   (as shown)
    Stanzas 2–3: (combine vv. 24–25):   107 syllables,
                         43 stresses, 50 words

If one divides only between stanzas two and three of each panel, separating only the final strophe as a refrain, there remains a balance between the corresponding stanzas in panels one and two:

Option C (combining stanzas one and two):
  I. Stanzas 1–2: (vv. 8–14): 191 syllables, 78 stresses,
                                88 words
     Stanza 3:   (vv. 15–17): 59 syllables, 21 stresses,
                                22 words
 II. Stanzas 1–2: (vv. 18–24): 192 syllables, 80 stresses,
                                83 words
     Stanza 3:   (v. 25):   54 syllables, 21 stresses,
                                25 words

The symmetry between the two halves of the whole, however it is divided, is clear. Yet there are additional indications of careful internal structure that give further indication of the unity of the pericope. For example, the use of a divine name occurs four times in each half.[9]

In 5:8–17, the name "Yahweh Seba$^\circ$oth" occurs in the first "woe" (line 9a) and "Yahweh" in the second "woe" (line 12c). There are no divine names in the "therefore" sections, but two in the final stanza: "Yahweh Seba$^\circ$oth" in 16a and "the Holy God" in 16b. In the first strophe of the second panel, 19c echoes the name used in the final strophe of the first panel: "the Holy One of Israel." There are no other names used in the "woe" stanzas of the second panel, but the 'therefore' (לכן) stanza has two: "Yahweh Seba$^\circ$oth" in 24e and "the Holy One of Israel" in 24f. Finally, v. 25, which is, in effect, an additional 'therefore' section (using על־כן), although it is, in fact, a concluding refrain, has "Yahweh" in 25a:

Panel I (vv. 8–17)   *Panel II (vv. 18–25)*

Stanza 1: יהוה צבאות (line 9a)   Stanza 1: קדוש ישראל (line 19c)
           יהוה (12c)

Stanza 2: [   ]   Stanza 2: יהוה צבאות (24e)
                                      קדוש ישראל (24f)

9. In passing, I would call attention to the fact that there are six uses of divine names or titles in 9:7–10:4 but none in the final "woe" stanza of 10:1–4. The eighth name in 5:8–25, however, appears in v. 25, which forms a link to 9:7ff. Both pericopes (5:8–25 and 9:7–10:4), therefore, have a combined total of 14 (2×7) divine names; seven within the stanzas containing "woes," seven within stanzas containing the refrain of 5:25ef. See below, p. 102.

Stanza 3: יהוה צבאות (16a)   Stanza 3: יהוה (25a)
האל הקדוש (16b)

Putting the corresponding sections together, one discovers (a) there
are three different names in the "woe" sections: Yahweh Seba⁾oth, Yahweh, the Holy One of Israel; (b) there are two different names in the
"therefore" (לכן) sections (none in vv. 13–14, two in v. 24): Yahweh Se-
ba⁾oth and the Holy One of Israel; and (c) there are three different names
in the refrain stanzas that close each panel: Yahweh Seba⁾oth, the Holy
God, and Yahweh:

Sanzas 1:	יהוה צבאות	(9a)
	יהוה	(12c)
	קדוש ישׂראל	(19c)
Stanzas 2:	יהוה צבאות	(24e)
	קדוש ישׂראל	(24f)
Stanzas 3:	יהוה צבאות	(16a)
	האל הקדוש	(16b)
	יהוה	(25a)

Furthermore, there are several instances of word play between and
among the parts. The verb עשׂה and its cognate noun מַעֲשֶׂה link 10bc
at the end of the first "woe" with 12d at the end of the second "woe." The
root occurs again in the first strophe of the second series of "woes," 19a
and forms not only an internal link between the two "woes" in the first
panel but also a link between the "woes" in the first and the second
panels.

The verbal root אכל appears in the very last line of vv. 8–17, and
one wonders if this is an allusion also to the voracious appetite of Sheol
in v. 14 as well as the insatiable quest for field and harvest discussed
in vv. 8–10. But just as the verb indicates a turning of the "table" in panel
I, its reappearance in the "therefore" section in panel II (line 24a) makes
the same point: the harvest will be consumed, but not by the intended
consumer.

The interplay of משׁפט, the root צדק, as well as טוב and רשׁע/רע
occurs in lines 16ab and 23ab (where noun or participle of the root צדק
is used three times!) and echoes lines 20ab. It is also likely that the use of
the particle אמרים in 19a and 20a in reference to what the people "say"
is contrasted by the assertion that "they refuse the אמרת קדושׁ-ישׂראל"
in 24f. Finally, I would again call to mind the echo of 8d (בקרב הארץ),
within the first strophe, in 25d (בקרב חוצות), within the last strophe.
Not only is man 'alone *in the midst of* the earth', but he is also now

described as being abandoned like corpses left as refuse '*in the midst of the streets*'.

To summarize, there is an intricate but clear structural pattern in Isa 5:8–25 on the level of stanzas and "panels," which indicates an overall unity to the composition. Further, there are a number of internal rhetorical features, such as wordplay and repetition, which attest to the integrity of the pericope as a unit. Structural and rhetorical analysis have confirmed the original hypothesis that the correct boundaries of this unit extend from v. 8 through v. 25.

Thought Progression

With the borders secured, it remains to show how this analysis has enhanced the understanding of the text. I have already noted instances where vocabulary repetition has nuanced the understanding of individual verses. Now I shall try to trace the thought progression of the composition as a whole.

The structure proposed divides the piece into two major "panels," each of which consists of an introductory series of "woes" (stanza 1) followed by two further stanzas of equivalent length (stanzas 2–3), which indicate the impending results of the actions the "woes" addressed. The first "woe" is expanded to include a hint of the conclusion of each panel: land, houses, and people will be destroyed. The second set of "therefores" is expanded in length to include further reason for the destruction (the כי clauses of lines 24ef) and to indicate that the threat of Yahweh's anger still remains (v. 25).

The first set of (two) "woes" (panel I, stanza 1) is equivalent in length to the second set of (four) "woes" (panel II, stanza 1). They are equivalent in length, but in the ratio of 1:2 in the number of "woes." The absence of the actual word הוי after the sixth woe leaves the question open whether there is, in fact, more to come.

The first two "therefores" (vv. 13–14) are complementary to one another,[10] and the shift from masculine to feminine is actually a linkage of the masculine "my people" with the feminine "Jerusalem" in 5:1–7 (see below

---

10. Thus I agree with Anderson (1988: 234–35) that the "double therefore" of vv. 13–14 is "not necessarily inelegant stylistically" in spite of the general view that "the connection between verses 13 and 14 is questionable" (see also Barth 1977: 192, as cited by Anderson). Anderson notes at least three other uses of the "double therefore" in Isaiah: 24:6, 30:18, 50:7. But Anderson still misses the real point: v. 14 follows logically upon v. 13: the second "therefore" has as its basis the first "therefore."

on larger structure, pp. 133ff. and 136ff.). However, the total length of
the two "therefore" strophes of stanza 2 of panel I is half that of the
"therefore" sections that conclude panel II, the second of which includes
a refrain to be found in materials that follow (9:7ff.).

The "therefore" sections are equivalent in the number of "therefores"
but in the ratio of 1:2 in length. The difference in length is made up at the
conclusion of panel I by a carefully crafted stanza, which includes a refrain
found in materials that have preceded this text (2:9, 11, 17). Thus, as
noted earlier, the first half of the poem links the theme of Yahweh's judgment to what has been previously discussed; the second half links to what
is yet to come.

The entire composition can be outlined thematically:

Panel I
    Stanza 1:   Two "woes" (vv. 8–12)
    Strophe A: "Woe" for what is done (economic exploitation)
                Hint of impending destruction
    Strophe B: "Woe" for what is done (wild living)
                and for what is not done (work of Yahweh)
    Stanza 2:   Two "therefores" (vv. 13–14)
    Strophe A: "My people" go into exile
    Strophe B: "Her" splendor goes into Sheol
    Stanza 3:   Refrain link to material beyond this poem (vv. 15–17)
                Man is debased; Yahweh is exalted
                Destruction of land
Panel II
    Stanza 1:   Four "woes" (vv. 18–23)
    Strophe A: "Woe" for what is done (sin)
                and for what is said (tempt Yahweh)
    Strophe B: "Woe" for what is said (good = evil)
    Strophe C: "Woe" for what is thought (self-delusion)
    Strophe D: "Woe" for what is done (wild living)
                and for what is done (perversion of justice)
                Are these all the woes?
    Stanza 2:   One "therefore" (v. 24)
    Destruction
    Because they rejected Yahweh's teaching
    Stanza 3:   One "therefore" (v. 25)
                refrain link to material beyond this poem (cf. 9:7ff.)
    Destruction
    But Yahweh's anger not past—is there another "woe" yet to
    be heard?

Chapter 3

Isaiah 9:7–10:4

Boundaries of This Unit

The overall unity of this larger section is not questioned. Although commentators may disagree regarding the contents and order of the original composition and its relationship to the material in 5:8ff., the unit is clearly ordered by the four refrains at the conclusion of what appear to be four stanzas: 9:7–11, 12–16, 17–20; and 10:1–4.

Clements, for example, places 10:1–4 immediately before 5:8ff. and discusses it at that point, although he suggests that the present dislocation has been deliberate. Likewise Kaiser, in his first edition (1963), moves 10:1–4 for discussion with chap. 5, although he places it *after* 5:24 (so also Wildberger). In his second edition (1979), however, Kaiser presents 9:7–10:4 as a whole unit in its appropriate place, as does Watts. Duhm would attach 5:25–30 as the conclusion to 9:7–10:4, but he deals with the latter material as a piece. Likewise, Gray adds 5:25/26–30 to 10:4 and speaks of a poem of five strophes, and he reconstructs several lines to produce 14 lines in each. Lack (1973) deals with 10:1–4 as a separate unit, but only because of its links to chap. 5.

In any case, the boundaries of 9:7–10:4 are not as issue as much as its relationship to the material in 5:8–30, which is not the topic here (but see below, pp. 96ff.). In their more-focused studies, both Sheppard (1985) and Anderson (1988) also take notice of the linkage with 10:5ff., but they deal with 9:7–10:4 as at least a subunit within their larger structures.

One is clearly on firm ground in dealing with this unit as a whole. It is marked at the beginning and the end in both CA and CL, as well as in 1QIsaᵃ. CL (BHS) shows a *setumah* before 9:7; CA has *petuchah*. The Qumran scroll shows only a minor break, indicating a closer connection to what comes before. At 10:4, CL again has a *setumah,* while CA again has a *petuchah*. In this case Qumran shows a larger break, equivalent to a *petuchah* (Oesch 1979, T [7+]).

I shall offer the hypothesis that, whatever conclusions are to be reached relative to 5:8–30, the unit of 9:7–10:4 can be discussed as a whole, and further, that its own structure can be analyzed as an integrated unit, independent of the material in 5:8ff.

	Text	Syllable Count	MT	Stress Count	MT
9:7a	דָּבָר שָׁלַח אֲדֹנָי בְּיַעֲקֹב	10	11	4	4
b	וְנָפַל בְּיִשְׂרָאֵל׃	7	7	2	2
8a	וְיָדְעוּ הָעָם כֻּלּוֹ	8	8	3	3
b	אֶפְרַיִם וְיוֹשֵׁב שֹׁמְרוֹן	8	9	3	3
c	בְּגַאֲוָה וּבְגֹדֶל לֵבָב לֵאמֹר׃	9/(10)	12	4	4
9a	לְבֵנִים נָפָלוּ	6	6	2	2
b	וְגָזִית נִבְנֶה	5	5	2	2
c	שִׁקְמִים גֻּדָּעוּ	5	5	2	2
d	וַאֲרָזִים נַחֲלִיף׃	(5)/6	7	2	2
10a	וַיְשַׂגֵּב יְהוָה אֶת־צָרֵי רְצִין עָלָיו	12	12	5	5
b	וְאֶת־אֹיְבָיו יְסַכְסֵךְ׃	8	8	2	2
11a	אֲרָם מִקֶּדֶם וּפְלִשְׁתִּים מֵאָחוֹר	10/(11)	12	4	4
b	וַיֹּאכְלוּ אֶת־יִשְׂרָאֵל בְּכָל־פֶּה	11	11	3	3
c	בְּכָל־זֹאת לֹא־שָׁב אַפּוֹ	7	7	3	3
d	וְעוֹד יָדוֹ נְטוּיָה׃	7	7	3	3
Verses 7–11		118/121 =119	127	44	44
12a	וְהָעָם לֹא־שָׁב עַד־הַמַּכֵּהוּ	10	10	3	3
b	וְאֶת־יְהוָה צְבָאוֹת לֹא דָרָשׁוּ׃	11	11	3	4
Verse 12		21	21	6	7
13a	וַיַּכְרֵת יְהוָה מִיִּשְׂרָאֵל	9	9	3	3
b	רֹאשׁ וְזָנָב כִּפָּה וְאַגְמוֹן	9	9	4	4
c	יוֹם אֶחָד׃	3	3	2	2
14a	זָקֵן וּנְשׂוּא־פָנִים הוּא הָרֹאשׁ	(9)/10	10	4	4
b	וְנָבִיא מוֹרֶה־שֶּׁקֶר הוּא הַזָּנָב׃	10	11	4	4
15a	וַיִּהְיוּ מְאַשְּׁרֵי הָעָם־הַזֶּה מַתְעִים	13	13	5	5
b	וּמְאֻשָּׁרָיו מְבֻלָּעִים׃	8/(9)	9	2	2

Translation

9:7a A word has Adonay sent into Jacob;
   b and it falls on Israel.
  8a The people—all of them—know
   b —Ephraim and the Resident of Samaria.
   c In pride and in greatness of heart, [they/he say/s]
  9a "Bricks have fallen;
   b [with] hewn stones we shall build.
   c Sycamores have been cut up;
   d [with] cedar we shall replace [them]."
  10a   Yahweh will raise up Rezin's foes against him,

   b   and his enemies he will stir up.
  11a   Aram from the east and the Philistines from the west:
   b   they will consume Israel with a whole mouth.
   c   **In all this his anger has not returned;**
   d   **still his hand is outstretched.**

  12a The people have not returned to the one who struck them;
   b Yahweh Sebaᵓoth they have not sought.

  13a Yahweh will cut off from Israel
   b head and tail, branch and reed
   c in one day.
  14a [An/The] elder, who is well respected—he is the head.
   b [A/The] prophet, who is a false teacher—he is the tail.
  15a The leaders of this people are leading astray;
   b and those of it (i.e., of this people) who are being led, are confused.

16a	עַל־כֵּן עַל־בַּחוּרָיו	6	6	2	2
b	לֹא־יִשְׂמַח אֲדֹנָי	6	6	2	2
c	וְאֶת־יְתֹמָיו וְאֶת־אַלְמְנֹתָיו	11	11	2	2
d	לֹא יְרַחֵם	4	4	2	2
e	כִּי כֻלּוֹ חָנֵף וּמֵרַע	8	8	3	4
f	וְכָל־פֶּה דֹּבֵר נְבָלָה	8	8	3	3
g	בְּכָל־זֹאת לֹא־שָׁב אַפּוֹ	7	7	3	3
h	וְעוֹד יָדוֹ נְטוּיָה׃	7	7	3	3
Verses 13–16		118/120 =119	121	44	45
17a	כִּי־בָעֲרָה כָאֵשׁ רִשְׁעָה	8	8	3	3
b	שָׁמִיר וָשַׁיִת תֹּאכֵל	6	7	3	3
c	וַתִּצַּת בְּסִבְכֵי הַיַּעַר	8	9	3	3
d	וַיִּתְאַבְּכוּ גֵּאוּת עָשָׁן׃	9	9	3	3
18a	בְּעֶבְרַת יְהוָה צְבָאוֹת	8	8	3	3
b	נֶעְתַּם אָרֶץ	3	4	2	2
c	וַיְהִי הָעָם כְּמַאֲכֹלֶת אֵשׁ	8	10	4	4
d	אִישׁ אֶל־אָחִיו לֹא יַחְמֹלוּ׃	8	8	3	4
19a	וַיִּגְזֹר עַל־יָמִין וְרָעֵב	9	9	3	3
b	וַיֹּאכַל עַל־שְׂמֹאול וְלֹא שָׂבֵעוּ	11	11	3	4
c	אִישׁ בְּשַׂר־זְרֹעוֹ יֹאכֵלוּ׃	9	9	4	3
20a	מְנַשֶּׁה אֶת־אֶפְרַיִם	6	7	2	2
b	וְאֶפְרַיִם אֶת־מְנַשֶּׁה	7	8	2	2
c	יַחְדָּו הֵמָּה עַל־יְהוּדָה	8	8	3	3
d	בְּכָל־זֹאת לֹא־שָׁב אַפּוֹ	7	7	3	3
e	וְעוֹד יָדוֹ נְטוּיָה׃	7	7	3	3
Verses 17–20		122	129	47	48
10:1a	הוֹי הַחֹקְקִים חִקְקֵי־אָוֶן	9	10	4	3
b	וּמְכַתְּבִים עָמָל כִּתֵּבוּ׃	9/(10)	9	3	3
2a	לְהַטּוֹת מִדִּין דַּלִּים	7	7	3	3
b	וְלִגְזֹל מִשְׁפַּט עֲנִיֵּי עַמִּי	10	10	4	4
c	לִהְיוֹת אַלְמָנוֹת שְׁלָלָם	8	8	4	4
d	וְאֶת־יְתוֹמִים יָבֹזּוּ׃	8	8	2	2
3a	וּמַה־תַּעֲשׂוּ לְיוֹם פְּקֻדָּה	9	10	3	3
b	וּלְשׁוֹאָה מִמֶּרְחָק תָּבוֹא	8/(9)	8	3	3
c	עַל־מִי תָּנוּסוּ לְעֶזְרָה	8	8	3	3
d	וְאָנָה תַעַזְבוּ כְּבוֹדְכֶם׃	10	10	3	3

16a   Therefore, concerning their chosen ones
  b   will Adonay not rejoice,
  c   and to their orphans and widows
  d   he will not show mercy.
  e   For every one of them is an apostate and evildoer;
  f   every mouth speaks sacrilege.
  g   **In all this his anger has not returned;**
  h   **still his hand is outstretched.**

17a   For wickedness burns like fire;
  b   thorns and briars it will consume.
  c   It will flare up in the thickets of the forest;
  d   they will go up in a cloud of smoke.
18a   In the rage of Yahweh Seba³oth
  b   [the] earth shakes,
  c   and the people are like fuel for fire.
  d   No one pities his fellow man.
19a   One cuts off what is on the right and is hungry;
  b   another eats what is on the left and is not satisfied;
  c   each eats the flesh of his seed.
20a   Manasseh [eats] Ephraim;
  b   and Ephraim Manasseh.
  c   Together they are against Judah.
  d   **In all this his anger has not returned;**
  e   **still his hand is outstretched.**

10:1a   Hey! You who decree decrees of evil,
  b   and writs of oppression they write
  2a   to twist the needy (of my people) from justice,
  b   and to rob the poor of my people of [their] rights;
  c   so widows become their spoil
  d   and orphans they plunder.
  3a   What will you do in the day of reckoning?
  b   In the devastation from afar that comes?
  c   To whom will you flee for help?
  d   Where will you leave your "glory?"—

		Syllables	MT	Stresses	MT
4a	בִּלְתִּי כָרַע' תַּחַת אַסִּיר	7	8	3	3
b	וְתַחַת הֲרוּגִים יִפֹּלוּ	8	9	3	3
c	בְּכָל־זֹאת' לֹא־שָׁב אַפּוֹ	7	7	3	3
d	וְעוֹד יָדוֹ נְטוּיָה:	7	7	3	3
Verses 1–4		115/(117)	119	44	43
Totals		494/501 = 496	517	185	187

Notes on Translation and Text

9:7a.   "Adonay"   The MT reads אדני, which may reflect the second-ary rendering of an original יהוה, attested by the reading in 1QIsaᵃ. In light of the common solo use of the divine name אדני in v. 16 and else-where in Isaiah (for example, 3:17, 18; 4:4; 6:1, 8, 11; 7:14, 20; 10:12; 11:11) it could well have been the original reading here, although it is more likely to have been changed from יהוה to אדני than vice-versa.

9:7b.   "it"   The antecedent דבר may seem awkward in light of the fact that it rarely forms the subject of the verb נפל; there is only one other occurrence in the Hebrew Bible: Ruth 3:18. Josh 21:45, 23:14; and 1 Kgs 8:56 suggest a slightly different idiom, 'a word has not "fallen"' = 'fallen out, been omitted', although the nuance of 'happen, occur' may bind the usages together. The LXX reads θανατον, reflecting (perhaps?) an original דֶּבֶר 'plague, pestilence' (= death). But this noun never serves as the subject of נפל; the idiom is that *men* "fall" because of a plague (for ex-ample, Ezek 6:11, 1 Chr 21:14).

"falls"   The tense is difficult, as the *waw* could be simple conjunction with the clear afformative, past tense שלח in line 7a. However, the *waw* could also be read as "consecutive" and translated as future. I have opted for the omnitemporal—and ominous—English present to stress the im-mediacy of the prophet's concern.

9:8b.   "Resident of Samaria"   The "Resident of Samaria" could be collective singular, although it is likely a reference to the singular resident, that is, the king (compare Amos 1:5, 8).

9:8c.   "In pride and in greatness of heart"   The translation is literal. The expression is likely hendiadys, 'in the great pride of their/his heart'.

"they/he"   If I am correct in suggesting that the "Resident of Samaria" is specifically the king (above, note to 8b), then "he" is likely also the

4a   except to crouch under prisoner[s]

b   and under [the] slain they will fall.

c   **In all this his anger has not returned;**

d   **still his hand is outstretched.**

---

one whose heart is enlarged with pride and who makes the following arrogant boast.

9:10a, 11b, 13a. **"will"** The MT preterite *waw* consecutive is read as the so-called prophetic perfect (that is, future). On the other hand, the verb is parallel to the preformative יסכסך (without prefixed *waw*) at the end of 10b, which would suggest a simple future tense. The question of the tenses is difficult (see Gray: 180–81, for a summary of issues and views), and I agree with him that, while vv. 7–8 are past tense, v. 10 begins "a succession of calamities that are to fall on Israel." The suggestion that v. 10 begins a new strophe (see below, p. 84) further supports this shift in tense.

9:10a. **"Rezin"** The deletion of רצין suggested in BHS and adopted by Clements (1980b: 68) attempts to resolve the tension within 10a and between 10a and 11a (how can Rezin's foes be identified with Aram?), but the omission is without textual evidence. Scribal error cannot be ruled out, but the addition of "Rezin" would be a mistake toward the "harder reading" and therefore unlikely. More likely is a reference to a possible or potential internal coup, whether real or simply in the prophet's mind: thus Aram against itself, encouraged no doubt, directly or indirectly, by Assyria.

Possibly the pronoun in line 10a ("against *him*") has as its antecedent "Israel" or even the "Resident of Samaria." Rezin's enemies are not understood as raised up against Rezin himself but against Israel, which is clearly the point of v. 11. In any case, a situation is presupposed in which the alliance of Aram under Rezin with the Northern Kingdom has disintegrated, and, instead of helping Israel, Aram is perceived as another attacker.

9:10b. **"he will stir up"** יְסַכְסֵךְ is presumably *Pilpel* from the root סוך 'excite, stir up, provoke'. It occurs only here and in Isa 19:2.

9:11b. **"with a whole mouth"** The translation is literal; in modern idiom one might suggest 'in one gulp'.

9:13c. **"in"** The preposition is added in translation, which is certainly understood here and used elsewhere (Isa 10:17).

9:14ab. **"who is"** The use of the conjunction in 14a is not paralleled in 14b. Combined with the fact that the הוא is singular in both lines, the *waw* is best taken epexegetically. The contrast between "well respected" and "false teacher" implies a sarcastic nuance to the first term, which may have come through in the tone of voice.

9:16b. **"rejoice"** I follow the MT. 1QIsaᵃ reads יחמול, which is a better parallel to ירחם and occurs in 18c.

9:17d. **"they will go up in a cloud of smoke"** The line is difficult. יתאבכו is a hapax legomenon, whose meaning can be derived only from context. (BDB [5] suggests a relationship with root הפך.) Furthermore, the meaning of גאות is not clear. Its basic meaning of 'majesty, something high' obtains elsewhere in Isaiah (for example, 12:5). BDB (145) relates the meaning here only to Ps 89:10, 'a "swelling" of the sea'. The suggested translation 'column' conveys the sense of a 'raising up', but my translation attempts to relate to American idiom. Since this is the only use of the word with עשן in the Hebrew Bible, any translation must remain tentative.

9:18b. **"shakes"** The root is another hapax legomenon. Moran (1950: 153–54: see also Hummel 1957: 94) suggested the more familiar root נוע (pf., 3 f. s.) plus enclitic *mem*, which is attractive in light of the use of this root in 6:4 and twice in 7:2. I follow, but with caution.

9:19bc. **"is not satisfied"** The verb is plural, the nouns singular, and the idiom is distributive, perceiving each as part of the collective whole.

9:19c. **"flesh of his seed"** I emend cautiously to זַרְעוֹ although good textual evidence is lacking. The Alexandrian LXX adds τοῦ ἀδελφοῦ, which is supported by the targum's translation קריביה and would suggest an original reading of רעו, 'his neighbor's flesh'. In light of line 18c, this is attractive and followed by most commentaries (for example, Gray, who then rearranges 18d to follow 19b). Wildberger (206) also considers the vocalization זַרְעוֹ ('his seed = offspring?') but concludes "was sich aber doch nicht glatt in den Zusammenhangeinfügt." The MT certainly has the "harder reading," but it is difficult to make sense of this expression. It is possible that the reference is to cannibalism of children, which may occur under siege conditions.

9:20a. **"eats"** Verse 20 seems to continue the reciprocal atrocities mentioned in v. 19, although the object marker could also be read as the preposition 'with', in which case 20ab anticipates 20c.

10:1b. **"writs of"** In view of the parallelism with the preceding line and the chiasm that links the two inside terms, it is very attractive to read מכתבים as the construct plural plus enclitic *mem* (so Hummel 1957: 94), and BHS notes at least one manuscript with the construct form. Since the parallel is the noun form cognate to חקק, I read מכתבי as a cognate noun (compare with the similar construction in 5:8ab).

10:2ab. **"of my people"** It is possible that משפט in line 2b is wrongly pointed as a construct and that instead it is parallel to (מ)דין in line 2a. Thus the preposition מן could be read as serving double duty with משפט and the *nomen rectum* עמי in 2b should serve double duty with דלים in 2a, perhaps with enclitic *mem*.

10:2c. **"so"** The English translation unfortunately destroys the syntactic parallel of three infinitives in a row.

10:3d. **"glory"** Quotation marks are used in contrast to the "glory" of Yahweh (compare 6:3). Compare also 5:13, where vain human "glory" is meant sarcasticxally.

10:4a. **"crouch"** Reading כרע as infinitive (expected after בלתי). The afformative 3d masculine-singular form could be retained and read as impersonal 'one crouches'. The meaning may well be better expressed as 'drop down dead'; compare the use of כרע, along with נפל, in Judg 5:27, where the meaning clearly refers to falling in death.

Lineation

Again an attempt is made to deal carefully and systematically with the problems of lineation. Decided on the basis of syntax and parallelism, I show a range from 66 lines (appendix 2A, in which every uncertain division is decided in favor of short lines) to 56 lines (appendix 2B, in which every difficulty is decided in favor of long lines).

In either lineation, however, it is clear that the most common line length is the 8-syllable colon, of which there are 17 (out of 66 = 25.8%) in appendix 2A and 17 (out of 56 = 30.4%) in appendix 2B. Well over half the lines have 7–9 syllables, and well over three-fourths of the lines have 6–10 syllables.

Appendix 2A (shortest possible lines)
lines with 8 syllables:	17	(25.8%)
lines with 7–9 syllables:	38	(57.6%)
lines with 6–10 syllables:	50	(75.8%)

Appendix 2B (longest possible lines):
lines with 8 syllables:	17	(30.4%)
lines with 7–9 syllables:	36	(64.3%)
lines with 6–10 syllables:	45	(80.4%)

Furthermore, if all difficult or questionable lines are eliminated from consideration and one analyzes only the lines that can be lineated clearly, the 8-syllable line again appears dominant:

v.	7ab:	10 + 7		v.	19bc:	11 + 9
v.	8ab:	8 + 8		v.	20abc:	6 + 7 + 8
v.	8c:	9		v.	20de:	7 + 7
v.	10ab:	12 + 8		v.	1ab:	9 + 9
v.	11ab:	10 + 11		v.	2ab:	7 + 10
v.	11cd:	7 + 7		v.	2cd:	8 + 8
v.	16ef:	8 + 8		v.	3ab:	9 + 8
v.	16gh:	7 + 7		v.	3cd:	8 + 10
v.	17ab:	8 + 6		v.	4ab:	7 + 8
v.	17cd:	8 + 9		v.	4cd:	7 + 7
v.	18d/19a:	8 + 9				

Of these 42 lines, the most common line length is 8 syllables (14 lines):

6-syllable lines:	2	10-syllable lines:	4
7-syllable lines:	12	11-syllable lines:	2
8-syllable lines:	14	12-syllable lines:	1
9-syllable lines:	7		

33.3% (14) of these lines have 8 syllables.
78.6% (33) of these lines have 7–9 syllables.
92.9% (39) of these lines have 6–10 syllables.

On the basis of the lines that can be lineated clearly, the 7–9 syllable lines account for over 76% of the cola (compare pp. 42–43 above).

With these data as a foundation, a lineation based simply on the 8-syllable, 3-stress lines has produced a poem of exactly 62 lines (appendix 2C). Obviously, this method ignores considerations of syntax and parallelism and allows for enjambment in favor of more balanced line lengths.

Neverthess, it has used the factor of line length to produce a number of lines within the limits of the 56–66 lines set by considerations of syntax and parallelism alone.

Using this figure as a target for the overall total number of lines, one can now return to the difficult questions of lineation and deal with them on a case by case basis in relationship to the overall pattern.

Verse 9. These 21/22 syllables divide syntactically into either 2 longer lines (appendix 2B) or 4 shorter lines. The latter seems more likely, since vv. 7–11 form a unit of 118/121 syllables, which should produce 15 lines. No other lines within this unit can be redivided or sub-divided along grammatical breaks.

Verse 12. Although the 21 syllables could form a tricolon (appendix 2C), the parallelism suggests a long bicolon. The verse illustrates the tension between syntax and meter. The decision to retain longer lines here forms a balance with the shorter lines already noted in v. 9.

Verse 13. The verse does not divide well as either a bicolon or a tricolon (compare appendixes 2A, B, C). The 9 stresses suggest 3 lines, and 21 syllables could form 3 lines of 7 syllables (or dividing at least at word breaks, 5 + 8 + 8, as in appendix 2C). I attempt to retain grammatical breaks, allowing a very short final line, possibly for emphasis (see discussion below, p. 85).

Verse 14. The lines could form a quatrain, with הוא הזנב // הוא הראש forming the second lines of each bicolon (see appendix 2A), but the lines would be unnecessarily short. As shown, the bicolon is balanced and only slightly longer than average.

Verse 15. Verse 15a is a long line but impossible to divide without enjambment. The configuration of the 21/22 syllables and 7 stresses of v. 15 into a more balanced tricolon is shown in appendix 2C, and this example reflects again the tension between meter and syntax.

Verse 16abcd. The total of 27 syllables and 8 stresses is somewhat short for a quatrain but very long for a bicolon. A third option is a tricolon, as in appendix 2C. In light of the longer lines in v. 15, I have shown the shorter lines of the quatrain here.

Verse 18abc. The lines divide awkwardly as either a bicolon or a tricolon. As in v. 13, I show a tricolon, which agrees with the 9 stresses (but see appendix 2C). The slightly greater number of syllables in vv. 17–20 may suggest an extra, shorter line.

By allowing parallelism, syntax, and metric considerations all to play a role, the suggested lineation has attempted to deal with uncertain circumstances in a careful and measured way. This method has been consistent with the method applied to Isa 5:8–25 (see pp. 42ff.). Based on instances in which lineation was clear, here, too the dominance of the 8-syllable (or 7–9 syllable) colon was established and then used to produce a target figure for the total number of lines.

In fact, as in 5:8–25, in a majority of cases (42 of 62 lines) the factors of grammar, parallelism, and line length overlapped so that there was no difficulty in lineation, which again suggests that these factors complement one another and operate interactively.

Nevertheless, as also in 5:8–25, there were a number of cases in which the "metric" consideration of line length (and, to a lesser degree) stress accents stood in tension with the grammatical divisions of lines. An alternate lineation based entirely on these "metric" features has again been provided, in appendix 2C.

In summary, both the tension and the harmony between the factors and features of lineation have been observed, and it has been noted and admitted that there are instances where more than one solution may be possible. While specific situations are generally resolved within each verse, the net result of individual decisions will affect the total number of lines. However, as has been argued, the dominance of the 8 (7–9)-syllable line indicates that there should be approximately 62 lines, which would perfectly match the unit in 5:8–25, previously discussed. It may well be that the poet/prophet used a certain amount of flexibility in lineation, so that the best one is able to do with the evidence at hand is to present a reasonable case for the decisions one makes.

Syllable Counts

The syllable count for this unit shows a range of 494–501. Seven instances of the prefixed conjunction account for the variables, and one should note the striking similarity to the counts discovered in Isa 5:8–25, where counts ranged from 494–500. (In contrast, the MT counts are not nearly so close: 517 in this section vs. 533 in 5:8–25.)

Again one must consider the fact that 62 8-syllable lines would result in 496 syllables, which is undoubtedly the correct number, however they might be counted. Therefore, it is logical, if arbitrary, to consider that five of the seven conjunctions were elided, and that two of the longer counts should be retained. For the purposes of further analysis I shall figure line 9d by the longer count (6 syllables), since that will balance the quatrain $(6 + 5 + 5 + 6)$, and also line 14a by the longer count, again to balance the verse $(10 + 10)$. In the other cases, I shall assume the shorter count.

In the notations indicated in the text (pp. 66ff.), I have placed the alternate number in parentheses.

While individual line lengths again show a wide diversity, ranging from 3–13 syllables, the 8-syllable colon is clearly dominant at the center (both median and mean) of the spectrum. The 62 lines as shown have the following colon lengths:

3-syllable lines:	2	9-syllable lines:	9
4-syllable lines:	1	10-syllable lines:	7
5-syllable lines:	2	11-syllable lines:	4
6-syllable lines:	6	12-syllable lines:	1
7-syllable lines:	12	13-syllable lines:	1
8-syllable lines:	17		

Of the 62 lines,

27.4% (17 lines) have 8 syllables,
61.3% (38 lines) have 7–9 syllables,
82.3% (51 lines) have 6–10 syllables.

The median line length is 8 syllables.
The average line length is 8.00 syllables per line (496/62).

Represented graphically, the distribution of line length appears again as a roughly bell-shaped curve, with the peak at 8 syllables per line:

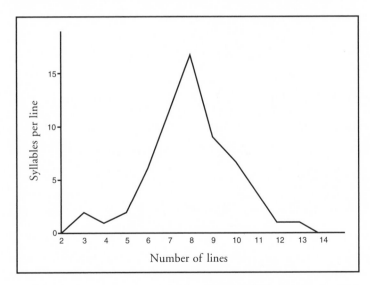

Fig. 3.1. Distribution of line lengths (in syllables): Isa 9:7–10:4

On the level of bicola, there is a higher number of 14–15 syllable bicola than of 16-syllable bicola. But these are balanced by a similar higher number of 17-18 syllable bicola:

v. 7:	10 + 7 = 17		v. 16gh:	7 + 7 = 14
v. 8ab:	8 + 8 = 16		v. 17ab:	8 + 6 = 14
v. 9ab:	6 + 5 = 11		v. 17cd:	8 + 9 = 17
v. 9cd:	5 + 6 = 11		v. 18d/19a:	8 + 9 = 17
v. 10:	12 + 8 = 20		v. 19bc:	11 + 9 = 20
v. 11ab:	10 + 11 = 21		v. 20de:	7 + 7 = 14
v. 11cd:	7 + 7 = 14		v. 1:	9 + 9 = 18
v. 12:	10 + 11 = 21		v. 2ab:	7 + 10 = 17
v. 14:	10 + 10 = 20		v. 2cd:	8 + 8 = 16
v. 15:	13 + 8 = 21		v. 3ab:	9 + 8 = 17
v. 16ab:	6 + 6 = 12		v. 3cd:	8 + 10 = 18
v. 16cd:	11 + 4 = 15		v. 4ab:	7 + 8 = 15
v. 16ef:	8 + 8 = 16		v. 4cd:	7 + 7 = 14

These 26 bicola are tabulated as follows:

11-syllable bicola:	2	17-syllable bicola:	5
12-syllable bicola:	1	18-syllable bicola:	2
13-syllable bicola:	0	19-syllable bicola:	0
14-syllable bicola:	5	20-syllable bicola:	3
15-syllable bicola:	2	21-syllable bicola:	3
16-syllable bicola:	3		

11.5 % (3) of the bicola have exactly 16 syllables.
65.4% (17) of the bicola have 14–18 syllables (7–9 per line).
80.8% (21) of the bicola have 12–20 syllables (6–10 per line).

The median length of the bicola is 16 syllables.
The average length of a bicolon in 16.38 syllables.

Represented graphically, the number of syllables per bicolon appears as shown in fig. 3.2.

The chart graphically displays the diversity of bicolon length around the 16-syllable norm as well as the fact that the average is slightly higher than the median. In addition to these 26 bicola, however, I have marked one monocolon and three tricola:

v. 8c:	9 syllables
v. 13abc:	9 + 9 + 3 = 21 syllables
v. 18abc:	8 + 3 + 8 = 19 syllables
v. 20abc:	6 + 7 + 8 = 21 syllables

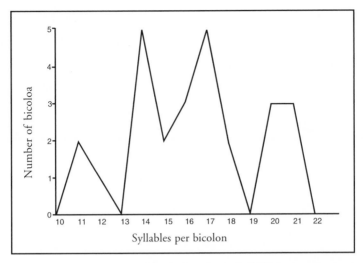

Fig. 3.2.   Distribution of bicola lengths (in syllables): Isa 9:7–10:4

All three tricola are short, averaging 20.3 syllables, and thereby tend to balance out the slightly longer average for the bicola.

It is of further interest to observe the way the individual lines within each bicolon relate in length. For example, in 8 of the 26 bicola, the first (or A) line is longer; in 8 bicola the second (or B) line is longer; in 10 bicola the 2 lines are exactly the same length. This gives an even greater sense of balance than was noted in reference to the bicola of 5:8–25 (see above, p. 47), where the A lines seemed longer, although attention was called to the artificial nature of that imbalance due to the extra stress of the "woe" and "therefore" lines.

If one considers a one-syllable difference between lines to be insignificant (as was also suggested above, on p. 47), there is an even higher number of perfectly balanced bicola:

bicola in which the A line is longer: 6
bicola in which the B line is longer: 2
bicola in which both lines are within one syllable: 18

In fact, if ones adds up all the A lines, plus all the B lines, there is a slight dominance to the A lines: 220 syllables + 206 syllables. This difference is reduced if the monocolon and the three tricola are factored in the same way as in the discussion of 5:8–25. The overall totals reflect a difference of only 3.2%:

number of syllables in A lines: 252
number of syllables in B lines: 244

In summary, there is again a wide divergence in length both on the level of the individual lines and on the level of combinations of lines into bicola and tricola. However, again there is also a sense of balancing, or evening out of these differences over the course of the longer unit. While line lengths range from 3–13 syllables, over 80% fall within the range of 6–10 syllables, with 5 lines under 6 syllables and 6 lines over 10 syllables. Bicola tended to be slightly longer than 16 syllables on average, but three tricola were significantly shorter than the anticipated 24-syllable average.

The initial, tentative conclusions suggested above on pp. 48–49, with reference to Isa 5:8–25, are thus strengthened by comparison with this second large unit. The overall dominance of the 8-syllable colon is clear, but there is, by way of contrast, also a wide variation from the norm. However, the deviations both above and below the norm produce a sense of balance. The evidence shows a second time that the poet/prophet appears to have worked with a clear sense of compensation in mind, so that shorter lines and verses would be balanced by longer lines and verses within the structure of the whole composition.

Stress Counts

The total 185 stresses that I have counted in this unit is so close to the 186 figure that could be projected on the basis of 62 three-stress lines that it is, for all practical purposes, equivalent. The Masoretic accents total 187. Individual lines have 2–5 stresses:

> 2-stress cola: 16 (25.8%)
> 3-stress cola: 33 (53.2%)
> 4-stress cola: 11 (17.7%)
> 5-stress cola: 2 (3.2%)

Thus 60 lines (96.8%) have 2–4 stresses.
The average number of stresses per colon is 2.98.

Represented graphically, the dominance of 3-stress cola is clear, as shown in fig. 3.3.

On the level of bicola, the dominance of the 6-stress bicolon stands out again, although oddly there are no 5-stress bicola:

> 4-stress bicola: 4 (15.4%)
> 5-stress bicola: 0 (0.0%)
> 6-stress bicola: 15 (57.7%)
> 7-stress bicola: 6 (23.1%)
> 8-stress bicola: 1 (3.8%)

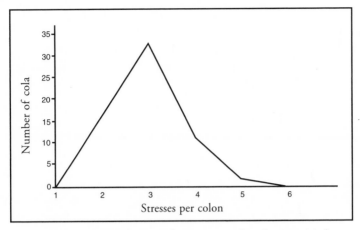

Fig. 3.3. Distribution of stresses per colon: Isa 9:7–10:4

Thus 100% of the bicola have between 4–8 stresses (2–4 per colon). The average number of stresses per bicolon is 6.00.

Represented graphically, the void at 5 stresses slightly distorts the image of the overall balance, which is nevertheless clear:

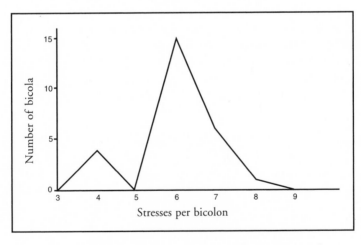

Fig. 3.4. Distribution of stresses per bicolon: Isa 9:7–10:4

The other verse configurations should also be noted:

v. 8c:	4 stresses
v. 13abc:	3 + 4 + 2 = 9 stresses
v. 18abc:	3 + 2 + 4 = 9 stresses
v. 20abc:	2 + 2 + 3 = 7 stresses

Taken as a unit, these lines confirm the same pattern: 10 lines with a total of 29 stresses is only one short of 3 stresses per colon.

Finally, I take note also of the balancing of the stresses between the lines of the bicola. Of the 26 bicola, the following stress patterns are found:

Balanced Bicola			*Unbalanced Bicola*			
2:2	4 bicola		A dominant:	4:2	1 bicolon	
3:3	13 bicola			4:3	2 bicola	
4:4	1 bicolon			5:2	1 bicolon	
			B dominant:	3:4	2 bicola	
monocolon:	4					
tricola:	3:4:2					
	3:2:4					
	2:2:3					

Of the 26 bicola, 18 are perfectly balanced. The most common stress pattern by far is the 3:3 bicolon (50%). Of the unbalanced bicola, 4 are more heavily stressed on the A lines, 2 on the B lines. The 3:4:2 and the 3:2:4 tricola balance each other out; the 2:2:3 tricolon leans slightly toward the B line category.

In sum, these figures confirm the dominance of the 3-stress colon and the 6-stress bicolon, which correspond to the 8/16 syllable counts for the same units. Further, this analysis has demonstrated a sense of balancing in the number of stresses between the lines of the bicola, similar to the overall balancing of the number of syllables. Although one must admit to a larger margin for error in dealing with accents, the figures are strikingly close to what should be expected on the basis of my hypothesis.

Prose Particles

Overall, the unit contains 19 prose particles, or 8.56% of the 222 words. Of these, almost half (9) are object markers; the others are uses of the article. The particles are scattered throughout the poem, although there is a fourfold use of the article in vv. 14–15a.

According to Freedman's hypothesis (1987a), this material falls into the middle range (*tertium quid*), although the percentage figure falls much closer to the classic poetry category than to prose. In light of the poetic features already noted and analyzed, this unit is rightly called a poem. It seems likely that both the article and especially the object marker were used intentionally and for a specific purpose, such as emphasis, to mark specific words in an otherwise unmarked environment.

Verse and Strophe Structure

As will be discussed in greater detail below, the unit is clearly divided into four stanzas, each of which concludes with the same refrain, also found in 5:25. Unlike the discussion of the unit in 5:8–25, however, where the larger structure suggested itself only after consideration of the smaller pieces, I shall anticipate further analysis and refer to the stanza divisions in discussing the verses and strophes. Each stanza, it will appear, can be understood as consisting of two strophes plus the refrain.

Stanza 1, Strophe A: Verses 7–9

The section begins with an emphatic accusative use of דָּבָר, which clearly serves double duty with line 7b, although its second use is as subject. While the final words of each line are a matched pair, this interplay in the first half of each line also helps bind the bicolon together. While דבר is understood in the second line, אדני is not. This creates an uneven line length between the two cola, yet the total of the bicolon is 17 syllables, only one off the 8 + 8 pattern.

Lines 8ab do present an 8 + 8 bicolon, and it continues the syntax of v. 7 by the use of the prefixed *waw* verb form. "Jacob" and "Israel" are summarized by the collective and articulated העם, which in turn is again divided in line 8b. Thus vv. 7–8b, I suggest, form the initial quatrain of the first strophe: 33 syllables and 12 stresses.

Lines 8c–9 form the second "verse": 31 syllables and 12 stresses. Despite the attempt of Gray et al. to discover a lost line, line 8c should best be left a monocolon, introducing the quotation in v. 9 (compare 5:9a). The pairing of the terms ובגדל לבב + בגאוה creates a sense of parallelism even within the single line, which is followed by the short but well-constructed quatrain in v. 9.

The 4 lines of v. 9 follow an ABAB pattern, each with inverted word order. The two A lines (9a and 9c) describe what has happened, each subject followed by an intransitive or passive verb. The two B lines (9b and 9d) exclaim what "we" (that is, the people and/or the king) will do, each verb preceded by the objective adverbial noun. Each A line ends with a *waw*; each B line begins with a *waw*. One should notice the chiastic alliteration within the first bicolon (9ab) between *b* and *n* sounds: נבנה // לבנים.

Lines 8c–9d continue the focus on the people begun in v. 7, and the use of the verb נפל in 7b and 9a binds the two verses into a strophe of 64 syllables and 24 stresses. No doubt the assertion made in line 8a (וידעו)

was turned to irony by the citation of their own words back upon them in v. 9 (compare the accusation that "my people do not *know*" in Isa 1:3).

Stanza 1, Srophe B: Verses 10–11b

Verse 10 begins with the common preterite *waw*-consecutive in normal word order (which is translated as "prophetic perfect"; see translation note to 9:10a, 11b, 13a, p. 71). Yahweh is again the subject as in 7a, so that the beginning of the second strophe shifts the focus back to God's action. Lines 10ab are another uneven bicolon (12 + 8 syllables) formed by the presence of both the double-duty term (יהוה) and the "ballast variant" in the same line. Both direct objects are marked by the object markers for emphasis, which calls attention also to the chiastic structure of the bi-colon. The final word balances the initial verb.

As העם is expanded by the terms "Jacob," "Israel," "Ephraim," and "the Resident of Samaria" in vv. 7–8, so the "foes of Rezin" are articulated as "Aram and Philistines" in vv. 10–11. I have already suggested (translation note to 9:10a, p. 71) that "Aram" likely refers to an internal threat to Rezin, but the real target in the poet/prophet's mind is Israel, which becomes explicit in v. 11b. Again the object marker is used; the action has moved from Yahweh to the enemies and from the enemies to Israel. Thus the stanza concludes with the direct interaction of Yahweh and Israel with which it began in v. 7. The initial preterite *waw*-consecutives in 10a and 11a bind the final two bicola into a strophe of 41 syllables and 14 stresses, which is followed by the refrain.

Interlude: Verse 12

Lines 12ab, I shall argue, form an independent strophe, loosely connected to the previous lines. In fact, it is tempting to suggest that this strophe forms the conclusion to 10–11ab, since its use of the object marker would bring the action full circle, from Israel (העם) back to "Yahweh Seba³oth." Further, the use of העם would form an inclusio with 8a and bind the unit together. If the refrain in 11cd is omitted from the figures, the second strophe would then consist of 10, 11ab, and 12: 62 syllables and 20 stresses, compared to the 64 syllables and 24 stresses of vv. 7–9.

However, the refrain intervenes, and v. 12 stands outside what I shall call the first stanza (vv. 7–11, see below, pp. 88ff.). On the other hand, the bicolon is clearly connected to what lies before. It does not begin the sec-ond stanza, contra Gray (177), who finds the first preservation of an origi-nal 14-line stanza in vv. 12–16. Rather, the links to both the first and second strophe already mentioned as well as the echo of the refrain in the use of the verb form שָׁב would attest to the reliability of the division made in both CA and CL, which have a *setumah*, and in 1QIsaᵃ, which has a *petuchah* break, *after* v. 12 (see further, p. 90).

Stanza 2, Strophe A: Verses 13–15

Line 13a begins both a new stanza and a new strophe, again with the initial preterite *waw*-consecutive and subject Yahweh, as in 10a. The relationship of Yahweh and Israel is clearly the topic, as in v. 7. I have shown v. 13 as a tricolon, with the two pairs that form the direct objects as the middle line and the adverbial but ominous יוֹם אֶחָד alone in the very short final colon.

Verse 14 expands and defines the first two terms in line 13b in a tightly parallel bicolon. I have already noted the distinctive and careful use of the *waw* in our translation notes (p. 72, note to 9:14ab). Each line has one conjunction: the first is used to mark an appositive; the second coordinates the two lines.

Verse 15 continues the thought, but its initial verb form and careful construction mark it as a separate verse. The play on verb forms between the *Piel* participles in the first line and the *Pual* participles in the second is striking, and an uneven bicolon (13 + 8 syllables) is created by having both the double-duty word (וַיְהִי) and the "ballast variant" in the same line (15a). Metrically, of course, the bicolon could be balanced as a 10 + 10/11 bicolon or even a tricolon (see appendix 2C). The four participles produce another series of four terms, echoing line 13b, and I suggest that vv. 13–15 together form one strophe of 62 syllables and 24 stresses (compare vv. 7–9; see below, p. 89).

Stanza 2, Strophe B: Verse 16abcdef

The second strophe begins with the only use of the עַל־כֵּן formula in 9:7–10:4 (compare 5:25a). The somewhat shorter lines of the quatrain form an ABAB pattern: each A line (16a and 16c) indicates the object of the verbs in each B line (16b and 16d).

The second A line (16c) doubles the single term of the first A line: עַל־בַּחוּרָיו // וְאֶת־יְתֹמָיו וְאֶת־אַלְמְנֹתָיו, although the first A line manages a double use of עַל (the first a part of עַל־כֵּן) to match the double use of אֶת in the second A line. Conversely, the first B line (16b) is reduced by the second B line (16d), in that the subject אֲדֹנָי is omitted, but understood, in 16d.

Lines 16ef are a regular bicolon of 8 + 8 syllables. The repetition of *kap* sounds forms alliteration begun in עַל־כֵּן in line 16a, but the specific vocable כֻּלּוֹ is repeated in כָל in lines 16ef (and g). Here three adjectival forms (two stative verbs and one transitive participle) are used in a listing, similar to the use of three nouns in 16a and c. The whole of 16abcdef forms a second strophe of 43 syllables and 14 stresses (compare vv. 10–11b; see below, pp. 88–89), followed by the refrain.

Stanza 3, Strophe A: Verses 17–18c

Verse 17 begins the next stanza with another quatrain, bound together by the fact that רִשְׁעָה in 17a is the subject of the first three lines. The first bicolon is chiastic in that the verbs are in the first and last segments (the interior elements are the subject of the first verb and object of the second), while lines 17cd are both verb-initial. The chiastic verbs are an alternation of the afformatives and preformatives, typical of early Hebrew poetry; the verbs in 17cd are both preterite *waw*-consecutives.

The second verse of this strophe (v. 18abc) returns to the tension between Yahweh and the people, already introduced by the causal clause that has preceded in v. 17, in which the "wickedness" was not clearly specified. The previous stanzas have listed specific "wickednesses" of "the people," but in vv. 17–18, "the people" appear as intransitive means, as "fuel" for the fire of (their own) wickedness. This interplay between "actor" and "acted upon" on the part of the people is overpowered by the "rage of Yahweh Sebaᵓoth" in line 18a, yet the subject-verb is the intransitive נעתם with אֶרֶץ: 'the earth shakes'. The effect is subtle: wickedness burns, the earth shakes, the people are like fuel, but the real actors are the people, who do the wickedness, and Yahweh Sebaᵓoth, who acts in rage to punish. The repetition of אֵשׁ at the end of 18c forms an inclusio with 17a and brings the strophe to conclusion: 50 syllables and 21 stresses.

Stanza 3, Strophe B: Verses 18d–20

Verses 18d–19c closely continue the thought with a well-crafted quatrain dealing with the individual effects of the burning wickedness within "the people": man is turned against his fellowman. Thus there is a link between the first and last lines (lines 18d and 19c), creating a sense of chiasm, that is, an ABBA quatrain.[1] Both begin with אִישׁ, which likely puns on the previous use of אֵשׁ, and both use the distributive "one to

---

1. Gray's rearrangement of 18d after 19b (so that 18d and 19c are adjacent) is thus quite unnecessary.

another" idiom. So also the interior lines (19ab) are matched by both syntactic and semantic parallelism: verb—adverb—coordinate result clause: "cuts off" // "eats," "right hand" // "left hand," "be hungry" // "not be satisfied."

On the other hand, the first and third lines (18d and 19b) share in common the concluding negated verb form, while the second and fourth lines conclude with a positive (but contrasting) verb: the stative 'be hungry' and the preformative 'they eat'. Finally, the last two lines show a small chiasm of their own in the repetition of the verb אכל at the beginning of 19b and end of 19c. Thus all four lines are tightly intertwined by a variety and mixture of structural features: a major ABBA pattern plus minor ABAB and AABB patterns.

The second verse of this strophe (lines 20abc) forms a tricolon with a 2 + 1 pattern. The first two lines continue the "one against his fellow man" motif, using the object marker twice (compare 10ab, 16c), but the third line dramatically shifts the focus away from the internal strife of Ephraim/ Manasseh, where it has been since v. 7 (Jacob/Israel), to Judah, in a way similar to that by which the enemies of Rezin (vv. 10–11a) were turned upon Israel in 11b. The emphatic pronoun not only links 20c to the previous lines of the tricolon (where its antecedent is found) but also highlights this important development in the theme of the whole poem.

The refrain concludes this third stanza, which, I suggest, consists of two strophes: vv. 17–18c (50 syllables and 21 stresses) and vv. 18d–20c (58 syllables and 20 stresses), followed by the refrain.

Stanza 4, Strophe A: Verses 10:1–2

The final stanza begins with the הוי + participle formula found six times (two with noun or adjective) in 5:8–25. The following line concludes with a 3 pl. finite verb, as has also been seen in 5:8 and 11. If I am correct in reading מכתבים as a construct plural noun form with enclitic *mem*, then the inside terms match as well. The wordplay on the verbal cognate nouns is catchy and reversed in each line: participle—noun / noun—preformative verb.

Verse 2 seems to be another quatrain. The first 3 lines all begin with ל + infinitive, but the final line (2d) inverts a marked object before a concluding finite verb, similar to line 1b. But cutting across the AAAB pattern is the fact that each bicolon has its own unifying structure. Lines 2ab are bound by the pairing of דין with משפט and of דלים with עניי עמי, by the double-duty use of the preposition מן with both דין and משפט, and by the double-duty use of עמי with דלים (see translation note to 10:2ab, p. 73). Further, the use of the word pair "widow and orphan" in 2cd binds these lines together. The same pair is used in reverse order in

9:16c. One should note also the juxtaposition of the noun שׁלל in 10:2c and the verb form from בזז in 2d, because they seem to form an intentional pun on the name of Isaiah's son מהר שׁלל חשׁ בז (see below, p. 103).

Syntactically, 10:1–2 are one sentence, and I suggest these two verses form the first strophe of this final stanza: 51 syllables and 20 stresses (compare vv. 17–18c and see below, p. 89).

Stanza 4, Strophe B: Verses 3–4b

The final strophe begins with the rhetorical question in 10:3a, which is followed by two similar questions in 3c and 3d, forming an ABAA pattern. Line 3b expands the second term of line 3a: the "day of reckoning" is when "destruction comes from afar."

Lines 4ab continue the sentence. Since these lines propose an answer to the questions not only of 3cd but also of all of v. 3abcd, they likely form a second verse, a bicolon following the quatrain (4 + 2) of v. 3. This is similar to but the reverse of the quatrain that follows a bicolon (2 + 4) in the previous strophe. Again one should note the interplay between the second and third persons, as v. 4ab switches to and concludes with the same 3d pl. form with which the first strophe ended (line 2d) and which (as perfect) followed the participle in v. 1.

The 6 lines of vv. 3–4b form the second strophe of the final stanza: 50 syllables and 18 stresses (compare vv. 18d–20, as well as 10:1–2; see Gross Structure), followed by the refrain.

Gross Structure

Having discussed the detailed structuring of the verse and strophes, and having already noted the presence of the four refrains that divide this unit into four stanzas, I now consider the structure of the entire unit, 9:7–10:4, as has already been outlined:

Stanza 1: (vv. 7–11)
Strophe A:	vv. 7–9:	64 syllables, 24 stresses, 24 words
Strophe B:	vv. 10–11b:	41 syllables, 14 stresses, 18 words
Refrain:	v. 11cd:	14 syllables, 6 stresses, 8 words
INTERLUDE: (v. 12)		21 syllables, 6 stresses, 10 words

Stanza 2: (vv. 13–16)
Strophe A:	vv. 13–15:	62 syllables, 24 stresses, 26 words
Strophe B:	v. 16a–f:	43 syllables, 14 stresses, 21 words
Refrain:	v. 16gh:	14 syllables, 6 stresses, 8 words

Stanza 3: (vv. 17–20)
 Strophe A: vv. 17–18c: 50 syllables, 21 stresses, 22 words
 Strophe B: vv. 18d–20c: 58 syllables, 20 stresses, 28 words
 Refrain: v. 20de: 14 syllables, 6 stresses, 8 words

Stanza 4: (10:1–4)
 Strophe A: vv. 1–2: 51 syllables, 20 stresses, 20 words
 Strophe B: vv. 3–4b: 50 syllables, 18 stresses, 21 words
 Refrain: v. 4cd: 14 syllables, 6 stresses, 8 words

On the basis of this outline, the following observations are made:

(1) If, as has been suggested, v. 12 is an independent bicolon perhaps loosely connected to vv. 7–11, but an interlude of some sort, then all four stanzas are of equivalent length:

Stanza 1 (vv. 7–11): 119 syllables, 44 stresses, 50 words
Stanza 2 (vv. 13–16): 119 syllables, 44 stresses, 55 words
Stanza 3 (vv. 17–20): 122 syllables, 49 stresses, 58 words
Stanza 4 (10: 1–4): 115 syllables, 44 stresses, 49 words

(2) Stanza 1 has two strophes of unequal length (64 + 41 syllables), plus the refrain, and so does stanza 2 (62 + 43 syllables). Thus within stanzas 1 and 2, the A strophes correspond to one another in length, as do the B strophes:

Stanza 1, Strophe A: 64 syllables, 24 stresses, 24 words
Stanza 2, Strophe A: 63 syllables, 24 stresses, 26 words

Stanza 1, Strophe B: 42 syllables, 13 stresses, 18 words
Stanza 2, Strophe B: 43 syllables, 13 stresses, 21 words

(3) Stanzas 3 and 4, however, have two strophes of relatively equal length:

Stanza 3, Strophe A: 50 syllables, 21 stresses, 22 words
Stanza 3, Strophe B: 58 syllables, 20 stresses, 28 words
Stanza 4, Strophe A: 51 syllables, 20 stresses, 20 words
Stanza 4, Strophe B: 51 syllables, 18 stresses, 21 words

One conclusion drawn from these observations is that this major section displays a linear, two-part structure, stanzas 1–2 forming the first half (panel) and stanzas 3–4 the second. Setting aside v. 12 for the moment, the total length of each half is strikingly similar:

Panel I (stanzas 1–2): 238 syllables, 88 stresses, 105 words
Panel II (stanzas 3–4): 237 syllables, 93 stresses, 107 words

In fact, the length is roughly equivalent to that of each of the two "panels" described in 5:8–25 (see above, pp. 59–60 and below, p. 99).

Furthermore, I note the use of divine names once in each strophe of stanzas 1–2, and in reverse order in each stanza: אדני (line 7a) . . . יהוה (line 10a) in stanza 1, but יהוה (line 13a) . . . אדני (line 16a) in stanza 2. Thus "Adonay" forms an inclusio from the first strophe of stanza 1 to the second of stanza 2. Likewise, the use of the form כלו, which occurs nowhere else in Isaiah 2–12, links 8a with 16e. Finally, both stanzas close with the expression כל־פה in the final line before the refrain (11b and 16d).

Such further links between stanzas 3–4, however, are not evident. For example, only one divine name occurs in all of stanzas 3–4, יהוה צבאות in line 18a. But it can be argued that the thought progression from the first to the second stanza is analogous to the one from the third to the fourth. Stanza 1 speaks a "word" of judgment against Jacob/Israel, which Yahweh will accomplish through the mediation of Rezin's foes, and stanza 2 articulates more clearly what specific evils are at issue. Stanza 3 describes the impending effects of wickedness in an intransitive, mediated mode, although it is clear that Yahweh Seba'oth is behind the judgment. The stanza ends by shifting attention from Jacob/Israel to Judah, and, I would argue, stanza 4 continues this focus with the same accusatory "woe" used against the specific sins of Judah in 5:8ff. Thus both stanzas 2 and 4 articulate more clearly the nature of the wickedness.

However, I have yet to take into consideration v. 12, which has been conspicuous by its absence in this analysis. It may be significant that the Masoretic divisions (see the discussion of this verse on p. 84), supported by the Qumran scroll, break 9:7–10:4 into *three* units, dividing between v. 12 and v. 13 (and *not* after the refrain in v. 11), and then again after the refrain in v. 20 (but not after the one in v. 16). The lengths of this tripartite structure would be as follows:

Part I (9:7–12):   140 syllables, 50 stresses, 60 words
Part II (9:13–20):   241 syllables, 91 stresses, 113 words
Part III (10:1–4):   115 syllables, 44 stresses, 49 words

This suggests a chiastic arrangement, and if parts I and III are added together, the following totals appear:

Parts I + III: 255 syllables, 94 stresses, 109 words
Part II: 241 syllables, 91 stresses, 113 words

The correspondence is not as close as the previous division into two "panels," but that analysis conveniently ignored v. 12. And the variation here is only 4–6% in the different categories.

It would be tempting to assume that the addition of v. 12 interrupted a precise structure of four stanzas, and that this is a clear example of a later redactional corruption. However, the text as it stands offers an example of an intentionally-worked structure that both includes and cuts across the more obvious divisions formed by the refrains. Whether this is the result of later redaction, or of a superimposition of a second structure upon an original poem, or whether it simply indicates an original but complex structure, is a matter of debate and beyond proof.

In any case, it seems reasonable to view the two structural analyses, one linear and the other chiastic, not as mutually exclusive, but as a sophisticated combination. Indeed, I have previously noted the juxtaposition of chiastic and linear verse structures within the same verse or strophe (for example, v. 17, vv. 18d–19c). If both techniques were available and used together on the level of line and verse, it is likely that they could be used in combination at a larger structural level as well.

The tripartite structure has a further integrity of its own. By including v. 12, the divine name יהוה צבאות is added to the first part, yielding three names in part I, (one אדני, one יהוה, one יהוה צבאות), three names in part II (one יהוה, one אדני, and one יהוה צבאות), and none in part III. Thus three uses occur in parts I and III, and three occur in part II:

Part I:	אדני	(7a)	*Part II:*	יהוה	(13a)
(vv. 7–12)	יהוה	(10a)	(vv. 13–20)	אדני	(16a)
	יהוה צבאות	(12b)		יהוה צבאות	(18a)
[+ *Part III*]					

It should also be noted that the midpoint of the entire poem lies in the same verse that forms the midpoint of the middle part: lines 16gh. Since this is the refrain that concludes the second "stanza," it could well be that even without a specific Masoretic division marker, this point in the whole poem would have been noticed as significant.

Furthermore, since the thought progression from stanza 1 to 2 is similar to the progression between stanzas 3 and 4, the progression between the material in stanzas 1 and 4, and between 2 and 3, also follows, except that the sequence would be reversed in 2–3. Thus parts I and III link the judgment of vv. 7–11 (stanza 1) with the specific indictments of stanza 4, while the middle section (part II) cites specific offenses before describing the resultant (self-) destruction. In fact, if I am correct in understanding 10:1–4 as an accusation against Judah in the mode of 5:8ff., the linkage to vv. 7–11 (that is, between parts I and III) is enhanced by the inclusion of v. 12, which alludes to the failure of Judah to "turn to the one striking them" by echoing the verbal root נכה from 5:25b. Thus part I also links the fate of Jacob/Israel to Judah, which is articulated in part III. Part II lists specific ills within Jacob/Israel but also turns the result of these sins upon Judah in line 20c.

However it may be divided into parts, and in addition to the logic of the thought progression, the whole of 9:7–10:4 is held together by other features as well. The verbal root נפל, which has been noted as a link between the beginning and end of the first strophe in vv. 7–9, also appears in the line preceding the final refrain, 10:4b. This inclusio not only binds together the whole piece, but it also suggests a thematic development between the word that "falls" in Israel and those who will fall (in both Israel and Judah) as a result.

The use of the somewhat difficult idiom גאות עשן in line 17d in describing the impending destruction due to the wickedness of the people calls to mind the accusation against their arrogance in 8c, where the noun גאוה is used.

Further, I note the repetition of the verbal root אכל, which appears in 11b in reference to the action of the enemies against Israel. In vv. 17ff. the same verb characterizes the internecine destruction in Israel, which gives a different nuance to the fact that "the people" Israel are described as מאכלת for the fire in 18c. Twice more the verb is used in 19bc to indicate the action of those within Israel against their own, and, as our translation shows, is likely to be the verb supplied in 20ab.

The word pair אלמנה and יתום is used in line 16c to describe the withdrawal of Yahweh's mercy, and in 10:2cd they appear in the less common[2] reverse order, describing the heinous action of the people. Further, the double use of the object marker (as in 16c) is found in 10ab and in 20ab. It also occurs in 5:24ef and thus may serve as a link back to the material in 5:8–25.

Likewise, the use of the noun עם serves both to bind 9:7–10:4 together as well as to echo 5:8ff. This noun appears once in each stanza of 9:7ff.: in 8a (העם), 15a (העם הזה), 18b (העם), and 10:2b (עמי). Furthermore, it occurs in v. 12 (העם), which, I have argued, can be understood not only as an independent piece of the structure of 9:7ff. but also as a link back to 5:25, where Yahweh is described as angry 'at his people' (בעמו, 5:25a).

In summary, it is proposed that there is a structural integrity to the unit 9:7–10:4 that goes beyond previous division of the piece simply into four stanzas, although this observation has certainly been the starting point. The balancing of the lengths of the various subunits has played a significant role, whether measured by syllables, accents, or even individual words. But I have also noticed the use of poetic and rhetorical devices, such as word play, repetition, chiasm, and inclusio, as structural markers.

---

2. Of 25 occurrences of the word pair in the Hebrew Bible, 20 have the order "orphan . . . widow." Of the four uses in Isaiah (the two discussed here plus 1:17, 23), only 10:2 shows this reversed order.

This careful, complex, and integrated structural unity suggests that the composition of 9:7–10:4 is structurally independent of the material in 5:8–25 and that my initial hypothesis (pp. 65–66) can be confirmed. However, many of the structural features in this unit do suggest links to the material in chap. 5, and this will be taken up in detail below (pp. 96ff.).

Thought Progression

Later I shall deal with the relation of this unit to chap. 5, to the intervening material in chaps. 6–8, and to the larger structure of chaps. 2–12. At this point my focus is on this one poem, although it cannot be understood apart from its larger context. While commentators are not unanimous, it is generally recognized that these chapters have in mind the events described in chaps. 7–8, dealing with the Syro-Ephraimite conflict, and the mention of Rezin in 9:10a is a clear reference to one of the central characters in that crisis.

The first stanza (9:7–11) speaks of Adonay's "word" which has been sent against Jacob/Israel, a word that the people and likely the king (the "Resident of Samaria") know but do not seem to understand, since they respond with pride and arrogance rather than with humility and repentance. The result is that Yahweh's destructive anger will fall upon them by means of the Gentile nations around them: Aram, Philistines, and Assyria (in the background). Nevertheless, the destruction of Israel does not bring Yahweh's anger to conclusion: "his hand is still outstretched."

If I am correct in separating v. 12 as an interlude that echoes 5:25, then this verse forms a link not only to the previous material (which deals primarily with Judah) but also between stanza 1 and what follows in chaps. 9–10. The use of העם may well be ambiguous: in 8a it has as referent the Northern Kingdom; yet it is used also of the South (1:3), and of both North and South together.

Thus there is in v. 12 an anticipation of the general theme that what happens in the North is linked, both by cause and by effect, to circumstances in the South. In fact, the theme of v. 12 could well be understood as the theme of the entire poem, expressed by the words לא שב, which are echoed in each refrain but with a different subject. Because the people have not returned/repented, Yahweh's hand has not returned/turned away.

Stanza 2, however, continues the direct focus on Israel, although it is possible that here the term also has a secondary reference to "all Israel," including the Southern Kingdom. In any case, the second stanza gives specific reasons for the punishment and destruction of Israel: her people, and above all her leaders, are apostates and evildoers. "Therefore" Adonay will punish all, showing no mercy even to the orphans and widows. And the refrain concludes with an ominous tone—even with the destruction of all in Israel, the hand of Yahweh's punishment has not yet turned away.

Stanza 3 now expands the picture beyond the Northern Kingdom. Wickedness spreads like a forest fire, the whole earth will shake and tremble before Yahweh's rage, and "the people" (line 18c)—whatever referent is understood—are like fuel for the fire. The specifics of lines 20abc are not completely clear, and perhaps some sort of confusion and chaos is just the point. It seems likely that internal conflict within the Northern Kingdom is pictured as expanding externally against Judah (probably a reference to the Syro-Ephraimite threat).

But whether the internecine terror in Ephraim and Manesseh refers to political strife, social injustice, something specific about which we have no information, or something general that includes all these possibilites, one cannot be certain. Whatever the situation, the aggression against Judah is portrayed as an extension of the fratricide within Israel and may well reflect the view that North and South are still to be considered brothers. In any case, the refrain indicates that the threat and attack now on Judah has still not brought Yahweh's anger to completion.

Stanza 4 brings into focus the real target of the whole poem: those who were assailed by the "woe" formula (calling to mind the invective in 5:8ff), who are primarily those in Judah and Jerusalem. The prophet now speaks specifically to—and about—the Southern Kingdom, whose apostasy and social sins against "my people" (2b) generally match those of their brethren to the north. Judah cannot glory in the impending fall of the North, since they will have their own "day of reckoning," for Yahweh's hand is still stretched out—against them.

As the refrain now brings the whole poem to conclusion, it still remains to be asked whether Yahweh's anger has, in fact, "returned," or at least will have been turned away when Judah is eventually punished. This would be consistent with the general theme of the poem against Judah, as a warning that what happens in the North may happen to them as well. However, vv. 17–18 have introduced the motif of Yahweh's anger against any place where wickedness burns, and the final refrain therefore leaves open the possibility of further anger and punishment, even beyond Judah. This theme is picked up in the following unit, 10:5ff, and will be discussed below (pp. 140ff. and 184ff.).

The following outline summarizes 9:7–10:4:

Stanza 1 (vv. 7–11)
    Strophe A: Yahweh's "word" rejected by Northern Kingdom
    Strophe B: Israel consumed
    Refrain: Yahweh's anger still not satisfied

Interlude (v. 12)

Theme of whole poem; link to material beyond this poem (5:25)

"'The people' do not repent (לא שב) =

Yahweh's hand does not return (לא שב)"

Stanza 2 (vv. 13–16)

Strophe A: Israel's leaders mislead the people

Strophe B: Adonay will not show mercy to anyone

Refrain: Yahweh's anger still not satisfied

Stanza 3 (vv. 17–20)

Strophe A: Yahweh's anger expands beyond Northern Kingdom

Strophe B: Northern Kingdom now against Southern Kingdom

Refrain: Yahweh's anger still not satisfied

Stanza 4 (10:1–4)

Strophe A: "Woe" to those in Judah (link to material beyond this poem, cf. 5:8ff.)

Strophe B: *Judah* will be destroyed

Refrain: Yahweh's anger *still* (?) not satisfied

Chapter 4

The Macrostructure of Isaiah 5:1–10:4

The Relationship of 5:8–25 and 9:7–10:4

Methodological Concerns and Previous Research

So far I have dealt with the two poems in Isa 5:8–25 and 9:7–10:4 as independent units, each of which reflects a carefully worked structure in itself. However, the interrelatedness of these chapters has long been noted, although no clear consensus on the nature of the relationship has been reached. The surface data focus on two rather obvious features. First, 5:8ff. presents a series of six "woes," each introduced by הוֹי, and 9:7–10:4 presents a series of four stanzas, each of which concludes with the same refrain:

בְּכָל־זֹאת לֹא־שָׁב אַפּוֹ
וְעוֹד יָדוֹ נְטוּיָה:

Second, an additional, "seventh" woe is found in 10:1, linking to the six in chap. 5; and another instance of the exact wording of the refrain is found in 5:25, forming a second (inter)linkage with 9:7ff.

Although it seems unlikely that the two data are independent, I shall first consider them individually, since commentaries do not necessarily deal with them as part of the same phenomenon. Concerning the refrain found in chap. 5, which is identical to the refrains in 9:7–10:4, one explanation offered is that the present position of 5:25 is due to accidental displacement, likely a result of an error of transmission (so Duhm, Marti, Gray, Eichrodt, Kaiser, and Wildberger). With this theory often come attempts at reconstructing the original text, usually accomplished by transposing 5:25 back as the conclusion to 9:7ff., either following 9:20 (for example, Wildberger) or after 10:1–4 (for example, Gray, though he leaves 5:25abc in position and suggests moving only 25d).

A second suggestion is that 5:25 was *intentionally* transposed to its present position due to deliberate redactional activity, a suggestion put forth most forcefully by Barth (1977), as well as Vermeylen (1977), and followed by Clements (1980b), Kaiser (1963, 1979), L'Heureux (1984), and Sheppard (1985). According to Barth's theory, this rearrangement was part of the process of the "Assur-redaction," done at the time of Josiah. This major piece of the redactional puzzle began with what is now 5:1, and the account of the summoning of the Assyrians in 5:26–30 was placed as the close of the initial indictment of Israel and Judah in 5:1–24, with 5:25 forming an intentional link to the material beyond the *Denkschrift.*[1]

In both schemes, 5:25 is considered as originally part of the poem in 9:7ff., and the verse represents either a truncated or reworked part of an original longer stanza. Its present position results from the intentional insertion of the *Denkschrift* after chap. 5, which interrupted the original poem in some way.

Related (though not necessarily so) is the question of the existence and possible location of a "seventh woe." For example, Duhm suggests that a seventh "woe" has been lost between 5:13 and 5:14, quite apart from consideration of 10:1–4. Hayes and Irvine believe that 5:23 originally began with הוי, and that a seventh "woe" was found there. Gray allows for additional "woes" at both vv. 14 and 23 and speaks of "six, or perhaps in the original text seven or more" sections (1912: 88).

On the other hand, Kaiser, Wildberger, Clements, and Watts argue that the "woe" found in 10:1 is indeed the seventh of the series, although it is not clear whether it was originally the first (Clements) or the final one (Kaiser,[2] Wildberger). Watts (1985: 142)[3] deals with 10:1–4 without further reference to chap. 5, admitting simply that "the relationships are complex".

However, if it is possible to suggest that intentional redactional activity has placed, if not "misplaced," 5:25, it seems likely that the same sort of intentional redactional activity may have placed 10:1–4 in its position as an intentional link to 5:8ff. Kaiser suggests a somewhat *quid pro quo* exchange of the two sections, "after the woe [10:1–4] had already been extended in terms of eschatological disaster, and before it had again been made contemporaneous by the addition of 5:24" (Kaiser 1979 = 1983: 111).

---

1. The term *Denkschrift* is used here as the common designation for the material in Isa 6:1–8:18 (9:6). The term describes these so-called memoirs, often assumed to be an early collection of Isaiah's writing, perhaps autobiographical in nature.

2. Interestingly, in his first edition, Kaiser (1963 = 1972) discusses 10:1–4(a!) in connection with 5:8–24, but in the second edition (1979 = 1983), he includes 10:1–4(b) with 9:7ff.

3. Watts suggests a further connection beyond 10:4 to 10:5, where the "woe" formula is continued, but without refrain. However, 10:5 is surely a new unit, and not, in my opinion, integral to the connection between 5:8ff. and 9:7–10:4.

These arguments for intentional "displacement" ("replacement" or, better still, "placement") have been further developed by L'Heureux (1984), Sheppard (1985), and Anderson (1988), as noted above (pp. 20–21), and they all suggest a much more intentionally structured unity to the larger piece, including the thought progression revolving around the *Denkschrift*. Thus L'Heureux (1984: 115) argues that the present state of the whole of 5:1–10:4 is the work of a single redactor (his "Primary Redactor"). Sheppard (1985: 194), who agrees with the suggestion of a "double inclusio" (see below, p. 100) sees such carefully worked "displacement" of pieces as an editorial technique that is a characteristic feature of the "Assur-Redaction."

Such attempts to reconstruct the redactional history follow upon the work of those whose primary concern was the reconstruction of the original text. Duhm and Gray, for example, represent an era characterized by textual reconstruction based precisely on the need for metrically balanced strophes, the lack of which can certainly be explained otherwise (see above, pp. 58ff. and 88ff.). The form-critical approach, which assumes an original, short, specific "woe" formula and thus also assumes that any cola or verses that go beyond the formal limits are later additions, bases many conclusions on a large amount of hypothetical reconstruction, falters on a lack of clear consensus,[4] and fails to do justice to the text as it now stands.

Barth, Vermeylen, Kaiser, and Clements, on the other hand, focus on intentional editorial activity in tracing the history of redaction, but they simply assume that the present text is the product of a long redactional process.[5] Although the reconstruction of the original text is not their primary concern, they must assume a specific original form in order to demonstrate and explain the way in which it was reworked. While one need not deny redactional activity or the possibility of the combination of originally distinct units, it is not logically—or methodologically—necessary to assume that a prior, original form, even if one could be determined convincingly, ever existed independently. In fact, I shall propose a compositional unity that bespeaks a coherent plan and organization to the text as it now stands. At this point, then, questions of redaction become simply matters of dating both the content of the text and the process of compo-

---

4. Wildberger's comments (1972: 183) are noteworthy: "Da es sich um eine Sammlung handelt, deren Einzelstücke einmal selbstständig waren, können diese zu sehr verschiedenen Zeiten gesprochen worden sein, und man müßte grundsätzlich versuchen, für jede ursprüngliche Einheit die Zeit zu bestimmen." However, he continues, "Aber es fehlen alle Anhaltspunkte, die zu einer chronologischen Festlegung dienen könnten. Vermutlich sind aber diese Rufe doch allesamt erhoben worden, bevor die assyrische Gefahr in bedrohliche Nähe gerückt war."

5. In contrast, I note the comment of Andersen and Freedman (1989: 4) in reference to the book of Amos, "We cannot assert that the book is mainly the work of post-exilic editors, a theory that is often repeated but seldom defended in detail."

sition, and if a date can be determined within the historical context of the prophet/poet to whom the work is attributed, questions of a prehistory of the text become unnecessary.[6]

Structural and Rhetorical Features

However one seeks to explain the cause and nature of the relationship between these poems, to which I shall return below, it is evident that they are in fact related (contra Brown 1990). In addition to the two interconnections between the "woes" and the refrain already noted, there is one striking and important feature that my analysis of each poem has determined and that previous research has not considered, namely, the length of each unit. Despite differences in internal structure of each poem, as I noted in chaps. 2 and 3, each unit can be understood as a combination of two "panels," roughly equivalent in length, so that a "side-by-side" or 1:1 correspondence has been built into each poem. More significantly, I would now call attention to the total length of each poem:

> Isa 5:8–25:   496 syllables, 200 stresses, 218 words, 62 lines
> Isa 9:7–10:4:   496 syllables, 185 stresses, 222 words, 62 lines

Even allowing for some margin of error, the correspondence in the number of syllables is striking. The poems are the same length. On the basis of the syllable counts, one is tempted to assert that they are *exactly* the same length.

This is confirmed by the other measurements as well. Although I have noted a number of "extra" emphatic accents that have raised the total number of stresses in the chap. 5 material (pp. 49–52), even the difference between 185 and 200 is a variance of only 8.1%. If the number of accents in 5:8–25 is reduced to 190, as suggested on p. 49, the figures would be even closer (2.7%). Finally, I note the close equivalency in the total number of words, as well, which suggests that this figure is another factor that merits inclusion in considerations of length, especially on the level of larger units.

This nearly exact correspondence is hardly the result of coincidence or haphazard redactional activity. Nor is it the result of simply exchanging one segment of two previously independent poems, since the length of the interchanged pieces is not the same. (The length of 5:25 is less than half the length of 10:1–4.) Moreover, since both 5:25 and 10:1–4 form integral parts of the structure of the poem in which they appear, as has been shown in the analysis of the gross structure of each larger unit (pp. 58ff. and 88ff.), these "pieces" cannot be understood as simply being "displaced." If intentional redactional activity has, indeed, taken place, then it

---

6. Wiklander (1984: 7 and 248) addresses this point in dealing with Isaiah 2–4, although he leaves the issue somewhat unresolved; see below, n. 9.

has been done with the utmost of creative care, so that the two poems as they now stand match each other very closely indeed.

Furthermore, this close and purposeful connection between the two poems suggests that other points of comparison and connection should be sought as well. In the analysis of the internal structure of each major unit, I noted that thematic and vocabulary links, the use of poetic inclusio, wordplay, and other rhetorical devices played a role in unifying part and whole, and it is likely that similar connections may operate between these major units as well. For example, both L'Heureux (1984) and Sheppard (1985) have noted the possible "double inclusio," between 5:8 and 10:4, in which the woe-sayings form the outer circle (5:8–24 and 10:1–4) and the refrain stanzas form the inner circle (5:25ff. and 9:7–10:4).

Moreover, other connections can also be found. For example, the use of עַל־כֵּן in 5:25a, in contrast to לָכֵן used elsewhere in 5:8–25 (lines 13a, 14a, 24a), corresponds to the עַל־כֵּן of 9:16a, the sole use of a word for 'therefore' in the second poem. In 5:25d, נְבֵלָה (from the root נָבֵל, BDB 615) refers to the corpses of the people, but in the "therefore" verse of 9:16(f), the same word (but likely from root נָבֵל II, BDB 614) describes the foolish "sacrilege" spoken by every mouth.

The wordplay involving the vocable פֶּה has already been observed within the individual sections, but it is interesting to contrast 5:14, where "Sheol opens wide its mouth," with 9:11, where Israel's enemies devour her with "a whole mouth." Further, the use of הַמַּכֵּהוּ in 9:12 is a clear link to the וַיַּכֵּהוּ in 5:25b, which, as has been noted, is the major point of contact with 9:7ff. Conversely, this suggests that 9:12 is to be heard in connection with 5:25 (note also the use of the root שׁוּב in 9:12a and the refrain repeated in 5:25ef).

In 5:9a, a monocolon follows an initial quatrain of 31 syllables and 13 stresses. This single line uses elliptical syntax to introduce a direct quotation: what Yahweh says, presumably in the divine council, which is overheard by the prophet and shared with the people. In parallel fashion, in line 9:8c, a monocolon follows an initial quatrain of 33 syllables and 12 stresses. This single line also uses an elliptical style to introduce a direct quotation: what the people say in pride and arrogance in response to the "word" of Adonay.

A clear indication of the interrelationship between these two poems results from confirmation that the "seventh woe" is, in fact, located in 10:1–4 and further, from the way that the seven "woe" strophes are arranged. I have already noted the disagreements over the proposed location of a "seventh woe," including some who argue that it is found within chap. 5 and apart from chaps. 9–10. Indeed, the expected place for it would seem to be 5:23a, where a pattern that is similar to the introduction of the other "woes" appears, but without the use of הוֹי. However, to generate a "lost" הוֹי (Hayes and Irvine, Gray, Duhm) is, at best, a possibility based on text-critical principles (though in this case without manuscript evidence) and, at worst, a re-creation ex nihilo. In light of the clear relationship between the two passages that has already been demonstrated, it is not only more logical but also much simpler to find, within the texts themselves, a seventh woe, ready-made, in 10:1–4.

Moreover, the sequence of the woes is significant. Kaiser, who agrees that the "seventh woe" is found in 10:1, suggests a "circular composition" to the seven woes, noting that "the first, fourth and seventh woes are concerned with transgressors of the law; the second and sixth with drunkards and the third and fifth with frivolity which is forgetful of God" (1979 = 1983: 97). I have come independently to a similar conclusion but would suggest that the chiastic arrangement is much more detailed than Kaiser had proposed.

For example, it is only the first and seventh woes (5:8 and 10:1) that are followed by 2 pl. verb forms (in 5:8d and 10:3a). Further, the topic of these first and last woes is not simply "transgressors of the law," as Kaiser summarized, but rather more specifically the social sins of monied injustice ("joining house to house" and "decreeing decrees of evil . . . to twist the needy from the justice due them"). This, I note in passing, is also the theme addressed in 5:23, which speaks of the perversion of justice, but where no הוי is used.

Further, the third and fifth woes (5:18–19 and 5:21) deal not so much with frivolity, as with the confusion of man's insight and wisdom compared to the "counsel of the Holy One of Israel." Finally, the fourth or middle woe (5:20) is a carefully structured strophe of three bicola, all of which begin with the plural participle (in no other woe are there three participles) followed by contrastive chiasm: "evil:good :: good:evil," "darkness: light :: light:darkness," "bitter:sweet :: sweet:bitter," all of which summarize the complete inversion of basic issues of right and wrong. Thus the full series, concluded in 10:1–4 presents the following pattern:

Woe #1: social sins: economic oppression (5:8)
  Woe #2: alchohol abuse (5:11)
    Woe #3: affront to Yahweh's counsel (5:18)
      Woe #4: confusion of good and evil (5:20)
    Woe #5: affront to true wisdom (5:21)
  Woe #6: alchohol abuse (5:22)
Woe #7: social sins: economic oppression (10:1ff.)

If one would consider only the unit in 5:18–23, which contains woes ##3–6 and forms the first stanza of the second "panel" of 5:8–25 (see above, pp. 58ff.), the fourth woe (v. 20) would turn out to be at the structural middle also of this smaller series. This is due to the fact that the strophe containing the third woe is so much longer than those of the fifth and sixth woes and therefore is equivalent to the total of both of them.

What is also interesting is that the content of 5:23, which follows upon
the sixth woe and speaks of justice and injustice, would also fit the expected theme of the seventh woe, although the הוי formula is not used in
that verse. Combined with the rhetorical feature of the shortening of the
strophe and the quickening of the pace through vv. 20–21 (see above,
pp. 58 and 62), the effect of reaching the sixth woe would likely have been
the anticipation of the seventh and final woe immediately after v. 22,
but the absence of the actual הוי would create doubt in the mind of the
hearer/reader whether the sequence was, in fact, at an end. The holding off
of the final woe until 10:1 has had the effect of keeping the hearer/reader
in suspense until the announcement of the final woe at the end of the
entire composition.[7]

Rather than inserting an additional הוי in order to create a seventh
woe in 5:23, which would destroy the rhetorical feature just observed, the
appearance of what might be called a "phantom," or at least rhetorically
ambiguous, seventh "woe" at that point (5:23) illustrates again the inter-
connection of the two poems and suggests that each must be understood in
light of the other. Thus the present position of the actual seventh woe in
10:1 is not the result of unintentional or even intentional dismembering
and displacement of an original unity (so Kaiser, Clements, and others) but
the conscious and careful binding of the message of 5:8–25 with the message of 9:7–10:4.

A further structural feature that can be found only by considering both
poems in relation to each other is the placement of divine names. I have
already noted the use of eight divine names in 5:8–25 and of six divine
names in 9:7–10:4 in the consideration of the gross structure of each unit
(see above, pp. 58ff. and 88ff.). It was observed that the eighth divine
name in 5:8–25 occurs in the section (v. 25) that most directly links with
the latter poem and that, conversely, the one stanza in 9:7–10:4 that lacks
any divine name (10:1–4) is the one that links directly with the former
poem. Thus there are exactly seven divine names in the "woe" material
and seven divine names in the refrained stanzas, even though they are
unevenly divided between the two poems:

5:8–25	*9:7–10:4*
v. 9: יהוה צבאות	v. 7: אדני (MT) [יהוה ?]
v. 12: יהוה	v. 10: יהוה

---

7. Thus Kaiser's concern "whether the series of seven woes had a previous history
of its own, or whether it was brought together for its present position" (1979 = 1983:
99) and his argumentation of how "at a last stage the last strophe of the refrain poem
was exchanged with the last woe" (p. 111 and also p. 221), while creative, thorough,
and consistent with his assumption about the redactional history, are, in my opinion,
simply unnecessary.

v. 16:	יהוה צבאות		v. 12:	יהוה צבאות
v. 16:	האל הקדוש		v. 13:	יהוה
v. 19:	קדוש ישראל		v. 16:	אדני
v. 24:	יהוה צבאות		v. 18:	יהוה צבאות
v. 24:	קדוש ישראל	⟵	[10:1–4: final "woe"]	
v. 25:	יהוה	⟶		

Since the order of the specific names is integrated into the structure of each poem, one cannot simply regroup the names without affecting the integrity of each individual poem. However, if one considers the two poems in combination, there appears a total of fourteen divine names. Reading אדני with the MT at 9:7, there is one pair of the title קדוש ישראל in the first poem and one pair of the title אדני in the second. Of the remaining ten names, nine are יהוה (five times with the addition of צבאות, three in the first poem and two in the second) plus the one variant האל הקדוש.

If one reads יהוה in 9:7, of course, then there are exactly ten uses of the tetragrammaton (two times alone plus three times with צבאות in the first poem; three times alone plus two times with צבאות in the second). The sole singleton in the first poem, האל הקדוש, would match the singular use of אדני in the second. However one reads the name in 9:7, therefore, a pattern emerges that indicates an intentional connection found only by regarding the two poems as complementary.

Finally, I would call attention to the somewhat awkward construction of 5:19a, in which two jussive verbs are juxtaposed asyndetically: "let him hasten, let him hurry [his work]," which might also be rendered as hendiadys, producing the English redundancy, 'let him quickly hurry [his work]'. The use of the two verbal roots מהר and חוש in a somewhat peculiar expression might have stood out in and of itself, but one's interest is drawn back to them also by the bicolon arrived at in 10:2cd. Here the inversion of the more common order of the word pair "orphan . . . widow" to "widows . . . orphans" would call attention to a verse in which one also finds the noun שלל in 10:2c matched by the use of the verbal root בזז in 10:2d.

Remembering that this verse occurs in the first strophe of 10:1–4, which, in turn, is the stanza that has the most direct link with 5:8–25, one's attention is returned to the awkward verbs in 5:19. Bringing these verses together produces an important juxtaposition of four vocables: מהר, plus חוש in the participial form in 5:19a (designated here as terms A + B); שלל, plus בזז in the nominal form in 10:2c (designated A′ + B′). These come together in the form A + A′ + B + B′ into the significant name of Isaiah's son, מהר שלל חש בז (8:3).[8]

---

8. One should note in passing the rhetorical feature of this name itself: 3 + 3 syllables plus 2 + 2 syllables, which provides a 6 + 4 "falling" rhythm, causing the very

If this is true, then there exists a link not only between the two poems in chaps. 5 and 9 but also between the two poems together and the intervening material, since Maher-shalal-hash-baz is one of the children who play a role within the *Denkschrift*. It is tempting to ask if any reference might be found to the other of Isaiah's sons featured in the *Denkschrift* material, שְׁאָר יָשׁוּב. While no reference can be found to the vocable שְׁאָר, the use of the verbal root שׁוּב is important both thematically and structurally as a key word in the five refrains and in the important assertion concerning "the people" in 9:12. Whether these instances are intended to call to mind the rather ambiguous meaning of שְׁאָר יָשׁוּב is difficult to determine, but it seems clear that there are several allusions to material in chaps. 6–8, and it is likely that the two poems in chaps. 5 and 9 have been intentionally placed around this intervening material.

In sum, several instances have been found in which poetic and rhetorical features have indicated a carefully worked bond between the two poems in 5:8–25 and 9:7–10:4, the most striking of which is the fact that they are the same length. These two poems have already been discussed as individual units (chaps. 2–3 above), and I have tried to show that each piece is, on its own, a carefully crafted unity. But the two poems so clearly complement each other that we must conclude that each has been composed with specific reference to the other and that they must be understood with this interrelationship in mind: the first by means of anticipating, the second by means of bringing a sense of conclusion to the other.

Since there is a sense of unity to each poem in its present state, however, any reconstruction of an earlier, more unified work is therefore rendered questionable. And any explanation of the redactional activity that has produced the present text that suggests accidental—or even intentional—displacement of material must first consider that the two pieces are so closely linked to one another that they have been constructed to be the same length, and that this phenomenon is most easily—if not also most logically—explained as the result of original craftsmanship rather than as the result of redactional reworking.[9]

---

utterance of the name to speed up and hasten to the end. Analogous to the order of the terms in 5:19 and 10:2, the matching of A + B with A′ + B′ would produce within the word order of the name itself a combination of 3:2 + 3:2.

9. Wiklander's conclusions (1984: 248) concerning Isaiah 2–4 offer a somewhat similar argument. Although he leaves open the possibility that this unit is either "an original, coherent and well-formed discourse intended for reading or oral public performance" or "a well-formed, redactional and literary unit consisting of originally self-contained speeches that were gradually shaped into a unified whole according to a fixed plan," he affirms that "the text-shape of Isa 2–4 as it emerges in the period of the earliest accepted texts is essentially the text produced by the author."

The Transitional Pieces: 5:26–30 and 8:19–23a

The thought progression indicated by this structural phenomenon will be discussed in greater detail below. Now I shall first consider the intervening material, since some connections have already been found between the poems in 5:8–25 and in 9:7–10:4 and the material associated with the so-called Isaianic memoirs, or *Denkschrift*, around which these two poems now seem intentionally placed and designed. Previous discussion of Isaiah 5ff. has certainly tried to make sense of the present literary context of the whole of these chapters, in spite of the various theories of the history and displacement of the text.

For example, although I have questioned the need for hypotheses that assume extensive redactional displacement and reworking of material, the theory that the *Denkschrift* of 6:1–8:18 was inserted at this particular point does, after all, offer some rationale for this redactional decision (see, for example, Barth 1977). Assuming that 5:26–30 speaks of an Assyrian invasion, the theme of the rise and, later, the impending fall of Assyria (articulated in 10:5ff.) would be enhanced by the material concerning the Syro-Ephraimite war, which "fills out the picture of the circumstances which occasioned the coming of the Assyrians and explains why their advent became a threat to Judah" (Clements 1980b: 55).

The seam at the conclusion of the *Denkschrift* is not nearly as obvious, however. Barth (1977) proposes that the oracle in 8:23b–9:6 was added at the time of his Assur-Redaktion, and he eliminates 8:19–23a completely as a still later addition. Kaiser defends the Isaianic origin of these verses in his first edition (1963 = 1972: 122), but in his second edition he assumes a postexilic date (1979 = 1983: 200). Wildberger (1972: 344) dates this passage to the exilic period. Clements (1980: 101) acknowledges that "the section that concludes chap. 8 is beset with considerable difficulties . . . " and argues that vv. 19–20 and vv. 21–22 represent two different units, both from the exilic time.

What is striking about the material in 8:19ff. is especially the "darkness and doom" vocabulary that echoes quite clearly the verse found at the end of chap. 5. Line 5:30b begins

$$\text{ונבט לארץ והנה־חשך צר}$$,

and 8:22 begins

$$\text{אל־ארץ יביט והנה צרה וחשכה}$$,

using the same vocabulary in different form and word order.

But before any structural relationship between these two smaller sections is developed, it is helpful to submit each text to poetic analysis.

Isaiah 5:26–30

Text

		Syllable Count		Stress Count	
			MT		MT
5:26a	וְנָשָׂא־נֵס לַגּוֹיִם֙ מֵרָחֹ֔וק	10	10	(3)/4	3
b	וְשָׁ֤רַק לֹו֙ מִקְצֵ֣ה הָאָ֔רֶץ	8	9	3	4
c	וְהִנֵּ֥ה מְהֵרָ֖ה קַ֥ל יָבֹֽוא׃	9	9	(3)/4	4
27a	אֵין־עָיֵ֤ף וְאֵין־כֹּושֵׁל֙ בֹּ֔ו	8	8	3	3
b	לֹ֣א יָנ֔וּם וְלֹ֖א יִישָׁ֑ן	7	7	2	4
c	וְלֹ֤א נִפְתַּח֙ אֵזֹ֣ור חֲלָצָ֔יו	9	9	3	4
d	וְלֹ֥א נִתַּ֖ק שְׂרֹ֥וךְ נְעָלָֽיו׃	9	9	3	4
28a	אֲשֶׁ֤ר חִצָּיו֙ שְׁנוּנִ֔ים	7	7	3	3
b	וְכָל־קַשְּׁתֹתָ֖יו דְּרֻכֹ֑ות	9	9	3	3
c	פַּרְסֹ֤ות סוּסָיו֙ כַּצַּ֣ר נֶחְשָׁ֔בוּ	9	9	4	4
d	וְגַלְגִּלָּ֖יו כַּסּוּפָֽה׃	7	7	2	2
29a	שְׁאָגָ֥ה לֹ֖ו כַּלָּבִ֑יא	7	7	2	3
b	וְשָׁאַ֣ג כַּכְּפִירִ֗ים	7	7	2	2
c	וְיִנְהֹם֙ וְיֹאחֵ֣ז טֶ֔רֶף	7	8	3	3
d	וְיַפְלִ֖יט וְאֵ֥ין מַצִּֽיל׃	7	7	3	3
30a	וְיִנְהֹ֥ם עָלָ֖יו	5	5	2	2
b	בַּיֹּ֣ום הַה֔וּא כְּנַהֲמַת־יָ֑ם	8	9	3	3
c	וְנִבַּ֣ט לָאָ֔רֶץ וְהִנֵּה־חֹ֑שֶׁךְ	9	11	4	3
d	צַ֣ר וָאֹ֔ור חָשַׁ֖ךְ בַּעֲרִיפֶֽיהָ׃	(8)/9	10	4	4

Totals		(150)/151	157	(55)/57	61
		Syllables	MT	Stresses	MT

Notes on Translation and Text

5:26a. **"nation(s) from afar"** Though possible, it is not necessary to regroup גוים מרחק to גוי ממרחק (see BHS) to agree with the singular pronoun. The sense of line 26a is that one nation will answer the call (or be selected by Yahweh). The word ממרחק, however, does occur in 10:3 and may well be the reading here. While not specifically named, Assyria is certainly the nation in view.

5:28a. **"—whose"** The relative pronoun is awkward, but clearly the antecedent is the nation being discussed.

Translation

5:26a He will raise a standard for the nation(s) from afar.
  b He will whistle for one from the end of the earth.
  c Look! Quickly, swiftly it comes.
  27a No one is weary; no one stumbles within it.
  b No one gets sleepy; no one falls asleep.
  c No waistband is loose;
  d No sandal-strap is torn.
  28a —whose arrows are sharpened,
  b and whose bows are bent;
  c whose horses' hoofs seem like flint,
  d and whose wheels (seem) like a whirlwind.
  29a Its roaring is like a lioness;
  b it roars like young lions.
  c It snarls and seizes prey;
  d it causes fugitives but there is no rescuer.
  30a And he will snarl against him
  b **on that day** like the snarling of the sea.
  c And he will look to the earth, and there is darkness.
  d Distress and light darken in her clouds!

5:28c. "flint" MT צַר is a hapax legomenon and may well be an alternate form of צֹר, which is attested by 1QIsaᵃ: צור. However, the MT may reflect a pun on the use of צַר from the root צרר II ('suffer distress'; compare line 30d) or צרר III (= צור III 'act as foe/enemy'). Possibly צור II may fit as well: 'besiege'.

5:29d. "causes fugitives" The meaning of root פלט in the *Hiphil* is not completely clear, occurring only here and in Mic 6:14, where the nuance is also not certain. The context of a severe attack would suggest something like 'cause to (try to) escape' = 'drive out', contra BDB (812) 'bring into security'. In Mic 6:14, I translate, 'you will not let anyone

escape, but if one of you does, I will send destruction'. In the Isaiah text
the second clause presents the negative.

5:30a. **"him"**   The antecedent is no longer clear, a problem linked
to the question of the subject of the verb: וינהם. Possibly the subject has
shifted from the invading nation to Yahweh, who will now ("on that day")
"snarl" against even the nation he has summoned (compare 10:5ff.). More
likely, the subject remains the same as in the previous use of the same
verb (29c), and the object of the preposition is the nation under attack.

5:30c. **"he"**   Again the antecedent is not clear. Here the subject
seems to be the same 3 s. m. used as the object of the preposition עליו
in 30a.

5:30d. **"and light"**   BHS suggests an accent shift, moving צַר to the
previous construction and beginning the second colon with the *waw*. The
MT, however, presents the more difficult reading in sense (although it
produces slightly better balance between the two lines) and should not be
ignored. The reference to "light" is strange in either case, and BHS demands
a paraphrase 'light [is/becomes] darkness . . .', which remains somewhat
awkward.

I follow the MT and suggest an oxymoronic coordination of otherwise
contradictory terms, a device used, for example, in Isa 1:13d: אָוֶן וַעֲצָרָה.
The theme here would be akin to Amos 5:18, where the prophet attempts to correct a misconception that the "Day of Yahweh" is necessarily "light" and not darkness. Possibly the "light" is to be understood as
lightning, which amidst the darkness of a storm is all the more threatening and distressful.

It is also possible that צַר could be understood from צרר III (= צור III)
'enemy, foe' (see 9:10), which would also fit the context. In any case, word
play is likely involved amongst all these verbal roots (see the discussion at
the note to 5:28c).

Lineation and Poetic Counts

My lineation shows 19 lines; the only difficulty is in dividing 30ab. I
have opted to include ביום ההוא in the second line of the bicolon to
avoid a very short line to which the MT gives only one accent. Enjambment would allow a division between these two words, forming a 7 + 6
bicolon.

The syllable count shows a small range, although the maximum number of 151 (MT: 157) is slightly shorter than 19 lines of 8 syllables, which
should yield (19 × 8 = 152). I count line 30d as 9 syllables:

> 5-syllable lines: 1
> 7-syllable lines: 7
> 8-syllable lines: 3
> 9-syllable lines: 7
> 10-syllable lines: 1

Of the 19 lines,
> 15.8% (3 lines) have 8 syllables,
> 89.5% (17 lines) have 7–9 syllables,
> 94.7% (18 lines) have 6–10 syllables.

I count 55–57 stresses (MT: 61). At 3 stresses per line, 19 lines would have 57. Tabulation is done on the basis of the higher number:

> 2-stress cola: 5 (26.3%)
> 3-stress cola: 9 (47.3%)
> 4-stress cola: 5 (26.3%)

The prose particle count is 3% (2/66 words).

Structure

Each verse could be understood as a separate "verse" or strophe, roughly equivalent in length:

> v. 26: 27 syllables, 11 stresses
> v. 27: 33 syllables, 11 stresses
> v. 28: 32 syllables, 12 stresses
> v. 29: 28 syllables, 10 stresses
> v. 30: 31 syllables, 13 stresses

A relationship between vv. 26 and 30 suggests a chiastic pattern. In both the first and last verse, Yahweh is the subject. There is an inclusio between הארץ/והנה in 26bc (describing the coming of Assyria) and לארץ/והנה in 30c (describing the result of Assyria's coming).

Furthermore, vv. 27 and 29 are matched by the repetition of אֵין, twice in v. 27a and again in 29d, and by the sound play between ינום in 27b and ינהם in 29c (the latter is also a link to 30a).

Cutting across this chiastic structure is the fact that the whole poem divides into two evenly balanced halves:

> vv. 26–28b: 76 syllables (60 + 16), 28 stresses
> vv. 28c–30: 75 syllables (16 + 59), 29 stresses

Isaiah 8:19–23a

Text

		Syllable Count		Stress Count	
			MT		MT
8:19a	וְכִי־יֹאמְרוּ אֲלֵיכֶם	8	8	3	2
b	דִּרְשׁוּ אֶל־הָאֹבוֹת	6	6	(2)/3	2
c	וְאֶל־הַיִּדְּעֹנִים	7	7	2	2
d	הַמְצַפְצְפִים וְהַמַּהְגִּים	8	9	2	2
e	הֲלוֹא־עַם אֶל־אֱלֹהָיו יִדְרֹשׁ	9	9	3	3
f	בְּעַד הַחַיִּים אֶל־הַמֵּתִים:	9	9	3	3
20a	לְתוֹרָה וְלִתְעוּדָה	7	7	2	2
b	אִם־לֹא יֹאמְרוּ כַּדָּבָר הַזֶּה	10	10	4	4
c	אֲשֶׁר אֵין־לוֹ שָׁחַר:	5	6	3	3
21a	וְעָבַר בָּהּ נִקְשֶׁה וְרָעֵב	9	9	3	4
b	וְהָיָה כִי־יִרְעַב וְהִתְקַצַּף	10	10	3	3
c	וְקִלֵּל בְּמַלְכּוֹ וּבֵאלֹהָיו	10	10	3	3
d	וּפָנָה לְמָעְלָה:	6	6	2	2
22a	וְאֶל־אֶרֶץ יַבִּיט	5	6	2	2
b	וְהִנֵּה צָרָה וַחֲשֵׁכָה	(7)/8	9	3	3
c	מְעוּף צוּקָה וַאֲפֵלָה מְנֻדָּח:	10/(11)	11	4	4
23a	כִּי לֹא מוּעָף לַאֲשֶׁר מוּצָק לָהּ	9	10	(4)/5	6
Totals		135/137	142	(48)/50	50
		=136			
		Syllables	MT	Stresses	MT

Notes on Translation and Text

8:19b. **"mediums"** 'Mediums' is from אוֹב (see 1 Sam 28:3). Watts reads אָבוֹת ('fathers') without explanation. It is also of interest to note that the use of דרשׁ with the preposition אל is not particularly common, especially with an object other than a divine name. Of the five occurrences in the Hebrew Bible, four are in Isaiah: 8:19 (2×), 11:10, and 19:3. The fifth is found in Deut 18:11, which deals with the same abomination addressed here: seeking the dead for sorcery.

8:20b. **"surely"** אִם־לֹא could be read literally, 'if they will not . . .', but the idiomatic translation is more likely. Compare 5:9.

Translation

8:19a   For when they say to you,
   b   "Seek the mediums
   c   and the soothsayers,
   d   who whisper and moan!
   e   Should a people not seek its 'god(s)'
   f   —the dead on behalf of the living—
   20a   for torah and testimony?"
   b   Surely they will talk according to this word
   c   for which there is no dawn!

   21a   But they will pass through in it hard pressed and hungry.
   b   And, when they are hungry, they will be enraged
   c   and curse against their king and against their god(s)
   d   and they will face upward.
   22a   But to the earth they will look,
   b   and there will be distress and darkness,
   c   gloom of oppression and darkness of banishment.
   23a   For there is no faint light for whom there is hardship.

8:21a. **"they"** The subject here and with the following verbs is the singular but collective עַם (19d), translated as plural.

"it" The antecedent is usually understood as "land," which makes good sense (see BHS footnote). If so, I suggest that the noun is the one found in 5:30, which indicates a connection between these two poems (see pp. 113–14). It is also possible that the pronoun is anticipatory of its own antecedent, which is found in 8:22a.

8:21b. **"will be enraged"** The *Hithpael* of קָצַף is used only here. Perhaps a reflexive sense is intended: 'get themselves into a rage'.

8:21c. **"against"** בְּ might indicate 'by' = 'in the name of', which may convey the same approximate meaning.

8:22b. "distress"   Again there is a wordplay on the various roots צרר and צור (see notes to 5:28c and 5:30d). Here the meaning is clearly 'distress'.

8:22c. "gloom"   The vocabulary is difficult. מעוף appears to be a construct noun from the root עוף II 'be dark' (so BDB).

8:23a. "faint light"   Difficulties increase. מועף is a hapax legomenon and clearly a play on מעוף in line 22c (previous note). BDB suggests מועף is also from root עוף II and means 'gloom'; Holladay suggests 'glimmer of light'(!).

The real crux is whether the line is to be understood as continuing the negative tones or introducing a sense of contrast. The problem is complicated by the possibility of reading לא as לו ('to him', suggested by the footnote in BHS). Thus there are four basic possibilites:

1. 'There is no (more) gloom . . .'   (לא = לא ;מועף = negative)
2. 'There is no glimmer of light (= hope) . . .'
   (לא = לא ;מועף = positive)
3. 'There is for them gloom . . .'   (לו = לא ;מועף = negative)
4. 'There is for them a glimmer of light (= hope) . . .'
   (לו = לא ;מועף = positive)

I prefer to read 23a as continuing the "doom and gloom" tone of the previous lines, retaining לא, as in the MT. The play between מעוף and מועף is therefore contrastive, not synonymous. Perhaps a sense of ambiguity is intended; my translation, 'faint light', might suggest a twilight that can lead either to darkness or light.

Lineation and Poetic Counts

The passage appears to be predominantly prose, although it allows for lineation according to the established norms. While parallelism is lacking, the constraint of line length appears to function.

I lineate as 17 lines and show a range of 135–37 syllables (MT: 142). An average of exactly 8 syllables per line would yield 136 syllables, which is the target figure. Individual lengths are fairly consistent:

5-syllable lines:	2	8-syllable lines:	3
6-syllable lines:	2	9-syllable lines:	4
7-syllable lines:	2	10-syllable lines:	4

Of the 17 lines,
   17.6% (3 lines) have 8 syllables,
   52.9% (9 lines) have 7–9 syllables,
   88.2% (15 lines) have 6–10 syllables.

I count 48–50 stresses (MT: 50), which is slightly low for 17 lines of 3 stresses per line (17 x 3 = 51). Using the higher counts, a typical range appears:

2-stress cola:	5	(29.4%)
3-stress cola:	9	(52.9%)
4-stress cola:	2	(11.8%)
5-stress cola:	1	(5.9%)

The prose particle count is 15.3% (9/59 words), confirming the prosaic nature of this section. In light of the context, in which poetic features have played a dominant role, it is possible to suggest that this material is an example of what might be called "poetic prose," that is, prose that is influenced by poetic features, such as the considerations of line length and stress accents.

Structure

There is a clear thematic break between v. 20 and v. 21, and a structural division occurs there as well:

vv. 19–20:	69 syllables, 25 stresses
vv. 21–23a:	67 syllables, 25 stresses

The Relationship of 5:26–30 and 8:19–23a

The analysis of 5:26–30 has demonstrated the integrity of these verses as a unit and in so doing has further confirmed the hypothesis that the previous section includes v. 25 (see above, p. 64). I have also shown that the piece in 8:18–23a, while much closer to prose than to poetry, picks up a major theme from the previous unit. Since these two pericopes fall on either side of the *Denkschrift*, it is likely that there is a literary relationship between them, especially in light of the clear link between the major poems in 5:8–25 and 9:7–10:4, which surround this intervening material.

The "darkness and doom" vocabulary within 5:26–30 concludes a poem dealing with the ominous advent of "the nation(s)," responding, apparently, to the signal (נס) raised by Yahweh, all of which seems, in historical context, to refer to the impending march of Assyria (although no nation is actually named[10]). This is certainly a transition to one of the major themes of the *Denkschrift*, namely, that Assyria will all but cover the land of Judah

10. P. Machinist (1983: 728) has shown, however, that the mention of devouring lions in 5:29 is likely an indirect reference to Assyria, since the lion is a known "cliché for Assyrian power in the Neo-Assyrian insciptions." In light of the convincing evidence throughout the article, one must conclude that Assyria is clearly in mind.

(7:18–25 and 8:6–8). The use of the verb for 'whistle' (שׁרק) in 5:26 to refer to the summoning of this nation echoes the remark in 7:18 that Yahweh will "whistle" for Assyria, which is the only other use of this verbal root in the entire book of Isaiah.

On the other side of the *Denkschrift*, the piece in 8:19–23a also concludes with the same "darkness and doom" vocabulary. This section deals with the distress of a people who have clearly suffered destruction and who seek explanation for what has happened, even cursing God and king. They have replaced the word of Yahweh with "this word" (8:20) of falsehood, like the "word" which will not stand (8:10). The true תעודה and תורה (8:16), which have been hidden away by Isaiah's disciples, has been replaced by a false search for תורה and תעודה (v. 20) in the cult of the dead. Thus both 5:26–30 and 8:19–23a have links not only to one another but also to the Denkschrift itself.

To be sure, the two sections 5:26–30 and 8:19–23a are different in literary style. Section 5:26–30 is clearly poetry, with a prose particle count of 3.4%. On the other hand, 8:19–23a is prosaic, with a prose particle count of 15.3%, although all the particles are in vv. 19–20, giving some credence to the idea that there is a shift in style in vv. 21–23a. The internal structure of 5:26–30 was noted as chiastic, the structure of 8:18–23a as two equal halves.

Nevertheless, taken as two units, 5:26–30 and 8:19–23a are roughly equivalent in length and, while not exact, do show a structural interrelationship:

5:26–30:   151 syllables, 57 stresses, 66 words
8:19–23a: 136 syllables, 50 stresses, 59 words

I conclude, albeit tentatively, that these two sections form a smaller, transitional circle around the *Denkschrift* in 6:1–8:18.

The Isaianic *Denkschrift*: 6:1–8:18

Although it is not my intention to offer a detailed structural analysis of the *Denkschrift* itself, it may be helpful to note some general features. In very broad outline, chap. 6 presents an autobiographical account of the commissioning of Isaiah, following his experience of "seeing" and hearing the activity in the heavenly council. His commission, however, is largely negative: to speak to those who will not hear or see or "turn" (שׁוב), although, if one does not exclude the final line, there was presented to the prophet a flicker of hope in a cryptic reference to a "holy seed."

Chapters 7–8 discuss the role of Isaiah as he interacted with King Ahaz in the face of the Syro-Ephraimite coalition, which had been formed to combat the growing presence and pressure of Assyria. Although Isaiah entreated the king to trust in the promise of Yahweh for the security of Zion and the Davidic line, the king is presented as a prime example of one who had not ears to hear or eyes to see.

As I shall argue, chaps. 7 and 8 offer somewhat parallel accounts, chap. 7 as biographical narrative and chap. 8 as autobiographical, although the events of chap. 8, especially the birth of another son to Isaiah, presumably followed those of chap. 7. The *Denkschrift* concludes with a soliloquy in which the prophet considers the fact that his word has been rejected (8:11–18).

In 7:1–9, Isaiah approaches Ahaz with a word of Yahweh, assuring the king that the Syro-Ephraimite coalition will not succeed. The presence of Isaiah's son שאר ישוב suggests that the meaning of his symbolic name is to be understood positively. But the final rhetorical flourish in 9b, punning on the root אמן, leaves the fate of Ahaz and Judah at least open to question, and the ambiguity of 'A Remnant Shall Return' is left somewhat unresolved.

Isa 7:10 introduces a second encounter between Yahweh and Ahaz, mediated through Isaiah, begun by the sentence:

$$\text{ויוסף יהוה דבר אל־אחז לאמר}$$

Here the focus is on the rejection of Ahaz of the sign of Yahweh's presence, signified by the symbolic name given to the child עמנו אל, whose name signifies God's presence not only as deliverer but also as destroyer. As a result of Ahaz's action against Yahweh, the presence of God will no longer be active in protection and deliverance but rather in summoning up Assyria as a means of destruction and punishment (vv. 18–25).

Chapter 8 presents a subsequent but private account that parallels the two encounters between Isaiah and Ahaz recorded in chap. 7. In 8:1–4, Isaiah reports the birth of a second son,[11] whose symbolic name, though also ominously ambiguous, is linked to an assurance that the threat of the Syro-Ephraimite coalition shall soon pass (8:4). Nevertheless, despite the identification in v. 4 that the "booty" and "plunder" is that of Damascus

---

11. It is not my purpose either to review or to enter into the discussion of the identity of the son Immanuel. Some have suggested, for example, that he is a son of Isaiah, and that possibly he is one and the same with Maher-shalal-hash-baz, especially in light of the sequence of material and the reiteration of the motif, "before the lad knows how to . . . ," which appears in 7:16 and in 8:4. While the summary presented here does not depend on the specific identification of Immanuel, it seems more likely to me that he is not a son of Isaiah but rather a royal son. This is in accordance (a) with the general theme of Yahweh's faithfulness to Zion and David, which is the basis of Isaiah's approach to Ahaz, (b) with the interpretation of the idiom "curds and honey" as a reference both

and Samaria, the mention of Assyria and the unspoken but real threat that she may, in fact, hasten on to claim other "booty and plunder" leaves the tension between Assyria as friend or foe somewhat unresolved.

Verse 8:5 introduces a second encounter between Yahweh and Isaiah, begun by the sentence:

ויסף יהוה דבר אלי עוד לאמר

This is a clear parallel to 7:10. Again, the focus is on the rejection by Ahaz of Yahweh's promise of protection. As a result, the presence of God is again described as no longer active in protection and deliverance but in summoning up Assyria as a means of destruction and punishment, culminating in a negative, sarcastic use of the vocative name, עמנו אל.

Finally, 8:9–10[12] continue and conclude the interpretation of the name עמנו אל by expanding its meaning to address "peoples . . . from the distant parts of the earth." The identification of these distant peoples is a major crux of the interpretive problem, but it is likely that both the Syro-Ephraimite coalition and the Assyrians are in view. Possibly the reference extends even beyond these specific peoples, since no nation is actually mentioned.[13] Therefore the passage asserts that the meaning of עמנו אל is greater than either threat to Ahaz, whose greatest peril is neither the Syro-Ephraimite league nor the Assyrians but rather his own pride and asserted independence of the promised protection of his God. Indeed, the plan and power of Yahweh are proclaimed as greater than the counsel and the might of any nation, from the threatened Ahaz to the mighty Assyria, and even beyond Assyria to whoever might follow her in the rise and fall of the king-doms of the earth. Thus the sign of "Immanuel" as signifying Yahweh's presence, while apparently ambiguous in meaning either salvation or judgment, is quite *un*ambiguous in reference to the ultimate plan and power of Yahweh over all peoples, including Judah under Ahaz.

The consequences of this message, however, as they were to be played out in the subsequent history of Judah are perceived by Isaiah himself to be long-range rather than immediate. This is indicated by the final section of the *Denkschrift* material, 8:11–18, which affirms the hiddenness of Yah-

---

to royal food as well as to wilderness rations, and (c) with the fact that the message of "Immanuel" in 7:10–25 and in 8:6–8 is not the deliverance of Judah, which seems to be the point of the names of Isaiah's two sons, but rather the punishment of Judah.

12. To be sure, there is debate over the authenticity of these verses. For example, Gray, Vermeylen, Barth, and Clements take them as a later addition; for Barth and Clements they are part of the Assur-Redaction, reflective of the triumphalistic interpretation of the events of 701 (e.g., Clements: 1980a). On the other hand, Duhm, Wildberger, and Kaiser allow for an Isaianic origin.

13. The apparent reference to Assyria without mention of any nation by name is similar to the summoning of the גוים in 5:26–30 (see above, see p. 106).

weh's plan before those who have not ears to hear and eyes to see, and which therefore anticipates the rejection of Yahweh's words as mediated through his prophet. Isaiah reports that he was instructed to seal up and hide away the testimony and the torah (v. 16) and remain, along with his symbolically designated scions, as a silent witness to his message. In this way, the *Denkschrift* ends with themes similar to those in chap. 6: the sovereign power of Yahweh in contrast to the stubborn rejection of "this people" (8:11, 12 and 6:9, 10) and the revelation and recognition of these realities for Isaiah, who would bear witness to them in his person and in his proclamation.

If the entire *Denkschrift* section is outlined accordingly, a somewhat circular arrangement emerges, with the parallel accounts in 7:1–25 and 8:1–10 forming the center of the message:

A. Isaiah's ministry hidden in Yahweh: 6:1–13

    B. The sign of Immanuel and the Syro-Ephraimite threat

        1. Biographical: Isaiah (Yahweh) vs. Ahaz: 7:1–25

            a. Round 1: Isaiah's child is sign of deliverance for Ahaz: 7:1–9

            b. Round 2: Ahaz rejects; Immanuel is sign of destruction: 7:10–25

        2. Autobiographical: Isaiah and Yahweh re Ahaz: 8:1–8

            a. Round 1: Isaiah's child is sign of deliverance: 8:1–4

            b. Round 2: Rejection; Immanuel is sign of destruction: 8:5–8

    B'. The sign of Immanuel and all peoples: 8:9–10

A'. Isaiah's ministry hidden in Yahweh: 8:11–18

If one again takes into consideration the feature of length, these pieces are not necessarily balanced, although I shall suggest that the total length of the whole of this section is significant in terms of the macrostructure of Isaiah 2–12 (see below, pp. 136ff. and 253ff.). Since much of the material is prose, I have not included stress accents in the counts. I have shown syllable counts as a range without detailing or defending a precise number.[14]

A. (6:1–13) 424–433 syllables and 188 words

    B. 1. 739–762 syllables and 345 words

        a. (7:1–9)   301–312 syllables and 139 words

        b. (7:10–25) 438–450 syllables and 206 words

      2. 251–254 syllables and 118 words

        a. (8:1–4)   122–124 syllables and 58 words

        b. (8:5–8)   129–130 syllables and 60 words

    B'. (8:9–10)   51 syllables and 21 words

A'. (8:11–18) 208–212 syllables and 86 words

---

14. For a full accounting of the statistical data, see appendix 3.

One striking feature of an analysis that considers length to be measured by syllables and words is the recognition that the center of the
entire *Denkschrift* falls precisely at the Immanuel sign of 7:14 (see below, p. 256). Yet there are other links that hold the piece together. I have
noted the vocabulary link between chap. 6 (A), with its double use of
העם הזה, and the similar double use of the same term in 8:11 and 12
(A'). The term occurs only one other time in this section, at 8:6, in
reference to the rejection of "this people," which is the underlying theme
in 6:1–13 and 8:11–18. One also finds the particle הנה in 8:7 (B.2.b),
introduced by לכן followed by אדני, the same combination found in 7:14
(B.1.b). The only other uses of הנה are found in the A sections: 6:7, in
reference to the atoning coal; 6:8, in reference to Isaiah's personal presence; and 8:18, in reference to the presence and significance of Isaiah and
his children.

If I am correct in suggesting that the transitional material in 5:26–30
and 8:19–23a forms a circle around the *Denkschrift*, then the chiastic
structure of the *Denkschrift* itself has another concentric ring added to it:

Isaiah 8:23b–9:6

Text

		Syllable Count	MT	Stress Count	MT
8:23b	כְּעֵת הָרִאשׁוֹן הֵקַל	7	7	3	3
c	אַרְצָה זְבֻלוּן וְאַרְצָה נַפְתָּלִי	11	11	4	4
d	וְהָאַחֲרוֹן הִכְבִּיד דֶּרֶךְ הַיָּם	9	10	3	3
e	עֵבֶר הַיַּרְדֵּן גְּלִיל הַגּוֹיִם:	9	11	4	4
9:1a	הָעָם הַהֹלְכִים בַּחֹשֶׁךְ	8	9	3	3
b	רָאוּ אוֹר גָּדוֹל	5	5	3	3
c	יֹשְׁבֵי בְּאֶרֶץ צַלְמָוֶת	7	9	3	3
d	אוֹר נָגַהּ עֲלֵיהֶם:	6	6	3	3
2a	הִרְבִּיתָ הַגּוֹי לֹא הִגְדַּלְתָּ הַשִּׂמְחָה	10/(12)	12	4	4
b	שָׂמְחוּ לְפָנֶיךָ כְּשִׂמְחַת בַּקָּצִיר	(12)/13	13	4	4
c	כַּאֲשֶׁר יָגִילוּ בְּחַלְּקָם שָׁלָל:	11	12	4	4
3a	כִּי אֶת־עֹל סֻבֳּלוֹ	6	6	2/(3)	3
b	וְאֵת מַטֵּה שִׁכְמוֹ	6	6	2	3

X. Darkness and distress (5:26–30): 151 syllables and 66 words
   A. Isaiah's ministry hidden in Yahweh: 6:1–13
       B. The sign of Immanuel and the Syro-Ephraimite threat: 7:1–8:8
       B'. The sign of Immanuel and all peoples: 8:9–10
   A'. Isaiah's ministry hidden in Yahweh: 8:11–18
X'. Darkness and distress (8:19–23a): 136 syllables and 59 words

The Two Remaining Pieces: Isaiah 8:23b–9:6 and 5:1–7

I shall now consider 8:23b–9:6, a passage which moves from the theme of darkness to the theme of light focused in the birth of a royal child, and from the location of the northern provinces of Israel to the Davidic throne in Jerusalem. Thus the motif of light and darkness links to what precedes this unit, both immediately in 8:19–23a and, further, in the conclusion to chap. 5. The signal birth of a Davidic son with significant names seems to carry forward the message of hope in the promises of Yahweh to Zion and David, which are the basis of Isaiah's message of salvation in chaps. 7–8.

Translation

8:23b   As the first time he dishonored
    c   the land of Zebulun and the land of Naphtali.
    d   But at the last (time) he will have honored The Way of the Sea,
    e   Transjordan, Galilee of the Goyim.
9:1a   The people walking in darkness
    b   will have seen a great light.
    c   Those dwelling in a land of deep darkness—
    d   a light will shine upon them.
    2a   You will multiply the rejoicing; you will increase the joy.

    b   They will rejoice before you as the joy in the harvest,
    c   as they rejoice in dividing the spoil.
    3a   For the yoke of his burden
    b   and the rod on his shoulder,

		Syllables	MT	Stresses	MT
c	שֵׁבֶט הַנֹּגֵשׂ בּוֹ	5	6	2/(3)	3
d	הַחִתֹּתָ כְּיוֹם מִדְיָן׃	7/(8)	8	3	3
4a	כִּי כָל־סְאוֹן סֹאֵן בְּרַעַשׁ	8	9	4	4
b	וְשִׂמְלָה מְגוֹלָלָה בְדָמִים	10	10	3	3
c	וְהָיְתָה לִשְׂרֵפָה מַאֲכֹלֶת אֵשׁ׃	10	12	4	4
5a	כִּי־יֶלֶד יֻלַּד־לָנוּ בֵּן נִתַּן־לָנוּ	11	12	4	4
b	וַתְּהִי הַמִּשְׂרָה עַל־שִׁכְמוֹ	9	9	3	3
c	וַיִּקְרָא שְׁמוֹ	5	5	2	2
d	פֶּלֶא יוֹעֵץ אֵל גִּבּוֹר	6	7	2	2
e	אֲבִי עַד שַׂר־שָׁלוֹם׃	6	6	2	2
6a	לְמַרְבֵּה הַמִּשְׂרָה	6	6	2	2
b	וּלְשָׁלוֹם אֵין־קֵץ	6	6	2	2
c	עַל־כִּסֵּא דָוִד וְעַל־מַמְלַכְתּוֹ	10	10	3	3
d	לְהָכִין אֹתָהּ וּלְסַעֲדָהּ	9	10	3	3
e	בְּמִשְׁפָּט וּבִצְדָקָה	7	7	2	2
f	מֵעַתָּה וְעַד־עוֹלָם	7	7	2	2
g	קִנְאַת יְהוָה צְבָאוֹת תַּעֲשֶׂה־זֹּאת׃	10	11	5	4
Totals		239/243 = 240	258	90/(92)	92
		Syllables	MT	Stresses	MT

Notes on Translation and Text

8:23b. **"he"** The subject is lacking; presumably "Yahweh" is to be understood (see note in BHS).

8:23c. **"land ... land"** 1QIsaᵃ reads ארץ ... הארץ without the final הָ, which appears to be directive. If the MT is correct, there may be an echo of the expressions ופנה למעלה (21e) and אל־ארץ יביט (22a) from the previous section: the focus is not up but down; the darkness and gloom have been played out "on earth." This would also suggest wordplay between the *Piel* of קלל in 21c and the *Hiphil* in 23b.

8:23d. **"will"** Read as future (so-called prophetic) perfect in light of the contrast between הראשון and האחרון.

"have honored" In Isa 6:9, the Hiphil use of כבד means 'make heavy', with negative overtones. In light of the contrast in the context (see previous note), it likely means quite the opposite here.

c   the staff of his taskmaster,

d   you will shatter as on the Day of Midian.

4a   For every boot tramping in quaking,

b   and (every) garment rolled in blood

c   will be for burning, fire's fuel.

5a   For to us will be born a child; a son will be given to us.

b   The governing authority will be upon his shoulder.

c   His name will be called

d   Wonder Counselor, God Warrior,

e   Father of Perpetuity (= Perpetual Father), Prince of Peace.

6a   Of the increase of the governing authority

b   and of peace, there is no end.

c   Upon the throne of David and upon his rule

d   to establish it and to found it

e   in justice and in righteousness

f   from now into perpetuity:

g   the zeal of Yahweh Seba³oth will do this.

9:1b. **"will have seen"**   I continue the future sense (see note to 8:23d).

9:1c. **"those dwelling in"**   The broken construct chain is not uncommon (Waltke and O'Connor 1990: 140 [9.3.d]). It is striking that several instances occur in this short passage: 9:2a, 2b, and, if one reads the two uses of ארצה in 8:23b as constructs with directive *he*, also there.

9:1d. **"a light will shine"**   I continue the future sense (see notes to 8:23d and 9:1b) here and into the verses following.

9:2a. **"rejoicing"**   Various attempts to solve the textual problem have been inconclusive. The accentuation in the MT suggests that לא should be read with what follows (compare the KJV, which negates the second verb). The Masoretic *Qere* (לו) is possible, but the antecedent of the proposed pronoun is by no means clear. Another, less convincing, suggestion is to read הגוי לא as one expression, 'a nation-not' (= 'not a nation') similar to לא עמי in Hosea 1.

In light of the poetic parallelism, the correction proposed in the BHS footnote is quite helpful and requires the assumption of only a minor scribal error: הגילה (= הגילא > הגוילא). Since the following line picks up the root שׂמח from 2aB and uses the verbal form, the verbal use of root גיל in 2c would logically follow from a use of the nominal גילה in 2aA, and I read accordingly.

9:2b.   "joy"   See note to 9:1c.

9:4a.   "boot"   Both סָאוֹן and סֹאֵן are hapax legomena, likely carrying the meaning of 'tramp, tread' (see BDB), thus 'boot' for the nominal form.

9:4c.   "burning"   Compare לבער in 5:5d and below, p. 127, translation note to 5:5d.

9:5b.   "governing authority"   משׂרה is another hapax legomenon, likely from root שׂרר (compare שׂר 'ruler, prince, chief'). Could the prophet be avoiding a more common term that would use the root מלך (but see note to 9:6c below)? Wordplay anticipates the title שׂר־שׁלום in 5e.

9:5de.   "Wonder Counselor, God Warrior, Father of Perpetual Future, Prince of Peace"   I make no attempt to deal in detail with the translation problems or the interpretation of the names (see commentaries and extensive secondary literature). In short, I suggest that the names are based on typical throne names but are, in fact, adaptations of such titles to indicate something other than the normal king, all of which would have been part of the messianic hope expressed further in v. 6. This may also relate to the prophet's use of the rare משׂרה to describe his rule and authority.

9:6a.   "increase"   Read with the MT *Qere* למרבה. The לם could be dittography following שׁלום, but the parallel to לשׁלום in 6b suggests that the *lamed* is correct; the final form of *mem* is perhaps scribal error.

9:6c.   "rule"   Here the more normal ממלכת is used as that upon which the rule will be based (see following line and note).

9:6d.   "it"   The antecedent is משׂרה.

Lineation and Poetic Counts

Lineation is difficult and somewhat arbitrary at many points, although decisions are basically whether to divide into longer or shorter bicola, since parallelism is common. For example, each colon in 2abc could be divided into a bicolon (adding three lines to the overall poem). On the other hand, 3abcd could be reduced to two bicola; 5c is short and might be combined with 5de into a 17-syllable bicolon. Thus there is a possible range in the number of lines from 27–33. My lineation into 30 lines falls in the middle of that range and is consistent with the number of syllables.

The syllable count also shows a range, 239–43 (MT: 258), depending on whether the second-person suffixes in 2a, 2b, and 3d are counted as extra syllables. Since the middle figure of 30 lines would yield 240 syllables at 8 per line, my calculations are very close. For the sake of tabulation, I shall count the lower figure in the afformative verb forms in 2a and 3d and the higher figure with the pronominal suffix in 2b, giving a fairly broad spectrum:

5-syllable lines:	3		10-syllable lines:	5
6-syllable lines:	7		11-syllable lines:	3
7-syllable lines:	5		12-syllable lines:	0
8-syllable lines:	2		13-syllable lines:	1
9-syllable lines:	4			

Of the 30 lines,
   6.7%   (2 lines) have 8 syllables,
  36.7% (11 lines) have 7–9 syllables,
  76.7% (23 lines) have 6–10 syllables.

Our stress count shows 90–92 stresses (MT: 92). At 3 stresses per line, 30 lines would yield 90 stresses, so that I shall opt for the lower figure. There is a typical distribution:

2-stress cola:	10	(33.3%)
3-stress cola:	11	(36.7%)
4-stress cola:	8	(26.7%)
5-stress cola:	1	(3.3%)

The prose particle count is 13.9% (15/108 words). Despite this relatively high count, the section displays a great number of poetic features. This may help describe further a category of "poetic prose," with a prose particle count in the 10–15% range, yet with clear poetic features.

Structure

Among the clear poetic features are several very well-crafted verses. For example, v. 2, which I have left as a series of longer cola, is a fine example of so-called staircase parallelism, in which the second line builds on the root שׂמח from the end of the first line, then expands it by a double use (line 2b). The third line (2c) expands on the comparison begun in the previous line ("as the joy in the harvest") by seconding it. The final line (2c) also picks up the root גיל from the first line (assuming the reading הגילה; see translation note to 9:2a).

The thought progression and thematic grouping of the verses suggests a five-part, chiastic outline:

8:23b–9:1:   62 syllables, 26 stresses
9:2:   34 syllables, 12 stresses
9:3–4:   52 syllables, 20 stresses
9:5:   37 syllables, 13 stresses
9:6:   55 syllables, 19 stresses

On the other hand, the whole piece divides very neatly into halves after v. 3, although this structural division cuts across the thematic outline:

8:23b–9:3:   120 syllables, 47 stresses
9:4–6:   120 syllables, 43 stresses

Isaiah 5:1–7

Text

		Syllable Count		Stress Count	
			MT		MT
5:1a	אָשִׁירָה נָּא לִידִידִי	7	7	3	3
b	שִׁירַת דּוֹדִי לְכַרְמוֹ	7	7	3	3
c	כֶּרֶם הָיָה לִידִידִי בְּקֶרֶן בֶּן־שָׁמֶן:	10	13	5	5
2a	וַיְעַזְּקֵהוּ וַיְסַקְּלֵהוּ	(10)/12	12	2	2
b	וַיִּטָּעֵהוּ שֹׂרֵק	7	7	2	2
c	וַיִּבֶן מִגְדָּל בְּתוֹכוֹ	7	8	3	3
d	וְגַם־יֶקֶב חָצֵב בּוֹ	6	7	2	3
e	וַיְקַו לַעֲשׂוֹת עֲנָבִים	(7)/8	8	3	3
f	וַיַּעַשׂ בְּאֻשִׁים:	5	6	2	2
3a	וְעַתָּה יוֹשֵׁב יְרוּשָׁלַם וְאִישׁ יְהוּדָה	14	15	5	5
b	שִׁפְטוּ־נָא בֵּינִי וּבֵין כַּרְמִי:	9	9	4	4
4a	מַה־לַּעֲשׂוֹת עוֹד לְכַרְמִי	7	8	3	3
b	וְלֹא עָשִׂיתִי בּוֹ	6	6	2	3

As the proposed macrostructure of the material between the major units in 5:8–25 and 9:7–10:4 continues to be constructed, there seems little place for the section 8:23b–9:6, just discussed above, to fit. However, based on the fact that the length of a given unit has provided a helpful clue to structural relationships, it is possible that the length of this section may provide a clue to its structural role as well. It is clear that there is no similar, corresponding unit within the material so far under discussion. However, if one considers the poem with which chap. 5 begins, the so-called Song of the Vineyard in 5:1–7, it is found to be exactly equivalent in length:

8:23b–9:6:   240 syllables, 90 stresses, 108 words
5:1–7:   240 syllables, 90 stresses, 100 words

While there may seem to be little connection between these two pieces, my structural analysis, which takes seriously the factor of length, has indicated that perhaps their connection should be considered, and I shall proceed with the methodological analysis of 5:1–7.

Translation

5:1a   Let me sing for my loved one
  b   a song of my friend for his vineyard.
  c   "My loved one had a vineyard on a fertile ridge.

2a   He worked the soil; he de-stoned it;
  b   he planted it (with) choice vines.
  c   He built a watch-tower in the middle of it.
  d   Also a wine-vat he hewed out in it.
  e   He expected [it] to yield grapes,
  f   but it yielded stench."

3a   So now, Resident of Jerusalem and man of Judah:
  b   judge between me and my vineyard!
4a   What was [there] yet to do for my vineyard
  b   which I had not done in it?

		Syllables	MT	Stresses	MT
c	מַדּוּעַ קִוֵּיתִי לַעֲשׂוֹת עֲנָבִים	10	12	4	4
d	וַיַּעַשׂ בְּאֻשִׁים׃	5	6	2	2
5a	וְעַתָּה אוֹדִיעָה־נָּא אֶתְכֶם	9	9	3	3
b	אֵת אֲשֶׁר־אֲנִי עֹשֶׂה לְכַרְמִי	10	10	4	4
c	הָסֵר מְשׂוּכָּתוֹ	6	6	2	2
d	וְהָיָה לְבָעֵר	6	6	2	2
e	פָּרֹץ גְּדֵרוֹ	5	5	2	2
f	וְהָיָה לְמִרְמָס׃	6	6	2	2
6a	וַאֲשִׁיתֵהוּ בָתָה	6/(7)	7	2	2
b	לֹא יִזָּמֵר וְלֹא יֵעָדֵר	9	9	(3)/4	4
c	וְעָלָה שָׁמִיר וָשָׁיִת	7	8	3	3
d	וְעַל הֶעָבִים אֲצַוֶּה	8	8	2	3
e	מֵהַמְטִיר עָלָיו מָטָר׃	7	7	3	3
7a	כִּי כֶרֶם יְהוָה צְבָאוֹת בֵּית יִשְׂרָאֵל	11	12	(4)/5	6
b	וְאִישׁ יְהוּדָה נְטַע שַׁעֲשׁוּעָיו	10	11	4	4
c	וַיְקַו לְמִשְׁפָּט וְהִנֵּה מִשְׂפָּח	(10)/11	11	4	4
d	לִצְדָקָה וְהִנֵּה צְעָקָה׃	9	9	3	3
Totals		236/241 = 240	255	(88)/90	94
		Syllables	MT	Stresses	MT

Notes on Translation and Text

5:1b. "friend" The relationship between יָדִיד and דּוֹד is not completely clear. While related, יָדִיד is normally adjectival; דּוֹד is the noun 'friend'. Thus שִׁירַת דּוֹדִי is literally a 'song of my friend'. A pun on the name דָּוִד may also be involved (see below, p. 131).

5:1c. "ridge" Although the translation 'hill' is widely accepted, this is the only such use of קֶרֶן in this sense in the Hebrew Bible. The context demands a *"geomorphologischer Ausdruck"* (Wildberger, 167), but the odd usage along with the juxtaposition with שֶׁמֶן calls to mind the motif of 'anointing', since 1 Sam 16:1, 13 and 1 Kgs 1:39 (also Ps 92:11) are the only other places where these words are used in the same context.

5:2f. "stench" The basic meaning of בָּאַשׁ is 'to stink'. Only here is it used to describe grapes.

    c   Why—[when] I expected [it] to yield grapes—
    d   did it yield stench?

5a   So now let me tell you
    b   that which I am about to do to my vineyard.
    c   (I am about to) remove its hedge,
    d   and it will be burned up.
    e   (I am about to) break down its wall,
    f   and it will become trampled.
6a   I will make it a 'waste.'
    b   It will not be pruned; it will not be cultivated.
    c   Briar and thorn will come up.
    d   Concerning the clouds I will command
    e   not to send rain upon it.

7a   For the vineyard of Yahweh Seba^ɔoth is the House of Israel,
    b   and the man of Judah is his delightful planting.
    c   He expected justice, but there was bloodshed.
    d   (He expected) righteousness, but there was outcry.

5:3a. **"Resident of Jerusalem"**   The idiom may refer to the king (compare 9:8: יושב שמרון).

5:4d. **"yield"**   1QIsa^a reads וישה, which is not from any clearly known root and destroys the parallelism with line 2f.

5:5b. **"about to do"**   I translate this "imminent future" idiom as 'to be about to . . .'.

5:5c. **"remove"**   The infinitive absolute substitutes for the appropriate verb form; I attempt to continue the sense of the infinitive in English from the previous lines: 'about to . . .'.

5:5d. **"burned up"**   This is literally, 'it will be for burning' (compare 6:13 and 9:4c above, p. 122 translation note).

5:5e. **"wall"**   1QIsa^a reads אסיר, which may well have carried a similar meaning: 'barrier', 'that which "imprisons"'.

5:5f. **"trampled"** The expression is parallel to the experession in the previous line, except here the noun is used. Compare 7:25, 10:6 (also 1:12).

5:6a. **"waste"** The translation of the hapax legomenon בָּתָה remains a crux. Watts (53) cites G. R. Driver's suggestion following Akkadian *batû* 'destroy', which certainly fits the context.

5:7c. **"bloodshed"** I make no attempt to reproduce the sound and the force of the pun between מִשְׁפָּט and מִשְׂפָּח here, or between צְדָקָה and צְעָקָה in the following line.

Lineation and Poetic Counts

Several decisions of lineation are difficult. I show line 1c as a rather long monocolon, but the following line, though only two words, is equally as long, if not longer. Likewise 3a is long, but, as has been seen before, shorter lines elsewhere will balance out. Longer lines return in the final quatrain. The number of lines could theoretically range from 28–32, but in light of the syllable count, 30 lines is most likely.

The syllable count also shows a slight range, from 236 to 241, depending on how several prefixed conjunctions are handled (MT: 255). Adjusting, as the poet certainly could have, on the basis of eliding prefixes if necessary, one could propose a count of 240 syllables, which would represent 30 lines of 8 syllables each. For the sake of tabulation, I therefore count line 2a as 12 syllables, 2e as 8 syllables, and 7c as 11 syllables, since all of them show the same prefix. I read 6a, however, as elided into 6 syllables.

5-syllable lines:	3	10-syllable lines:	4
6-syllable lines:	6	11-syllable lines:	2
7-syllable lines:	7	12-syllable lines:	1
8-syllable lines:	2	13-syllable lines:	0
9-syllable lines:	4	14-syllable lines:	1

Of the 30 lines,
6.7% (2 lines) have 8 syllables,
43.3% (13 lines) have 7–9 syllables,
76.7% (23 lines) have 6–10 syllables.

I count 88–90 stresses (MT: 94). The higher figure would correspond with the total of 30 lines, but there is a fair diversity:

2-stress cola:	12	(40%)
3-stress cola:	9	(30%)
4-stress cola:	6	(20%)
5-stress cola:	3	(3%)

The prose particle count is exacly 4.0% (4 out of 100 words). Interest-ingly, three of the four particles appear in the same bicolon, 5ab, where there are two object markers and one relative pronoun. The prosaic nature of this verse highlights it as the beginning of the second major part of the poem (see below). One article appears, in line 6d.

Structure

Individual verses display a variety of structure. Bicola seem to dominate, although my lineation shows a long monocolon (1c) at the beginning, fol-lowing the introductory bicolon. The other three sections begin with long bicola. Verse 6abc is the sole tricolon.

The poem divides into four sections as marked by breaks:

vv. 1–2:	69 syllables,	25 stresses
vv. 3–4:	51 syllables,	20 stresses
vv. 5–6:	79 syllables,	29 stresses
v. 7:	41 syllables,	16 stresses

Divided into two stanzas, the poem has two equal parts, the second begin-ning with the prosaic 5ab:

Stanza 1:	(vv. 1–4)	120 syllables, 45 stresses
Stanza 2:	(vv. 5–7)	120 syllables, 45 stresses

The parts are carefully interrelated. For example, stanza 1, strophe A (vv. 1–2) describes what has been done to the vineyard, and strophe B (vv. 3–4) involves the audience. In stanza 2, strophe A (vv. 5–6) describes what will be done to the vineyard, and strophe B (v. 7) involves the au-dience. Both stanzas begin with a cohortative verb form + נא (lines 1a and 5a).

On the other hand, the two middle strophes (vv. 3–4 and vv. 5–6) both begin with עתה and are, apparently, direct quotes in the first person. But strophes A + B of stanza 1 are held together by the parallelism of 2ef with 4cd. The verb form קוה reappears in 7c.

Seven verbs are linked by *waw*-consecutive in stanza 1, A (v. 2); seven verbs are used to describe the action to be taken in stanza 2, A (vv. 5c–6e). The noun כרם appears in every strophe, 2× each in the two strophes in Stanza 1, once in each of the strophes in stanza 2.

The Relation of 5:1–7 and 8:23b–9:6

In spite of the fact that these two poetic pieces have not been considered in relationship to each other, there is a significant link between them: they are the same length. Moreover, once this consideration of length has indicated a connection, other structural and thematic relationships become apparent. The climactic concern of the Song of the Vineyard is an indictment against the "house of Israel" and the "man of Judah" for a lack of משפט and צדקה (5:7), and these words—and the same concern—form the climax to the poem in 8:23b–9:6. In the second poem, the Davidic scion is portrayed as presiding over a reign of universal peace, which he has established במשפט ובצדקה (9:6e). In fact, this word pair is used only one other time in all of Isaiah 2–12, and that is with reference to Yahweh himself in the conclusion to the first part of the poem in 5:8–25 (5:16).

Furthermore, the Song of the Vineyard has important ties to the other material within this larger section. In 5:3, the "man of Judah," which is idiomatic for the ordinary citizen, is indicted along with the 'Resident of Jerusalem' (יושב ירושלם), a term which is strikingly parallel to the יושב שמרון in 9:8, where I have argued the reference is likely to the king himself. In 5:6, the use of the word pair 'thorns and briars' (שמיר ושית) indicates the result of destruction in the vineyard, but in 9:17 the same pair describes that which is consumed by wickedness out of control. The pair is used three times in close connection, as well as in reference to the destruction of the land within the central section of the *Denkschrift*, in 7:23, 24, 25. Thus there are distinctive vocabulary links between 5:1–7 and the two poems in 5:8–25 and in 9:7–10:4, as well as to the intervening material within the *Denkschrift*.

More important, however, is the motif dealing with the combination of responsibility on the part of both people and king. This is also brought out in 8:23b–9:6, where *the people* walking in darkness rejoice, as in the common joy of harvest, in expectation and anticipation of the ideal *king*. And it is the relationship of people to king, or more precisely, the responsibility of king over people, that forms a major theme in the *Denkschrift*. In this central section Ahaz stands out as the prime example of one of "this people" who hear without hearing and see without seeing. But more than just one of the people, Ahaz is the one in whom the fate of the people is sealed before the threat of the Syro-Ephraimite coalition, before the threat of the Assyrians, and before the threat even of Yahweh as the ultimate one whose presence can mean either deliverance or destruction.

The Song of the Vineyard deals with the *lack* of "justice and righteousness" and concludes in a verdict of destruction for the vineyard. This corresponds to the concern for the *establishment* of "justice and righteousness" in the victorious reign of peace for which the throne of David is responsible, under the power and presence of the zeal of Yahweh Seba>oth (9:6g).

Further, I have suggested the possibility that 5:1–7 has been entitled a "love song," based on the verbal root דוד, as a pun on the name David (see translation note to 5:1b on p. 126). In light of this connection with the Davidic hope expressed in 8:23b–9:6, the likelihood that this is an intentional, though indirect, reference is strengthened. Likewise, the suggestion that the phrase usually translated 'fertile hill' is intentionally using the vocabulary of anointing (translation note to 5:1c) would fit well into this interpretation.

Of course, "my beloved" is a reference to Yahweh, although it is possible to understand the "vineyard" as belonging to the Davidic king. Indeed, it is precisely this tension created by the question of ownership that may well lie at the heart of the problem being addressed: who is, in fact, the vineyard's owner, its master, its king? Chapter 6, dated to the year in which King Uzziah died, clearly asserts that in spite of the uncertainties of human accession, Yahweh is the king (6:5). The relationship between 5:1–7 and 8:23b–9:6 would indicate that whoever the royal heir might be, in whom the "man of Judah" might place hope, this human king must realize that the name and lineage of David imply a great responsibility and special relationship with Yahweh himself.

The Two Major Poems (5:8–25 and 9:7–10:4) and the *Denkschrift*

Having observed interconnections among the pieces within the larger structure of Isa 5:1–10:4, I return to the first two poems considered, 5:8–25 and 9:7–10:4, in order to note further connections between them and the intervening *Denkschrift* material, which has been shown as structurally integral to the positioning of these two major poems.

I have already noted the play on the name Maher-shalal-hash-baz found by combining 5:19a with 10:2cd, the importance of the root שׁוב, and the thematic importance of the motif of the presence of God as a two-edged sword (Immanuel), all of which link the poems to the symbolic names of the three children in Isaiah 7–8. And, of course, the direct reference to Rezin in 9:10a, however one interprets the verse, clearly calls to mind the situation introduced in 7:1.

I have further observed the elliptical introductions to direct quotations in 5:9a and in 9:8c (the fifth line of each poem). In chap. 5, the citation comes from the mouth of Yahweh, when he announces the destruction of the land. In chap. 9 it comes from the mouths of the people and king of Israel, who continue to threaten Judah by their pride and arrogance in the face of initial defeat and destruction.

Within the opening chapter of the *Denkschrift*, the prophet relates, in first-person account, his participation in the heavenly council in which Yahweh announced the impending destruction of the land. The vocabulary of 6:11bc is strikingly similar to that of 5:9bcde, especially in the use of שׁממה, בתים (compare שׁמה in 5:9c), and the idiom מאין יושׁב, which is used only in these two places in the whole of Isaiah.

Although vocabulary links are not as striking, the *Denkschrift* concludes with a first-person account of a divine word in which the prophet is exhorted not to listen to the words of the people, by which they express their fear and doubt in the face of the pride and the plans of the Northern Kingdom, whose words are reported in 9:8–9.

There are further connections in vocabulary as well. For example, the verbal root מאס occurs only three times in Isaiah 2–12: in 7:16, where the lad Immanuel will know how to "refuse the evil"; in 8:6, where, by contrast, "this people" has "refused" the peaceful waters of Shiloah; and in 5:24, where those against whom the woes are uttered are described as having "rejected" the torah of Yahweh, which is the theme reiterated in 8:11–18 and again in 8:19ff.

What is more, the one instance in which this "refusal" motif has a positive connotation—namely, the text with the lad Immanuel in 7:16—contrasts his rejection of "evil" with his ability to choose "good." This pairing of רע and טוב appears only one other place in all of Isaiah 1–39, in 5:20, which, as we have observed, forms the "middle woe" of the series of seven and focuses on the complete confusion of good and evil that lies at the heart of the problem addressed.

On the other side of the *Denkschrift*, one finds further links within the poem of 9:7–10:4. The word pair 'thorns and briars' (שמיר ושית), which appears seven times in the whole of Isaiah 1–39, occurs three times in close proximity in 7:23, 24, 25 in reference to the impending desolation of the land. In 9:17, where the thought progression has begun to expand from a focus on the Northern Kingdom to the consequences for the South and, indeed, for all the earth (9:18), one finds the startling statement that "wickedness will consume thorns and briars (שמיר ושרת)." This seems to indicate that even the remains of destruction are subject to more destruction. I have already noted the use of the same pair in the Song of the Vineyard and will note another occurrence (in 10:17) below (see pp. 184ff.). The fact that this word pair appears in such close connection, with three of the usages in the central section dealing with the sign of Immanuel, suggests some intentional thematic structuring.

As the conflagration expands in 9:17c, the thickets 'of the forest' (יער) also go up in a cloud of smoke, and one notes an allusion to the response of Ahaz and the people, described in 7:2 as the "shaking (נוע) of the trees of the forest (יער)." Indeed, the fear and false trust of Ahaz is probably also implied as the poem in 9:7ff. continues toward the wrath of Yahweh Sebaʾoth, before which the "earth shakes"[15] (9:18b). Indeed, the power of God filling all the earth was emphatically introduced along with the

---

15. This assumes that my translation of the form נעתם is correct (see p. 72, translation note to 9:18b).

'shaking' (root נוע) of the doors in 6:1–4. And the further destruction of that which is already destroyed is introduced also in chap. 6, where in v. 13 the already "decimated" land (actually, only the tenth *remained*!) will again be burned.

These interconnections not only between the major poems in 5:8–25 and 9:7–10:4 but also between the two poems and the intervening material strongly suggest that they have been constructed under a common bond. Against the theory that the *Denkschrift* formed a major insertion *into* previously existing material, creating displacement and the need for redactional reworking, I propose that the intricate structuring of 5:8–25 and 9:7–10:4, as well as of the *Denskschrift* itself, suggest that these chapters were intentionally constructed *around* the intervening material and continue the chiastic pattern begun within the *Denkschrift* and expanded by the transitional material in 5:26–30 and 8:19–23a.

Thought Progression of 5:1–10:4

The introductory work of L'Heureux (1984), Sheppard (1985), and Anderson (1988), I believe, is basically on the right track in perceiving a certain sense of unity within the larger structure that includes the whole of chaps. 5:1–10:4. My analysis has not only confirmed their basic observation, it has gone into much greater detail. Although I disagree concerning the role and even existence of his "Primary Redactor" as well as his need to reconstruct an original, prior text, I do agree with L'Heureux (1984: 115), for example, when he speaks of "a coherent and logical redactional whole" that "bespeaks a single undisturbed redactional plan."

L'Heureux concludes that the structuring of the material around the *Denkschrift* was intended to make clear that the Assyrian threat to Judah in the wake of the Syro-Ephraimite war was due to social injustice on the part of the upper classes. This indictment, however, is not articulated in the intervening material, where the blame falls instead upon Ahaz's failure to trust the promises of Yahweh regarding Zion and David. Thus, according to L'Heureux, the interplay between the poems in 5:8–25 and 9:7–10:4 is found in the fact that while the "woe-sayings" in 5:8–25 clearly addressed the upper classes, the point of the "Outstretched-Hand Poem" was originally a condemnation against the whole people ("head and tail," 9:13). In its reworked form, the second poem now articulates more clearly that the blame falls on the leadership class, and the clue is the fact that v. 14 has been carefully rewritten to identify the "head and tail" as elder and prophet.

While L'Heureux has supported the view that this material indicates a careful structuring, his suggestion of the reworking of the material is simply unnecessary. While it is true that the poem castigates the leadership class who have "led the people astray" (9:15), there is more to the juxtaposition of these two poems than simply the concern for social injustice.

Anderson (1988: 242ff.), on the other hand, attempts a linear outline of chaps. 5–10(11) that moves from the rebuke of Yahweh's own people to the execution of his judgment upon them by the hand of Assyria to the judgment upon Assyria. He brings out the theme that Yahweh's plan (compare 55:10–11) includes the *opus alienum* of destruction and judgment against even his own people, but that, in the end, his judgment has within it an eschatological hope, which is picked up in chap. 11 and, finally, chap. 12.

Anderson (1988: 241) does not discuss the date of this redaction, although it is clear that he is dealing with the "final relecture" of the Isaianic tradition. Nevertheless, his thematic approach is helpful in summarizing some of the motifs basic to this material, although my analysis suggests that it should be understood in a more circular, rather than linear, fashion, even if it was read or heard in a linear way.

If one begins in the center with the *Denkschrift* or so-called Book of Immanuel, the meaning of Yahweh's presence and promise is seen in tension with the threat to Judah and Jerusalem presented by the Syro-Ephraimite coalition. Ahaz stands as "exhibit A" of "this people," who hear and see but do not hear and see (6:9). In fact, the role and responsibility of the Davidic king vis-à-vis Yahweh were introduced at the beginning of chap. 6, where the uncertainty at the end of the long and stable rule of Uzziah was answered by the assertion that *Yahweh* was truly king (6:5).

According to Isaiah's personal experience recounted in 6:5, the presence of sin and guilt in the presence of the holy Yahweh meant judgment. Nevertheless, in his humble acknowledgment of his own uncleanness, the prophet found his sin removed (6:7). Assuming that the "house of David" (7:2) knew its proper place under *the* true king (6:5), Isaiah assured Ahaz that the Syro-Ephraimite threat would not stand. However, Yahweh's presence was a "two-edged sword": "if you do not affirm, you will not be confirmed" (7:9).

In 7:10–25, Ahaz refused the protective presence of Yahweh, and Isaiah predicted that the plan of Ahaz to trust Assyria for help would bring into action the second edge of Yahweh's sword, now turned against Judah. This is the point of 8:5–8 as well: Assyria would overflow its banks, like a flood out of control, and engulf Judah up to the latter's neck.

Nevertheless, Isaiah affirmed Yahweh's ultimate power and control, over Assyria and even over all peoples (8:8–10). Then he retreated into silent witness to the impending darkness of those who see but do not see (8:11–18, 8:19–23a) and who will suffer from the advance of the distant nations, rallying to the banner raised by Yahweh (5:26–30).

Around this are placed the two poems in 5:8–25 and 9:7–10:4, the first of which attacks the social sins in Judah, introduced by the Song of the Vineyard in 5:1–7. The major theme is not necessarily social injustice as such but the fact that evil and good, darkness and light, bitter and sweet are completely reversed (so the "middle woe" in 5:20) and that the man/men of Judah have placed their plan and their wisdom above that of Yahweh (5:19, 21). The poem ends with one woe yet to come and the ominous threat that Yahweh's anger is not yet turned away.

At this point, the hearer/reader would understand that the context of these six woes is the (present?) situation of the Syro-Ephraimite war and the resultant threat of Assyria not simply as friend but also as foe to Judah. This has been foreshadowed by the transitional piece in 5:26–30, in which the agent of Yahweh's wrath is not yet directly named, and which is complemented by the darkness and distress vocabulary that is linked to the rejection of Yahweh's word in 8:19–23a, following the *Denkschrift* material.

The second major poem, in 9:7ff., connects the "outstretched-hand" refrain, addressed in 5:25 along with the "woes" against Judah, to a "word" now addressed to Jacob/Israel. As the two poems are connected, so the actions and fate of both Israel and Judah are closely intertwined. The intramural conflict of Israel *against* Judah, described in 7:17 as a situation second only to the separation of Israel *from* Judah, is reflected by the internal conflict *within* Israel (articulated specifically in 9:21ab), which, in turn, has climaxed in the attack of both Ephraim and Manasseh *against* Judah (9:21c).

The "word" against Jacob/Israel in 9:7ff. is therefore also a "word" for Judah and Jerusalem. Isaiah's words to Ahaz in 7:1–9 make clear his position that trust in Yahweh (and not in Assyria) would bring the threat of the Syro-Ephraimite coalition to an end. Ahaz's rejection of that plan in the face of the sign of Immanuel would spell eventual disaster also for Judah. This is the same message articulated in 9:7ff. Whatever the fate of the Northern Kingdom, presumably about to be destroyed by both external and internal forces, the angry hand of Yahweh's judgment is still stretched out, not just against Israel but also against Judah.

This is brought home by the return in 10:1 of the theme of woe and judgment against Judah. As 5:25 anticipated the anger of Yahweh against even his own people, 10:1–4 reminds them that, in spite of the sins of and the judgment against the North, the situation in Judah is still of grave concern. The significance of the name Maher-shalal-hash-baz, which is interpreted as a word of deliverance for Judah against the Syro-Ephraimite threat in 8:4, becomes, in the face of an apparent misinterpretation within Judah that bred a sense of false confidence and arrogance before Yahweh (5:19) and a continued sense of injustice before one another (10:2), a reminder that Yahweh's anger and outstretched hand are yet anticipating a "day of visitation" (10:3a).

The use of the noun דבר in 9:7 may, in fact, refer to the torah and testimony that Isaiah had sealed away for future reference (along with the names of his children) in 8:16–18 and that stand in contrast to 'this [false] word' (הדבר הזה) in 8:20. These are the only two uses of the noun דבר in Isaiah 2–12 apart from the superscription in 2:1 and initial oracle in 2:3. In light of the rather limited and seemingly careful use of the noun elsewhere in Isaiah 1–39,[16] it is likely that it is deliberately used here as well. This would confirm that "the word" that falls upon Jacob/Israel in 9:7 is indeed to be understood as a word also against Judah/Jerusalem, which is precisely the major emphasis not only of this poem but also of the connection of this poem with the one in 5:8–25, as well as of the combination of both poems in relation to the *Denkschrift* material.

An oracle has been placed in between 9:7–10:4 and the *Denkschrift* and slightly out of symmetric kilter. It picks up the theme of Yahweh's plan and power over all nations from 8:9–10 and looks beyond the impending darkness and doom to the light of a new day under a new Davidic king: 8:23b–9:6. The reason for the placement of this unit here may be simply stylistic variation. But in light of the larger macrostructure of chaps. 2–12 (see below, pp. 138 and 253ff.), it is possible to suggest a thematic intent. This theme was that the hope in a Davidic heir, which might have followed upon the birth of the child Immanuel, would be tempered, if not negated, by the continued state of affairs described by the complementary piece in 9:7–10:4. This is especially likely if Immanuel is identified as a royal heir, at whose birth the Davidic line would have been perceived as established for another generation. While Isaiah would affirm the promise to David and Zion, on which his original counsel to Ahaz was based, the placement of this oracle at this point would qualify this promise by the continued (and prior) need to deal with the arrogance of both king and people.

The Macrostructure of 5:1–10:4

I conclude by summarizing the structural outline for this major section of Isaiah 2–12. I began this chapter by noting the close correspondence

---

16. A detailed excursus on the further use of דָּבָר is beyond the scope of this study, but it is worth noting that, apart from 16:13, it is always used in reference to Judah and Jerusalem and concentrated in chaps. 28–30 (28:13, 14; 29:21; 30:12) and in the exchanges between Isaiah and Hezekiah in chaps. 36–39 (36:5, 21; 37:22; 38:4, 7; 39:2, 4, 5, 6, 8).

that exists between the two major poems that were analyzed in detail in chaps. 2 and 3:

5:8–25:   496 syllables, 200 stresses, 218 words, 62 lines
9:7–10:4:   496 syllables, 185 stresses, 222 words, 62 lines

We have also seen the correspondence in length between the smaller sections within this large unit:

5:1–7:   240 syllables, 90 stresses, 100 words, 30 lines
8:23b–9:6:   240 syllables, 90 stresses, 109 words, 30 lines

5:26–30:   151 syllables, 57 stresses, 66 words, 19 lines
8:19–23a: 136 syllables, 50 stresses, 59 words, 17 lines

I have suggested that 5:26–30 and 8:19–23a form a smaller border, encircling the *Denkschrift* material in 6:1–8:18. Around this are the remaining poems, which are exactly matched:

A	B	A′
I. 5:1–7	5:26–30	I. 8:23b–9:6
II. 5:8–25	6:1–8:18	II. 9:7–10:4
	8:19–23a	

In this way, the total length of A matches A′:

A : 736 syllables, 290 stresses, 318 words, 92 lines
A′: 736 syllables, 275 stresses, 331 words, 92 lines

The smaller units A I and A′ I match, as do A II and A′ II:

A   I: 240 syllables,   90 stresses,   100 words,   30 lines
A′ I: 240 syllables,   90 stresses,   109 words,   30 lines
A   II: 496 syllables, 200 stresses,   218 words,   62 lines
A′ II: 496 syllables, 185 stresses,   222 words,   62 lines

However, if the smaller units that surround and form the transitions to the middle, predominantly prose *Denkschrift* (B I and III) are combined with the larger sections, A and A′, an even greater sense of symmetry of length is dicovered:

A	B	A′
I. 5:1–7	6:1–8:18	I. 8:19–23a
II. 5:8–25		II. 8:23b–9:6
III. 5:26–30		III. 9:7–10:4

In this scheme, A is still matched to A′; the deviation from the mean in syllables is 0.8%, in stresses 4%, and in words 0.8%:

A   (5:1–30):   887 syllables, 347 stresses, 384 words, 111 lines
A′ (8:19–10:4):   872 syllables, 325 stresses, 389 words, 109 lines

Of course, my hypothesis suggests a crossing over of individual parts between A and A':

> A I matches A' II
>
> A II matches A' III
>
> A III matches A I

If A' II and III were reversed, the matches would work out chiastically (A I with A' III, and so forth), but, as has already been suggested, this is likely a deliberate variation on an otherwise simple scheme, even if carried out over a larger and complicated body of material. In fact, the reversal of these pieces actually creates an interlocking mechanism, not unlike the interlocking of the two poems in 5:8–25 and 9:7–10:4 themselves. The overall pattern is presented as follows:

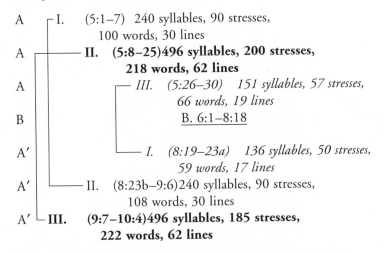

A   ┌ I.   (5:1–7) 240 syllables, 90 stresses,
                100 words, 30 lines

A   ├──── **II.   (5:8–25)496 syllables, 200 stresses,**
                218 words, 62 lines

A   │   ┌── *III.   (5:26–30)   151 syllables, 57 stresses,*
     │   │   *66 words, 19 lines*

B   │   │   B. 6:1–8:18

A'   │   └── *I.   (8:19–23a)   136 syllables, 50 stresses,*
     │   *59 words, 17 lines*

A'   └──── II.   (8:23b–9:6)240 syllables, 90 stresses,
                108 words, 30 lines

A' └ **III.   (9:7–10:4)496 syllables, 185 stresses,**
                222 words, 62 lines

Finally, combining the larger A with the A' section, one discovers that they are, added together, roughly equivalent to the B section:

> A (5:1–30) + A' (8:19–9:6):   1759 syllables, 774 words
>
> B (*Denkschrift*):   (ca.)[17] 1700 syllables, 749 words

While quite close, the correspondence is, however, not nearly as exact as has been found between the two poems in 5:8–25 and 9:7–10:4, or, for example, between the smaller units in 5:1–7 and 8:23b–9:6, where the syllable counts were exactly matched. Yet certainly there is a sense of balancing that extends beyond verses and strophes, and even beyond the composition and structure of individual poems or pericopes. The fact that

---

17. See appendix 3, where the range is shown as 1673–1712. At this point we arbitrarily fix a round number near the median, but see below, p. 255).

a sense of symmetry is apparent even in larger structural configurations should prompt one to look both for further confirmation of this hypothesis and for further implementation of this methodological consideration in an even larger body of material. In the next two chapters, I shall turn attention to the next circle of prophetic rhetoric beyond Isa 5:1–10:4 and consider both the major block that follows, 10:5–12:6, and the block that precedes, chaps. 2–4.

Chapter 5
Isaiah 10:5–12:6

Boundaries of This Unit

Having discussed the independent yet complementary poems in Isa 5:8–25 and 9:7–10:4, not only in relationship to each other but also within their larger literary context in Isa 5:1–10:4, I shall now move beyond the boundary of 10:4 to explore the literary, poetic style of the prophetic rhetoric in the next major section of Isaiah 2–12. In so doing, I shall explore the possibility that a structural and thematic relationship may exist between the chapters so far analyzed and what follows in Isa 10:5–12:6.

Isaiah 10:5–34

Text

		Syllable Count	MT	Stress Count	MT
10:5a	הוֹי אַשּׁוּר שֵׁבֶט אַפִּי	6	7	4	4
b	וּמַטֶּה־הוּא בְיָדָם זַעְמִי׃	9	9	3/(4)	3
6a	בְּגוֹי חָנֵף אֲשַׁלְּחֶנּוּ	9	9	3	3
b	וְעַל־עַם עֶבְרָתִי אֲצַוֶּנּוּ	10	10	3	3
c	לִשְׁלֹל שָׁלָל וְלָבֹז בַּז	8	8	4	4
d	וּלְשִׂימוֹ מִרְמָס כְּחֹמֶר חוּצוֹת׃	9/(10)	11	4	4
7a	וְהוּא לֹא־כֵן יְדַמֶּה	7	7	3	3
b	וּלְבָבוֹ לֹא־כֵן יַחְשֹׁב	7/(8)	8	3	3
c	כִּי לְהַשְׁמִיד בִּלְבָבוֹ	7	7	3	3
d	וּלְהַכְרִית גּוֹיִם לֹא מְעָט׃	8/(9)	9	3/(4)	4
8a	כִּי יֹאמַר	3	3	1/(2)	2
b	הֲלֹא שָׂרַי יַחְדָּו מְלָכִים׃	9	9	4	4
9a	הֲלֹא כְּכַרְכְּמִישׁ כַּלְנוֹ	8	8	3	3
b	אִם־לֹא כְאַרְפַּד חֲמָת	7	7	3	3
c	אִם־לֹא כְדַמֶּשֶׂק שֹׁמְרוֹן׃	8	9	3	3

This large section breaks down into three parts, 10:5–34, chap. 11, and chap. 12, although there are, in fact, connections that suggest that these subsections are somewhat artificially distinguished. Nevertheless, for the sake of this analysis, I shall first deal with each of these three parts and then discuss any interconnections that may become apparent. Due to the larger amount of material, the analysis will be abbreviated slightly, although the method employed continues to pay close attention to poetic and stylistic details.

Translation

10:5a	Hey! Assyria, the staff of my anger,
b	the rod of [= to carry out] my curse is he in my hand.
6a	Into an apostate nation I send him forth,
b	and against a people of [= who have incurred] my rage I commission him,
c	to take booty and to seize plunder
d	and to make them trampled like street mud.
7a	But he—not thus does he think!
b	and his mind—not thus does it consider!
c	But to destroy is on his mind,
d	and to cut down nations not a few.
8a	For he says,
b	"Are not kings like all my princes?
9a	Is not Calno like Carchemish?
b	Surely Hamath like Arpad?
c	Surely Samaria like Damascus?

10a	כַּאֲשֶׁר מָצְאָה יָדִי	7	8	3	3
b	לְמַמְלְכֹת הָאֱלִיל	7	7	2	2
c	מִירוּשָׁלַ͏ִם וּמִשֹּׁמְרוֹן: וּפְסִילֵיהֶם	13/(14)	15	3	3
11a	הֲלֹא כַּאֲשֶׁר עָשִׂיתִי	7	8	3	3
b	לְשֹׁמְרוֹן וְלֶאֱלִילֶיהָ	8/(9)	10	2	2
c	כֵּן אֶעֱשֶׂה לִירוּשָׁלַ͏ִם וְלַעֲצַבֶּיהָ:	11/(12)	15	3/(4)	4
Verses 5–11		168/(174)	184	63/(67)	66
12a	וְהָיָה כִּי־יְבַצַּע	7	7	2	2
b	אֲדֹנָי אֶת־כָּל־מַעֲשֵׂהוּ	8	8	2/(3)	2
c	בְּהַר צִיּוֹן וּבִירוּשָׁלָ͏ִם	9	10	3	3
d	לְבַב מֶלֶךְ־אַשּׁוּר אֶפְקֹד עַל־פְּרִי־גֹדֶל	11	13	4/(5)	4
e	וְעַל־תִּפְאֶרֶת רוּם עֵינָיו:	7	8	3	3
13a	כִּי אָמַר	3	3	1/(2)	2
b	בְּכֹחַ יָדִי עָשִׂיתִי	7	7	3	3
c	וּבְחָכְמָתִי כִּי נְבֻנוֹתִי	9/(10)	10	3	3
d	וְאָסִיר גְּבוּלֹת עַמִּים	8	8	3	3
e	וַעֲתִידֹתֵיהֶם שׁוֹשֵׂתִי	8	9	2	2
f	וְאוֹרִיד כַּאבִּיר יוֹשְׁבִים:	8	8	3	3
14a	וַתִּמְצָא כַקֵּן יָדִי לְחֵיל הָעַמִּים	12	12	5	5
b	וְכֶאֱסֹף בֵּיצִים עֲזֻבוֹת	8	9	3	3
c	כָּל־הָאָרֶץ אֲנִי אָסָפְתִּי	8	9	3	3
d	וְלֹא הָיָה נֹדֵד כָּנָף	8	8	3/(4)	4
e	וּפֹצֶה פֶה וּמְצַפְצֵף:	(7)/8	8	3	3
15a	הֲיִתְפָּאֵר הַגַּרְזֶן עַל הַחֹצֵב בּוֹ	12	12	4	5
b	אִם־יִתְגַּדֵּל הַמַּשּׂוֹר עַל־מְנִיפוֹ	11	11	3	3
c	כְּהָנִיף שֵׁבֶט וְאֶת־מְרִימָיו	9	10	3	3
d	כְּהָרִים מַטֶּה לֹא־עֵץ:	7	7	3	3
Verses 12–15		167/169 =168	177	59/(63)	62
16a	לָכֵן יְשַׁלַּח הָאָדוֹן יְהוָה צְבָאוֹת	13	13	5	5
b	בְּמִשְׁמַנָּיו רָזוֹן	6	6	2	2
c	וְתַחַת כְּבֹדוֹ יֵקַד יְקֹד כִּיקוֹד אֵשׁ:	12	13	5	6
17a	וְהָיָה אוֹר־יִשְׂרָאֵל לְאֵשׁ	9	9	3	3
b	וּקְדוֹשׁוֹ לְלֶהָבָה	7/(8)	8	2	2
c	וּבָעֲרָה וְאָכְלָה שִׁיתוֹ	10	10	3	3
d	וּשְׁמִירוֹ בְּיוֹם אֶחָד:	(7)/8	8	3	3

10a   As my hand has found [its way]

  b   to the idol-kingdoms—

  c   and their images [were more] than Jerusalem['s] or Samaria['s]—

11a   will I not, as I have done

  b   to Samaria and to her idols,

  c   so also do to Jerusalem and to her idols?"

12a   And it will happen, when (Adonay) will complete

  b   Adonay all his work

  c   on Mount Zion and in Jerusalem,

  d   "I will punish the fruit of the greatness of the mind of the king of Assyria

  e   and the pride of the arrogance of his eyes,

13a   for he has said,

  b   'By the strength of my hand I have acted,

  c   and [it is] by my [own] wisdom that I have discernment.

  d   I remove the border of peoples,

  e   and their preparations I plunder,

  f   like a bull I bring down inhabitants.

14a   And my hand will find, like a nest, the wealth of the peoples,

  b   as abandoned eggs are gathered,

  c   [so] I will gather all the earth.

  d   There is no flapping wing

  e   or opening mouth or chirping.'

15a   Will the ax exalt itself over the one who chops with it?

  b   Will the saw magnify itself over the one wielding it,

  c   like a staff wielding those who raise it,

  d   like a rod raising [someone] not of wood."

16a   Therefore the Lord Yahweh Seba'oth will send forth

  b   leanness into his fat ones,

  c   and instead of his honor, a kindling will be kindled, like kindling a fire.

17a   And the Light of Israel will become fire,

  b   and its Holy One a flame.

  c   It will burn and consume his briars

  d   and his thorns in one day.

18a	וּכְב֤וֹד יַעְרוֹ֙ וְכַרְמִלּ֔וֹ	8/(9)	9	3	3
b	מִנֶּ֥פֶשׁ וְעַד־בָּשָׂ֖ר יְכַלֶּ֑ה	9	10	3	3
c	וְהָיָ֖ה כִּמְסֹ֥ס נֹסֵֽס׃	7	7	3	3
19a	וּשְׁאָ֥ר עֵ֛ץ יַעְר֖וֹ מִסְפָּ֣ר יִֽהְי֑וּ	9/(10)	10	4/(5)	5
b	וְנַ֖עַר יִכְתְּבֵֽם׃	5	6	2	2

Verses 16–19		102/106 =103	109	38/(39)	40

20a	וְהָיָ֣ה בַּיּ֣וֹם הַה֗וּא	7	7	3	3
b	לֹֽא־יוֹסִ֨יף ע֜וֹד שְׁאָ֤ר יִשְׂרָאֵל֙	9	9	4	4
c	וּפְלֵיטַ֣ת בֵּֽית־יַעֲקֹ֔ב	6/(7)	8	2	2
d	לְהִשָּׁעֵ֖ן עַל־מַכֵּ֑הוּ	8	8	2	2
e	וְנִשְׁעַ֗ן עַל־יְהוָ֛ה קְד֥וֹשׁ יִשְׂרָאֵ֖ל בֶּאֱמֶֽת׃	13	14	5	5
21a	שְׁאָ֥ר יָשׁ֖וּב שְׁאָ֣ר יַעֲקֹ֑ב	8	9	4	4
b	אֶל־אֵ֖ל גִּבּֽוֹר׃	4	4	2	2
22a	כִּ֣י אִם־יִהְיֶ֞ה עַמְּךָ֤	6/(7)	7	3	3
b	יִשְׂרָאֵל֙ כְּח֣וֹל הַיָּ֔ם	7	7	3	3
c	שְׁאָ֖ר יָשׁ֣וּב בּ֑וֹ	5	5	2/(3)	3
d	כִּלָּי֥וֹן חָר֖וּץ שׁוֹטֵ֥ף צְדָקָֽה׃	10	10	4	4
23a	כִּ֥י כָלָ֖ה וְנֶחֱרָצָ֑ה	7	8	3	3
b	אֲדֹנָ֥י יְהוִ֖ה צְבָא֑וֹת	8	8	3	3
c	עֹשֶׂ֖ה בְּקֶ֥רֶב כָּל־הָאָֽרֶץ׃	7	9	3	3

Verses 20–23		105/(107)	113	43/(44)	44

24a	לָכֵ֗ן כֹּֽה־אָמַ֞ר אֲדֹנָ֤י יְהוִה֙ צְבָא֔וֹת	13	13	5	5
b	אַל־תִּירָ֥א עַמִּ֖י	5	5	2	2
c	יֹשֵׁ֣ב צִיּ֑וֹן מֵֽאַשּׁ֔וּר	7	7	3	3
d	בַּשֵּׁ֣בֶט יַכֶּ֑כָּה	5	6	2	2
e	וּמַטֵּ֥הוּ יִשָּׂא־עָלֶ֖יךָ	(8)/9	9	3	3
f	בְּדֶ֥רֶךְ מִצְרָֽיִם׃	4	6	2	2
25a	כִּי־ע֖וֹד מְעַ֣ט מִזְעָ֑ר	6	6	3	3
b	וְכָ֣לָה זַ֔עַם וְאַפִּ֖י עַל־תַּבְלִיתָֽם׃	11	12	4	4
26a	וְעוֹרֵ֨ר עָלָ֜יו יְהוָ֤ה צְבָאוֹת֙ שׁ֔וֹט	11	11	5	5
b	כְּמַכַּ֥ת מִדְיָ֖ן בְּצ֣וּר עוֹרֵ֑ב	9	9	4	4
c	וּמַטֵּ֖הוּ עַל־הַיָּ֔ם	7	7	2	2
d	וּנְשָׂא֖וֹ בְּדֶ֥רֶךְ מִצְרָֽיִם׃	(7)/8	10	3	3

Verses 24–26		(93)/95	101	38	38

18a	The honor of his forest and of his fertile field
b	from life to flesh it will finish off.
c	It will be like the falling of a standard
19a	and the remnant of the wood of his forest will be [such] a number
b	that a child can write them down.

20a	It will happen **in that day,**
b	no longer will the Remnant of Israel
c	and the fugitive(s) of the house of Jacob
d	rely upon the one who strikes,
e	but they will rely on Yahweh, the Holy One of Israel, in truth.

21a	"A-Remnant-Will-Return"—the Remnant of Jacob—
b	to El Gibbor.
22a	For though your people (Israel) will be . . .
b	Israel (will be) . . . like the sand of the sea,
c	"A-Remnant-Will-Return" amongst them.
d	Destruction is decided—overflowing [with] righteousness
23a	—but destruction is determined!
b	Adonay Yahweh Seba'oth
c	is about to act in the midst of all the land.

24a	Therefore, thus says Adonay Yahweh Seba'oth,
b	"Do not be afraid, my people,
c	inhabitant(s) of Zion, of Assyria.
d	With (his) staff he will strike you,
e	And his rod he will raise upon you
f	in the Way of Egypt,
25a	But only a little while
b	and my curse will be completed as well as my anger toward their destruction.
26a	Yahweh Seba'oth will rouse up upon him (them) a calamity
b	like the striking by Midian at Rock Oreb
c	and his rod over the sea—
d	his lifting (it) up in the Way of Egypt.

27a	וְהָיָה בַיּוֹם הַהוּא	7	7	3	3
b	יָסוּר סֻבֳּלוֹ מֵעַל שִׁכְמֶךָ	(9)/10	10	4	4
c	וְעֻלּוֹ מֵעַל צַוָּארֶךָ	(8)/9	9	3	3
d	וְחֻבַּל עֹל מִפְּנֵי־שָׁמֶן:	8	9	3	3
28a	בָּא עַל־עַיַּת עָבַר בְּמִגְרוֹן	9	9	4	4
b	לְמִכְמָשׂ יַפְקִיד כֵּלָיו:	7	7	3	3
29a	עָבְרוּ מַעְבָּרָה	6	6	2	2
b	גֶּבַע מָלוֹן לָנוּ	5	6	2/(3)	3
c	חָרְדָה הָרָמָה	6	6	2	2
d	גִּבְעַת שָׁאוּל נָסָה:	6	6	3	3
30a	צַהֲלִי קוֹלֵךְ בַּת־גַּלִּים	8	8	3	3
b	הַקְשִׁיבִי לַיְשָׁה	5	5	2	2
c	עֲנִיָּה עֲנָתוֹת:	6	6	2	2
31a	נָדְדָה מַדְמֵנָה	6	6	2	2
b	יֹשְׁבֵי הַגֵּבִים הֵעִיזוּ:	9	9	3	3
32a	עוֹד הַיּוֹם בְּנֹב לַעֲמֹד	7	8	3	4
b	יְנֹפֵף יָדוֹ הַר בֵּית [בַּת] צִיּוֹן	9	9	4	4
c	גִּבְעַת יְרוּשָׁלָ͏ִם:	6	7	2	2
Verses 27–32		(127)/129	133	50/(51)	52
33a	הִנֵּה הָאָדוֹן יְהוָה צְבָאוֹת	10	10	4	4
b	מְסָעֵף פֻּארָה בְּמַעֲרָצָה	9	10	3	3
c	וְרָמֵי הַקּוֹמָה גְּדוּעִים	9	9	3	3
d	וְהַגְּבֹהִים יִשְׁפָּלוּ:	8	8	2	2
34a	וְנִקַּף סִבְכֵי הַיַּעַר בַּבַּרְזֶל	10	12	4	4
b	וְהַלְּבָנוֹן בְּאַדִּיר יִפּוֹל:	10	10	3	3
Verses 33–34		56	59	19	19
Totals		818/836 = 824	876	310/(321)	321
		Syllables	MT	Stresses	MT

Notes on Translation and Text

10:5b. **"the rod of my curse"** I am reading ומטה ... זעמי as a broken construct chain, parallel to שבט אפי. See Freedman (1980: 339).

"in my hand" Freedman further suggests that the suffix on בידם should be read as first-person singular plus enclitic *mem*. Based on the parallelism and structure demonstrated in the previous note, it is likely also that הוא בידם matches הוי אשור, thus: 'Hey, Assyria is in my hand'.

27a It will happen, **in that day,**
  b his burden will be removed from your shoulder,
  c and his yoke from your neck—
  d —(his) yoke will be broken because of fatness.
28a He has come against Aiath; he has crossed through Migron;
  b at Michmash he deposited his equipment;
29a They have crossed the Pass,
  b "Geba is a lodging place for us."
  c Ramah is terrified;
  d Saul's Gibeah has fled.
30a Cry out your voice, daughter Gallim!
  b Pay attention, Laish.
  c Poor is Anathoth;
31a Madmenah has fled.
  b The inhabitants of Gebim sought refuge;
32a even today [one is] to stand still at Nob;
  b He shakes his hand at the mount of daughter Zion,
  c at the hill of Jerusalem.

33a Behold, the Lord Yahweh Seba°oth
  b is about to lop off the bough with a crash,
  c and the high haughtiness will be hewn down;
  d the arrogance will be brought low.
34a The thickets of the forest will be hacked away with iron,
  b and Lebanon by might will fall.

10:6d. **"them"** The antecedent of the pronoun is not completely clear. Most likely it refers to the "people" and "nation" of the previous line.

10:8b. **"like"** Based on the close parallelism with the following line, it is likely that the comparative preposition כ also serves this line as well.

"princes" שׂר is likely a play on Assyrian *sarru* 'king'. See Machinist (1983: 734–35). If a comparison is intended (see previous note), there is also a play on the Hebrew meaning of שׂר 'lesser official'.

10:12d. **"I"**   The shift to direct discourse with the use of the first person is abrupt but not uncommon. No Hebrew manuscript supports the LXX shift to the third person, which reflects a change toward the easier reading.

10:13e. **"preparations"**   *Kethiv* and *Qere* may reflect alternate spellings of the same word, from the root עתד 'be ready'. BDB (800) suggests a deliberate change to indicate a specialized use here. Watts (1985: 146) reads the *Qere* as from עַתּוּד 'he-goat' and suggests a metaphor for "leaders," but he then opts for the *Kethiv* as better fitting the parallelism.

   "plunder"   Read as from root שסה.

10:15d. **"not of wood"**   The idiom seems awkward, but possibly simply unknown to moderns. The attempt to emend לֹא עֵץ to לוֹחֵץ is attractive but unnecessary and without any textual evidence.

10:16c. **"will be kindled"**   יְקֹד appears to be an infinitive construct, as is יְקוֹד in the following line, from the root יקד 'burn, be kindled'. (1QIsaᵃ spells the first plene, the second without the mater.) There may be wordplay on the root קדד 'to bow down, pay homage'.

10:18a. **"fertile field"**   Although כרמל seems to refer to a field on the way to becoming a יער (compare Isa 29:17, 32:15, 37:24 [= 2 Kgs 19:23]; and Mic 7:14), the terms are used in tandem and in this case may form a double *nomen rectum* for the bound form כְּבוֹד. See Avishur (1984: 171, 695) for the word pair, and Waltke and O'Connor (1990: 139, 9.3b) for the construction.

10:18b. **"from life to flesh"**   נפש and בשׂר are also a word pair (though not so noted in Avishur 1984)—see, for example, Ps 63:2, 84:3; Job 13:14, 14:22—and likely form a merismus similar to "body and soul" in English.

10:18c. **"falling of a standard"**   Both words in the *Qal* are hapax legomena. Most translators follow BDB in citing נסס I, 'to be sick', which is not impossible in light of line 16b. However, the 'falling standard' better fits the overall context with its theme of the proud being humble and of the falling ("felling") of trees, and my translation suggests anticipatory wordplay on the נֵס (from BDB נסס II) in 11:10, 12.

10:20a. **"in that day"**   Boldface type draws attention to the emphatic role this phrase plays.

10:20c. **"fugitive(s)"**   This word is singular in the collective sense.

10:21a. **"A-Remant-Will-Return"**   Though here a sentence, the words explain the name of Isaiah's son mentioned in 7:3.

10:23a. **"destruction"** Note the wordplay in Hebrew between the cognates כִּלָּיוֹן and כָּלָה, both of which are translated 'destruction'.

10:24d. **"his"** I read the pronominal suffix on מַטֵּהוּ as double duty.

10:24f. **"Way of Egypt"** Watts's suggestion (1985: 157) that דֶּרֶךְ מִצְרָיִם should be taken as a geographical site has merit. Although the context deals with the manner of and deliverance from past oppression, the reference to the otherwise unknown "Rock of Oreb" in v. 26 and the repetition of the term there indicates a specific locale.

10:25b. **"my"** This pronoun stems from reading the pronominal suffix on אַפִּי as double duty (see note to 10:24d).

10:26c. **"and his rod over the sea—"** My translation is literal; the two lines in 26de form one unit: 'and (like) his lifting up his rod upon the sea at the Way of Egypt'.

10:26d. **"Way of Egypt"** See the note to 10:24f, above. Here, too, the translation 'in the manner of Egypt' = 'the way it was with Eygpt' is attractive. But, as noted, the parallel with בצור עורב indicates that a specific place-name is likely intended. One cannot dismiss the possibility of a double meaning and paronomasia with דרך.

10:27d. **"because of fatness"** Against the suggestion that וחבל belongs with 27c and that the remainder of 27d belongs to the list of place-names that follows ('He has ascended from Pene-Yeshemon' [Watts 1985: 159 and other commentators]), I note: (a) עֹל is only a hypothetical verb form from עלל; (b) the MT verse division carries significant weight; (c) Pene-Yeshemon is not known as a place-name (though it could well be one); (d) the list of place-names that follows contains fourteen names, culminating in Zion/Jerusalem. A fifteenth name would be odd and unnecessary. (e) line 27d makes reasonable sense as a conclusion to 27bc. While the meaning of 'because of fatness' could well be questioned, 6:10 makes clear the metaphor of fatness for unresponsiveness to the Word of Yahweh (likely caused by over-affluence, including, literally, "fatness"). Here the metaphor is applied to Assyria, as it is also in line 16b.

10:32b. **"daughter"** I am reading the *Qere*, בת for בית.

10:33b. **"is about to lop off the bough"** The common translation of the hapax legomena מסעף פארה follows meanings given in BDB and is based on the similarity to the following lines. That פארה should be left as the *Kethiv*, as Watts suggests (164), is not without warrant, but more likely it is meant to be a pun on תִפְאָרָה (compare 3:18, 4:2, as well as the פְּאֵרִים of 3:20; and 10:12).

10:33c. **"high haughtiness"** The immediate referent is the high treetops; the metaphor recalls the haughtiness of man, first of Israel/Judah (2:9, 11, 17) and now of Assyria.

10:34a. **"will be hacked away"** I read וְנִקַּף as *Niphal* with the force of the singular הַיַּעַר as subject, or, possibly, a case of plural subject with singular verb.

Lineation

The passage presents numerous problems, due especially to a wider range in the potential number of lines as well as in the syllable counts. Although there are possible variations, my method suggests a text of 103 lines. While difficult, decisions have been made in line with my methodological considerations and are therefore not simply arbitrary or without explanation.

For example, the following lines are long and might be divided: line 10c (but without natural division), line 11c (but without easy division), line 12d (5 stresses is long, but 11 syllables is not unreasonably long), line 14a (possibly to be divided after יָדִי), lines 15ab (could be a quatrain), line 16a (long, but not divisible without separating the divine name), line 16c (syntactically difficult to divide), line 20e (very long, but concludes a quatrain of 36 syllables and 13 stresses), line 24a (leave divine name intact), lines 25b and 26a (neither of which is excessively long; five stresses is "heavy" for 26a, but the line does not divide easily). The final unit, vv. 33–34, is very long for 6 lines (56 syllables), but the accent count is closer to a 6-line unit, and the lines as I show them reflect syntactical and semantic boundaries.

On the other hand, the following lines are short and might possibly be combined to reduce the number of cola: lines 8a and 13a, which have been left as individual lines; lines 22abc (2 lines?); 24be; 24def (2 lines?).

These variables offer a range in the number of lines from 98 to 116. The syllable count offers a range of 818 to 836 (see below, p. 151). Based on the norm of 8 syllables per line that has been found to be operative and dominant throughout the texts under study, this syllable count would suggest 102–5 lines, with 103 or 104 the most likely numbers. Anticipating also the consideration of the gross structure of this unit (see below, p. 157), a balancing of the syllable counts in vv. 5–11 and 12–15, and in vv. 16–19 and 20–23 suggests the lower number of syllables and therefore confirms the lower number of lines.

Syllable and Stress Counts

The range of the syllable count, 818–36, is the result of several variables, the most frequent of which is the prefixed conjunction before shewa (*šureq*), in which cases both a high and low count are shown, assuming the possibility of elision.

Working within the range, I have reached the total of 824 syllables (MT: 876), which is appropriate to the 103 lines. Although the lineation has shown a large variety of line lengths, from very short lines (2 or 3 syllables) to several that are quite long in either (or both) syllable or stress counts, the overall sense of balance is remarkable:

3-syllable lines:	2		9-syllable lines:	19
4-syllable lines:	2		10-syllable lines:	7
5-syllable lines:	6		11-syllable lines:	5
6-syllable lines:	11		12-syllable lines:	3
7-syllable lines:	22		13-syllable lines:	4
8-syllable lines:	22			

Of the 103 lines,
   21.4% (22 lines) have 8 syllables,
   61.2% (63 lines) have 7–9 syllables,
   78.6% (81 lines) have 6–10 syllables.

The median line length is 8 syllables.
The average line length is 8.00 syllables per line (824/103).

The stress count also shows a fairly large range, 310–21 (MT: 321). Several lines carry an extra stress, such as the הוי in line 5a and לכן in 16a and 24a, as well as other lines with a "heavy" number of accents. At 3 stresses per line, the 103 lines should have 309 stresses, which is very close to the lower number of the range. Thus I shall tabulate on the basis of all lower numbers, including the very unusual cases in lines 8a and 13a, where I would show a one-stress line, which is at least compatible with the (also) very short 3 syllables:

1-stress cola:	2 (1.9%)
2-stress cola:	24 (23.3%)
3-stress cola:	54 (52.4%)
4-stress cola:	17 (16.5%)
5-stress cola:	6 (5.8%)

Thus 95 lines (92.2%) have 2–4 stresses.
The average number of stresses per colon is 3.01 (= 3.00).

Prose Particles

The prose particle percentage of the entire unit is 6.72% (24/357 words). Of the 24 prose particles, 20 are the definite article. Two object markers appear in vv. 12 and 15, and two occurrences of כאשר are found (vv. 10 and 11).

Although the overall count is close to the suggested 5% maximum figure for poetry, the particles are not evenly distributed. Verses 5–11, for example, contain only 3 particles (out of 72 words) for a count of 4.16%. But a higher concentration is found in vv. 12–15 (including the two object markers), where 7 of the 74 words give a figure of 9.46%. The highest count is found in vv. 33–34, where 5 out of 19 words gives a percentage of 26.32%, although the only prose particle used is the article, and the lines show parallelism in 33bcd as well as in 34ab.

There can be little doubt that these final lines, as well as other lines within the unit display characteristics of both prose and poetry and fall between the two categories. Yet taken as a whole, the count for the entire unit is much closer to that of poetry than prose.

Verse and Strophe Structure

Verses 5–11

The section begins with a masterfully crafted bicolon, which, as has been observed in the translation notes, takes the construct with which the first line ends and divides it to form an envelope around the second line. Not only do the words 'anger' and 'hand' form a link to the refrain of the previous section, but the word pair מטה//שבט also introduces a motif that will be heard in 15cd and 24de.

The two bicola of v. 6 are carefully ordered in linear parallelism, with final verbs matched in 6ab and initial infinitives in 6cd. The alliteration of the *lamed* (9 times in v. 6) carries over into v. 7 as well, where again the first 2 lines have final verb forms, and the second 2 have infinitives in the first element.

Whether classified as four bicola or as two quatrains, vv. 6–7, added to v. 5, form the first half (and therefore likely a strophe) of vv. 5–11. If the strophe is divided at v. 7, it, in turn, consists of two parts: vv. 5–6, 6 lines totaling 51 syllables and 21 stresses, and v. 7, 4 lines totaling 29 syllables and 12 stresses.

This is nearly a mirror image of the second strophe, vv. 8–11, in which the first part is the 4 lines of vv. 8b–9 (plus the introductory 8a), totaling

32 (+ 3) syllables and 13 (+ 1) stresses, and the second is vv. 10–11, consisting of 53 syllables and 16 stresses. In any case, the total of both strophes is roughly equivalent: 80 syllables and 33 stresses in vv. 5–7 and 88 syllables and 30 stresses in vv. 8–11.

The second strophe consists of a speech in the mouth of an arrogant Assyria. The first quatrain (8b, 9abc) is a series of four rhetorical questions, the first two introduced by הֲלֹא, the second by אִם־לֹא. The preponderance of *kap* sounds is striking, but the first line omits the comparative preposition, which should be understood (see p. 147 translation note to 10:8b).

Verses 10–11 appear to be two tricola of 27 and 26 syllables each. The first begins with כַּאֲשֶׁר, continuing the alliteration and sound play; the second combines כַּאֲשֶׁר with the הלא used in 8b–9a, a combination that binds these verses together. The repetition of אליל in 10b and 11b further links v. 10 and v. 11, and the arrogant use of ידי by Assyria in contrast to the invective of Yahweh in line 5b ties the two strophes together.

Verses 12–15

Verse 12 begins a second unit (stanza, see below, pp. 157ff.) with the prosaic והיה. Were it not for the parallel repetition of an על־ phrase in 12de, the verse could be read as prose. Here a direct quotation of Yahweh is introduced abruptly, while in v. 13 another citation from the mouth of an arrogant Assyria is introduced by the perfect כי אמר (compare 8a). Both speeches by Assyria are really indirect within direct discourse by Yahweh (through the prophet), so that line 12d simply picks up where v. 11 left off. Verse 12abc serves, by way of interruption, both to close the indirect quote within the previous quote and to introduce what follows.

Assyria's second speech proceeds in ten poetic lines, with theme and content similar to the ten-line speech in vv. 8b–11. The first bicolon is linear, the second is chiastic. A chiasm appears between the verb forms of root אסף in 14bc. Repetition of ידי in lines 13b and 14a and of עמים in lines 13d and 14a form internal links. And the final line (14e) not only continues the "bird" metaphor (compare 8:8), but it also combines *pe* and *ṣade* sounds with great effect.

As Assyria's speech in vv. 8b–11 was also contained in 10 lines, so the overall length of both speeches is equivalent. Verses 8b–11 have 85 syllables and 29 stresses (34 words) compared to the 84 syllables and 31 stresses (33 words) in vv. 13b–14. Further, v. 15, with 39 syllables and 13 stresses, balances v. 12, with 42 syllables and 15 stresses, so that the total of v. 12 + v. 15 (81 syllables and 28 stresses) is equivalent to the total of the Assyria speech in between, just as vv. 5–7 are balanced in length by vv. 8–11.

Thus vv. 5–11 divide equally between an A and a B strophe (vv. 5–7 and vv. 8–11), while vv. 12–15 follow an A-B-A′ pattern, with the total of A + A′ equivalent to the B section. In each case, the B section is a speech in the mouth of Assyria.

Lines 15ab begin as negative rhetorical questions (cf. vv. 8–9). The root of the last word of the second line begins the third, and the root of the last word of the third line begins the fourth. The final word עץ is the common denominator of all the instruments described in the previous 4 lines. The final bicolon also pairs שבט and מטה (compare v. 5).

This concluding verse clearly links to v. 12 through the use of vocabulary as well. The roots of גדל (12d) and פאר and רום (12e) appear in lines 15b (יתגדל), 15a (יתפאר), and 15c and d (רום). And it is tempting to suggest that הַמַּשּׂור (line 15b) is a pun on מֶלֶךְ־אַשּׁוּר (line 12d; also compare 5a).

Verses 16–19 and 20–23

The word לכן (line 16a) introduces the judgment pronounced upon Assyria's pride. Whether or where vv. 16–19 should be broken into strophes is difficult to determine. The term והיה occurs at the beginning of lines 17a and 18c. Alliteration appears in 16c and 18c. Verses 17c–18b are held together by the chiastic placement of verbs only at the beginning and end of the quatrain, and one hears sound play between ואכלה and יכלה. The word יער links lines 18a and 19a.

Verses 20–23, however, which are the same length as vv. 16–19 (see below, p. 157) seem to divide after v. 21, yielding two strophes of 55 syllables and 22 stresses (vv. 20–21) and of 50 syllables and 21 stresses (vv. 22–23). On analogy, it is therefore possible to divide vv. 16–19 after 17b, forming strophes of 47 syllables and 17 stresses (vv. 16–17b) and of 56 syllables and 21 stresses (vv. 17c–19), a shorter-longer // longer-shorter pattern similar to but the reverse of what was found in vv. 5–11 // vv. 12–15.

I have previously noted the difficulties in lineation in v. 20. Decisions were made based on viewing 20bcde as a quatrain, following the introductory, prosaic 20a. Line c expands the subject of line b in a way similar to the expansion of the object of the preposition from line d to line e. The first 3 lines, however, are bound syntactically; the final line both parallels line d (also by the use of the same verbal root) and contrasts it by specifying an object of reliance *other* than that of line d, although one major theme of the whole poem plays on the tension of identifying "the one who struck them." Here it seems to be Assyria in contrast to Yahweh. Yet Yahweh has claimed to be the one working in and through Assyria (for example, v. 5).

Verse 21 concludes this strophe by twice repeating the key word שאר from the beginning of the previous quatrain and focusing it on אל גבור, another divine title that parallels the name in 20e.

With a change to the second person, the second strophe begins with line 22a. Against the versification in MT, I suggest the possibility that 22abc forms a tricolon, followed by the bicolon of vv. 22d–23a and a final bicolon in 23bc. The initial כי in 22a and 23a, as well as the alliteration with other *kap* sounds, holds these lines together. There is interesting play between the roots כלה and חרץ in the bicolon of 22d–23a. The final bicolon (23bc) consists simply of subject plus predicate, and the divine name bridges to the first line of the following strophe.

Verses 24–26

Verse 24 begins with a second לכן (compare line 16a) and introduces the direct discourse of Adonay Yahweh Seba²oth with the כה אמר formula, which is not found previously, in spite of the fact that Yahweh has spoken before (for example, 12c). The third-person narrative returns in v. 26; and if v. 26 is added to the introduction in line 24a, one finds that this narrative section of 48 syllables and 19 stresses is equivalent to the quotation of 47 syllables and 19 stresses. This is very similar to the circular strophic division noted in vv. 12–15, where the narrative around the speech by Assyria was equivalent in length to the speech itself. Here, however, both the speech and the entire unit are slightly less than half as long as those of both vv. 5–11 and 12–15. It is tempting, though speculative, to suggest that Yahweh is depicted as needing half as many words, or, conversely, that the boasting of Assyria is expansive and overdone.

In any case, Yahweh's speech is a tightly constructed unit bound together by the use of שבט and מטה in 24de and זעם and אפי in 25ab. Thus the two construct chains introduced in 5ab, one of which was already broken in 5b, are here further divided, expanded, and articulated. The "rod" and "staff" are identified as belonging to Assyria (מטהו) in 24e, while the "rage" and "anger" are again described as belonging to Yahweh. This tension is precisely the point of the whole passage: Assyria (and secondarily, Judah) does not understand that it is Yahweh who stands behind the events of Assyria's success. Assyria should realize that as Yahweh has given, so he can take

away, and Judah will come to know that as he has taken away, so he can also
give. The narrative conclusion in v. 26 repeats the allusion to the events
of the Exodus, בדרך מצרים (compare 26d with 24f). The final 2 lines begin
with מטה and the root נשא, echoing line 24e.

Verses 27–32

Verse 27 seems to begin a new unit with the same formula found at the
beginning of vv. 20ff. The rest of v. 27 appears to be a tricolon, held
together by the use of מֵעַל in the first 2 lines and of עֹל in the second and
third (see p. 149, translation note to 10:27d, regarding מפני־שמן as part
of this verse). The repetition of the *ᶜayin* and *lamed* sounds carries over
into the next lines as well.

A new strophe begins with v. 28. These five verses (vv. 28–32) present
a list of fourteen place-names, culminating in Zion/Jerusalem. The first
2 lines form a 9 + 7 = 16 bicolon (4 + 3 stresses), with a third-person singular subject.

With v. 29, however, the subject shifts to the plural, and then to the
first-person plural in the following line. In fact, the 10 lines in vv. 29–32a
are five bicola of generally shorter length, a fact that gives the rhetorical
effect of hurried movement. Bicolon 29ab begins and ends with the plural
-û suffix; 29cd begins and ends with feminine verb forms; 30ab begins with
a feminine imperative; 30c–31a uses feminine forms; 31b–32a returns to
the third-person plural, echoing 29a and bringing this subunit to conclusion with another 9 + 7 bicolon.

With 32bc the third-person *singular* returns, linking back to 28ab and
forming an envelope around the five bicola in between. The climax of the
whole strophe is reached with the fourteenth place-name, a double reference to Jerusalem.

That the climactic focal point of this section is therefore Jerusalem is
clearly enhanced by the verse structure. What is not clear is what is being
described by this advance upon daughter Zion from the near north. The
context would suggest Assyria, but this theory has been challenged on historical grounds, since the advance of Sargon in 711 B.C.E. or the better-
documented approach of Sennacherib in 701 B.C.E. was apparently from the
(south)west. Two other suggestions are summarized by Clements (1980b:
117–18): either some other historical occasion or a typical, "stylized" advance of any Mesopotamian power; and Clements, at least, opts for the latter.
Hayes and Irvine (1987: 208–9; so also Scott 1956) argue for the Syro-
Ephraimite attack, relating to the situation described in Isaiah 7, and this
is also a likely possibility.

My analysis of the verse structure, however, indicates that two different subjects are involved. I suggest that the third-person singular, which is the subject in v. 28 and again in 32bc is, in fact, an enemy, perhaps known but intentionally unnamed. On the other hand, the plural verbs are describing the flight of the local inhabitants before the face of the approaching enemy, as indicated by the first-person plural in 29b and the reference to the "inhabitants" in 31b, two "clues" within the first and final bicola of the inside unit. The inhabitants, in turn, are "surrounded" by the enemy, who reaches Jerusalem in 32bc.

Verses 33–34

The unit concludes with a sudden appearance of Yahweh, whose impending action will powerfully stop those who act in haughtiness and pride, presumably those about to attack Jerusalem. As I have already noted, the unit is long for 6 lines, but it is also difficult to lineate any other way. The previous lines were generally shorter, and longer lines here offset them and result in a sense of balancing.

Gross Structure

In the discussion of verse and strophe structure I have already begun to deal with certain larger divisions, which have been found to serve the logical sense of both the parts and the whole. These divisions also correspond to the scribal divisions in the major manuscripts. At least two and usually all three (CL, CA, 1QIsaᵃ) manuscripts indicate demarcation into units consisting of vv. 5–11, 12–15, 16–19, 20–23, 24–26 (here only the Dead Sea scroll marks a break, but it is a major indicator [Oesch 1979: 216]), 27–32, and 33–34.

The following data are noteworthy:

1. The lengths of the first two sections (vv. 5–11 and 12–15) are equivalent:
   - vv. 5–11:   168 syllables, 63 stresses, 72 words
   - vv. 12–15:   168 syllables, 59 stresses, 74 words
2. There is strong indication of inclusio and echoing between vv. 5 and 15.
3. Verses 5–11 begin with הוי, and vv. 12–15 begin with והיה.
4. The lengths of the third and fourth sections are equivalent:
   - vv. 16–19:   103 syllables, 38 stresses, 42 words
   - vv. 20–23:   105 syllables, 43 stresses, 51 words

5. The next two sections are shorter and longer than the previous two, but on average are only slightly longer:

vv. 24–26: 95 syllables, 38 stresses, 43 words

vv. 27–32: 129 syllables, 50 stresses, 56 words

Avg., vv. 16–23: 104 syllables, 40.5 stresses, 46.5 words

Avg., vv. 24–32: 112 syllables, 46.5 stresses, 49.5 words

6. Verses 16–19 begin with לכן, followed by vv. 20–23, which begin with והיה. Similarly, vv. 24–26 begin with לכן and are followed by vv. 27–32, which begin with והיה.

7. There is further use of the inclusio from vv. 5 and 15 in vv. 24–25.

8. The final paragraph forms a climactic conclusion and is structurally overloaded in terms of poetic lines.

9. The repetition of לכן (which is used only seven times in all of Isaiah 2–12 and not since 8:7) in 16a and v. 24, as well as the introductory והיה in vv. 12, 20, and 27, along with other vocabulary links, suggests a sense of unity.

Clearly vv. 5–11 and 12–16 are matched. I have already noted the similarity in the length of each of their strophes, including the matching speeches in the mouth of Assyria, which is preceded by a full strophe in the first stanza and centered around a split strophe in the second stanza. Verse 11 concludes with the boast of Assyria concerning what 'I will do' (root עשׂה), and v. 12 begins with a description of what Adonay will have done (מעשׂהו). The specific vocable אַשּׁוּר, with which the pericope begins (and which has not been used since 8:7) is repeated in the opening lines of the second stanza, 12d.

The concluding lines of the second stanza offer an outstanding example of structural links both within the second stanza and between the first and second stanzas. I have noted certain internal links within the stanza (for example, the root פאר in lines 15a and 12e, root גדל in lines 15b and 12d, root רום in lines 15c and d and 12e). In addition, one should compare the rhetorical questions in 15ab with the ones in the first stanza (vv. 8b–9): in 15ab the first question begins with הלא, which, in the first stanza, introduces the first two rhetorical questions (vv. 8b–9a). The second begins with אם, which introduces the second two questions in 9bc. It is likely that the noun מַשּׂוֹר in 15b is a pun on the use of אַשּׁוּר in vv. 5 and 12, and that the *Hiphil* of root נוף in 15c (הניף; see also מניפו at the end of 15b) puns on חָנֵף in 6a. Finally, the use of שבט and מטה in 15cd form a clear inclusio with 5ab.

Verses 16–19 appear to link to what has gone before, most importantly in regard to thematic considerations, since the לכן now introduces the judgment resultant from the "woe" that has been articulated and developed in vv. 5–15. Moreover, there is a vocabulary link between the repetition of עֵץ in the final verse of vv. 16–19 (19a) and the final verse of vv. 12–15 (15d). There could also be a pun between גַּרְזֶן in 15a and רָזוֹן in 16b.

On the other hand, the length equivalency between vv. 16–19 and vv. 20–23 suggests that these two stanzas are to be matched. Thematically, the message of v. 20 is dependent on the judgment against Assyria pronounced in vv. 16–19. The "remnant" theme of vv. 20–22 is introduced indirectly in reference to the "remnant of the forest of Assyria" in 19a.

Finally, I note the combination of the word לכן, which begins vv. 16–19, with the phrase והיה ביום ההוא, which begins vv. 20–23. This corresponds to the same alternation in the following two stanzas: vv. 24–26 begin with לכן, which is followed in the next section by an introductory והיה ביום ההוא (vv. 27–32).

In spite of these interrelationships, no single, clear structural plan is evident, and several possibilities emerge. One possibility, for example, is that vv. 5–11 and vv. 12–15 are a first part, or panel, and the following four stanzas a second part:

Panel I:
    Stanza 1 (vv. 5–11): 168 syllables, 63 stresses, 72 words
    Stanza 2 (vv. 12–15): 168 syllables, 59 stresses, 74 words

Panel II:
    Stanza 1 (vv. 16–19): 103 syllables, 38 stresses, 42 words
    Stanza 2 (vv. 20–23): 105 syllables, 43 stresses, 51 words
    Stanza 3 (vv. 24–26):   95 syllables, 38 stresses, 43 words
    Stanza 4 (vv. 27–32): 129 syllables, 50 stresses, 56 words

In this scheme, the equivalent length of the two stanzas in panel I is clear, as is the matched length of stanzas 1 and 2 in panel II, as well as the roughly equivalent average length of stanzas 3 and 4. However, the overall length of the two panels is not very close:

Panel I: 336 syllables, 122 stresses, 146 words
Panel II: 432 syllables, 169 stresses, 192 words

However, if the conclusion in vv. 33–34 is added to the total for panel I, the figures are somewhat closer, especially the syllable count:

Panel I (+ conclusion): 392 syllables, 141 stresses, 165 words
Panel II: 432 syllables, 169 stresses, 192 words

On the other hand, it seems likely that vv. 33–34 form the conclusion to the whole piece (and should not be added to panel I). Thus other structural arrangments may be possible. It could be that vv. 5–11 and 12–15 are matched in order to be separated into different parts of the structure so that they complement each other and tie the larger unit together. In fact, if the pieces are arranged as follows, one discovers a further grouping on the basis of the opening lines:

Panel I		*Panel II*	
1. vv. 5–11:	הוי	1. vv. 12–15:	והיה
2. vv. 16–19:	לכן	2. vv. 20–23:	והיה ביום ההוא
3. vv. 24–26:	לכן	3. vv. 27–32:	והיה ביום ההוא

vv. 33–34: הנה

In this scenario, the individual stanzas alternate between the two parts. The 1 stanzas match, the 2 stanzas match, and the 3 stanzas match. However, the total length of the two panels is not equivalent:

Panel I

Stanza 1 (vv. 5–11):	168 syllables,	63 stresses,	72 words
Stanza 2 (vv. 16–19):	103 syllables,	38 stresses,	42 words
Stanza 3 (vv. 24–26):	95 syllables,	38 stresses,	43 words
Totals, Panel I	366 syllables,	139 stresses,	157 words

Panel II

Stanza A′ (vv. 12–15):	168 syllables,	59 stresses,	74 words
Stanza B′ (vv. 20–23):	105 syllables,	43 stresses,	51 words
Stanza C′ (vv. 27–32):	129 syllables,	50 stresses,	56 words
Totals, Panel II	402 syllables,	152 stresses,	181 words

However, the interplay between the four stanzas of each panel that I have labelled stanzas 2 and 3 may suggest a different grouping. Read in a linear way, each "therefore" stanza is followed by one that begins "in that day," so that they might be regrouped as follows:

Panel I		*Panel II*	
Stanza 1 (vv. 5–11)	הוי	Stanza 1′ (vv. 12–15)	והיה
Stanza 2 (vv. 16–19)	לכן	Stanza 3 (vv. 24–26)	לכן
Stanza 2′ (vv. 20–23)	והיה	Stanza 3′ (vv. 27–32)	והיה
	ביום ההוא		ביום ההוא

Conclusion (vv. 33–34) הנה

Adding the factor of length to this scheme, there is a much better sense of equivalency, although in this case the stress and word totals are closer than the syllable counts:

Panel I

Stanza 1	(vv. 5–11):	168 syllables,	63 stresses,	72 words
Stanza 2	(vv. 16–19):	103 syllables,	38 stresses,	42 words
Stanza 2′	(vv. 20–23):	105 syllables,	43 stresses,	51 words
Totals, Panel I		376 syllables,	144 stresses,	165 words

Panel II

Stanza 1′	(vv. 12–15):	168 syllables,	59 stresses,	74 words
Stanza 3	(vv. 24–26):	95 syllables,	38 stresses,	43 words
Stanza 3′	(vv. 27–32):	129 syllables,	50 stresses,	56 words
Totals, Panel II		392 syllables,	147 stresses,	173 words

Although one cannot be decisive about any of these structural schemes, there can be little doubt that the piece is carefully and intricately interwoven. There is a clear relationship between vv. 5–11 and vv. 12–15, which seem to form a unit together and yet also possibly form the structural basis for two major divisions. Likewise, vv. 16–19 and vv. 20–23 are matched, although they stand in relationship to vv. 24–26 and vv. 27–32 as well. These latter two stanzas, added together, total 224 syllables (88 stresses, 99 words), a sum that exactly matches the sum of vv. 5–11 added to the concluding vv. 33–34: 224 syllables (82 stresses, 91 words). This fact may indicate a further relationship between the beginning stanza and the conclusion.

Thought Progression

The structural interrelationships also carry over into the thematic progression of the piece. The major focus is certainly the judgment against Assyria, introduced by the initial הוֹי in 10:5. (The fact that this is a thematic link to the previous material will be discussed below on p. 187) There are two "therefore" (לָכֵן) sections, which should logically follow up the "woe." However, the "woe" stanza is followed by a second stanza, introduced by וְהָיָה. Each "therefore" stanza is followed by a stanza introduced by וְהָיָה בַּיּוֹם הַהוּא. The general theme of the entire poem is that Assyria, who was used as the "rod" of Yahweh to punish Judah, will fall because of her arrogant boast in taking credit for what was Yahweh's doing, and that Judah and Jerusalem will have hope, but only after "righteous" judgment and punishment.

Verses 5–11 and 12–15 match two speeches in the mouth of Assyria to show her arrogance, the result of which follows in the "therefore" section of vv. 16–19. Here Yahweh will "burn" against Assyria, reducing her to a small and insignificant "remnant" (v. 19).

Verses 20–23 follow, indicating the future result (וְהָיָה) of Yahweh's destruction of Assyria: a "remnant" of Israel will return and learn to trust
Yahweh, whose "righteous destruction" falls upon both Israel and Assyria.
This hopeful theme is carried over into the following "therefore" section,
which also applies the destruction of Assyria as a word of comfort ("fear
not," line 24b) to Zion. However, vv. 27–32 reiterate the motif of the as-
sault and attack on Judah, forcing refugees from Judean cities and culminating in the threat to Jerusalem, all of which may well indicate that the
threat of enemy advance has not yet passed.

Finally, vv. 33–34 bring the whole section to conclusion with an introductory הִנֵּה. Here the prophet makes final allusion to the destruction
of Assyria, for which the metaphor of the forest is echoed from v. 18.
These concluding verses clearly counter the attack described in vv. 27–32
and return to the major theme of Yahweh's power not only against Assyria
but against any and all who are רָמֵי הַקּוֹמָה or גְּבֹהִים. With the use of the
verb שָׁפֵל (33d) this vocabulary is reminiscent of a major theme found in
Isa 2:11, 17; and 5:15. The final יִפֹּלוּ echoes the exact word with which
the previous pericope ended (10:4b) and which served there as an inclusio
with 9:7b.

Following the scheme proposed on p. 163, this outline summarizes
what has just been said in a more visual manner.

Isaiah 11:1–16

Text

		Syllable Count MT		Stress Count MT	
11:1a	וְיָצָא חֹטֶר מִגֵּזַע יִשָׁי	8	10	4	4
b	וְנֵצֶר מִשָּׁרָשָׁיו יִפְרֶה׃	8	9	3	3
2a	וְנָחָה עָלָיו רוּחַ יְהוָה	8	9	3/(4)	4
b	רוּחַ חָכְמָה וּבִינָה	6	7	3	3
c	רוּחַ עֵצָה וּגְבוּרָה	(6)/7	8	3	3
d	רוּחַ דַּעַת וְיִרְאַת יְהוָה׃	7	9	3	4
3a	וַהֲרִיחוֹ בְּיִרְאַת יְהוָה	(8)/9	9	3	3
b	וְלֹא־לְמַרְאֵה עֵינָיו יִשְׁפּוֹט	9	9	3	3
c	וְלֹא־לְמִשְׁמַע אָזְנָיו יוֹכִיחַ׃	9	10	3	3
4a	וְשָׁפַט בְּצֶדֶק דַּלִּים	7	8	3/(4)	4
b	וְהוֹכִיחַ בְּמִישׁוֹר לְעַנְוֵי־אָרֶץ	10	12	3	3

Panel I

   Stanza 1 (vv. 5–11) הוי   Woe to Assyria
     Strophe A (vv. 5–7)   Assyria is Yahweh's rod to punish his
                                     own people.
     Strophe B (vv. 8–11)   Assyria's arrogant boast
   Stanza 2 (vv. 12–15) והיה   What will happen
     Strophe A (vv. 12+15)   Assyria will be punished
     Strophe B (vv. 13–14)   Assyria's arrogant boast

Panel II

   Stanza 1 (vv. 16–19) לכן   Lord Yahweh vs. Assyria
   Stanza 2 (vv. 20–23) והיה ביום ההוא A hope for a remnant *after*
                                     righteous destruction
   Stanza 3 (vv. 24–26) לכן   Hope for Zion "in a little while,"
                                     after the curse is completed
   Stanza 4 (vv. 27–32) והיה ביום ההוא Jerusalem still under threat
                                     of enemy attack
   Conclusion (vv. 33–34)   Yahweh punishes haughtiness and
                                     arrogance

Translation

11:1a And a shoot will go out from the stump of Jesse,
    b and a branch from his roots will bear fruit,
    2a and the spirit of Yahweh will rest upon him:
    b the spirit of the wisdom and of the understanding (of Yahweh),
    c the spirit of the counsel and of the strength (of Yahweh),
    d the spirit of the knowledge (of) and of the fear of Yahweh;
    3a and he will inspire him in the fear of Yahweh.
    b Not by what his eyes see will he judge,
    c nor by what his ears hear will he decide.
    4a But he will judge—in righteousness—the (earth's) poor,
    b and he will decide—in fairness—for the earth's afflicted.

c	וְהִכָּה־אֶרֶץ בְּשֵׁבֶט פִּיו	7	9	3	3
d	וּבְרוּחַ שְׂפָתָיו יָמִית רָשָׁע׃	(9)/10	11	4	4
5a	וְהָיָה צֶדֶק אֵזוֹר מָתְנָיו	8	9	4	4
b	וְהָאֱמוּנָה אֵזוֹר חֲלָצָיו׃	10	10	3	3
6a	וְגָר זְאֵב עִם־כֶּבֶשׂ	6	7	3	3
b	וְנָמֵר עִם־גְּדִי יִרְבָּץ	8	8	3	3
c	וְעֵגֶל וּכְפִיר וּמְרִיא יַחְדָּו	(8)/10	11	4	4
d	וְנַעַר קָטֹן נֹהֵג בָּם׃	7	8	3/(4)	4
7a	וּפָרָה וָדֹב תִּרְעֶינָה	8	8	3	3
b	יַחְדָּו יִרְבְּצוּ יַלְדֵיהֶן	8	8	3	3
c	וְאַרְיֵה כַּבָּקָר יֹאכַל־תֶּבֶן׃	9	10	3	3
8a	וְשִׁעֲשַׁע יוֹנֵק עַל־חֻר פָּתֶן	8	10	4	4
b	וְעַל מְאוּרַת צִפְעוֹנִי	8	8	3	3
c	גָּמוּל יָדוֹ הָדָה׃	6	6	3	3
9a	לֹא־יָרֵעוּ וְלֹא־יַשְׁחִיתוּ	9	9	2	2
b	בְּכָל־הַר קָדְשִׁי	5	5	2	2
c	כִּי־מָלְאָה הָאָרֶץ	6	7	2	2
d	דֵּעָה אֶת־יְהֹוָה	5	5	2	2
e	כַּמַּיִם לַיָּם מְכַסִּים׃	7	8	3	3
Verse 1–9		(228)/233	257	91/94	95
10a	וְהָיָה בַּיּוֹם הַהוּא	7	7	3	3
b	שֹׁרֶשׁ יִשַׁי אֲשֶׁר עֹמֵד	7	8	4	4
c	לְנֵס עַמִּים	4	4	2	2
d	אֵלָיו גּוֹיִם יִדְרֹשׁוּ	7	7	3	3
e	וְהָיְתָה מְנֻחָתוֹ כָּבוֹד׃	10	10	3	3
Verse 10		35	36	15	15
11a	וְהָיָה בַּיּוֹם הַהוּא	7	7	3	3
b	יוֹסִיף אֲדֹנָי שֵׁנִית יָדוֹ	9	9	4	4
c	לִקְנוֹת אֶת־שְׁאָר עַמּוֹ	7	7	3	3
d	אֲשֶׁר יִשָּׁאֵר מֵאַשּׁוּר	8	8	3	3
e	וּמִמִּצְרַיִם וּמִפַּתְרוֹס	8	9	2	2
f	וּמִכּוּשׁ וּמֵעֵילָם	7	7	2	2
g	וּמִשִּׁנְעָר וּמֵחֲמָת	8	8	2	2
h	וּמֵאִיֵּי הַיָּם׃	6	6	2	2
12a	וְנָשָׂא נֵס לַגּוֹיִם	7	7	3	3
b	וְאָסַף נִדְחֵי יִשְׂרָאֵל	8	8	3	3
c	וּנְפֻצוֹת יְהוּדָה יְקַבֵּץ	(9)/10	10	3	3
d	מֵאַרְבַּע כַּנְפוֹת הָאָרֶץ׃	7	8	3	3

c   He will strike the (wicked of the) earth with the staff of his mouth,

d   and with the spirit ('breath') of his lips he will put to death the wicked (of the earth).

5a   Righteousness will be the belt for his loins

b   and truth the belt for his waist.

6a   Wolf will stay with lamb;

b   leopard will rest with goat.

c   Calf and young lion and yearling together—

d   a young lad will lead them.

7a   Cow and bear will graze;

b   together their young will rest.

c   Lion(s) will eat straw like cattle.

8a   An infant will play upon a cobra's hole;

b   upon a viper's den

c   a weaned child will put his hand.

9a   They will do no evil; they will do no harm

b   on the whole of my holy mountain,

c   because the earth will have become filled

d   with knowing Yahweh

e   as the waters cover the sea.

10a   It will happen **on that day**—

b   the root of Jesse, which will be standing,

c   will become a standard for the nations—

d   to it the nations will come seeking.

e   And its place of rest will be "glory."

11a   It will happen **on that day**—

b   Adonay will [take] a second time his hand

c   to acquire the remnant of his people

d   that remains from Asshur

e   and from Egypt and from Pathros

f   and from Cush and from Elam,

g   from Shinar and from Hamath

h   and from the islands of the sea.

12a   He will raise a standard for the nations.

b   He will gather the outcasts of Israel,

c   and the shattered of Judah he will bring together

d   from the four corners of the earth.

13a	וְסָרָה֙ קִנְאַ֣ת אֶפְרַ֔יִם	7	8	3	3
b	וְצֹרְרֵ֥י יְהוּדָ֖ה יִכָּרֵ֑תוּ	11	11	3	3
c	אֶפְרַ֙יִם֙ לֹֽא־יְקַנֵּ֣א אֶת־יְהוּדָ֔ה	10	11	3	3
d	וִיהוּדָ֖ה לֹֽא־יָצֹ֥ר אֶת־אֶפְרָֽיִם׃	9	10	3	3
14a	וְעָפ֨וּ בְכָתֵ֤ף פְּלִשְׁתִּים֙ יָ֔מָּה	11	11	4	4
b	יַחְדָּ֖ו יָבֹ֣זּוּ אֶת־בְּנֵי־קֶ֑דֶם	9	10	3	3
c	אֱד֤וֹם וּמוֹאָב֙ מִשְׁל֣וֹחַ יָדָ֔ם	9	9	4	4
d	וּבְנֵ֥י עַמּ֖וֹן מִשְׁמַעְתָּֽם׃	(7)/8	8	3	3
15a	וְהֶחֱרִ֣ים יְהֹוָ֗ה אֵ֚ת לְשׁ֣וֹן יָם־מִצְרַ֔יִם	11	13	4	5
b	וְהֵנִ֥יף יָד֛וֹ עַל־הַנָּהָ֖ר	9	9	3	3
c	בַּעְיָ֣ם רוּח֑וֹ	4	4	2	2
d	וְהִכָּ֙הוּ֙ לְשִׁבְעָ֣ה נְחָלִ֔ים	10	10	3	3
e	וְהִדְרִ֖יךְ בַּנְּעָלִֽים׃	7	7	2	2
16a	וְהָיְתָ֣ה מְסִלָּ֔ה לִשְׁאָ֖ר עַמּ֑וֹ	11	11	4	4
b	אֲשֶׁ֥ר יִשָּׁאֵ֖ר מֵאַשּׁ֑וּר	8	8	3	3
c	כַּאֲשֶׁ֤ר הָֽיְתָה֙ לְיִשְׂרָאֵ֔ל	9	10	3	3
d	בְּי֥וֹם עֲלֹת֖וֹ מֵאֶ֥רֶץ מִצְרָֽיִם׃	9	11	4	4

Verses 11–16		(242)/244	255	87	88

Totals		(505)/512	548	193/(196)	198
		Syllables	MT	Stresses	MT

Notes on Translation and Text

11:3a. **"and he will inspire him"** The translation of וַהֲרִיחוֹ is difficult. The form is *hiphil* infinitive construct of the root *ריח/רוח, which
means 'smell' transitively. There could well be allusion to the sacrificial
idiom with רֵיחַ 'his (soothing, acceptable to God) smell', but the *Hiphil*
form is more likely to be understood in the transitive sense (compare
Amos 5:21). The prevailing suggestion is to read the suffix as subjective:
'his "delighting" (= he delights) in . . .' . Based on the apparent inclusio
that this line forms with line 2a around the three pairs (compare 6:2!)
of construct chains (and contra the suggestion in BHS to delete due to
dittography!), I read 3a in connection with 2a: "spirit of Yahweh" is subject, the pronoun suffix on the *hiphil* verb is objective, and, whatever
lexical data are chosen to translate the verb, it is connected to and likely
a play on the noun רוּחַ.

13a	The jealousy of Ephraim will go away,
b	and the harassers of Judah will be cut off.
c	Ephraim will not be jealous of Judah,
d	and Judah will not harass Ephraim.
14a	They will fly ('swoop down') on the shoulder of the Philistines on the west.
b	Together they will plunder the sons of the East:
c	Edom and Moab will be under their power,
d	and the Ammonites will obey them.
15a	Yahweh will dry up the tongue of the sea of Egypt,
b	and he will wave his hand over the "River"
c	with the strength of his wind.
d	He will strike it into seven streams
e	and make it possible to walk thereon with sandals.
16a	There will be a highway for the remnant of his people
b	who remain from Asshur,
c	as there was for Israel
d	**in the day** they came up from the land of Egypt.

11:4cd. "(wicked of the) earth . . . wicked (of the earth)" I combine the phrase רשע ארץ from 4c and 4d into a construct chain, which has been split across this bicolon. It is parallel to the chain ענוי־ארץ in the previous line (4b).

11:8c. "will put" The verb הדה is a hapax legomenon. The meaning is suggested only by context.

11:9d. "knowing" Read the noun as verbal, marked by the use of the object marker.

11:10e. "glory" Translated literally, if awkwardly. While English favors an adjective, the Hebrew suggests a noun.

11:13ab. "jealousy of . . . harassers of" The genitives are subjective: "Ephraim's jealousy" and "those within Judah who harass (Ephraim) . . . ," as indicated by lines c and d.

11:15c. **"with the strength"** בעים is without clear explanation. Hummel (1957: 94) suggests the root בעה ('boiling of water') plus enclitic *mem*. The context indicates something along the lines of 'power, might'. Watts (1985: 178) gives a helpful survey of suggestions.

Lineation

Several difficult decisions should be noted. Verse 9 is problematic (see below, p. 171), since there is little parallelism. The verse could be divided into 4 lines, with cd combined, giving an 11-syllable, 4-stress line. Verse 10 could be lineated as a quatrain; 35 syllables is perhaps closer to 4 lines than 5. Yet the accent count is right for 5 lines of 3 stresses. Metrically, 10bc would better be divided after the relative pronoun, yielding lines of 5 + 6 syllables and 3 + 3 stresses.

Verse 11defgh is difficult to divide, yet, as shown, it falls quite neatly into the 5-line pattern, with three pairs of place-names enclosed by one each in the first and final lines. Verse 15abc has been lineated as shown, even though the final line is rather short. As only 2 lines, the verse would be a 11 + 13 = 24 / 4 + 5 = 9 bicolon, which is too long. The 24 syllables and 9 stresses, however, are exactly right for 3 lines, even if unevenly balanced, and one could easily divide into 3 lines of 8 syllables, with enjambment. Line 16a could be divided into 2 lines of 7 + 4 syllables and 2 + 2 stresses.

Thus the range falls between 62 and 65 lines. The range of the syllable count, 505–12, suggests 63–64 lines, although 63 lines of 8 syllables should produce 504 syllables, one short of the minimum. Thus I show 64 lines and 512 syllables. The larger structure (vv. 1–9, v. 10, vv. 11–16; see below, p. 173) might divide them into units of 30 + 4 + 30. My lineation, however, shows 30 + 5 + 29, although vv. 1–9 have fewer syllables than vv. 11–16. Nevertheless, I have tried to retain grammatical divisions and to avoid enjambment, and in spite of this method, the total number of lines corresponds to the syllable total.

Syllable and Stress Counts

The total syllable count is 505/512 (MT: 548). The lineation of 64 cola (× 8) would suggest a total of 512, so I shall consider the longer counts in each case. The tabulation of line lengths reveals a familiar pattern:

4-syllable lines:	2	8-syllable lines:	15
5-syllable lines:	2	9-syllable lines:	12
6-syllable lines:	5	10-syllable lines:	8
7-syllable lines:	16	11-syllable lines:	4

Of the 64 lines,

> 23.4% (15 lines) have 8 syllables,
> 67.2% (43 lines) have 7–9 syllables,
> 87.5% (56 lines) have 6–10 syllables.

The median line length is 8 syllables.
The average line length is 8.00 syllables per line (512/64).

The total stress count shows a range of 193 to 196 (MT: 198). Five cases of an apparent extra stress occur in vv. 1–9, where line lengths are somewhat short for the number of accents. In vv. 11–16, however, the number of stresses is exactly 3 per line, although here the number of syllables is high for the number of lines. Thus, taken as a whole, the totals balance out, and the overall minimum count is quite close to what would be expected for 64 lines of 3 stresses (=192). Again the dominance of the 3-stress line is clear, with 2- and 4-stress lines fairly evenly balanced:

> 2-stress cola: 11 (17.2%)
> 3-stress cola: 41 (64.1%)
> 4-stress cola: 12 (18.8%)

Thus 64 (100%) of the lines have 2–4 stresses.
The average number of stresses per colon is 3.01 (= 3.00).

Prose Particles

The prose particle count in vv. 1–9 is 2.80%, very low and indicative of poetry. Of the three particles (out of 107 words), two are the article and one is the object marker. In vv. 10–16, however, there are five articles, five object markers, and four relative pronouns, for a particle percentage of 12.5% (14/112 words), which is much closer to a prose pattern, although poetic features are apparent and important.

In a way similar to what has been observed in dealing with lineation and line lengths, therefore, the two major parts of the poem display quite different features. However, if one takes the entire chapter as a whole, these figures combine into a total prose particle count of 7.76% (17/219), again falling into the 5–10% range suggested for prophetic rhetoric.

Verse and Strophe Structure

Verses 1–5

Rather regular bicola dominate this initial strophe, with an additional stress in the first and final bicola. The longest bicolon falls in the middle, where the 9 + 9 syllables (3 + 3 stresses) of 3bc form a bicolon that displays linear parallelism with exact corrrespondence between all parts, both semantically and syntactically. Inverted word order emphasizes the adverbial phrases that begin each line.

Lines 1ab are chiastic; the verbs come at the beginning and end, a perfect *waw*-consecutive followed by an imperfect. The subjects are semantically parallel; "Jesse" is echoed in the second line by the use of the pronoun suffix.

I consider vv. 2–3a a 5-line verse that consists of a split bicolon (lines 2a + 3a) wrapped around a tricolon (2bcd). The three middle lines are held together by repetition of the initial word, each followed by parallel pairs as compound *nomina recta*. The final pair is expanded by the further bound form יראת, and it culminates in the divine name יהוה, which thus becomes the final *nomen rectum* for all the pairs in 2bcd (see translation).

As suggested in the translation notes (p. 166, note to 11:3a), line 3a seems to form an envelope with 2a through the use of a verb form from the root רוח and the repetition of יהוה. In line 2a the divine name is part of the subject; in 3a it is in the predicate. Line 3a links to 2d by repeating יראת, and lines 2a + 3a link to 2bcd by the use of רוח. All this forms a tightly knit unit with the divine name used three times—once in each line of the bicolon, and once in the tricolon—and רוח used once in every line.

Following lines 3bc, lines 4ab repeat the use of the verbal roots שפט and יכח, now as an afformative and in the initial position. The noun ארץ likely serves double duty with the first line. Together, vv. 3bc–4ab form a quatrain of 35 syllables and 12 stresses.

Lines 4cd pick up the use of ענוי־ארץ, parallel to the "poor of the earth," in a broken or separated construct chain spread over the bicolon (see translation note to 11:4cd, p. 167). In 4d the sixth use of the root רוח appears, forming an inclusio with v. 2. Lines 5ab conclude the strophe by focusing no longer on the work but on the description of the person of this descendant of Jesse. Perhaps the article is added in the second line for an alliterative effect. Taken together, vv. 4cd–5ab form another quatrain of 35 syllables (compare vv. 3bc–4ab), although here I find 14 stresses.

Verses 6–8

Lines 6ab also show chiastic parallelism, with the verbs at beginning and end, a perfect *waw*-consecutive followed by an imperfect, and, along with the introduction of the animal motif, suggests a new strophe. The bicola are quite regular and balanced; 5 of the 10 lines have 8 syllables and 3 stresses.

The middle bicolon (7ab), however, is the only 16/6 bicolon, and it draws further attention by combining in 7b the verbal root רבץ (used in 6b) and the word יחדו (used in 7c). This verse may be transitional, since the quatrain formed by 6abcd would match the 4 lines in 7c–8abc in having 31 syllables and 13 stresses each.

Verse 9

I suggest that v. 9 forms an independent strophe (see below, p. 174). Although prosaic, the verse is easily broken down into poetic lines. The first is somewhat long for a 2-stress colon, and, possibly, lines c + d could be combined into a longer 11/4 line. While 32 syllables may suggest 4 lines, my method takes into consideration the fact that shorter lines here will balance longer lines later in the poetic piece.

The use of two prose particles (one article and one object marker) adds to the unusual nature of this verse; it appears to form a conclusion. The repetition of דעה and the use of the divine name, not heard since 3a, form an inclusio with 2d and the first strophe.

Verse 10

Verse 10 forms an independent, transitional verse (see below, p. 173). Like v. 9, it is prosaic and somewhat arbitrarily delineated. The 35 syllables suggest 4–5 lines; the 15 stresses confirms my five-cola lineation, but the division of 10bc is very difficult. Metrically (see above, p. 168) one should divide after the relative pronoun. It is also possible to divide before it, leaving 2 lines of 3 + 8 syllables (2 + 4 stresses). My lineation places the short line (10c) in the middle.

Thus the *lamed* that begins line c may link syntactically with the initial verb instead of with the participle עמד in the previous line: not "standing as a standard," but "it will become a standard," as my translation has suggested. Lines c and d are bound by the word pair גוים//עמים. The final line begins with the perfect *waw*-consecutive of root היה, as did the first line.

Verses 11–12

As shown, this strophe divides into three quatrains of roughly equal length. Verse 11abcd, while virtually a prose sentence, breaks down neatly into 4 lines, the second pair incorporating the relative pronoun into the sound play of the *ʾalep-šin-reš* sounds. The verse consists of 31 syllables and 13 stresses.

The second quatrain is simply a list of seven place-names, divided into 2 + 2 + 2 + 1, although the final description is expanded to contain 2 stresses as well. It is possible that the three pairs plus one are intended to echo in reverse the one plus three pairs of *nomina recta* used with רוח in 2a + bcd. The 29 syllables are roughly the same length as both v. 11abcd and v. 12.

The 32 syllables of v. 12 (12 stresses) conclude this strophe and echo the נס motif from v. 10c. Since the middle bicolon is chiastically structured, bound by the verbs קבץ//אסף, it is possible that lines 12a and d form a split bicolon that could be read together: "he will raise a standard to the nations from the four corners of the earth," possibly implying that it is not just the remnant of Israel and Judah that will be gathered.

Verses 13–14

This strophe divides as two quatrains of equal length. The initial bicolon is chiastically structured, with the afformative/preformative verb alternation forming the outside terms. Lines 13cd pick up the two roots from the nouns in 13ab (קנא and צרר) and use their verbal forms in the second bicolon.

The "togetherness" of Ephraim and Judah is accented in v. 14, where יחדו echoes its use in vv. 6–7. The 37 syllables (14 stresses) of v. 14 match the 37 syllables (and 12 stresses) of v. 13. Lines 14ab are held together by the "west-east" pair, and lines cd are parallel. The "sons of Ammon" balance the combination of Edom and Moab and together expand the "sons of the East" from line b.

Verses 15–16

Verse 15 is lineated as a tricolon plus a bicolon (see above, p. 168). Although line lengths are unbalanced, 41 syllables and 14 stresses likely represent five cola. The internal structure, however, is rather intricate. Lines 15a + c combine as a bicolon (11/4 + 4/2 = 15/6): "Yahweh will dry up the tongue of the sea of Egypt . . . by the strength of his wind." The middle line of the tricolon (15b) actually goes with the following bicolon in 15de: "he will wave his hand over the 'River'; he will strike it into seven streams. . . ." The final line (15e) likely is a conclusion to the double thought expressed by the 4 previous lines: "he will make it possible to walk thereon with sandals." Thus the 5 lines do not break down into a 3 + 2 pattern, but a 4 + 1, ABABC pattern.

The final quatrain, with 37 syllables and 14 stresses, roughly matches the previous 5-line unit. The first bicolon forms an inclusio with 11cd, repeating the second line exactly. The second bicolon continues the sound play with כאשר (and likely also ישראל) and uses the verb form היתה from line 16a, which also links back to the transitional v. 10(e). The concluding reference to the Exodus from Egypt also echoes the "second exodus" theme with which this stanza began in v. 11. The idiom ביום + infinitive construct picks up the phrase ביום ההוא of both 11a and 10a. The phrase מארץ מצרים in 16d matches the manifold use of מן in 11d–h, which culminates in מארבע כנפות הארץ in 12d.

Gross Structure

It seems relatively clear that chap. 11 forms a single unit, although there are certainly connections with what precedes and follows. I have already suggested the transitional nature of 10:33–34, and on the other side, chap. 12 continues the theme of a renewed exodus under the motif of "that day." Both the CL and CA show a *setumah* break at the end of chap. 10, although it should be noted that neither shows a break after chap. 11. 1QIsaᵃ, however, shows a major break at both beginning and end of chap. 11.

Within the chapter, the manuscripts confirm the pivotal role of v. 10, which is set off by *petuchah* markers in CL, by *setumah* markers in CA, and by a major and minor break in the Dead Sea scroll. Since CL and CA show no break at the end of the chapter, the possiblity should be kept in mind that 11:10–11ff. may relate also to chap. 12.

I have already observed some differences between 11:1–9 and 11:10–16 in terms of line length, verse length, and poetic particles. Nevertheless, certain thematic and vocabulary links between these two major sections have been noted, and the combination of them has displayed an overall balancing effect regarding the apparent diversities in line lengths and poetic particle percentage.

Furthermore, if v. 10 is separated from vv. 10–16, as it is in all three manuscripts, it becomes a clear hinge between vv. 1–9 and vv. 11–16. In common with the verses before, it reiterates the exact terms שֶׁרֶשׁ יִשַׁי, which appear in 1ab and do not occur in what follows. Further, the repetition of the root נוח in the noun מְנֻחָתוֹ is an echo of the use of the verb in 2a.

On the other hand, v. 10 connects this "rootstock of Jesse" with the נֵס עַמִּים (10c), which, along with the use of גּוֹיִם, is a clear link to 12a. The idea of the root left standing (10b) complements the theme of the remnant, which is a major motif in vv. 11–16. Finally, I note the use of the וְהָיָה form in 10a and 11a (also line 5a in vv. 1–9 contains וְהָיָה), and of וְהָיְתָה in 10e and 16a.

I conclude, therefore, that chap. 11 is a unified whole, held together by v. 10, which functions as a "hinged pivot," linking both backwards and forwards. If both halves are considered a "stanza," they are of somewhat equivalent length:

Stanza 1 (vv. 1–9): 233 syllables, 91 stresses, 107 words
Pivot (v. 10): 35 syllables, 15 stresses, 15 words
Stanza 2 (vv. 11–16): 244 syllables, 87 stresses, 97 words

Interestingly, stanza 2 has 9 more syllables, but 4 fewer stresses and 10 fewer words than stanza 1. The overall balance and interrelationship of all three measurements indicates eqivalency.

With this general structure in mind, the following further observations are made:

1. Each stanza consists of three strophes of varying lengths:

    Stanza 1 (vv. 1–9)
       Strophe A: vv.   1–5   123 syllables and 48 stresses
       Strophe B: vv.   6–8   78 syllables and 32 stresses
       Strophe C: v.   9   32 syllables and 11 stresses
    Stanza 2 (vv. 11–16)
       Strophe A: vv. 11–12 92 syllables and 33 stresses
       Strophe B: vv. 13–14 74 syllables and 26 stresses
       Strophe C: vv. 15–16 78 syllables and 28 stresses

2. The seven uses of the noun רוח are divided between the first and last strophes: 6× in stanza 1, strophe A and 1×(15c) in stanza 2, strophe C. Note also the use of the afformative of the root נכה in 4c and 15d.

3. Of the six divine names found in this chapter, four of the five uses of יהוה are in these same first and last strophes, and they are again divided unevenly: 3× in stanza 1 A (2a, 2d, 3a) and 1× in stanza 2 C (15a).

4. The two remaining divine names are found at the end of stanza 1 (strophe C, line 9d: יהוה) and the beginning of stanza 2 (strophe A, line 11b, אדני).

5. The middle strophes (B) of each stanza contain no divine names. Here one finds three uses of the word יחדו, (which is used only seven other times in Isaiah 1–39, two other times in chaps. 2–12), twice in stanza 1 B (6c and 7b) and one in stanza 2 B (14b).

6. The final strophe (vv. 15–16) indicates an inclusio not only with the beginning of the second stanza but also with the first stanza (see items 2 and 3 above). The word מי, which appears in this final strophe (15a), is used in every strophe of the second stanza (11h, 14a [in the directive ימה]), and also in the final line of the first stanza, further binding the two stanzas together.

Thus the whole of chap. 11 displays a much greater sense of structural unity than may appear at first glance. In fact, there is a chiastic pattern between the three strophes of each stanza: ABC:CBA, with v. 10 forming a middle, hinged pivot that links to the material both before and after this verse.

While the strophes in the second stanza are roughly equivalent in length, the three strophes in the first stanza are not. However, stanza A (123/48) plus stanza C (32/11) together (155/59) equal twice stanza B (78/32 × 2 = 156/64), indicating some sense of balance among the three.

Finally, there is a thematic unity among and between the parts. Stanza 1 deals with the establishment of the peaceful reign under the scion of Jesse, in the midst of which (strophe B) there will be peace between otherwise natural and bitter enemies. Stanza 2 focuses attention on the future, reconstructed remnant of Israel/Judah, in the midst of which (strophe B) the bitter enmity between Ephraim and Judah is replaced by peace and cooperative conquest and dominance.

Thought Progression

The major theme of the chapter assumes an Assyrian conquest (although it may be perceived as a future event), from which a remnant of both the Davidic line and the Israelite populace will be restored. The image of a second exodus and conquest lies at the heart of the second stanza. The image of new creation and of a peace even within nature lies at the heart of the first stanza. Foreign nations—indeed all the earth—will not be the only source of the remnant (11e–h) but also those who respond to the raising of Yahweh's standard. Thus not only the remnant but also the nations themselves will seek the root of Jesse, from whom universal peace flows and fills the earth "as the waters cover the sea" (line 9c).

In the structural middle of the entire poem the rallying point is found, the נס עמים, who will stand as (become?) a standard even for the "nations." A second reference to the "root" of Jesse (compare v. 1) again traces the lineage not simply to David but to the generation before David. The central focus of the poem places hope in something greater and more "radical" than simply another descendant of the Davidic line: clearly a "second David" is in mind.

The following thematic outline is proposed:

Stanza 1: (vv. 1–9) The perfect king to come
Strophe A: (vv. 1–5) Perfect rule, empowered by the Spirit (breath) of Yahweh: ultimate "justice and righteousness"
Strophe B: (vv. 7–8) Perfect peace
Strophe C: (v. 9) Peace of the holy mountain will cover the earth
PIVOT: (v. 10) This "root of Jesse" will become a standard for all the nations to seek
Stanza 2: (vv. 11–16) A remnant will return
Strophe A: (vv. 11–12) As in the Exodus from Egypt, a remnant will return from Assyria and ultimately from all lands
Strophe B: (vv. 13–14) Reunified, "all Israel" will be at peace with itself and will reestablish the conquest
Strophe C: (vv. 15–16) As at the Reed Sea, Yahweh will act by the power of his wind (breath)

Isaiah 12:1–6

Text

		Syllable Count	MT	Stress Count	MT
12:1a	וְאָמַרְתָּ בַּיּוֹם הַהוּא	(7)/ 8	8	3	3
b	אוֹדְךָ יְהוָה כִּי אָנַפְתָּ בִּי	(8)/ 9/(10)	10	4	5
c	יָשֹׁב אַפְּךָ וּתְנַחֲמֵנִי׃	(9)/10/(11)	11	3	3
2a	הִנֵּה אֵל יְשׁוּעָתִי	7	7	3	3
b	אֶבְטַח וְלֹא אֶפְחָד	6	6	3	3
c	כִּי־עָזִּי וְזִמְרָת יָהּ יְהוָה	9	9	4	4
d	וַיְהִי־לִי לִישׁוּעָה׃	(6)/ 7	7	2	2
3a	וּשְׁאַבְתֶּם־מַיִם בְּשָׂשׂוֹן	(7)/ 8	9	2/(3)	2
b	מִמַּעַיְנֵי הַיְשׁוּעָה׃	(7)/ 8/(9)	7	2	2
Verses 1–3		66/ 75 =72	74	26/(27)	27
4a	וַאֲמַרְתֶּם בַּיּוֹם הַהוּא	(7)/8	8	3	3
b	הוֹדוּ לַיהוָה	5	5	2	2
c	קִרְאוּ בִשְׁמוֹ	4	4	2	2
d	הוֹדִיעוּ בָעַמִּים עֲלִילֹתָיו	10	10	3	3
e	הַזְכִּירוּ כִּי נִשְׂגָּב שְׁמוֹ׃	8	8	3	4
5a	זַמְּרוּ יְהוָה כִּי גֵאוּת עָשָׂה	10	10	4	5
b	מְיֻדַּעַת זֹאת בְּכָל־הָאָרֶץ׃	7/(8)	10	3	3
6a	צַהֲלִי וָרֹנִּי יוֹשֶׁבֶת צִיּוֹן	9	11	4	4
b	כִּי־גָדוֹל בְּקִרְבֵּךְ קְדוֹשׁ יִשְׂרָאֵל׃	11	11	4	4
Verses 4–6		71/73 =72	77	28	30
Totals		137/148 =144	151	54(55)	57
		Syllables	MT	Stresses	MT

Notes on Translation and Text

12:1c. **"let"** Despite the suggestion of BHS, the form should be read
as the jussive that it is (contra LXX), and so also the following ותנחמני.
Wildberger (1972: 477) is correct in admitting that the jussive and im-

Translation

12:1a   You (sg.) will say **in that day,**

b   "I will thank you, Yahweh, for you were angry at me;

c   let your anger turn back and may you comfort me!

2a   Look, O God of my salvation,

b   I will trust and not be afraid!

c   for 'my strength and my protection is Yah,' O Yahweh,

d   'and he has become my salvation.'"

3a   You (pl.) will draw water with joy

b   from the springs of salvation,

4a   and you (pl.) will say **in that day,**

b   "Give thanks to Yahweh!

c   Call on his name!

d   Make known among the nations his deeds!

e   Cause to be remembered that his name is exalted!

5a   Sing of Yahweh, for he has done majestically!

b   This is to be made known in all the earth."

6a   Cry out and shout for joy, inhabitant Zion,

b   for great in your midst is the Holy One of Israel.

---

perfect "fallen in einem Danklied . . . auf," but he is also correct in rejecting the majority's view of emending: "Es ist aber doch fraglich, ob man auf diese Weise dem Text von 𝕸 seine nonkonformistische Kühnheit nehmen darf." So also Watts (1985: 180).

What the meaning of the jussive implies is another question, since it suggests that salvation has not yet been accomplished. This is, of course, consistent with the meaning of the refrain in 5:25 and 9:7ff., which employ the same vocabulary.

12:2a.   "O God"   In light of the vocative in line 1b, I read the divine name as vocative also here, and not as the subject of a verbless sentence (the majority view). 1QIsaᵃ has אל אל, which is either the addition of the preposition: "to El," or a doubling of the name as in 2c, or dittography. My translation suggests that the entire first psalm (vv. 1b–2d) is addressed to Yahweh in the second person.

12:2c.   "'my strength and my protection is Yah'"   The direct citation of Exod 15:2 is put in quotation marks, since it is being quoted back to Yahweh as a reminder of his salvation and the basis for the appeal and assertion of trust in Yahweh's assumed and anticipated response. This also explains the double divine name at the end of line 2c: the first is within the embedded citation; the second is another vocative, as observed in 1b and 2a.

12:5b.   "to be made known"   It is likely that the *Hophal* participle indicated as the *Qere* should be read, although the *Pual* participle represented by the *Kethiv* would result in a similar meaning. The use of the *Pual* of ידע, however, is rare, and the *Hiphil* use of ידע in 4d suggests a link to the *Hophal*.

12:6a.   "inhabitant Zion"   Reading ציון as an epexegetical appositive, not *nomen rectum*. In 10:24 "my people" are addressed as ישׁב ציון (using the *masculine* bound form). The likely explanation for the use of the feminine יושׁבת here is that it refers specifically to Zion and is therefore not to be read as the bound form. Compare בת ציון (*Qere*) in 10:32.

Lineation

Again one is confronted with difficult decisions. Line 1b might be divided on the basis of the second clause, yielding 2 lines of 4 + 5 syllables and 2 + 2 stresses. Although this alternative gives much shorter-than-average lines, either way of lineating falls within the norms. I have left 1b as one line to form a bicolon with 1c, since the other lines within the context all form bicola: 2ab, 2cd. But I recognize enough variety to admit that this is not necessarily the determining factor.

On the other hand, I divide lines 4bc, although one line of 9 syllables might be preferred. Since bicola continue to dominate (compare 4de, 5ab, and 6ab), I treat 4bc as a bicolon.

Lines 4e and 5a present problems similar to 1b: a main clause plus a subordinate clause within the same line. I admit the possibility that these should be divided, although, again, much shorter-than-average lines would result. However, to divide line 4e after the main clause (הזכירו) would leave only this single word as the first line. Furthermore, the parallelism of 4e with 4d suggests a bicolon. Thus, if 4e is left undivided, 5a, which has the same syntactic structure, should also be left as one line, and the parallelism of 5a with 5b indicates that they form another bicolon.

Thus my lineation shows 18 lines. At 8 syllables per line, the poem would have 144 syllables, near the middle of the range of 137–148.

Syllable and Stress Counts

Although 12:1–6 is a rather short piece, the syllable count shows a disproportionately large range, 137–48, due in large part to several second-person suffixed forms and three cases of the prefixed conjunction before *shewa*. In general, I read the afformative verbs as full syllables (1a, 1b) and the pronominal suffixes as single syllables (1b, 1c). Both words in 8b may have had an additional syllable; I have compromised at 8, one more than MT. Line 5b is read with the Qere, but I acknowledge both possibilities (see translation note to 12:5b, p. 178). The prefixed conjunctions are in this instance read as full syllables.

Within the range of syllable counts, I therefore suggest a total of 144, which is consistent with the proposed lineation into 18 lines. In fact, the poem divides equally into halves of 9 lines and 72 syllables (see below, p. 181).

The 18 lines are tabulated as follows:

4-syllable lines:	1	8-syllable lines:	5
5-syllable lines:	1	9-syllable lines:	3
6-syllable lines:	1	10-syllable lines:	3
7-syllable lines:	3	11-syllable lines:	1

Of the 18 lines,
27.8% (5 lines) have 8 syllables,
61.1% (11 lines) have 7–9 syllables,
83.3% (15 lines) have 6–10 syllables.

The median line length is 8 syllables.
The average line length is 8.00 syllables (144/18).

Concerning stresses, my total indicates exactly the 54 stresses (MT: 57) that would be expected from 18 lines of 3 stresses each. Again the dominance of the 3-stress line and the balancing of the 2- and 4-stress lines should be noted:

2-stress cola:	5 (27.8%)
3-stress cola:	8 (44.4%)
4-stress cola:	5 (27.8%)

Thus 100% of the lines have 2–4 stresses.

The average number of stresses per colon is 3.00.

Prose Particles

Only four prose particles appear, all of them the article and two of them in the prosaic introductions in lines 1a and 3a–4a. With a total of 62 words, the prose particle count is 6.45%.

Verse and Strophe Structure

Most notable in the piece as a whole are the twin introductions in 1a and 4a, the first in the second-masculine singular, the second in the second-masculine plural. Each uses the prosaic formula ביום ההוא. Taken together, they would form a parallel bicolon of 8 + 8 syllables.

Verses 1b–3b

Lines 1bc form a bicolon; each line has two verb forms (clause predicators). The noun form אפך in line 1c puns on the verb אנפת in 1b, and the lines are end rhymed.

Line 2a continues the end rhyme, although the introductory הנה begins a new verse unit. My translation suggests that direct address continues and that 2cd forms a quotation within the quotation, citing from Exod 15:2. The 4 lines of v. 2 are more carefully interwoven. Lines cd have rhyme both at the beginning (וַיְהִי־לִי / כִּי־עָזִּי) and at the end (לִישׁוּעָה/יָהּ). But lines a and d form an inclusio with the use of the noun יְשׁוּעה, and the paired verb forms in line b match the paired nouns in line c, creating an ABBA pattern within the quatrain.

Verse 3 concludes the first half by introducing the second-person plural verb form, to be picked up in line 4a. Thus the structure of these 8 lines (vv. 1b–3b) is 2 + 4(ABBA) + 2, plus the introductory line.

Verses 4b–6b

As already noted, the lineation of 4bc is difficult. One line of 9 syllables and 4 stresses is not impossible, but the parallelism supports 2 independent lines and continues the series of bicola.

In contrast to 4bc, a longer bicolon follows, which is part of a well-structured quatrain. The first 3 lines all begin with plural imperative verb forms, forming an AAAB pattern. But the first and last lines (4d and 5b) begin with a form of ידע respectively, and בעמים is echoed by בכל־הארץ,

forming an ABBA pattern, which is confirmed by the fact that the middle lines (4e and 5a) follow the imperative with the subordinate כִּי clause. Thus, like the middle quatrain in vv. 1–3 (2abcd), this quatrain (4de–5ab) reflects an ABBA chiasm.

This quatrain also relates to the bicolon in 4bc by the repetition of יהוה from 4b in the second bicolon of the quatrain (5a), and by the repetition of שְׁמוֹ from 4c in the first bicolon of the quatrain (4e).

Just as v. 3 concludes vv. 1–3, v. 6 concludes vv. 4–6 and shifts the subject, here to the second feminine. This final bicolon is long, especially when compared to the short bicolon in 4bc. Nevertheless, the lengths are balanced over the 9-line unit. Again I note the same pattern of lines observed in vv. 1–3: 2 + 4(ABBA) + 2, plus the introductory line.

Gross Structure

This short chapter is more complicated than would appear at first sight. The subject changes five times in these 18 lines, a fact barely noted and rarely explained in commentaries. Clearly the basic structure consists of the two parts already mentioned, which begin with virtually the same introduction and are exactly the same length:

I. (vv. 1–3): 72 syllables, 26 stresses, 30 words
II. (vv. 4–6): 72 syllables, 28 stresses, 32 words

Furthermore, within each half, the same smaller structure occurs:

A. Prosaic introduction (1a and 4a):
each is 8 syllables, 3 stresses
B. 8-line unit, structured 2 + 4 + 2 (vv. 1b–3b and vv. 4b–6b):
each is 64 syllables and 23/25 stresses

Within the B units, the final bicolon (v. 3 and v. 6) changes the subject and focus. Part I, which uses the first person, concludes in v. 3 with the second-person plural, which anticipates part II. Part II, in turn, concludes in v. 6 with the second-person singular, focusing on Zion and Jerusalem as a corporate whole.

Final evidence of the integrity of the poem as a whole is the fact that there are seven uses of divine names, divided between the halves as 4 + 3:

I. (vv. 1–3): Yahweh + El + Yah + Yahweh
II. (vv. 4–6): Yahweh + Yahweh + the Holy One of Israel

The occurrence of the two short names, "El and "Yah" in part I, is balanced by the single use of the construct name "Holy One of Israel" in part II.

Thought Progression

Each introductory line features the expression ביום ההוא, which forms
an integral link to a major motif in the material that has gone before. The
explicit citation of Exodus 15 calls to mind the salvation of the Exodus
event, to which reference has also already been made (10:24, 26; 11:11,
15–16). Thus the general theme of chap. 12 expresses thanksgiving and
joy for an action of Yahweh reminiscent of the Exodus event and Reed
Sea rescue.

The changes in subject play an important role not only in the structure
of the poem but also in the thematic movement. The use of the singular in
part I and the plural in part II indicates the expression of joy on both the
individual and corporate level. The shift in v. 3 anticipates part II, and the
shift in v. 6 brings the focus back from the many to the one, to Zion
herself, in whose midst is the "Holy One of Israel."

The following thematic outline is proposed:

    I. Individual praise (vv. 1–3)
       A. Introductory call to praise (1a)
       B. On the basis of Yahweh's (past) actions, "I" will praise you (1b–2)
       C. Future joy of community (v. 3)
    II. Corporate praise (vv. 4–6)
       A. Introductory call to praise (4a)
       B. On the basis of Yahweh's (future?) actions, "you" (plural) declare
          his name (4b–5)
       C. Future joy of Zion (v. 6)

Isaiah 10:5–12:6 as a Unified Whole

The three major parts of Isa 10:5–12:6 have now been discussed as individual units. I have found a consistency in the use of poetic stylistics
throughout this material and have analyzed a sense of structural unity and
integrity to each of these parts. For the sake of reference, the statistical
data concerning the measurement of length are summarized:

10:5–34:	824 syllables,	310 stresses,	357 words,	103 lines
11:1–16:	512 syllables,	193 stresses,	219 words,	64 lines
12:1–6:	<u>144 syllables,</u>	<u>54 stresses,</u>	<u>62 words,</u>	<u>18 lines</u>
Total:	1480 syllables,	557 stresses,	638 words.	185 lines

Next I shall consider the possibility that there is an even greater unity
to the whole of these three parts. For example, I have already called attention to the fact that the paragraph markers in both CL and CA indicate a
connection between 11:10–16 and chap. 12, and it is not difficult to understand that chap. 12 forms the doxological conclusion to the expression

of future hope and peace in chap. 11. In fact, the allusion to a "second exodus" in 11:11–16 is a clear link to both the first Exodus and the actual citation of Exod 15:2 that forms the basis of chap. 12.

I have also noted the role of 10:33–34 as a conclusion to 10:5–34, in which the scope of the previous section is expanded to include Yahweh's control not only over Assyria but also over any and all who are "haughty" or "arrogant." The vocabulary used is that of cutting off the trees of the forest, and certainly chap. 11 begins with this image applied to the "family tree" of the Davidic king. Thus one may rightly see 10:33–34 as a transitional section, both expanding the theme of the previous section and focusing the impending judgment of Yahweh on the house of David, the cutting down of which is the assumption with which the following chapter begins.

In fact, the secondary theme of the whole of 10:5–34 deals with the return of the remnant of Israel, *after* the punishment of Assyria for its arrogance in taking credit for the destruction of Israel. The return of the remnant, punning on the name of Isaiah's first son in 7:3, is stated clearly in 10:21–22 and described in terms of the Exodus in 10:24–26 (the double use of the expression בדרך־מצרים). This is precisely the point of 11:11–16, picked up further in chap. 12.

The use of the idiom ביום ההוא has already been noted in the two introductory lines in chap. 12, lines 1a and 4a. These seem to be a clear link to the same expression in chap. 11, where it appears in the transitional v. 10 and in the first line of the second stanza, 11a. This stanza (11:11–16) closes with the variant idiom ביום + infinitive construct, which forms an inclusio between the end of this second stanza (11:16b) and the beginning (11:11a). In every case the reference to "that day" is a positive one, indicating the "day" of Yahweh's deliverance in accord with his past action in the Exodus event (compare Exod 14:30).

Moving back into 10:5–34, one recalls two additional and carefully positioned occurrences of the same formula: ביום ההוא in 10:20 and in 10:27 (see above, p. 161). In both instances the motif of "that day" indicates future deliverance from the oppression of Assyria. Added to the two uses of this expression in chap. 12 and the three in chap. 11, the two occurrences in 10:5–34 make a total of exactly *seven* instances of the theme "that day" or "day of Yahweh" in Isa 10:5–12:6. All of them indicate hope for and confidence in a future deliverance, and they serve to bind together the three parts into the whole of this larger section.

Finally, I shall summarize the thought progression of this entire unit to suggest that such a unifying structural device serves the meaning and understanding of the text. Following the seven "woes" issued against Judah and Jerusalem in the major section in 5:1–30 and 8:19–10:4 (which, in turn, surrounds the material in 6:1–8:18, dealing with the role of Assyria as a solution to the Syro-Ephraimite threat to Judah and Jerusalem), 10:5 turns the "woe" formula against Assyria.

The point is not that Judah will be spared, but that the same pride and arrogance by which Judah (specifically Ahaz, the "house of David" in 7:13) failed to recognize the role of Yahweh will also become the downfall of Assyria (and, 10:33–34, of everyone who is "high and haughty"). As Yahweh has used Assyria as his instrument to punish even his own people ("complete all his work on Zion and in Jerusalem," 10:12), so Yahweh will punish Assyria, cutting down the כבוד of his forest 'like the falling of a standard' (כמסס נסס), 10:18.

This first "therefore" stanza (10:16–19) is followed by the first "in that day" stanza, which indicates the other side of Yahweh's destruction of Assyria, namely the gathering of a remnant of Jacob, *after* their righteous destruction. The second "therefore" stanza (10:24–26) is directed more toward Zion than Assyria, further developing the theme of hope and rescue "in the way of Egypt" (10:24, 26).

The final stanza of 10:5–34, however, reiterates the advance of the enemy toward Jerusalem as a reminder that the punishment is not yet past. Nevertheless, the ultimate power of Yahweh over any who are arrogant is asserted in the conclusion of chap. 10 (10:33–34), which also forms a transition to the next section.

Chapter 11 follows by describing a "radical" restoration of Yahweh's messianic kingship, right from the very root—not from David but from Jesse. The new king will establish a perfect reign of peace. "On that day" Adonay will gather the remnant from Assyria and from every part of the earth in the way he rescued his people from Egypt. The "way of Egypt" has become again a highway through the sea (11:15). "On that day" the root of Jesse will become the נס (a pun on מסס נסס), whose place of rest (= salvation) is described as simply כבוד (compare the destroyed כבוד of Assyria in 10:18).

Finally, "on that day" Zion will again sing psalms of praise (chap. 12) and make known the deeds of Yahweh to the nations, who have presumably been drawn to the root of Jesse as a "standard" for the peoples (11:10).

The Relationship of 10:5–12:6 and 5:1–10:4

If 10:5–12:6 are to be understood as a thematically unified piece following the content and message of 5:1–10:4, then it is likely that other structural and surface connections might be found between these major sections as well. If I am correct in asserting that the motif of "that day" serves to unite 10:5–12:6, then the thematic function of the same expression should be noted elsewhere. Interestingly, the term does not occur at all in the two poems in 5:8–25 and 9:7–10:4, which have been previously discussed in detail. However, the term is found four times in close connection within the central section of the *Denkschrift* material, in 7:18, 20, 21, 23. In every case, the motif brings an ominous tone, indicating the destruction that is predicted because Yahweh will bring "the king of Assyria" (7:17) upon Judah as his medium of punishment. In fact, this is the first direct naming of Assyria in the book of Isaiah, and it certainly sets a theme that is continued in 10:5ff. (compare 10:12, where מלך אשור is used explicitly, as in 7:17). In this latter section, however, the tables have been turned. Assyria, too, will be punished for its arrogance, and for Judah "that day" becomes a day of deliverance.

Another, more oblique reference to Assyria is found in the transitional section in 5:26–30, where the march of presumably Assyria (see above, p. 106 and Machinist 1983: 728) is described as relentless and irresistible. In 10:28–32 one finds another expression of such a march of an enemy upon Jerusalem, but it is tempered by the surrounding context, which describes the ultimate defeat of Assyria "in that day." Yet it is precisely within the description of the march in 5:26–30 that yet another use of the motif of "that day" occurs (5:30). There it carries a threatening sense of destruction, which is countered by way of contrast in 10:5ff.

Futhermore, 5:26 begins this smaller section with the statement that "Yahweh will lift up a standard (ונשא־נס) for the nations (לגוים)," strikingly parallel to 10:12, where the "standard" seems to be the royal seed of Jesse. What is not clear is the referent in 5:26. It may well be Assyria itself, in which case there is another contrast between the material in 5:26–20 and 10:5–12:6.

However, it seems likely that Assyria is pictured as a representative nation *responding* to the unidentified "standard" in 5:26–30. In this case, the "standard" is not Assyria, but neither is it otherwise identified. The play on the word נס in reference to Assyria in 10:18 (מסס נסס) would further distinguish Assyria from Yahweh's "true" נס. It is possible, therefore, that the "standard" in 5:26 is intentionally cryptic and refers to whatever means by which Yahweh might summon the nations for his purposes. If this is the case, then the identification of the "standard" in chap. 11 is intended to make explicit what had previously been only implicit.

Again, the contrasts are important. If the "standard" in 5:26 is the Davidic king, then the action by which the nations are summoned is the faithless reaction of Ahaz to the Syro-Ephraimite threat, in which he himself called on Assyria for help. In chap. 11, the scion of Jesse becomes the "standard" that the nations seek in order not to destroy Yahweh's people but rather to hear and learn from them of Yahweh's deeds of deliverance.

In the material on the other side of the *Denkschrift*, I have called attention to the vocabulary of "yoke" and "burden," of "rod" and "shoulder," in

9:3, likely another oblique reference to Assyria's power (Machinist 1983: 728). Clearly this is in mind in 10:27, where סבל is paired with שכם in 27b, and על appears twice in the following lines. Thematically, this agrees with the content of 8:23b–9:6, describing a day when the "yoke" and "burden" will be removed (9:3). Direct reference to the "rod" is not found here, but rather at the very beginning of 10:5ff., that is, line 5b, where the theme of "staff of my anger" and "rod of my wrath" is set forth. This motif reappears in the first "that day" strophe of 10:5ff., which is 10:20–23, where it is said that the remnant will no longer rely on the 'one striking them' (מכהו, line 20d). This is, then, another reference to the "rod" of Assyria, on whom Ahaz had relied, leading Yahweh to use the rod to punish the Davidic king and people.

In 10:24 the same motif is reiterated. Assyria is described as the "staff" and "rod" (24de). This strophe also turns the tables on Assyria, exhorting "my people" not to fear, for "in a little while" Assyria will be overcome "in the way of Egypt." It is interesting to note that the expression אל־תירא occurs only three times in all of Isaiah 1–39: in 37:6, here in 10:24b, and in 7:4, in the heart of the *Denkschrift* material, in which Isaiah offers to Ahaz the solution of trust and obedience, which, in turn, Ahaz chooses to decline.

Further evidence of contrast by way of similarity appears in 11:11–16. Future peace between Ephraim and Judah will be restored; together (יחדו) they will reenact the conquest (11:13–14). This is in direct reversal of the statement in 9:20, in which Ephraim and Manasseh are described as being together (יחדו) against Judah. In light of the relatively infrequent use of יחדו (see above, p. 174, #5), the similarity of the two passages is likely not coincidental.

I have observed that the symbolic names of Isaiah's children, featured in chaps. 7–8, are carried over into the surrounding context, specifically in the use of the roots מהר and חוש in 5:19 and שלל and בזז in 10:2. Section 10:5ff. begins with the declaration that Yahweh has sent Assyria 'to take booty and to seize plunder' (לשלל שלל ולבז בז), picking up where 10:2 left off. The difference is that in 5:19 and 10:2, these verbs are predicated of Judah and Jerusalem; they describe the evil attitudes and actions of Yahweh's people. In 10:5 they are predicated of Assyria, who is to punish Judah, described as "an apostate nation" (10:5).

Further, there can be little doubt that the name of Isaiah's other son שאר ישוב lies behind the assertions in 10:20–23, especially in the virtual citation of the name as a sentence in 21a and 22c. The theme carries over into chap. 11, with the specific use of שאר in 11:11d and 11:16b, and of the root בזז in 14b, now with a reunited Ephraim/Judah as the *subject*, no longer the object of Assyria's swift plundering.

Finally, I return to the major, complementary poems in 5:8–25 and 9:7–10:4. The theme of the first poem was focused on the sixfold use of הוי, in decreeing "woe" specifically against Judah and Jerusalem. I also noted the use of "therefore" strophes, following each series of woes and using the initial לכן three times (5:13, 14, 24) and על־כן once (5:25, a link to chap. 9). The seventh use of "woe" appears in 10:1.

While 10:5 clearly begins a new unit, the initial הוי is striking and certainly a link to what has gone before, except that here it is directed against Assyria. As suggested in the discussion of the structure of 10:5–34 (see above, pp. 157ff.), the interplay between the introductory use of הוי in 10:5 and of לכן in 10:16 and 10:24 is certainly a thematic and structural feature, similar to the way in which the "therefores" follow the "woes" in 5:8ff. Thus the structure of this first major part of 10:5–12:6 echoes the structural markers found in 5:8ff. However, in 10:5ff. the "therefores" bring hope and comfort to Judah and Jerusalem, while in 5:8ff. they announced judgment and punishment.

In the other, complementary poem in 9:7–10:4, I observed the unifying, structural role of the refrain "his anger is not turned away, his hand is still outstretched," which is also linked to the content and structure of 5:8–25. The "hand of my anger" appears in separated form in the opening lines of 10:5ff., namely, 5ab (see translation note to 10:5b, p. 146), where both the "woe" and now the "hand of Yahweh" are directed against Assyria. In 9:7–10:4, the ominous message that Yahweh's judgment had not yet been completed was a "word" against false hope in Judah and Jerusalem. In 10:5ff., the extension of judgment in the "hand of anger" reaches also to Assyria.

In the concluding part of 10:5–12:6, there is an anticipatory psalm of thanks based on an expression of trust (12:1b–2), which prays, "let your anger turn back, and may you comfort me." Here, at the end of this major unit, which began with reference to the hand of Yahweh, the juxtaposition of אף with the verbal root שוב presents another use of part of the motif that is essential to the refrain in 9:7ff.

The occurrence of the refrain in 5:25, which served to bind together the two poems in 5:8–25 and 9:7–10:4, is, in fact, a double use. The actual refrain is contained in the final bicolon (5:25ef) and concludes the entire poem (5:8–25), but the initial bicolon of v. 25 (5:25ab) also uses the expressions "anger" and "hand," so that the vocabulary of the refrain appears twice in 5:25. If this is true, then the complementary poems in 5:8ff. and 9:7ff. use the vocabulary of this refrain a total of six times. If the outstretched "hand of anger" in 10:5 (at the beginning of 10:5–12:6) is combined with the idiom of "anger turned back" in 12:1b–2 (at the end of 10:5–12:6), this split use combines to form the seventh occurrence of the motif.[1] If I am correct in translating 12:1c as a jussive, the expectation of the final "return" of Yahweh's anger is still perceived as a future hope.

In sum, I have argued that the major section 10:5–12:6, while consisting of three parts, nevertheless indicates a unity of theme and message that is reflected in the use of poetic stylistics and structural markers. Furthermore, I have attempted to show that this large section builds upon both the theme and the structural features found in the material that precedes it, both in the *Denkschrift* and in the material surrounding the *Denkschrift* in 5:1–10:4. If the major section in 10:5ff. forms another unit beyond what has been discussed so far, the final question in terms of the whole of Isaiah 2–12 is whether the material that lies *before* chap. 5 is related thematically and structurally to what has been found so far. Attention is therefore drawn to a discussion of Isaiah 2–4.

---

1. There is at least one more use of the refrain beyond Isaiah 2–12, which is clearly an echo of its thematic use here, namely, 14:24–27, which builds on this material and is thematic, for example, in the redactional reconstruction of Barth (1977). Note also the reuse of the vocabulary of "yoke," "burden," and "shoulder" in 14:25.

Chapter 6

Isaiah 2–4

Boundaries of This Unit

In the same way that the whole of Isa 10:5–12:6 has been dealt with as a larger unit, so now Isaiah 2–4 is likewise considered. Although I shall pay attention to details of poetic structure and style within each subsection, my goal is to determine, first, if these chapters as an entity exhibit any indication of unity, and second, whether they are to be considered part of a structural whole that includes Isaiah 5–12.

This major section breaks into subsections, generally indicated by paragraph markers in the manuscripts and followed by the commentaries: 2:2–4(5), 2:(5)6–22, 3:1–4:1, and 4:2–6, and I shall use these subdivisions as starting points. Structural considerations will either confirm or call into question the integrity of these smaller units.

Two problems must be noted. First, the chapter division between Isaiah 3 and Isaiah 4 is generally ignored, since 4:1 quite clearly concludes the previous section. The paragraph markers in both the CL and the CA attest to a break between 4:1 and 4:2. One must observe, however, that 1QIsaᵃ does not indicate a break. In fact, it shows a break between 3:26 and 4:1 and another between 4:2 and 4:3.

Second, the position of 2:5 as the conclusion to the unit 2:2–5 is not as obvious as may seem. In light of an envelope construction between 2:5 and 2:22, which will be discussed below (see pp. 202–3), I suggest that 2:5 does not conclude 2:2–4 but rather begins 2:5–6ff., in spite of the fact that most commentaries, as well as the text format in BHS, include 2:5 with 2:2–4. This latter assumption, of course, is consistent with the sense of the verse; it appears to conclude the section with an exhortation. Further, it is roughly parallel to the conclusion in the similar poem found in Mic 4:2–5.

However, both CA and CL, as well as the Qumran scroll, show a paragraph break after Isa 2:4, placing v. 5 with vv. 6ff. Further, although v. 5 is undoubtedly similar to Mic 4:5b, the Micah passage does not present the verbs as cohortatives. Upon closer inspection, other differences are also to be found. In fact, the only similarity is the use of the verb הלך and the divine name יהוה (בשם־יהוה אלהינו in Mic 4:5b, but באור יהוה in Isa 2:5). Moreover, the Micah passage includes several additional lines (vv. 4–5a) before 5b, and the formulaic "for the mouth of Yahweh Seba'oth has spoken" in Mic 4:4b ordinarily indicates closure.

It is not my intent to discuss in detail the passage in Micah or to study its relationship with Isa 2:2–4(5), except to note the obvious parallels that

---

Isaiah 2:5–22

Text

		Syllable Count		*Stress Count*	
			MT		MT
2:5a	בֵּית יַעֲקֹב לְכוּ	5	6	3	3
b	וְנֵלְכָה בְּאוֹר יְהֹוָה:	8	8	3	3
6a	כִּי נָטַשְׁתָּה עַמְּךָ בֵּית יַעֲקֹב	(9)/10	10	(3/4)/5	5
b	כִּי מָלְאוּ מִקֶּדֶם	6	7	2	3
c	וְעֹנְנִים כַּפְּלִשְׁתִּים	8	8	2	2
d	וּבְיַלְדֵי נָכְרִים יַשְׂפִּיקוּ:	(8)/9	9	3	3
7a	וַתִּמָּלֵא אַרְצוֹ כֶּסֶף וְזָהָב	10	11	4	4
b	וְאֵין קֵצֶה לְאֹצְרֹתָיו	9	9	3	3
c	וַתִּמָּלֵא אַרְצוֹ סוּסִים	8	8	3	3
d	וְאֵין קֵצֶה לְמַרְכְּבֹתָיו:	9	9	3	3
8a	וַתִּמָּלֵא אַרְצוֹ אֱלִילִים	9	9	3	3
b	לְמַעֲשֵׂה יָדָיו יִשְׁתַּחֲווּ	8	10	3	3
c	לַאֲשֶׁר עָשׂוּ אֶצְבְּעֹתָיו:	8	9	3	3
9a	וַיִּשַּׁח אָדָם וַיִּשְׁפַּל־אִישׁ	9	9	(3)/4	3
b	וְאַל־תִּשָּׂא לָהֶם:	6	6	2	2
Verses 5–9		(120)/122	128	(43)46	46
10a	בּוֹא בַצּוּר וְהִטָּמֵן בֶּעָפָר	10	10	4	4
b	מִפְּנֵי פַּחַד יְהֹוָה	6	7	3	3
c	וּמֵהֲדַר גְּאֹנוֹ	7	7	2	2
11a	עֵינֵי גַּבְהוּת אָדָם שָׁפֵל	8	8	4	4
b	וְשַׁח רוּם אֲנָשִׁים	6	6	3	3
c	וְנִשְׂגַּב יְהֹוָה לְבַדּוֹ בַּיּוֹם הַהוּא:	12	12	5	5
Verses 10–11		49	50	21	21

suggest some interdependence or, what is most likely in my opinion, common dependence on a third source, possibly a well-known oracle similar to but different from either the Isaiah or Micah passage. In any case, I shall begin with the hypothesis that Isa 2:5 actually belongs with the verses that follow and forms the introduction to the section in 2:5–22. Thus this section will be dealt with first, and I shall return to the smaller poem in 2:2–4 at the end of the discussion.

Translation

2:5a House of Jacob, come
  b let us walk in the light of Yahweh!
  6a For you (Yahweh) have abandoned your (own) people, the house of Jacob!
  b For they have filled—from the east—
  c sorcerers like the Philistines!
  d With sons of foreigners they have oversupplied.
  7a His land has been filled with silver and gold;
  b there is no end to his treasures!
  c His land has been filled with horses;
  d there is no end to his chariots!
  8a His land has been filled with worthless things:
  b the product of his hands they worship—
  c what his fingers have produced.
  9a Humanity has sunk, and each man has stooped.
  b Do not forgive them!

  10a Go into the rock and hide in the dirt
  b away from the presence of the Dread of Yahweh,
  c away from [the presence of] His Majesty's Splendor.
  11a Man's arrogant eyes are to be stooped;
  b sunk will be men's haughtiness,
  c for exalted will be Yahweh alone **on that day.**

12a	כִּי יֹום לַיהוָה צְבָאֹות	8	8	3	4
b	עַל כָּל־גֵּאֶה וָרָם	6	6	3	3
c	וְעַל כָּל־נִשָּׂא וְשָׁפֵל:	8	8	3	3
13a	וְעַל כָּל־אַרְזֵי הַלְּבָנֹון	9	9	3	3
b	הָרָמִים וְהַנִּשָּׂאִים	8	8	2	2
c	וְעַל כָּל־אַלֹּונֵי הַבָּשָׁן:	9	9	3	3
14a	וְעַל כָּל־הֶהָרִים הָרָמִים	9	9	3	3
b	וְעַל כָּל־הַגְּבָעֹות הַנִּשָּׂאֹות:	11	11	3	3
15a	וְעַל כָּל־מִגְדָּל גָּבֹהַ	7	7	3	3
b	וְעַל כָּל־חֹומָה בְצוּרָה:	8	8	3	3
16a	וְעַל כָּל־אֳנִיֹּות תַּרְשִׁישׁ	8	8	3	3
b	וְעַל כָּל־שְׂכִיֹּות הַחֶמְדָּה:	9	9	3	3
Verses 12–16		100	100	35	36
17a	וְשַׁח גַּבְהוּת הָאָדָם	7	7	3	3
b	וְשָׁפֵל רוּם אֲנָשִׁים	7	7	3	3
c	וְנִשְׂגַּב יְהוָה לְבַדֹּו בַּיֹּום הַהוּא:	12	12	5	5
18	וְהָאֱלִילִים כָּלִיל יַחֲלֹף:	9	10	3	3
19a	וּבָאוּ בִּמְעָרֹות צֻרִים	8	8	3	3
b	וּבִמְחִלֹּות עָפָר	6	6	2	2
Verses 17–19b		49	50	19	19
c	מִפְּנֵי פַּחַד יְהוָה	6	7	3	3
d	וּמֵהֲדַר גְּאֹונֹו	7	7	2	2
e	בְּקוּמֹו לַעֲרֹץ הָאָרֶץ:	7	9	3	3
20a	בַּיֹּום הַהוּא יַשְׁלִיךְ הָאָדָם	9	9	4	4
b	אֵת אֱלִילֵי כַסְפֹּו	6	6	2	3
c	וְאֵת אֱלִילֵי זְהָבֹו	8	8	2	3
d	אֲשֶׁר עָשׂוּ־לֹו לְהִשְׁתַּחֲוֹת	9	10	3	3
e	לַחְפֹּר פֵּרֹות וְלָעֲטַלֵּפִים:	10	10	3	3
21a	לָבֹוא בְּנִקְרֹות הַצֻּרִים	8	8	3	3
b	וּבִסְעִפֵי הַסְּלָעִים	8	8	2	2
c	מִפְּנֵי פַּחַד יְהוָה	6	7	3	3
d	וּמֵהֲדַר גְּאֹונֹו	7	7	2	2
e	בְּקוּמֹו לַעֲרֹץ הָאָרֶץ:	7	9	3	3
22a	חִדְלוּ לָכֶם מִן־הָאָדָם	8	8	3	3
b	אֲשֶׁר נְשָׁמָה בְּאַפֹּו	8	8	3	3
c	כִּי־בַמֶּה נֶחְשָׁב הוּא:	6	6	3	3
Verses 19c–22		120	127	44	46

Totals		(438)/440	455	(162)/165	168
		Syllables	MT	Stresses	MT

12a   For Yahweh Seba'oth has **a day**

    b   against everyone proud and arrogant,

    c   against everyone raised up and to be brought down,

13a   against all the cedars of Lebanon

    b   —high and raised up—

    c   against all the oaks of Bashan,

14a   against all the high mountains,

    b   against all the raised hills,

15a   against every high tower,

    b   against every fortified wall,

16a   against all the ships of Tarshish,

    b   against all the vessels of a splendid place.

17a   Sunk will be mankind's arrogance,

    b   and stooped will be men's haughtiness,

    c   for exalted will be Yahweh alone **on that day**.

18   The entirety of worthless idols will disappear;

19a   they will go into caves in rocks

    b   and into holes in dirt—

    c   away from the presence of the Dread of Yahweh,

    d   away from His Majesty's Splendor,

    e   when he rises to terrify the earth.

20a   On that day mankind will throw away

    b   the idols of his silver

    c   and the idols of his gold,

    d   which they made for themselves to worship,

    e   to the moles and to the bats,

21a   to come into the crevices of the rocks

    b   and into the clefts of the cliffs—

    c   away from the presence of Yahweh's Dread,

    d   and away from His Majesty's Splendor

    e   when He rises to terrify the earth.

22a   Cease from the man (= humanity)

    b   in whose nostrils is breath,

    c   for of what value is he?

Notes on Translation and Text

2:6a. **"For you have abandoned your (own) people, the house of Jacob!"**   The translation of v. 6 is difficult and much debated in the commentaries. Watts (1985: 32) appeals to the LXX text, which he translates, 'for it applies to his people, the house of Jacob', and then he reconstructs the hypothetical Hebrew *Vorlage*, כי נטה את העמו, which involves at least minor emendation. Several problems are apparent, not the least of which is the fact that, granting his proposal, the MT would preserve the "harder reading," from which the LXX seems a secondary clarification. Moreover, there is no evidence that ἀνίημι was ever used to translate נטה as he retranslates and emends. The LXX verb does translate נטש in Exod 23:11, and its meaning of 'leave alone' or 'abandon' fits perfectly well in Isa 2:6 without need to appeal to a less likely text. The targum confirms the original sense of the verb but reads it as second plural in reference to the house of Jacob: 'you have forsaken the fear of the Mighty One'.

It is also possible that עמך is a divine epithet, 'your (divine) kinsman', in which case the word is an object and "house of Jacob" is vocative: 'you have abandoned your Kinsman, O house of Jacob!' Wiklander (1984: 65) argues that עמך is a "reciprocal kinship term" and translates, 'you have abandoned your kin'.

In light of the question of structure (see below, pp. 201ff.), there may be a connection between v. 5 and v. 6, by which בית־יעקב begins line 5a and ends line 6a. However, the shift from second-person *plural* to second-person *singular* suggests different subjects, so that "house of Jacob" in 6a is more likely an appositive than a vocative. The subject of 6a is therefore "Yahweh," who is the subject of the other second-masculine-singular verb in the poem, found in 9b, with which 6a forms an inclusio (see below, pp. 201ff.).

2:6b. **"have filled"**   The verbal root מלא in the *Qal* can be transitive (though more often stative). Where the *Qal* stands in context with the *Niphal*, which is transitive-passive (for example, 6:1–4), it makes sense to regard it as transitive-active, as here. The translation of lines 6b–d is based on its poetic structure and discussed below.

2:6d. **"have oversupplied"**   From שׂפק (BDB II), not ספק as שׂפק (BDB I). Although one should note the reasonable attempt to relate the root of ישׂפיקו to ספק, it is not altogether clear whether ספק ever had the sense of 'clapping hands to make a bargain', as is usually presumed, even if one should emend 6d from ילדי to ידי. Furthermore, the use of the *Hiphil* would be as unique to ספק (= שׂפק I) as to the root שׂפק II. Of course, שׂפק II is far less attested, occurring only elsewhere at 1 Kgs 20:10 (and there in the *Qal*) with the meaning of 'be sufficient', which is reflected also in the nominal use in Job 20:22. What is attractive about the meaning of שׁפק II is that it may well overlap with the semantic field of מלא, with which it is matched by the chiastic inclusio (see below on verse structure, pp. 198–99). I read the *Hiphil* as intensive.

2:10a. **"Go into the rock and hide in the dirt"** 1QIsa[a] omits vv. 9b–10, but this appears to be haplography, due to the similarity of 9a to v. 11. The MT preserves the more difficult reading; it is much harder to explain why these lines, with their intrusive use of the second-person singular, would have been added.

2:10bc, 19cd, 21cd. **"Dread of Yahweh . . . His Majesty's Splendor"** I read these terms as divine names.

2:11a. **"are to be stooped"** Reading שׁפל as an infinitive absolute solves the problem of a feminine subject with a masculine verb form. A similar line in 5:15 adds a third clause, עיני גבהים תשפלנה, and 1QIsa[a] also shows the verb in 2:11 as תשפלנה.

2:11c, 12a, 17c. **"on that day . . . a day"** Boldface type attempts to indicate the emphatic role this theme and phrase will play in the overall structuring of chaps. 2–4.

2:12c. **"raised up and to be brought down"** שָׁפֵל seems contradictory in meaning to the sense of the rest of the line (exalted vs. humble) but nevertheless consistent and compatible with the wordplay. In light of the context, in which the proud are described as inevitably humbled, I translate with the stative sense used in v. 11.

2:16b. **"vessels"** שׂכיות is a hapax legomenon, likely related to the Egyptian word for 'ship'. See Wildberger (1972: 94) for further discussion.
"vessels of a splendid place" שׂכיות החמדה is a construct chain, parallel to 'ships of Tarshish'. That the *nomen rectum* could be translated as an adjective cannot be denied, but better balance with the first colon suggests a place, possibly a place-name.

2:19e. **"to terrify"** ערץ can mean 'shake' (transitive or intransitive), and in light of the context many commentators have found this to be a threat of an earthquake. This may well be true but not necessarily so. My translation leaves the question open.

2:20d. **"they made for themselves"** The alternation of third plural with third singular is more awkward in English than in Hebrew. The collective sense of "man/mankind" is grammatically either singular or plural or, here, perceived as both. 1QIsaᵃ has what appears to be [עצב]עותיו in a broken line, 'which his fingers [have made]'.

2:20e. "moles" The translation of MT לַחְפֹּר פֵּרוֹת is notoriously difficult. 1QIsaᵃ reads it as one word, so transliterated by Theodotion. The LXX (τοῖς ματαίοις 'worthless things') seems a guess at best. Context suggests some correspondent to עטלפים, hence the translation 'mole' or, better, some cave-dwelling creature.

2:22. Verse 22 is omitted in the LXX and considered a later addition by many commentators (for example, Duhm, Gray, Wildberger, Kaiser, Clements). We must not assume a priori that the MT is to be preferred over the LXX and its Vorlage, but the reasons usually given for the verse's inauthenticity are the same for its likely and later omission: it does not seem to fit very well. My structural analysis will attempt to defend its inclusion.

2:22a. "cease" The redundant לָכֶם (so–called "ethical dative") is best left untranslated.

2:22c. "for of what" The construction is awkward, but possible. Wiklander notes that the construction of ב with חשב is attested elsewhere only in the Dead Sea Scrolls, and he follows Dahood in reading במה = בהמה = 'beast'.

Lineation

Only a few major problems are apparent. I have divided the very first line against the MT *atnaḥ* to include the initial imperative with the vocative (compare Isa 2:3b, discussed on p. 234, below). Line 6a is left as a longer line; to divide would leave "house of Jacob" as a second line. As it is, 9/10 syllables is not unusually long, but the number of stresses is high. The greatest concern is how to handle the three uses of the idiom ביום ההוא (11c, 17c, and 20). In spite of the prosaic nature of the phrase, I have left each one attached to a poetic line, forming 2 rather long 12-syllable lines in 11c and 17c. All of 20–21b is quite prosaic, but one is able to lineate into 55 rather normal poetic lines nevertheless.

Syllable and Stress Counts

The second-person suffix in line 6a and the prefixed conjunction in 6d are shown as variables. At 8 syllables per line, the 55 lines should yield 440 syllables, and the total count is 438/440 (MT: 455). Therefore, I shall count the conjunction in 6d (= 9 syllables) and leave the suffixed עמך in 6a as a 3-syllable word (line 6a = 10 syllables).

In spite of the two 12-syllable lines, the distribution is quite typical:

5-syllable lines:	1	9-syllable lines:	12
6-syllable lines:	10	10-syllable lines:	4
7-syllable lines:	8	11-syllable lines:	1
8-syllable lines:	17	12-syllable lines:	2

Of the 55 lines,
  30.9% (17 lines) have 8 syllables,
  67.3% (37 lines) have 7–9 syllables,
  92.7% (51 lines) have 6–10 syllables.

The median line length is 8 syllables.
The average line length is 8.00 syllables per line.

The stress counts offer several difficulties. Line 6a, even with 10 syllables, is rather short for the 5 stresses of the MT. The 2 monosyllabics may or may not be counted. I agree with the MT in light of the overall number of accents. My count in line 9a is based on the four content words, although the final monosyllabic word could be combined with the previous word, as in the MT. One should also note the additional accents (which I have not counted) marked by the MT in 20bc, where the object markers are not bound as proclitic.

Thus I show a range of 162–65 (MT: 168). At 3 stresses per line, my 55 lines would total 165 stresses, which is the maximum number reached. Although the two instances of the ביום ההוא formula have given two 5-stress lines, the overall pattern is very typical:

2-stress cola:	11 (20.0%)
3-stress cola:	36 (65.5%)
4-stress cola:	5 (9.1%)
5-stress cola:	3 (5.5%)

Thus 94.5% (52 cola) have 2–4 stresses.
The average number of stresses per line is 3.00.

Prose Particles

The prose particle count falls in the 10–15% range; 25 particles out of 183 words gives a percentage of 13.7%. It should be noted that a high concentration of the definite article occurs in vv. 12–16, which I shall argue is the central section. The two object markers fall in the prosaic v. 20, where the MT accents them for emphasis. Thus the use of the prose particles appears to be focused and intentionally placed in certain subsections.

Verse and Strophe Structure

Verses 5–9

As will be argued below (pp. 201ff.), v. 5 actually begins this section with
a hortatory bicolon, followed by an apparent monocolon in 6a. However,
the repetition of בית יעקב at the end of 6a forms a natural inclusio, linking vv. 5–6a structurally, and the resultant tricolon may anticipate the
final tricolon in v. 22, where the only other use of the plural imperative
occurs. Verses 5–6a have 23 syllables and 11 stresses; v. 22 has 22 syllables and 9 stresses. However, line 6a also links to line 9b, and together
they frame the intervening verses with the only two uses of the vocative
addressed to Yahweh (see translation note to 2:6a, p. 194, and the further discussion of structure on pp. 201ff.).

Lines 6bcd are another tricolon, also fraught with translational difficulties. The subject changes to third person, now describing the situation introduced by line 6a. The tricolon is marked by a chiastic inclusio
of the two verbs, in an afformative/preformative sequence, at the beginning and end. The assumption, therefore, that מלאו is matched in
some way by ישׂפיקו has influenced my translation of the latter's debated
root and unique form (see translation note to 2:6, p. 194). Whether or
not one takes מלאו as transitive, as argued in the translation notes, the
direct or oblique object is lacking: "they are full . . . of what?" or "they
have filled . . . what?" The answer is suspended until v. 7: "they have filled
. . . the earth."

The inclusio or envelope structure also helps explain the seeming awk-
wardness of מקדם in v. 6, which, taken alone, lacks a referent. The proposed structure would link 6b with 6d, in which case the first prepositional
phrase modifies the second, ילדי נכרים. In fact, it is likely that the two
verbs relate as a hendiadys, in which case the paraphrase means something
like "they have sufficiently filled (oversupplied) [. . . the earth] with foreigners' sons from the east."

Line 6c, tucked into the envelope, should likely be the focal point of the
tricolon, in which case the phrase serves as an appositive to the "sons of
foreigners." It could also be argued that those described in 6c and 6d are
distinct, both lines noting different but similar atrocities "from the east."
The coordinates *waw . . . waw* should then be translated 'both . . . and'.

Verse 7 begins a new strophe with a neatly balanced quatrain of two
parallel bicola. It is linked to v. 6 by further expanding the theme of מלא,
now in the passive. Here the object of the "filling" of 6b is clarified: it is
the land, "his" land. Verse 7 contrasts with v. 6 by switching to third-person

singular, which links back to the singular "house of Jacob." It further expands the thought of 6b–d by adding inanimate and animate objects to the list: silver and gold (= treasures), horses (= chariots).

In v. 8 the initial line continues the preterite *waw*-consecutives using the *Niphal* of מלא, as in lines 7a and 7c. However, unlike 7a and 7c, which are followed by a seconding line that states "there is no end . . . ," 8a is followed by two parallel lines (8b and 8c). Thus v. 8 forms a tricolon of 25 syllables and 9 stresses. This matches the tricolon of 6bcd, which has 23 syllables and 7 stresses, so that vv. 6b–8c form a subunit in which two tricola are wrapped around two bicola (v. 7). One wonders if the absence in v. 8 of ואין קצה, repeated in 7a and 7c, might evoke the question whether there *is* now to be an end.

In any case, the use of אלילים seems a clever choice of word, punning on אלהים. Though often used in the sense of 'idols', it simply means 'worthless things', which in and of itself would inform and attempt to reform the observations in v. 7 concerning the abundance of things of apparently great worth. But 8bc specifies what is left somewhat general in 8a: these are not just worthless objects of false worth; they are objects of false worship. What are here separated as כסף וזהב (line 7a) and אלילים (8a) are later combined into parallel construct chains in v. 20: אלילי כספו and אלילי זהבו.

The lines of 8bc are well structured. Both start with ל and sibilant alliteration. The play of מעשה with its verbal counterpart is obvious. The whole of 8c is a good example of a so-called ballast variant, 8 syllables matching the 5 syllables of 8bA. The word ישתחוו of 8bB becomes a pivot-hinge; it governs the noun phrase/clause both before and after, as my translation has tried to indicate by the absence of punctuation.

Line 9a introduces what will become an important theme, repeated in v. 11 and v. 17. The line is somewhat overstressed, but combined with the shorter second line, the bicolon has 15 syllables and 6 stresses. Line 9b concludes this first stanza with an inclusio that matches the second-person address to Yahweh in 6a (see translation note to 2:6a, p. 194).

Verses 10–11

Like line 9a, line 10a also has 4 stresses but is followed by the short bicolon in 10bc, forming a tricolon of 23 syllables and 9 stresses.

Verses 11 and 17 form an envelope around vv. 12–16 (see below, p. 201), and they are both tricola with an overloaded final line, likely emphatic, caused by the phrase ביום ההוא. Each has 26 syllables and 11 (v. 17) or 12 (v. 11) stresses.

Verses 12–16

Verses 12–16 are a series of five bicola of 3 + 3 stresses each, introduced by
a monocolon in line 12a and interrupted by the monocolon in line 13b.
(Interestingly, 12a and 13b together would form an additional bicolon
of 16 syllables.) The five bicola are very carefully structured in listing
paralleled objects of judgment, and the monotonous drone of repetition
builds a rhetorically powerful effect, not unlike the *dies irae* passage in
Zeph 1:14–16. The first pair is general, presumably dealing with anyone
and anything "high," which is a figure of speech for "arrogant." The next
two pairs (13a + c and v. 14) threaten things in nature; the final two
threaten man-made objects, specifically objects tarnished by a spirit of
man's pride.

Breaking up the list by breaking up the second bicolon is line 13b,
which plays on the vocabulary of רום and נשא. Of the nine prose particles
in vv. 12–16, all of which are the article, eight occur in vv. 13–14. In
v. 13, the participial adjectives in line b are distributed as a hinge to the
lines before and after: "all the *high* cedars of Lebanon; all the *lifted-up* oaks
of Bashan." The same two adjectives then are used to modify the "mountains" and "hills" in the bicolon of v. 14, so that four articles occur in v. 13
and four in v. 14.

Furthermore, the placement of 13b divides the whole list of ten cola
into a group of 3 and a group of 7. (One might note the list in 3:18–23 of
3 *times* 7 items, see below p. 237.) This produces an interplay of various
groupings: each bicolon cites *two* items; line 13b intrudes after *three* cola;
vv. 13–14 group *four* items, as do vv. 15–16; vv. 13c–16 consist of *seven*
cola; and the entire list turns on the *ten*fold use of כָּל, presenting a
striking impression of completeness.

The ambiguity of 12bc (man and/or nature) is clarified as the forceful
repetition of וְעַל־כָּל moves from 4 lines about nature to 4 lines about
man. This theme carries over into the surrounding concentric circle (v. 10
+ vv. 18–19b), where both man and his worthless idols seek refuge in
nature. Ironically, man goes down into the rocks and dirt; in his self-
exaltation he stoops to hiding, and he literally stoops to hide. The intransitive verbs in vv. 11 and 17 add to the effect; it is not clear if man humbles
himself in fear before Yahweh or if man is humbled by Yahweh, or if, in
the prophet's mind, the two nuances are intended to overlap.

Verses 17–19b

Verse 17 clearly echoes v. 11. The roots שפל and שחח appear in reverse
order. The article is added to אדם, so that the variation changes the 8 + 6

bicolon in 11ab to a 7 + 7 bicolon in 17ab. The c line in each verse is identical.

Verses 18–19b form a tricolon, although the second and third lines form a complete sentence that is coordinate to the initial line. Wordplay echoes line 10a.

Verses 19c–22

Line 19c appears to begin a new strophe, marked by the inclusio of 19cde with 21cde, similar to the way an inclusio links 9b and 6a. This unit (19c–21) is followed by a conclusion (v. 22), just as vv. 6–9 are preceded by the introduction in v. 5. The first 2 lines of 19cde are the same 6 + 7 bicolon as 10bc, but the verse is expanded by the addition of a third line.

As has been noted, v. 20 appears to be very prosaic, with five prose particles. However, its structure, as delineated, breaks down into a 5-line unit of relatively normal line lengths. Lines 20bc consist of parallel noun phrases used as a compound direct object. Line 20e is the adverbial complement to 20a and as such forms an envelope around lines b–d ("man will cast away . . . to the 'moles and bats'"). However, since 21ab continues the thought of 20e, the 7 lines should be divided into a quatrain (20abcd) followed by a tricolon.

Section 21cde is an exact repetition of 19cde, and v. 22 concludes the poem with a tricolon of 22 syllables and 9 stresses (compare vv. 5–6a, with 23 syllables and 11 stresses). This equivalence between v. 22 and 5–6a is further indication that v. 5 does, in fact, belong with vv. 6–22.

Gross Structure

Duhm's comment (1922: 39) that "dies Stück ist das schlechtest erhaltene des ganzen Buches" has been echoed in most commentaries since. Gray (1912: 49) asserts that "obviously v. 6 is not the beginning of a poem," and he proceeds to construct his own strophic arrangement, modestly noted to be "only an approximation to that of the original poem." Clements (1980b: 43), following Barth, moves in the opposite direction: "the unevenness of the material can be better explained as a result of the progressive expansion of an original Isaianic unit of smaller compass".

I have already hinted at the kind of connections that may indicate the larger structure, beginning with the suggestion that v. 5, despite common opinion but in concert with the *petuchah* marker in BHS (that is, in the CL but also in the CA), belongs to this unit. The analysis of verse structure has shown that vv. 5–6a are matched by the concluding exhortation in v. 22, both in content and in length. The only other MT paragraph marker appears after v. 11, where the CL has a *setumah* and the CA has a *petuchah*.

The interplay of vocabulary within the semantic fields of "high" (= arrogant, proud) and "low" (= humble, humiliated) is notable throughout the piece. The words of 9a are mixed and rematched in 11ab, then reversed again in 17ab:

9a: (אֹ‎ישׁ +) שָׁפֵל‎ // . . . //   שׁחח‎ (+ אדם)   [V–S // V–S]
11ab: שׁחח + רום אנשׁים‎ // . . . // שׁפל + גבהות אדם‎   [S–V // V–S]
17ab: שׁפל + רום אנשׁים‎ // . . . // שׁחח + גבהות האדם‎   [V–S // V–S]

In addition, the following observations are worthy of note:

1. Verses 12–16 clearly form a unit around which the rest of the poem is structured.
2. Verse 11 and v. 17 form an inclusio around vv. 12–16. Verse 11 has a further link to v. 9, which forms an inclusio with 6a in the use of the second-person vocative addressed to Yahweh.
3. Line 10a has a clear link to vv. 18–19b and to v. 21, and 10bc is repeated and expanded in 19cde and in 21cde.
4. Section 19cde and 21cde are the same and form an inclusio around vv. 20–21ab.
5. Verses 7–8 have theme and vocabulary links to v. 20: כסף‎ (7a and 20b), זהב‎ (7a and 20c), אלילים‎ (8a and 20bc), the root השתחוה‎ (8b and 20d), the root עשׂה‎ (8bc and 20d).
6. Verses 20–21ab form a strophe of 4 + 3 lines with links to vv. 7–8, which form a strophe of 4 + 3 lines.

On the basis of these links, the structure of Isa 2:5–22 can be outlined as follows:

Stanza 1 (vv. 5–9)
    Introduction (v. 5):   13 syllables and 6 stresses
    Strophe (vv. 6–9):   109 syllables and 40 stresses
Stanza 2 (vv. 10–11)
    Strophe A (v. 10):   23 syllables and 9 stresses
    Strophe B (v. 11):   26 syllables and 12 stresses
Stanza 3 (vv. 12–16)   100 syllables and 35 stresses
Stanza 4 (vv. 17–19b)
    Strophe A (v. 17):   26 syllables and 11 stresses
    Strophe B (v. 18–19b): 23 syllables and 8 stresses

Stanza 5 (vv. 19c–22a)
  Strophe (vv. 19c–21):   98 syllables and 35 stresses
  Conclusion (v. 22):   22 syllables and 9 stresses

The general chiastic pattern is clear, and the stanzas are well matched in length:

Stanza 1 (vv. 5–9):   122 syllables and 45 stresses
Stanza 2 (vv. 10–11):   49 syllables and 21 stresses
Stanza 3 (vv. 12–16):   100 syllables and 35 stresses
Stanza 4 (vv. 17–19b):   49 syllables and 19 stresses
Stanza 5 (vv. 19c–22): 120 syllables and 44 stresses

Stanza 1 begins with a hortatory introduction (v. 5), which is matched by the conclusion in stanza 5 (v. 22). These two verses contain the only uses of the plural imperative in the poem, and their relationship confirms the suggestion that v. 5 does, in fact, belong to this unit and not to 2:2–4 (see above, p. 189).

The rest of stanza 1 consists of the inclusio formed by 6a and 9b around material that is linked by theme and vocabulary (vv. 7–8) to vv. 20–21b in the final stanza. These lines in stanza 5 are embraced by the inclusio formed by the repetition of 19cde and 21cde.

Stanzas 2 and 4 match in length and in content. Line 10a links to vv. 18–19b; v. 11 parallels v. 17. Thus vv. 10–11 relate to vv. 17–19b in an AB::BA chiasm. Furthermore, one line from stanza 1 (9c) anticipates both stanza 2 (11ab) and stanza 4 (17ab), where the theme is expanded into 2 lines. Likewise stanza 2 anticipates stanza 5, where the 2 lines of 10bc are expanded into the 3 lines of 19cde and 21cde. In fact, 10a is expanded in 19ab and echoed in 21a, while 10b is expanded in 19cde and in 21cde.

The middle is clearly stanza 3, which is a self-contained unit, set off after v. 11 by the paragraph markers in the MT. Here the one instance of the divine name יהוה צבאות occurs, as well as the one use of יום ליהוה (צבאות), a variant of the formula ביום ההוא, which occurs once each in vv. 11 and 17 (stanzas 2 and 4) and once in 20a (stanza 5).

Furthermore, a total of ten divine names appears, exactly seven of which use the name יהוה:

Stanza 1: יהוה (5b)
Stanza 2: פחד יהוה (10b)
           הדר גאנו (10c)
           יהוה (11c)
Stanza 3: יהוה צבאות (12a)

Stanza 4:   יהוה (17c)

Stanza 5:   פחד יהוה (19c)

           הדר גאנו (19d)

           פחד יהוה (21c)

           הדר גאנו (21d)

Thus stanzas 1 and 5 contain a total of five names, 2 and 4 contain a total of four names, and 3 has one. Of the seven uses of יהוה, stanzas 1 and 5 together have three; 2 and 4 together have three, and stanza 3 has the single use of צבאות יהוה.

Thought Progression

The focal point of the entire poem is the "Day of Yahweh" section in the structural and thematic middle (stanza 3). The "day" is against *all* that is "high" and "lifted up," vocabulary that echoes v. 9 in stanza 1, v. 11 in stanza 2, v. 17 in stanza 4, and v. 20 in stanza 5. The "day" affects both nature and humanity.

Stanza 2 (10bc) further describes the effects of the "day," when mankind will be humbled "before the terror of Yahweh," and stanza 5 expands this theme of 10bc by adding "when he rises to terrify the earth" in 19e and 21e. In v. 10, mankind is commanded to hide in rocks and dust, which, ironically, is one way in which man will be "brought low." In stanza 4, v. 18 applies the same motif to the worthless gods, brought with those who try to run and hide.

Isaiah 3:1–4:1

Text

		Syllable Count		Stress Count	
			MT		MT
3:1a	כִּי הִנֵּה הָאָדוֹן יְהוָה צְבָאוֹת	11	11	4	5
b	מֵסִיר מִירוּשָׁלַם וּמִיהוּדָה	10	11	3	3
c	מַשְׁעֵן וּמַשְׁעֵנָה	6	6	2	2
d	כֹּל מִשְׁעַן־לֶחֶם	4	5	2	2
e	וְכֹל מִשְׁעַן־מָיִם:	5	6	2	2
2a	גִּבּוֹר וְאִישׁ מִלְחָמָה	7	7	3	3
b	שׁוֹפֵט וְנָבִיא	5	5	2	2
c	וְקֹסֵם וְזָקֵן:	6	6	2	2

Stanzas 1 and 5 focus on the real issues, using the third person to describe those who are addressed: false gods, false worship, a land full of things but without faithfulness to Yahweh. Thus the exhortations with which the poem begins and ends appeal to the "house of Jacob" to "walk in the light of Yahweh," on the one hand, and to "put away the human standards," on the other.

The following thematic outline is proposed:

Stanza 1 (vv. 5–9)
    Introduction (vv. 5):   "Turn to Yahweh"
    Strophe (vv. 6–9):   Land filled with worthless things = false gods; Yahweh has abandoned his people, may not forgive

Stanza 2 (vv. 10–11)
    Strophe A (v. 10):   Man hides in rocks
    Strophe B (v. 11):   Man humbled, Yahweh exalted

Stanza 3 (vv. 12–16)   The Day of Yahweh against all

Stanza 4 (vv. 17–19b)
    Strophe A (v. 17):   Man humbled, Yahweh exalted
    Strophe B (vv. 18–19b): Idols disappear into rocks

Stanza 5 (vv. 19c–22)
    Strophe (vv. 19c–21):   Worthless things = false gods abandoned before Yahweh's wrath.
    Conclusion (v. 22):   "Forsake purely human things"

Translation

3:1a   Surely the lord Yahweh Seba³oth
    b   is about to remove from Jerusalem and from Judah
    c   supply and support—
    d   the whole supply of food
    e   and the whole supply of water,
    2a   warrior and foot soldier,
    b   judge and prophet
    c   and diviner and elder,

3a	שַׂר־חֲמִשִּׁים וּנְשׂוּא פָנִים	8/(9)	9	(3)/4	3
b	וְיוֹעֵץ וַחֲכַם חֲרָשִׁים	8/(9)	9	2	2
c	וּנְבוֹן לָחַשׁ׃	(3)/4	5	3	3
Verses 1–3		73/76 = 74	80	(28)/29	29
4a	וְנָתַתִּי נְעָרִים שָׂרֵיהֶם	10	10	3	3
b	וְתַעֲלוּלִים יִמְשְׁלוּ־בָם׃	8	9	2	2
5a	וְנִגַּשׂ הָעָם אִישׁ בְּאִישׁ	8	8	4	4
b	וְאִישׁ בְּרֵעֵהוּ	6	6	2	2
c	יִרְהֲבוּ הַנַּעַר בַּזָּקֵן	8	9	3	3
d	וְהַנִּקְלֶה בַּנִּכְבָּד׃	7	7	2	2
6 a	כִּי־יִתְפֹּשׂ אִישׁ בְּאָחִיו בֵּית אָבִיו	10	10	(4)/5	5
b	שִׂמְלָה לְכָה קָצִין תִּהְיֶה־לָּנוּ	10	10	4	4
c	וְהַמַּכְשֵׁלָה הַזֹּאת תַּחַת יָדֶךָ׃	10/(11)	11	4	4
7a	יִשָּׂא בַיּוֹם הַהוּא לֵאמֹר	8	8	4	4
b	לֹא־אֶהְיֶה חֹבֵשׁ	5	5	2	2
c	וּבְבֵיתִי אֵין לֶחֶם וְאֵין שִׂמְלָה	9/(10)	11	5	5
d	לֹא תְשִׂימֵנִי קָצִין עָם׃	8	8	4	4
Verses 4–7		107/(109)	112	(43)/44	44
8a	כִּי כָשְׁלָה יְרוּשָׁלִַם	8	9	3	3
b	וִיהוּדָה נָפָל	5/(6)	5	2	2
c	כִּי־לְשׁוֹנָם וּמַעַלְלֵיהֶם אֶל־יְהֹוָה	13	13	4	3
d	לַמְרוֹת עֵנֵי כְבוֹדוֹ׃	7	7	3	3
9a	הַכָּרַת פְּנֵיהֶם עָנְתָה בָּם	10	10	(3)/4	4
b	וְחַטָּאתָם כִּסְדֹם	6	6	2	2
c	הִגִּידוּ לֹא כִחֵדוּ	7	7	3	3
d	אוֹי לְנַפְשָׁם	4	4	2	2
e	כִּי־גָמְלוּ לָהֶם רָעָה׃	8	8	3	3
Verses 8–9		68/(69)	69	(25)/26	25
10a	אִמְרוּ צַדִּיק כִּי־טוֹב	6	6	3	3
b	כִּי־פְרִי מַעַלְלֵיהֶם יֹאכֵלוּ׃	10	10	3	3
11a	אוֹי לְרָשָׁע רָע	5	5	3	3
b	כִּי־גְמוּל יָדָיו יֵעָשֶׂה לּוֹ׃	9	9	4	4
12a	עַמִּי נֹגְשָׂיו מְעוֹלֵל	8	8	3	3
b	וְנָשִׁים מָשְׁלוּ בוֹ	7	7	3	3
c	עַמִּי מְאַשְּׁרֶיךָ מַתְעִים	(8)/9	9	3	3
d	וְדֶרֶךְ אֹרְחֹתֶיךָ בִּלֵּעוּ׃	(9)/10	11	3	3
Verses 10–12		(62)/64	65	25	25

3a   official of fifty and well respected,
   b   and advisor and wise craftsman,
   c   and skilled charmer.

4a   And I am about to make adolescents their officials;
   b   capricious children will rule over them;
5a   and the people will be oppressed—man against man
   b   and man against his fellowman.
   c   They will turn on each other—adolescent against elder
   d   and the dishonorable against the honorable.
6a   Surely one will seize his brother, his own kinsman:
   b   "You have a cloak! A leader you will be for us
   c   and this rubble will be under your authority. . . ."
7a   He will raise [his voice] **on that day**,
   b   "I will not be a binder [of wounds];
   c   in my house is neither food nor cloak.
   d   You will not make me leader of the people."

8a   For Jerusalem will have stumbled
   b   and Judah will have fallen.
   c   For their speech and their deeds are before Yahweh
   d   to act rebelliously [in] the eyes of his "glory."
9a   The expression of their faces testifies against them;
   b   their sin (is) like Sodom;
   c   they report; they do not conceal.
   d   Woe to themselves,
   e   for they have earned for themselves evil.

10a   Say [to the] righteous that it is well,
   b   for the fruit of their labors they will eat.
11a   Woe to the wicked, for it is bad,
   b   for the reward of his hands will be done to him.
12a   My people—their oppressors act like children;
   b   women rule over them!
   c   My people—your leaders are misleading;
   d   they confuse the way of your paths.

13a	נִצָּב לָרִיב יְהוָה	6	6	3	3
b	וְעֹמֵד לָדִין עַמִּים:	7	7	3	3
14a	יְהוָה בְּמִשְׁפָּט יָבוֹא	7	7	3	3
b	עִם־זִקְנֵי עַמּוֹ וְשָׂרָיו	8	8	3	3
c	וְאַתֶּם בִּעַרְתֶּם הַכֶּרֶם	8	9	3	3
d	גְּזֵלַת הֶעָנִי בְּבָתֵּיכֶם:	10	10	3	3
15a	מַלָּכֶם תְּדַכְּאוּ עַמִּי	9	9	3	3
b	וּפְנֵי עֲנִיִּים תִּטְחָנוּ	(8)/9	9	3	3
c	נְאֻם־אֲדֹנָי יְהוָה צְבָאוֹת:	10	10	3	3

Verses 13–15	(73)/74	75	27	27

16a	וַיֹּאמֶר יְהוָה	5	5	2	2
b	יַעַן כִּי גָבְהוּ בְּנוֹת צִיּוֹן	9	10	4	5
c	וַתֵּלַכְנָה נְטוּוֹת גָּרוֹן	9	9	3	3
d	וּמְשַׂקְּרוֹת עֵינָיִם	(6)/7	8	2	2
e	הָלוֹךְ וְטָפֹף תֵּלַכְנָה	8	8	3	3
f	וּבְרַגְלֵיהֶם תְּעַכַּסְנָה:	(8)/9	9	2	2
17a	וְשִׂפַּח אֲדֹנָי	6	6	2	2
b	קָדְקֹד בְּנוֹת צִיּוֹן	6	6	3	3
c	וַיהוָה פָּתְהֵן יְעָרֶה:	8	8	3	3

Verses 16–17	(65)/67	69	24	25

18a	בַּיּוֹם הַהוּא יָסִיר אֲדֹנָי	9	9	4	4
b	אֵת תִּפְאֶרֶת הָעֲכָסִים	7	8	3	3
c	וְהַשְּׁבִיסִים וְהַשַּׂהֲרֹנִים:	10	11	2	2
19	הַנְּטִיפוֹת וְהַשֵּׁירוֹת וְהָרְעָלוֹת:	13	13	3	3
20a	הַפְּאֵרִים וְהַצְּעָדוֹת וְהַקִּשֻּׁרִים	14	14	3	3
b	וּבָתֵּי הַנֶּפֶשׁ וְהַלְּחָשִׁים:	10	11	3	3
21	הַטַּבָּעוֹת וְנִזְמֵי הָאָף:	9	9	3	3
22a	הַמַּחֲלָצוֹת וְהַמַּעֲטָפוֹת	9	11	2	2
b	וְהַמִּטְפָּחוֹת וְהָחֲרִיטִים:	10	10	2	2
23a	וְהַגִּלְיֹנִים וְהַסְּדִינִים	10	10	2	2
b	וְהַצְּנִיפוֹת וְהָרְדִידִים:	10	10	2	2

Verses 18–23	111	116	29	29

24a	וְהָיָה תַחַת בֹּשֶׂם מַק יִהְיֶה	8	10	5	5
b	וְתַחַת חֲגוֹרָה נִקְפָּה	7	8	3	3
c	וְתַחַת מַעֲשֶׂה מִקְשֶׁה קָרְחָה	8	10	4	4
d	וְתַחַת פְּתִיגִיל מַחֲגֹרֶת שָׂק	8	11	4	4
e	כִּי־תַחַת יֹפִי [בֹשֶׁת]	5	5	3	2

13a   Yahweh is about to hold court

  b   and about to stand to judge [the] peoples.

14a   Yahweh will enter into judgment

  b   with the elders of his people and their officials.

  c   "You have burned the vineyard;

  d   the plunder of the poor [is] in your houses.

15a   Why do you crush my people;

  b   and the face of the poor you grind?"

  c   Oracle of lord Yahweh Seba°oth.

16a   And Yahweh said,

  b   "Because the daughters of Zion are arrogant

  c   and walk [with] outstretched neck[s]

  d   and winking eyes,

  e   tripping along they walk,

  f   and with their feet they jingle,

17a   Adonay will smite with a scab

  b   the scalp of the daughters of Zion

  c   and Yahweh will expose their pelvis."

18a   **On that day**, Adonay will remove

  b   the beauty of: the anklets

  c   and the headbands and the crescents,

19   the earrings and the bracelets and the veils,

20a   the diadem and the anklets and the sashes,

  b   and the "life boxes" and the charms,

21   the finger rings and the nose rings,

22a   the festal robes and the outer robes,

  b   and the cloaks and the purses,

23a   and the lingerie and the undergarments,

  b   and the turbans and the stoles.

24a   It will happen instead of perfume, stench will be;

  b   and instead of a belt, a rope;

  c   and instead of a hairdo, baldness;

  d   and instead of fine clothes, a girding of sackcloth;

  e   for, instead of beauty, shame.

25 a	מְתַיִךְ בַּחֶרֶב יִפֹּלוּ	7	9	3	3
b	וּגְבוּרָתֵךְ בַּמִּלְחָמָה:	(8)/9	9	2	2
Verses 24–25		(51)/52	62	24	23
26a	וְאָנוּ וְאָבְלוּ פְּתָחֶיהָ	(10)/11	11	3	3
b	וְנִקְּתָה לָאָרֶץ תֵּשֵׁב:	8	9	3	3
4:1a	וְהֶחֱזִיקוּ שֶׁבַע נָשִׁים	7	9	3	3
b	בְּאִישׁ אֶחָד בַּיּוֹם הַהוּא	8	8	3	3
c	לֵאמֹר לַחְמֵנוּ נֹאכֵל	7	7	3	3
d	וְשִׂמְלָתֵנוּ נִלְבָּשׁ	7	7	2	2
e	רַק יִקָּרֵא שִׁמְךָ עָלֵינוּ	9/(10)	10	4	4
f	אֱסֹף חֶרְפָּתֵנוּ:	6	6	2	2
Verses 3:26–4:1		62/64 = 63	67	23	23
Totals		672/686 = 680	715	(248)/251	250
		Syllables	MT	Stresses	MT

Notes on Translation and Text

3:1a, 6a. **"surely"** I take כִּי as an asseverative.

3:1b. **"is about to remove"** The word הנה plus a participle are taken as the "imminent future."

3:1c. **"supply and support"** Why מַשְׁעֵן is here spelled with an initial *a* vowel is not clear, especially since it is spelled *i–a* in lines d–e. Furthermore, the feminine form is attested only here; the two forms may be paired with variant spellings for inclusiveness and emphasis. So Holladay (221) and also BDB (1044), which notes the use of the terms of both genders "to exhaust the category = support of every kind."

3:3c. **"charmer"** The exact sense of לחשׁ is not clear; it may be a term for "snake charming" or another specific referent. My translation leaves a general sense.

3:4a. **"I"** The shift to first person is retained, as in the MT. Duhm (1922: 45) suggests reading נתן י as an abbreviated "Yahweh will . . . ," but that seems a forced attempt to maintain the third person, which is not necessary.

25a Your men will fall by the sword
  b and your heroes in battle.

26a Her gates will lament and mourn,
  b and she will be stripped; on the ground she will sit.
4:1a Seven women will take hold
  b of one man **on that day**,
  c saying, "Our bread we will eat,
  d and our clothes we will wear,
  e just let us have your name;
  f take away our shame."

"am about to make" The "imminent future" is likely linked to the construction in 1b by *waw*-consecutive.

3:4b. **"capricious children"** תעלולים in this form (never singular) is used only here and in Isa 66:4, where it has an abstract sense; so BDB (760). But the parallel to נערים as well as the perceived pun on עוֹלֵל suggests the reference includes overtones of *children's* actions (so Duhm 1922: 45, '*Bübereien*'). I suggest one step further: not just the children's actions, but 'capricious children'. The wordplay is picked up in line 12a.

3:6a. **"his own kinsman"** Taken as an appositive rather than adverbial 'in his father's house'.

3:6b. **"leader"** קצין is emphatic by position, and based on its use in Josh 10:24 and Judg 11:6, may recall the premonarchic period, when like Jephthah, anyone could become "leader" by acclamation or necessity. It is used in the prophets only here, in 1:10 and in 22:3, and in Mic 3:1, 9, all of which are accusatory and threatening.

3:6a. **"rubble"** מכשלה is used only here and in Zeph 1:3, where a specific meaning is also not clear. The verbal root כשל (see 8a) means 'to stumble'; the more common noun מִכְשׁוֹל usually means an 'occasion for stumbling', as in Isa 8:14 (צור מקשׁול). One notes again the use of a variant spelling with an initial *a* vowel (instead of *e* vowel) as in 1c. Line 8c uses the verbal root, and whether the reference here is to the buildings that will have fallen ('rubble') or the people who will have stumbled ('rabble') is not clear.

3:8a. "will have stumbled" Translation of the afformative tense is difficult and related to the question of historical context and referents. The general tone of the passage and description of "that day" is future, hence I take these verbs as "future (so–called prophetic) perfect."

3:8c. "before Yahweh . . . in the eyes of his 'glory'" The bicolon is very difficult. It is possible to read אל־יהוה as 'against Yahweh', since אֶל and עַל may overlap. In the second line, עני might be read as 'humble', which seems to underlie the sense of the LXX διότι νῦν ἐταπεινώθη, but the subject there is ἡ δόξα αὐτῶν. Overall, the LXX seems an awkward attempt to make sense out of awkward Hebrew. Wiklander (1984: 67) suggests 'they distress the humble regarding his glory', also reading עני as 'humble'. There is a sense, however, in which עני כבודו is somewhat parallel to the אל־יהוה of the first line, if one reads עני as עיני ('eyes of' = presence of).

Finally, the *Hiphil* infinitive (למרות for להמרות) could either take the following phrase as object, which is not impossible (and suggested by BDB 598), 'to act rebelliously toward = to provoke the eyes of his glory'; or as an adverbial, 'in the eyes of his glory', for which I have opted in light of the previous line.

3:9bc. "their sin (is) like Sodom; they report; they do not conceal" One could read הגידו (+ לא כחדו ?) in 9c as the verb, in which case כסדם is (likely) adjectival (rather than adverbial): 'their "Sodom-like" sin they report'. Possibly the entire tricolon, 9abc, is to be read together: 9c continues the sense of 9a, speaking of self-convicting actions. It is also likely that חטאתם is to be read as plural and as the subject of the verbs: 'their sins tell against them . . .'.

3:9d. "to themselves" נפשׁ could imply 'their life' or simply the pronoun, 'to them'. Though awkward English, the reflexive sense of the previous and following lines is continued in translation.

3:10a. "say" אמרו is difficult and much discussed. Attempts to restore a proposed אַשְׁרֵי via אסר ('to bind') via LXX Δήσωμεν are not helpful, since the LXX begins εἰπόντες, which is clearly from the root אמר (Watts 1985: 40). The imperative seems quite intrusive, as does the sudden reference to a "righteous one," but the contrast of righteous/wicked is easier to explain than the second-masculine plural verb. Apparently the prophet is exhorting the people, specifically the wicked ones, to observe in the lives of the righteous the same "reap what you sow" effect that will affect them negatively. Possibly צדיק could be read adverbially: 'speak righteously, for it [is] good . . .', but the shift back to third plural in 10b then becomes awkward.

3:10a, 11a. "to" . . . "for" I read the preposition (ל) here, based on the relationship of this verse with v. 11. The *lamed* in line 11a is taken as serving double duty back to line 10a. Conversely, the כי in 10a serves double duty and is read in 11a.

3:12a. "their" Though attractive, it is unnecesary to read נגשׂיו as נגשׂים, either taking the *mem* from מעולל or replacing a *mem* lost by haplography. The simple plural would make a better parallel to 12b (נשׁים), but the suffixed form is repeated in 12c, and the tension between the third- and second-person pronouns is upheld by the use of the third-singular masculine pronoun in 12b. The LXX reads the pronoun in 12a as second plural: οἱ πράκτορες ὑμῶν.

"children" Despite the targum, which takes עלל in the sense of 'glean', the previous wordplay involving the senses of both 'capricious action' and 'child' likely carries over here, as well (see v. 4 and note to 3:4b, above). The theme is the same as in v. 4, where the משׁלו־בם is echoed in the משׁלו בו of line 12b. Note that the root נגש is also used in line 5a.

3:13a. "about to hold court" I read the participle here, and again in 13b, as a continuation of the imminent future of v. 1 (see the note to 3:1b above). My translation of נצב + לריב attempts to reproduce the Hebrew idiom with an English idiom.

3:13b. "peoples" The plural seems odd, especially in light of the singular in 14b. Hummel (1976: 100) notes that this is possibly עמו plus enclitic *mem*.

3:14c. "you" The direct quotation is indicated by the concluding נאם formula.

3:15a. "why" Reading the *Qere* מה לכם. Compare, for example, Jonah 1:6.

3:17a. "Adonay" The use of the third person within a quotation of Yahweh (16a) is not impossible. The syntax clearly makes 17a the main clause; lines 16b–f are governed by יען כי. The repetition of בנות ציון is a further link within the one sentence.

"will smite with a scab"   The meaning of שׂפַח is assumed to be from the root ‏*ספח‎, presumably a denominative from ספחת 'scab'. See BDB 705.

3:17c.   "pelvis"   If the reading is correct, the only other use of the noun is 1 Kgs 7:50 in reference to door sockets (BDB 834). The context demands a body part, the exposure of which is denigrating. My translation is a guess.

3:18b.   "anklets"   It is beyond my purpose to document and defend the translation of the various individual items in the following list of women's accesories. Many of the words are hapax legomena and translations will inevitably involve guesswork. All seem to be luxury items. The structure and ordering of the list will be discussed below, but I have tried to reproduce the groupings by faithfully translating each conjunction.

3:23a.   "lingerie"   'Tablet' or polished surface (BDB 163) may imply a 'mirror', but the other items in v. 23 seem to be articles of clothing. Though a guess, גליֹן might be related to the root גלל a 'wrap' (?), or, in my translation, to the root גלה, implying something 'revealing'.

3:24e.   "for, instead of beauty, shame"   The integrity of כי is questioned; the whole line (24e) is lacking in the LXX. 1QIsaᵃ, however, retains the line with the addition of בשת, which is adopted here as the original reading. One should note the pun between this restored בשת and the word בשׂם in 24a.

3:26b.   "will be stripped"   נקה regularly has the sense of 'be innocent', which would make sense here only if sarcastic. The translation assumes the negative sense of the context, 'stripped *clean*' in an action of humiliation.

Lineation

The unit exhibits a wide diversity in line lengths and verse structures. Verses 13–15, for example, lineate quite easily along typical poetic patterns, but vv. 18–23 consist of a list of nouns with little apparent parallelism or meter, where lineation appears quite arbitrary. Hence I admit to a certain variance in the question of the number of lines.

For example, lines 1cde are the length of a bicolon and could be lineated accordingly, but the structure favors a 3-line unit. Verse 2bc could just as easily be a longer, single line of 11 syllables and 4 stresses, but the grouping by pairs in the context suggests that it should be understood as 2 lines of one pair each. Nevertheless, the singleton at the end of the section (line 3c) is left as a very short line.

Verse 9bcd could also be combined into a bicolon; I have left it as 3 lines. The long list in vv. 19–23a has been divided on the basis of syntax and the groupings of the conjunctions, although other configurations are possible (see below, p. 219).

Several longer lines cannot be easily divided without destroying a sense of syntax or sense, such as lines 1a and 8c. Hence, while allowing for certain variables and following a method that respects syntactical and semantic borders, the lineation into 85 lines does appear reasonable. Moreover, this is consistent with the total syllable count, which falls between 672 and 686. At 8 syllables per line, 85 lines would yield 680 syllables, approximately in the center of the range.

Syllable and Stress Counts

The range shown is somewhat large, 672–86 syllables. Of the fourteen variables, nine are the prefixed conjunction before shewa, of which six are prefixed *šureq*. Five uses of the second-person pronominal suffix appear in vv. 6c, 12c, 12d, 25b, and 4:1e. The third-feminine suffix in 26a is read as long (as in the MT). At 8 syllables per line, the syllable count would indicate either 84 (672) or 85 (680) lines, and I have worked toward the higher count, since it falls more in the middle of the range and is consistent with my lineation.

Despite the wide diversity of line lengths, including some very long lines in vv. 19–20, which have simply been retained as they are, there is a remarkable overall balance:

4-syllable lines:	3	10-syllable lines:	15
5-syllable lines:	7	11-syllable lines:	2
6-syllable lines:	9	12-syllable lines:	0
7-syllable lines:	14	13-syllable lines:	2
8-syllable lines:	19	14-syllable lines:	1
9-syllable lines:	13		

Of the 85 lines,
   22.4% (8 lines) have 8 syllables,
   54.1% (46 lines) have 7–9 syllables,
   82.4% (70 lines) have 6–10 syllables.

The median number of syllables per line is 8.
The average number of syllables per line is 8.00.

Concerning stress counts, a rather small range is shown, 248–51. I have opted for the higher number, since even this is slightly low for 85 lines ($\times$ 3 = 255). One should recognize the possibility of unmarked secondary stress, especially in cola such as 16f and 25b, where two words form a line of 9 syllables, which ordinarily would have 3 stresses. Five additional examples fall within the list of nouns in vv. 18–23: lines 18c, 22a, 22b, 23a, 23b; each colon has 9–10 syllables but only 2 stresses, and one must admit to some uncertainty in this unusual situation.

Further, vv. 19 and 20a offer examples of 13–14–syllable lines with only 3 stresses, and likely one could add a 4th, but secondary, accent to each of these. However, for the sake of more objective tabulation without adding any accents arbitrarily, I shall consider the lines as indicated, with a total of 251 stresses:

2-stress cola:	25 (29.4%)
3-stress cola:	42 (49.4%)
4-stress cola:	15 (17.6%)
5-stress cola:	3 (3.5%)

Thus, 96.5% of the cola (82 lines) have 2–4 stresses.

The average number of stresses per line is 2.95 and could be exactly 3.00 with the addition of secondary stresses.

Prose Particles

The prose particle count is greatly affected by the heavy use of the article (21×) in vv. 18–23. In fact, the rest of this section has a relatively low count and uses no particle other than the article. Nowhere does the relative pronoun occur; the one object marker appears within vv. 18–23. If one factors out the 21 articles, one object marker, and 29 words in vv. 18–23, the prose particle count is 4.6%. On the other hand, the count in vv. 18–23 is 75.9% (!) for this short section, indicating that it is a highly specialized and unusual, if not unique, unit. It appears to be neither poetry nor prose but simply a list.

Nevertheless, this list is embedded within otherwise poetic material, and even with vv. 18–23 included as part of the entire piece, the overall count is 33 particles out of 267 words, or 12.34%, well within the higher limits (10–15%) of the type of prophetic rhetoric I have sought to describe. The highly focused and concentrated use of the article in these verses, in contrast to the rest of the poem, must certainly be intentional.

Verse and Strophe Structure

Verses 1–3

The unit begins with a prosaic bicolon, long but not unusually so. I have divided syntactically, with the extended subject in line 1a and the predicate in line 1b. Section 1cde, however, quickly balances with shorter lines. In this tricolon the second and third lines expand the word pair of the first line, each adding a word of an additional word pair, "bread and water." The pair in line c forms one comprehensive unit (see translation note to 3:1c, p. 210), so that the tricolon cites three items.

Line 2a introduces the remainder of the list with a single pair, including one one-word and one two-word item. Lines 2bc note four one-word items and lines 3abc note four two-word items, with the additon of יועץ in line 3b. Added to the three items in 1cde and the pair in 2a, there are four items in 2bc and five in 3abc, for a total of fourteen items in the entire list.

Verses 4–7

Verses 4–5 are three bicola (18 + 14 + 15 syllables), with the third picking up the theme of the first: children (or their equivalent) will rule. The middle bicolon (5ab) really shows a tripartite structure (2:2:2 stresses) but is in length clearly a bicolon, either 2:4 (5 + 9 syllables) or, as shown, 4:2 (8 + 6 syllables).

Verse 6 continues the "one against another" motif, although the theme moves from oppression and anger to the pathos of a leaderless people. The translation difficulties of v. 6 have already been discussed; as I lineate, it is a long, but balanced tricolon of 10 + 10 + 10 syllables and 5 (4?) + 4 + 4 stresses.

If the translation is correct, v. 7 offers the response, by the one seized, to the incident described in v. 6, introduced by reference to the thematic motif of "on that day." Word repetitions bind the two verses together: בית אביו in 6a is echoed by בביתי in 7c; שמלה לכה in 6b is punned in reverse order by לחם . . . שמלה in 7cd; קצין occurs in 6b and 7d. The word תהיה in 6b is answered by אהיה in 7b.

Verses 8–12

Verse 8 appears to begin a new subsection (see below, pp. 220–21). Five of the seven initial כי clauses that occur in vv. 1–12 appear here. The verb כשל links back to the previous section via the noun formation הממשלה in line 6c. Lines 8ab give the reason for the previous situation; 8cd gives the reason for 8ab.

Lines 9abc form a tricolon, but the three verbs are distributed in the first and last lines. Whether the middle line is to be read as an independent verbless sentence or as dependent on at least one of the following verbs is not clear (see translation note to 3:9b, p. 212).

The 6 lines of vv. 9d–11 form three bicola. Each second line contains the כי clause subordinate to the first line. The first and last bicola, dealing with those who do evil, are contrasted by the middle bicolon, dealing with those who do good, the fruit of whose מעללים is thus contrasted with the מעללים previously mentioned in 8c. The repetition of אוי, the root גמל, and רע/רעה in 9de and v. 11 all serve to interlock these bicola, the second building on the meaning of the first. In 9de, "they" are identified as working "evil"; in v. 11, the individual "evil one" will receive the results of his work back upon himself, which seems to reiterate the point of 9d.

Verse 12 is a tightly arranged quatrain of two interlocked bicola, with a total of 34 syllables and 12 stresses. Lines ab, which speak of "my people" in the third person, are matched by lines cd, which speak of "my people" as second person. Conversely, lines a and c have the same grammatical structure, focus noun→substantive participle→verbal participle, while lines b and d use finite, afformative verbs, line b with a subject, line d with an object. While this may have produced some intentional ambiguity, it seems likely that the meaning of these lines follows the grouping of lines a and c, lines b and d. Thus "your leaders" are, in fact, "their oppressors," and "the women" who rule over them are those who "consume the way of your paths."

Verses 13–15

Verses 13–15 are the most balanced lines in the whole piece, dividing quite naturally into four parallelistic bicola, with a total of 64 syllables and 24 stresses (exactly 8/3 per line), plus a final, slightly longer monocolon as a conclusion to the oracle. As discussed below (p. 220, #4; p. 222), this unit plays a central role in both the structure and the theme of the entire piece.

Verses 16–17

Verses 16–17 are not as easily lineated or paired. These nine lines are, on the average, shorter, with a total of 67 syllables and 24 stresses. A short monocolon introduces direct discourse, as the longer monocolon in the previous verse (line 15c) concluded it. The following 8 lines seem to divide into two tricola surrounding the bicolon in 16ef. The כי clause in 16b precedes the main clause, and the subordinating conjunction governs the 5 lines of 16bcdef, followed by the main clause in the final tricolon, v. 17. The phrase בנות ציון holds the verses together (lines 16b and 17b).

Verses 18–23

This unit is, as already noted, the most difficult to treat. Nevertheless, structural features are quite apparent. Although vv. 18–23 are really one long sentence, the extended list of 21 items that forms the compound direct object is quite carefully worked. All of them are marked by the definite article and all of them are grammatically the *nomina recta* to which the initial תפארת is bound, itself marked by the only object marker in all of 3:1–4:1.

The initial bicolon of 16 syllables (18ab) introduces the first item. Verses 18c–20a list eight single terms, as do vv. 22–23. In the first list of eight (vv. 18c–20a), the use of *waw* divides the items as 2 + 3 + 3, while in vv. 22–23 the list is arranged as simply 1 + 7 (or as four pairs).

In between lies the chiastic bicolon of vv. 20b–21, a list of four items. The first and last are two-word units that are construct chains. The initial *waw* in line 20b links to what precedes; the asyndetic v. 21 links to what follows.

Thus the entire list is arranged as one item (18ab) + 8 items (18c–20a) + 4 items (20b–21) + 8 items (22–23): 1 + 8 + 4 + 8 = 21. On the other hand, dividing the middle chiasm (20b–21) and forming three units, 18ab, 18c–20b, and 21–23, the items are grouped as 1 + 10 + 10 (= 21). In syllable counts, the units divide as 16 + 37 + 19 + 39; or, again dividing 20b–21, 16 + 47 + 48, either of which indicates a sense of balancing and deliberate structuring.

A total of 112 syllables (versus the 111 that I count) would yield exactly 14 lines averaging 8 syllables, which could be achieved by arbitrarily grouping the 12 lines that follow the initial bicolon as 8 lines of two items (= 16) and 4 lines of one item (= 4, + 16, plus the one in 18ab = 21 items).

Verses 24–25

Verse 24 both continues and develops the thought, from removal to replacement, using תחת five times in a list of ten nouns, five substituting for five. Wordplay abounds, beginning and ending with בשת/בשם (see translation note to 3:24e, p. 214). There is also interplay between מק and שׁק in lines a and d, and of מעשׂה and מקשׁה in the center line (c).

Verse 25 concludes this section with a bicolon (compare 18ab) that addresses the women directly.

Verses 3:26–4:1

Verse 26 begins the final section by shifting back to the third person and suggesting that the women described are not simply the women of

Jerusalem but Jerusalem herself, whose "gates" will mourn. Although 4:1 is quite prosaic, it nevertheless lineates into 8 relatively balanced lines that continue the theme of v. 24: the loss of men to war will be the ultimate and awful symbol of the replacement of beauty by shame.

Gross Structure

Although seemingly long and diverse, the unit displays a number of features that suggest a unifying working of the material. The Masoretic paragraph markers in both the CL and the CA, confirmed also by the Qumran scroll, indicate breaks after vv. 12, 15, 17, and 4:1,[1] and these correspond to certain structural divisions as will be shown. It seems clear that v. 13 begins a new major section, right in the middle of the whole unit, with another major break after v. 15. The following general observations are to be made:

1. Two "lists" are basic to the content of this section: 7 pairs (=14) describing the male leadership in vv. 1–3, and 21 items (3×7) of women's luxuries, all marked with the definite article, in vv. 18–23. In addition, both sections begin with a use of the verbal root סור: מסיר in 1b and יסור in 18a.
2. The section following vv. 1–3 (vv. 4–5) describes the replacement of normal leaders by children; men will be turned against one another. The section following vv. 18–23 (vv. 24–25) describes the replacement of luxury beauty items with their opposites.
3. Verses 6–7 describe one man seizing another and begging him for leadership on the basis of his 'cloak' (שׂמלה) and 'food' (לחם). The final section, 3:26–4:1, describes seven women grabbing one man and begging him for his name with no obligation to provide them with a 'cloak' (שׂמלה) or 'food' (לחם).
4. Central to the entire piece are vv. 13–15 (the center by syllables lies in 14b; the center by stresses lies in 13a; the center by words falls in 12c). This middle unit consists of the most balanced lines: 8 lines with 64 syllables and 24 stresses, plus the concluding monocolon in 15c. The divine names יהוה and אדני יהוה צבאות form an inclusio between 13a and 15c.
5. Verse 16 picks up the theme of the women, first introduced in v. 12, and they become the focus of the rest of the larger unit, in contrast to vv. 1–12, where men are the dominant topic. Mention of the "men" returns at the very end, in 4:1.

---

1. Again 1QIsaᵃ shows a minor break after 3:26, corresponding to the chapter division in BHS, which is universally ignored by including 4:1 in this section. Further, the scroll shows a break after 4:2!

On the basis of these observations, I suggest a three-part structure, or, more precisely, two larger sections around a focus, or hinge, that is central to both structure and theme:

Stanza 1: vv. 1–12:   313 syllables, 124 stresses
Middle focus: vv. 13–15:   74 syllables, 27 stresses
Stanza 2: vv. 16–4:1:   293 syllables, 99 stresses

Stanzas I and II are roughly equivalent in length. Furthermore, each breaks down into four strophes:

Stanza 1 (vv. 1–12)
  Strophe A: vv. 1–3:   74 syllables, 29 stresses
  Strophe B: vv. 4–7:   107 syllables, 44 stresses
  Strophe C: vv. 8–9:   68 syllables, 26 stresses
  Strophe D: vv. 10–12:   64 syllables, 25 stresses
Stanza 2 (vv. 3:16–4:1)
  Strophe A: vv. 16–17:   67 syllables, 24 stresses
  Strophe B: vv. 18–23: 111 syllables, 29 stresses
  Strophe C: vv. 24–25:   52 syllables, 23 stresses
  Strophe D: vv. 3:26–4:1: 63 syllables, 23 stresses

Some vocabulary links have already been noted in the discussion of verse and strophe structure, in addition to the large inclusio using the terms "cloak" and "bread" between 3:7 and 4:1. One might also observe the use of the verbal root נפל in 8b, in reference to Judah, and in 25b, in reference to the soldiers of Judah. Likewise, two of the male terms from vv. 1–3 (איש מלחמה and גבור) are echoed by גבורתך במלחמה in 25b.

Thought Progression

The structural connection between the "lists" in vv. 1–3 and vv. 18–23 has already been noted. These are not only thematic to this section but also a clear link to the material in Isa 2:5–22, in which the land was described as "full." The characteristic use of the number seven certainly plays a role in indicating the "fullness" of the land, and 3:18–23 lists in almost hyperbolic detail the kinds of luxury items (אלילים in 2:8) that have overfilled these poetic lines as well.

However, the main issue is not simply this overabundance. The real tension lies in the judgment of Yahweh, which will result not only in the replacement of luxury with loss but also in the destruction of male leadership due to war. Thus the concern of stanza 1 is the loss of male leadership. The "list" in vv. 1–3 (strophe A) consists of various descriptions of leadership positions, turned upside down in vv. 4–5 (strophe B).

Verses 6–7 describe the ultimate lack of any leader: whoever has a cloak will be pressed upon to lead; yet the reply denies either cloak or food.

The third strophe indicates (1) the real problem: Jerusalem will stumble and fall (8ab); and (2) the real reason: they have openly rebelled against Yahweh (8cd). In contrast to the righteous, yet analogous to them, the evil will reap the reward of their hands.

The final strophe of the first stanza (v. 12) introduces the theme of the women, although the meaning of v. 12 is somewhat ambiguous. The verse could refer to the fact that women will be forced into ruling positions due to the lack of men. Possibly the men are still perceived as holding the positions, but they are so overcome and preoccupied with the women— whose enticing baubles and bangles are described in vv. 16ff.—that the women are actually the ones who can be described as "misleading" the people.

Verses 13–15 form the structural and thematic focus, and the protagonist comes into center court. In a tightly structured 8-line oracle, Yahweh is described as about to enter into judgment against his own people, specifically the leadership, for their self-centered oppression of the people.

This becomes the bridge to the second stanza, in which full attention is drawn in exaggerated detail to the possessions of the women. A land so "full" of silver and gold and idolatrous things (2:7–9) that an attempt at an exhaustive list nearly exhausts both speaker and hearer is a land about to be emptied. The women, to whom leadership is entrusted by default, are themselves deprived of that which brought them status. Not only are their things gone, their men are gone as well. The lack of men means not only lack of leadership but also lack of supply and support (1cde).

Isaiah 4:2–6

Text

		Syllable Count		Stress Count	
			MT		MT
4:2a	בַּיּוֹם הַהוּא יִהְיֶה צֶמַח יְהוָה	9	10	(4)/5	5
b	לִצְבִי וּלְכָבוֹד	(5)/6	6	2	2
c	וּפְרִי הָאָרֶץ	(4)/5	6	2	2
d	לְגָאוֹן וּלְתִפְאֶרֶת	6/(7)	8	2	2
e	לִפְלֵיטַת יִשְׂרָאֵל [וִיהוּדָה]	9	6	3	[2]
3a	וְהָיָה הַנִּשְׁאָר בְּצִיּוֹן	9	9	3	3
b	וְהַנּוֹתָר בִּירוּשָׁלַ͏ִם	8/(9)	9	2	2

That the "daughters of Zion" are at once both the actual women of Judah and Jerusalem and a metaphor for the city and land is confirmed by v. 26. "On that day," it will be not simply the women but Judah and Jerusalem who will be stripped of both luxury and necessity and who will sit on the ground, lament, and mourn.

The structure of 3:1–4:1 has moved from Judah and Jerusalem, through the male leadership and lack thereof, to the female leadership and lack thereof, and back again to the city and land. The reasons given in 3:8–12 and 16–17 focus on the evil deeds of the men and the self-centered indulgence of the women. Verses 13–15 make plain that the removal both of men and of the luxuries of the women are to be understood as the verdict of the Lord, Yahweh Seba²oth.

The following outline is proposed:

Stanza 1
    Strophe A (vv. 1–3):   List of leadership to be removed
    Strophe B (vv. 4–7):   Lack of leaders, now removed
    Strophe C (vv. 8–9):   The reason: rebellion (sin)
    Strophe D (vv. 10–12): Summary conclusion: wickedness, no
                             leaders, women may have to rule
Middle focus (vv. 13–15): Yahweh judges

Stanza 2
    Strophe A (vv. 16–17): Women judged for arrogance (sin)
    Strophe B (vv. 18–23): List of luxuries to be removed
    Strophe C (vv. 24–25): Lack of luxuries, now removed
    Strophe D (vv. 26–4:1): Lack of men

Translation

4:2a **In that day** the branch of Yahweh will become
   b   majesty and glory,
   c and the fruit of the land [will become]
   d   pride and beauty
   e for the fugitive(s) of Israel and Judah.

  3 a Then, what is left in Zion
    b and what remains in Jerusalem

		Syllables	MT	Stresses	MT
c	קָד֖וֹשׁ יֵאָ֥מֶר לֽוֹ	6	6	2	3
d	כָּל־הַכָּת֥וּב לַחַיִּ֖ים בִּירוּשָׁלָֽםִ׃	11	12	3	3
4a	אִ֣ם רָחַ֣ץ אֲדֹנָ֗י	6	6	3	3
b	אֵ֚ת צֹאַ֣ת בְּנוֹת־צִיּ֔וֹן	7	7	3	3
c	וְאֶת־דְּמֵ֥י יְרוּשָׁלַ֖ם	8	9	2	2
d	יָדִ֣יחַ מִקִּרְבָּ֑הּ	5	6	2	2
e	בְּר֥וּחַ מִשְׁפָּ֖ט וּבְר֥וּחַ בָּעֵֽר׃	8/(9)	9	4	4
5a	וּבָרָ֣א יְהֹוָ֡ה עַל֩ כָּל־מְכ֨וֹן הַר־צִיּ֜וֹן	12	12	5	5
b	וְעַל־מִקְרָאֶ֗הָ עָנָ֤ן יוֹמָם֙ וְעָשָׁ֔ן	12/(13)	13	4	4
c	וְנֹ֛גַהּ אֵ֥שׁ לֶהָבָ֖ה לָ֑יְלָה	9	9	4	4
d	כִּ֥י עַל־כָּל־כָּב֖וֹד חֻפָּֽה׃	7	7	3	3
6a	וְסֻכָּ֛ה תִּהְיֶ֥ה לְצֵל־יוֹמָ֖ם מֵחֹ֑רֶב	11	12	4	4
b	וּלְמַחְסֶה֙ וּלְמִסְתּ֔וֹר	8	8	2	2
c	מִזֶּ֖רֶם וּמִמָּטָֽר׃	6	7	2	2
Totals		166/172 = 168 Syllables	177 MT	(61)/62 Stresses	62 MT

Notes on Translation and Text

4:2e. **"fugitive(s)"** The feminine singular form is to be taken as the abstract, which stands for the masculine plural and is here translated in a collective sense.

"Israel and Judah" 1QIsaᵃ adds ויהודה, which is likely the original reading, lost by homoeoarchton with והיה. Since Jerusalem is clearly the referent in v. 3, both Israel and Judah are in view. The word is restored according to the Dead Sea scroll manuscript.

4:4a. **"when"** The translation of אם is difficult. The sense seems to rule out the more common conditional usage ('if . . .'). The temporal conjunction is more likely (so BDB 50). The structural analysis will suggest that the apodosis lies in the perfect *waw*-consecutive constructions in both v. 3 and v. 5.

4:4e. **"of burning"** 1QIsaᵃ reads סער for בער, which may be the more likely reading, although it might reflect adjustment *ad sensum* to the storm imagery of v. 6. The MT appears to have the "harder reading," although בער fits well with v. 4 and with the vocabulary of chap. 6 (compare 6:13a).

c   will be called holy—
d   all [that are] written for life in Jerusalem;
4a   When Adonay washes
b   the filth of the daughters of Zion,
c   and the bloodstains of Jerusalem
d   he purges from her midst
e   by a wind of judgment and by a wind of burning,

5a   Yahweh will create upon all the sanctuary of Mount Zion
b   and upon all her assemblies a cloud by day and smoke
c   and light of fiery flame by night.

d   Surely over all [her] glory—a canopy
6a   and a hut will become shade by day from heat
b   and shelter and protection
c   from storm and rain.

4:5a. **"sanctuary"** מכון is used elsewhere in Isaiah only in 18:4, where it refers to the dwelling place of Yahweh (compare with Exod 15:17; also 1 Kgs 8:13, where Yahweh is to dwell in the temple, but also vv. 39, 43, 49, where he dwells in the heavens). The reference here seems also to have the temple in mind, and it is paralleled in the following line by מקרא, which is used in Isaiah 1–39 only here and in 1:13, also with reference to assembly in the temple.

4:5b. **"assemblies"** The MT vocalization is plural, but the consonantal text is actually singular.

Lineation

BHS sets this section as prose, although the prose particle count is hardly decisive (see below, pp. 226–27). The influence of poetic features is present, but lineation is difficult. I show v. 2, for example, with shorter lines, according to the poetic parallelism between 2b and 2d. On the other hand, with only two fewer syllables, v. 5 is shown as a three-line unit, since it cannot be easily divided unless syntactic barriers are ignored.

Nevertheless, the 21 lines as shown fall within the range of my syllable count, indicating that the short and long lines do balance out over the entire unit.

Syllable and Stress Counts

The syllable count shows a range of 166–72, including four instances of the conjunction as *šureq*. The lineation into 21 lines would suggest a syllable count of 168, so I shall read the *šureq* in the two shortest lines (2b and 2c) as a full syllable.

In spite of both rather short and long lines, the overall pattern is quite balanced:

5-syllable lines:	2	9-syllable lines:	4
6-syllable lines:	5	10-syllable lines:	0
7-syllable lines:	2	11-syllable lines:	2
8-syllable lines:	4	12-syllable lines:	2

Of the 21 lines,
    19.0% (4 lines) have 8 syllables,
    47.6% (10 lines) have 7–9 syllables,
    71.4% (15 lines) have 6–10 syllables.

The median line length is 8 syllables.
The average line length is 8.00 syllables.

I count 61–62 stresses (MT: 62) and adopt the higher count, which is still slightly short overall for 21 lines ($\times$ 3 = 63). The two 5-stress cola seem quite overloaded, but they balance out the shorter lines. Oddly, the highest number is of 2-stress cola:

2–stress cola:	9 (42.9%)
3–stress cola:	6 (28.6%)
4–stress cola:	4 (19.0%)
5–stress cola:	2 (9.5%)

Thus 19 lines (90.5%) have 2–4 stresses.
The average number of stresses per colon is 2.95 (= 3.00).

Prose Particles

In spite of the prosaic nature of this material, there are only two object markers and five articles. The object markers are both in v. 4, which appears to be the central verse, and they are therefore likely intentional and emphatic. Overall, the prose particle count is 7/71 words, or 9.86%, higher than more normal poetry but lower than other sections of this prophetic rhetoric.

Verse Structure

Verse 2

The individual verses display many features of careful structuring, including the use of parallelism. For example, v. 2 begins with an apparently prosaic line, containing the formula ביום ההוא. But the verb of 2a also governs 2c. Since 2b and 2d are parallel, the first 4 lines form a double bicolon in an ABAB pattern. The final line, 2e, continues the alliteration of the *lamed* sound but really completes the predicate begun in the first line. Thus the whole verse shows an ABABC or, better, ABABA′ pattern. In spite of the extra stresses in 2a, the syllable counts as indicated mirror this symmetry: 9 + 6 + 5 + 6 + 9.

Verse 3

Similarly, v. 3 has a carefully worked structure. The verb in 3a does double duty with v. 3b; the subjects in each line are parallel. Line 3c completes the predicate, continuing 3ab as though the unit were a tricolon. The final line seems to explain further the meaning of the "remnant" vocabulary in 3ab but, in fact, links also to the sense of קדוש in 3c, so that the 4 lines hold together as a quatrain.

Verse 4

In the center of the whole piece, v. 4 contains the two object markers in a nicely chiastic 4-line unit, with the verbs in 4a and 4d, thus ABBA. Line 4e concludes the predicate, using a double adverbial phrase to modify both the verbs in the A lines. The five-colon verse has an ABBAC, or, better, ABBAA′ pattern.

Verse 5

Verse 5 has a type of "staircase" parallelism, built around word pairs. The phrase על כל־מכון הר־ציון in 5a is matched by the similar phrase על־מקראה in 5b. In the second half of this line, the pair ענן . . . ועשן closely surrounds the adverb יומם, which is then matched by the "fiery flame" vocabulary in the final line, where the match to יומם is found in לילה.

Line 5d has been shown as attached to the following verse, in light of the larger structural analysis (see below, Gross Structure), although it could well be argued that the MT versification is quite right. But the rhyme between חָפָּה and סֻכָּה links 5d to 6a, and the initial כי clause may well begin a new unit.

Verse 6

Each of lines 6bc expands one of the terms in 6a: לצל־יומם is paralleled by two further *lamed* phrases in 6b, and מחרב is paralleled by two further מן phrases in 6c.

Gross Structure

If line 5d is combined with v. 6, as indicated, the section breaks down into five verses of approximately equal length:

v. 2:	35 syllables, 13 stresses
v. 3:	34 syllables, 11 stresses
v. 4:	34 syllables, 14 stresses
v. 5(abc):	33 syllables, 13 stresses
v. 6(+ 5d):	32 syllables, 11 stresses

A chiastic pattern (ABCBA) emerges by combining vv. 2 + 6 (A) and vv. 3 + 5abc (B):

v. 2 + v. 6(+ 5d):	67 syllables and 24 stresses
v. 3 + v. 5(abc):	67 syllables and 24 stresses

There are other links between the verses, as well. The preformative verb form יהיה (2a) is echoed in תהיה in the last verse (6a). On the other hand, the two perfect *waw*-consecutive forms begin vv. 3 and 5.

 Verse 2 and vv. (5d–)6 are further linked by the use of כבוד in 2b and 5d, as well as by the alliterative effect of the initial *lamed* in lines 2b, d, e, and 6ab. On the other hand, vv. 3 and 5 are further linked by the use of the word pair "Zion/Jerusalem," which occurs as a pair in v. 3ab and then as a divided pair in 3d and 5a.

 Clearly v. 4 falls directly in the middle, and the emphatic nature of this verse has already been observed through its own chiastic structure and use of the two object markers. Here is to be found an additional use of the word pair "Zion/Jerusalem." And, if my translation of the particle אם is correct (see above, p. 224, translation note to 4:4a), v. 4 forms the protasis of the two perfect *waw*-consecutive clauses in vv. 3 and 5.

 Finally, the three uses of the divine name are carefully distributed within the ABCBA pattern. The name יהוה occurs once in the A verses (vv. 2 and 6), in 2a, and once in the B verses (v. 3 and v. 5abc), in 5a, but in the central v. 4, the name אדני appears.

Thought Progression

While I shall argue that the theme of this section builds on what has gone before, linked, for example, to 3:1–4:1 by the phrase "daughters of Zion" in 4a, the message conveyed here is certainly in contrast to the judgment and destruction previously described. Nevertheless, I would question Clements' assessment (1980b: 53) that the contrast is so great that "virtually all modern commentators . . . have argued that these verses do not come from Isaiah, and this verdict must unquestionably be upheld." It must be kept in mind that the theme of these verses is a *future* restoration and purification of a remnant, which implies the judgment just described. In fact, the "filth" of the daughters of Zion seems a clear link to the previous chapter, and my structural analysis has shown this verse to be the thematic middle of the section. Further, the discussion of the macrostructure of all of these chapters will attempt to demonstrate a larger sense of unity (see below, pp. 237ff.).

In any case, the passage begins with the "that day" motif, which has also been noted before, although here the emphasis is on the transformation of the "branch" of Yahweh into something glorious for the fugitives from the impending destruction. If vv. 5d–6ab are intended to complement v. 2, then the fugitives are also described as covered and protected by the "canopy" of Yahweh's glory as they return to Zion, imagery that evokes the cloud and smoke and fire that accompanied the Exodus and Yahweh's presence in the wilderness (see Exod 19:16–18, Num 9:15–22).

Verse 3, then, deals directly with what will remain in Zion and Jerusalem: it will be purified. According to my structural analysis, vv. 3 and 5 should be read with v. 4: the "wind/spirit" of judgment and burning will, in fact, be a purging and washing of the filth, so that Zion will be called holy and be re-created as the place of Yahweh's sanctuary.

To outline:

Strophe A (v. 2):	Glory for the fugitives
Strophe B (v. 3):	Zion restored
Strophe C (v. 4):	Washing = purging by burning judgment
Strophe B′ (v. 5abc):	Zion restored
Strophe A′ (v. 5d–6):	Glory for the fugitives

Relation of Isaiah 4:2–6 and 2:5–4:1

The discussion of the thought progression of 4:2–6 began by noting the contrast to the previous material, a factor that has led many commentators to conclude that 4:2–6 must be distinct from, though later attached to, chaps. 2–3. I have suggested a more cautious approach, based on the fact that the message of 4:2–6 assumes the same impending judgment of which the previous chapters have spoken but that also stands in tension with a promise of hope and continuity that may look beyond judgment.

It has already been noted that the thought progression of 10:5–12:6 builds on the judgment pronounced on Assyria as the basis for a rather grandiose expression of hope and peace in the messianic line. Moreover, the "remnant" motif, expressed by the symbolic name of Isaiah's child שאר ישוב, is clearly picked up in the vocabulary of 4:3a.

Such connections will be discussed below, but the point here is that 4:2–6 may well form a conclusion to the previous material and one that has links to suggest a sense of unity, rather than disunity. I have already noted the use of the "daughters of Zion" motif in 4:2, which connects with the thought of 3:16, where the focus shifts to both the women of Jerusalem and the metaphor of Jerusalem as a woman. In fact, the *nomen regens* of the long list of items begun in 3:18b is תפארת, precisely the same word used in 4:2d, indicating that the luxuries of 3:18ff. are not simply to be removed but are to be replaced by the very "fruit of the land," which is parallel to the "branch of Yahweh." Furthermore, the second term in 4:2d, גאון, is found in Isaiah 1–12 elsewhere only in the phrases הדר גאונו in *chap. 2* (2:19d and 21d). Chapter 4 turns this term of "terror" into a term of "pride."

Finally, one should note the thematic use of "that day" at the beginning of 4:2–6, which although described previously as a day of judgment, is nevertheless thematic to both of the subsections in 2:5–22 and 3:1–4:1. There are three uses of the ביום ההוא formula in 2:5–22 (11c, 17c, 20a, plus one variant, יום ליהוה in 12a; see above, p. 203). There

---

Isaiah 2:1–4

Text

		Syllable Count	MT	Stress Count	MT
2:1a	הַדָּבָר֙ אֲשֶׁ֣ר חָזָ֔ה	7	7	3	3
b	יְשַֽׁעְיָ֖הוּ בֶּן־אָמ֑וֹץ	7	7	3	2
c	עַל־יְהוּדָ֖ה וִירוּשָׁלָֽ͏ִם׃	(8)/9	9	(2)/3	2

are three more uses of the exact "in that day" formula in 3:1–4:1 (3:7a, 18a; 4:1b).

Thus the occurrence of the ביום ההוא phrase in 4:2 is the seventh use of this formula. The first six are negative; the seventh is positive. The thematic variant in 2:12a (יום ליהוה) becomes a seventh negative expression, so that of the eight instances, two different groupings of seven appear: seven negative expressions, six of the same formula (ביום ההוא) plus one variant (יום ליהוה); and seven uses of the exact same formula (ביום ההוא), six negative and the final one positive.

If it is possible, therefore, to argue that 4:2–6 continues and completes the thought progression from chaps. 2–3 with a sense of unity and structural integrity that views these chapters as a whole, it remains to be asked whether the initial poem in 2:2–4 is also part of this unit.

Isaiah 2:1–4

We now arrive at the very beginning of the large literary unit that was demarcated in the introduction (p. 18). Isa 2:1–4 is the last piece to be fit into the overall structure of Isaiah 2–12. Although 2:1 is the superscription, it, too, will be included in the analysis. This will further test the hypothesis that all of chaps. 2–12 form a coherent block and that 2:1 is a part of the whole.

The role of v. 5 was discussed at the beginning of this chapter. Based on the structural analysis of the text that follows it in vv. 6–22, we determined that v. 5 forms an inclusio with v. 22 and is therefore better understood as part of the unit 2:5–22.

Thus the unit for discussion here is defined as 2:1–4, although the detailed poetic analysis will focus on the poem in vv. 2–4.

Translation

2:1a The word that . . . saw
   b Isaiah ben Amos
   c concerning Judah and Jerusalem:

		Syllables	MT	Stresses	MT
2a	וְהָיָה בְּאַחֲרִית הַיָּמִים	9	10	3	3
b	יִהְיֶה הַר בֵּית־יְהֹוָה	6	6	3	3
c	נָכוֹן בְּרֹאשׁ הֶהָרִים	7	7	3	3
d	וְנִשָּׂא הוּא מִגְּבָעוֹת	8	8	3	2
e	וְנָהֲרוּ אֵלָיו כָּל־הַגּוֹיִם׃	10	10	3	3
3a	וְהָלְכוּ עַמִּים רַבִּים	8	8	3	3
b	וְאָמְרוּ לְכוּ	6	6	2	2
c	וְנַעֲלֶה אֶל־הַר־יְהֹוָה	7	8	3	2
d	אֶל־בֵּית אֱלֹהֵי יַעֲקֹב	7	8	3	3
e	וְיֹרֵנוּ מִדְּרָכָיו	8	8	2	2
f	וְנֵלְכָה בְּאֹרְחֹתָיו	9	9	2	2
g	כִּי מִצִּיּוֹן תֵּצֵא תוֹרָה	8	8	(3)/4	4
h	וּדְבַר־יְהֹוָה מִירוּשָׁלָ͏ִם׃	(8)/9	9	3	2
4a	וְשָׁפַט בֵּין הַגּוֹיִם	7	7	3	3
b	וְהוֹכִיחַ לְעַמִּים רַבִּים	8	9	3	3
c	וְכִתְּתוּ חַרְבוֹתָם לְאִתִּים	10	10	3	3
d	וַחֲנִיתֽוֹתֵיהֶם לְמַזְמֵרוֹת	(9)/10	10	2	2
e	לֹא־יִשָּׂא גוֹי אֶל־גּוֹי חֶרֶב	7	8	4	4
f	וְלֹא־יִלְמְדוּ עוֹד מִלְחָמָה׃	9	9	3	3
Totals		(173)/176	181	(62)/64	59
		Syllables	MT	Stresses	MT

Notes on Translation and Text

2:2a. "Future" The translation of אַחֲרִית הַיָּמִים is difficult. The debate over its understanding as a technical term is linked to a reconstruction of the history of eschatological thought, and it is used only here in the
whole of the book of Isaiah. That it does *not* mean 'last days' in the sense
of the 'end' seems clear ("nicht das Ende, sondern die Vollendung der Geschichte," Kaiser 1963: 20). Clements (1980b: 40) is correct in suggesting
that "it is a broad, and relatively undefined, reference to the exact period
of time when the change will take place, and means rather loosely, 'in the
future,'" but his juxtaposition of the adjectives "undefined" and "exact"
betray the tension.

My translation attempts to leave the temporal referent vague but
nevertheless to indicate some specificity in that the content (what will

2a When the Future comes,
 b the mountain of the house of Yahweh will be
 c established at the head of the mountains,
 d and [it (will be)] raised above the hills.
 e Then all the nations will stream to it;
3a then many peoples will come,
 b and they will say, "Come,
 c let us go up to the mountain of Yahweh,
 d to the house of the God of Jacob,

 e so that he may instruct us from his ways,
 f so that we may walk in his paths."

 g For out of Zion will go forth Torah,
 h and the Word of Yahweh from Jerusalem.
4a Then he will judge between the nations;
 b then he will adjudicate for many peoples;
 c then they will hammer out their swords into plowshares
 d and their spears into pruning hooks.
 e Nation will not lift up sword against nation,
 f and they will no longer learn warfare.

---

happen) is linked to some referent in the present, in the way that fulfillment is linked to promise. This seems consistent with the use of the term in Gen 49:1, where it refers to the accomplishment of what is predicted, and likewise in Num 24:14, in reference to the conquest of Moab and Edom. This is not really the "Vollendung der [ganzen] Geschichte," but the completion or fulfillment of a specific issue in, or period of, history.

2:2c. **"established"** The placement of נכון before יהיה (BHS) seems syntactically awkward, especially in light of the more normal order in Mic 4:1, which I have adopted here. The change in position from line c to line b may have been a secondary development after the הוא was lost in 2d (see following note), so that 2c and 2d were better balanced.

2:2d. **"[it will be]"** הוא is restored, as in Mic 4:2. Its omission is explained here as homoeteleuton with ונשא.

"raised above"   Prefixed מִן is likely comparative, 'raised [higher] than [all the] hills'.

2:3e. "so that"   The imperfect/jussive with simple *waw* may indicate a final clause, especially after the imperative/cohortative of line 3c.

2:3g. "Torah" is left as a proper noun; one could articulate ('the Torah') in light of the parallelism with "the Word of Yahweh"

Lineation

The lines divide quite naturally. Even the prosaic v. 1 easily lineates into 3 lines. I have divided 3bcd into the natural tricolon suggested by the syllable count, although 2 longer lines might be possible. As shown, there are 22 lines.

Syllable and Stress Counts

The range in the syllable count is 173–76 (MT: 181), with the variables caused by the prefixed conjunctions in 1c, 3h (*šureq*), and 4d. Since 22 lines of 8 syllables would yield 176 syllables, I accept all the longer counts. The line lengths are typical:

6-syllable lines:	2	9-syllable lines:	5
7-syllable lines:	7	10-syllable lines:	3
8-syllable lines:	5		

Of the 22 lines,
   22.7% (5 lines) have 8 syllables,
   77.3% (17 lines) have 7–9 syllables,
   100% (22 lines) have 6–10 syllables.

The median line length is 8 syllables per line.
The average line length is 8.00.

As was also found in 4:2–6, there is a slightly low stress count for the number of lines. Twenty-two lines of 3 stresses should total 66 stresses; I count 62–64 (MT: 60). Taking the higher count, I tabulate:

2-stress cola:	4 (21.1%)
3-stress cola:	16 (68.4%)
4-stress cola:	2 (10.5%)

Thus 100% of the cola have 2–4 stresses.
The average number of stresses per colon is 2.91 (= 3.00).

Prose Particles

In the poem in 2:2–4, only four particles appear, all of them the definite article. With only 61 words, however, the count is slightly above the 5% mark: 6.6%. The count in Mic 4:1–4 is 3.3.%, which confirms the poetic nature of the piece and implies that the articles have been added in the Isaiah text.

The heading in 2:1 contains one article and one relative pronoun, so that the count for these nine words is 22.3%, definitely prosaic. However, if the counts are combined and 2:1–4 is considered as a whole, the total count still falls within the 5–10% range, 6/70 words yields a count of 8.6%.

Verse and Strophe Structure

Verse 1

Verse 1 is, of course, the superscription, which, as it turns out, does form the heading for the whole of Isaiah 2–12. The poetic analysis will focus on the poem of 2:2–4.

Verse 2

Verse 2 is an introductory monocolon, followed by a tricolon in 2bcd. The verse structure supports the text-critical argument for moving נכון to 2c, in which case 2c and 2d each begin with the paraphrastic participle. As the lines are shown (contra MT), 2cd contains a couplet that expands the initial line (line 2b).

Verses 2e–3f

Verses 2e–3a are neatly parallel bicolon, with the כל־הגוים matched by עמים רבים in the second line. I have lineated 3bcd as a tricolon, with the initial line introducing the quotation and the following bicolon exactly matched in length. The phrase from 2b, הר בית־יהוה, is now divided into "mountain of Yahweh" and "house of the God of Jacob," forming an inclusio that, I suggest, brings the first strophe to conclusion.

The following bicolon, 3ef, lies at the very center of the poem, where two nonconversive preformative verb forms indicate the purpose clause at the heart of the matter. The first verbal root (ירה) will form a link to the noun תורה in the following bicolon; the second (הלך) echoes the imperative spoken in 3b.

Verses 3gh–4ab

Verse 3gh reverts to narrative, and this chiastic bicolon begins the final strophe, echoing in "Zion" and "Jerusalem" the "mountain of the house of Yahweh" phrase in 2b and 3cd. Verse 4ab repeats the עמים רבים + הגוים vocabulary from vv. 2e–3a.

Verse 4cdef

Just as the rest of 3bcdef describes what the nations would say, 4cdef describes what they will do. The first bicolon indicates positive action, and by use of two long words in 4d, the three words in 4c are matched in length. The second bicolon describes what they will *not* do, six very short words in 4e matching the three word units in 4f.

Gross Structure

The poem is somewhat difficult to analyze and displays a structure either altered from or simply different from that of the poem in Mic 4:2–4(5). Based on the structural feature of length equivalencies, a three-part structure presents itself, with 3ef as a middle pivot bicolon:

Strophe A (vv. 2a–3d):   68 syllables, 26 stresses
Middle pivot (v. 3ef):   17 syllables, 4 stresses
Strophe B (vv. 3g–4f):   68 syllables, 25 stresses

In this way, both strophes are matched in length, as well as in general thought progression. The middle pivot concludes strophe A, by bringing the direct quotation to completion, but it also links to strophe B by shifting the focus to what actually happens on the mountain. Further, both verbs within this middle bicolon are linked to each strophe, but in reverse order: ירה (3e) to the second strophe (3g), הלך (3f) to the first strophe (3b).

Thought Progression

Like 4:2–6, this poem deals with expectations of future hope and peace, and the time setting as the future age is clearly indicated in the very first line. That the mountain of Yahweh's temple will be established and raised in the future indicates also an intermediate, previous stage, also in the future, in which it is to be destroyed and razed. No longer bringing the threat of destruction, foreign nations are here described as coming (actually as flowing uphill!) to listen and to learn.

The second half of the poem links this instruction with the "Torah and Word of Yahweh" on Zion, on the basis of which the nations now refashion the implements of war into agricultural tools and abandon both hostility and the study of warfare.

This outline summarizes:

Strophe A (vv. 2a–3d): Zion raised; nations respond
Middle pivot (v. 2ef):   Nations instructed and walk in Yahweh's ways
Strophe B (vv. 3g–4f): Zion is source of instruction; nations respond

Isaiah 2–4 as a Unified Whole

In concluding the discussion of 4:2–6 (see above, p. 229), I noted a few connections with the material previous to that unit. I suggested that the whole of Isa 2:5–4:6 can be understood with a sense of unity and integrity, especially in the sevenfold use of the "day of Yahweh" motif within the judgmental material in 2:5–4:1 and across the judgmental material into 4:2.

The two subsections 2:5–22 and 3:1–4:1 both deal with themes of judgment and destruction. Section 2:5–22 has as its focus the "day of Yahweh" (2:12–16) against everything and everyone high and lifted up. The surrounding stanzas make clear that this day of judgment applies specifically to the people of Yahweh, who have filled their land with worthless things (= idols), and the pericope begins and ends with the exhortation to the "house of Jacob" to forsake vain humanity (2:22) and instead to walk in the light of Yahweh (2:5).

Chapter 3 features two carefully structured lists of persons and things that "fill the land" (compare 2:6–8) and will be destroyed: seven pairs (= 14) as designations of male leadership and 21 items of female luxuries. These lists likely also call to mind the list in 2:12–16, where the objects of Yahweh's destructive day are described by the tenfold use of כל (see above, pp. 200–201). That list, too, displays a careful division into a group of three and a group of seven.

The focus of chap. 3 is also the judgment of Yahweh, described in 3:13–15 in the courtroom motif of judging the people(s) (plural if עמים is read in 13b), specifically his own people.

However, 4:2–6 reverses the theme of "that day" from judgment, or, better, *past* judgment, to restoration and new creation. In this way, the unit 4:2–6 presents a theme similar to that of 2:2–4, where Zion and Jerusalem are raised, and the nations come to learn of Yahweh rather than to destroy his people and city. The combination "Zion and Jerusalem" appears in chaps. 2–4 only in 2:3gh and then in 4:3ab and

4bc,[2] and the theme of replacing instruments of war with implements of agriculture is echoed in the "fruit of the land" image in 4:2c.

In fact, the introductory באחרית הימים sets the future tone for both 2:2–4 and 4:2–6, and one wonders if the plural use of "days" may be intended to introduce the multifaceted understanding of the "day of Yahweh" as a day of both judgment *and* restoration by washing and purging. Further, with the inclusion of 2:1, the unit 2:1–5 is quite similar in length to the concluding unit in 4:2–6:

> 2:1–5:   176 syllables, 64 stresses, 70 words, 22 lines
> 4:2–6:   168 syllables, 62 stresses, 71 words, 21 lines

In light of the structural use of divine names elsewhere, it is of interest to observe that 2:2–4 has four divine names: יהוה used three times (2b, 3c, 3h) and אלהי יעקב used once (3d). I have already discussed the threefold use of divine names in 4:2–6, where two uses of יהוה are combined with one use of אדני. It is tempting to see a deliberate link between the two units; between the two poems, there are a total of seven divine names.

If there is, indeed, a structural chain connecting the component parts of Isaiah 2–4, then there should also be a thematic unity to the section as well. The thought progression of all of Isaiah 2–4 begins with a statement of the future: restoration of Zion and peace among the nations. The major subsections, however, deal with the present reality: a land not full of the fruit of the glory of Yahweh but filled with worthless things, a great deal of them, many lists of them. In contrast to the day when the mountain of the house of Yahweh will be 'raised' (נשא), Yahweh first has a day against all who are 'raised' up in pride and arrogance (נשא, 2:12c).

After the seventh occurrence of the motif of "that day" in a negative, judgmental sense, however, another seventh "in that day" appears in 4:2, which continues the themes with which the whole unit began in 2:2–4. In this way, 2:2–4 and 4:2–6 form structural brackets, like "bookends," or a larger-scale inclusio around the major, intervening materials. The message of the overall piece begins and points to a hopeful future, but only after the present reality has been punished and purged.

The Relationship of Isaiah 2–4 and 10:5–12:6

At the conclusion of chap. 5 of this book, I suggested that the larger unit of Isa 10:5–12:6 not only displays a sense of unity and integrity as a whole but also shows thematic and structural links to the previous material, Isa 5:1–10:4. Having now studied what precedes Isaiah 5, namely

---

2. The only other combination of these terms in Isaiah 1–12 appears in chap. 10: vv. 12 and 32.

chaps. 2–4, I have discovered the same basic patterns of poetic structures, of line lengths, stress counts, and prose particles that were observed as normative in the other poetic sections of Isaiah 2–12. If I am correct in suggesting a circular pattern of poetic structures, building from the *Denkschrift* outward, then it remains to consider whether chaps. 2–4 will fit into this structural scheme. If they do, they should in some way match or correspond to 10:5–12:6, completing the outer circle around the two complementary poems in 5:8–25 and 9:7–10:4.

It has been shown that 10:5–12:6 is held together by, among other devices, the sevenfold use of the "that day" theme (see above, p. 183). This same motif has helped to indicate the structural unity found in chaps. 2–4. Although there are a total of nine occurrences in chaps. 2–4 (counting the phrase באחרית הימים in 2:2), various groupings of seven were discovered, each with its own integrity. In the rest of Isaiah 2–12, there are only five additional uses of the motif, four in close connection within the *Denkschrift* (7:18, 20, 21, 23) and one in the transitional verse, 5:30. Thus the use of this theme is concentrated in Isaiah 2–4 and 10:5–12:6, where there is a total of sixteen occurrences (9 + 7). Added to the five uses in the intervening material, there is a total of twenty-one occurrences of this motif in the whole of Isaiah 2–12, focused especially in chaps. 2–4 and 10:5–12:6.

Closer examination reveals numerous links in other thematic material as well as in vocabulary. The following is to be noted:

1. The combination "Zion and Jerusalem," which was observed as a link between 2:2–4 and 4:2–6, is used only two other times in Isaiah 2–12. The pair occurs in 10:12, where, after Adonay will have completed his work on "Mount Zion and in Jerusalem," he will punish the fruit (פרי; compare 4:2!) of the greatness of the the king of Assyria. It appears again in 10:12, at the end of the march against Zion and Jerusalem.

2. This same verse, 10:12, which pronounces judgment on the king of Assyria for the "fruit of his greatness," parallels the phrase with תפארת רום עיניו, which again echoes the juxtaposition of פרי with תפארת in 4:2. In fact, the noun תפארת occurs in all of Isaiah 1–39 only in 4:2, 3:18 (see above, pp. 229–30), and 10:12.

3. The term "house of Jacob" is used in all of Isaiah only in 2:5–6 (chaps. 2–4), 8:17 (*Denkschrift*), and 10:20 (10:5–12:6). In 8:17, Yahweh is described as "hiding his face" from the house of Jacob. In 10:20 (introduced by והיה ביום ההוא), the "remnant" of Israel is paralleled by the expression "fugitive of the house of Jacob."

4. The term 'fugitive' (פליטת) is found in Isaiah 1–39 only in 4:2 and 10:20.

5. The verbal root שׁען, which is important in the noun forms in 3:1, is used only one other time in Isaiah 1–12, in 10:20, in which the remnant or fugitive will no longer 'rely on' (Niphal) the one who struck him (= Assyria).

6. The vocable עמך, specifically with the second-singular suffix, is used only in 2:6, 7:17 (where Ahaz is addressed threateningly), and 10:22 ("though 'your people' Israel will be as the sand of the sea, a remnant will return . . .").

7. The combination of roots רום, שׁפל, and גבה, appears in 2:9, 11, 17, and also in 10:33. Likewise, 12:4 (נשׂגב שׁמו) is an echo of the same vocabulary.

Further, there are thematic links between the contents of chaps. 2–4 and the contents of 10:5–12:6. The importance of the "day of Yahweh" motif has already been indicated, and its dominance as a structural tie both in chaps. 2–4 and in 10:5–12:6 is a major link connecting these sections.

In the latter section, the theme of "that day" becomes one predominantly of deliverance, salvation, and restoration. The thought in 10:5ff. progresses from "woe" and judgment *upon* Assyria for her arrogance to deliverance *from* Assyria for the "remnant" and "fugitive" of Israel. This will happen when Yahweh comes to cut down the arrogance and haughtiness of the "forest" (10:33–34), and it is very much like his coming "to terrify the earth" in 2:19, 21, also in response to the arrogance and haughtiness of mankind.

Chap. 11 describes how the nations will respond to the standard that Yahweh will raise (נשׂא) from the roots of Jesse, whose place of rest will be "glory," (11:10, the middle pivot of chap. 11), calling to mind the distinctive and thematic use of כבוד in 4:2b and 4:5d, in the first and final verses of 4:2–6. The coming of the עמים and גוים in 11:10 also links to the same theme in 2:2–4. Moreover, the revived messianic line described in chap. 11 rules in justice and righteousness, empowered by the רוח of Yahweh. The use of the verbs שׁפט and יכח in 11:3 and, predicated of Yahweh in 2:4, are the only two places in Isaiah 1–39 where these two verbs appear together.

Verse 4:4, which is the thematic middle of 4:2–6, describes the purifying by Yahweh as a רוח משׁפט. The use of רוח in 4:4 and the sevenfold use in chap. 11 are the only occurrences of the noun in Isaiah 2–12, apart from 7:2, where the heart of Ahaz is said to shake "like the shaking of the trees of the forest before the wind." It is tempting to suggest a play on the judgmental "wind" of Yahweh, before which Ahaz had every right to shake.

The imagery of a new exodus is a major motif in 10:5–12:6, for example, the "way of Egypt" in 10:24–26, the references to Egypt and a "second time" in 11:11–16, and the direct citation of Exodus 15 in Isa 12:2. Likewise, the Exodus imagery appears in the restoration material in 4:2–6, especially in recalling the awesome yet protecting presence of the cloud and smoke and fire (4:5–6).

Finally, the factor of length is taken into consideration. Adding up all the subsections, the total length of chaps. 2–4 is comparable with 10:5–12:6. While not exactly the same, the two units are quite close in length:

2:1–4:6:   1464 syllables, 542 stresses, 591 words, 183 lines
10:5–12:6: 1480 syllables, 557 stresses, 638 words, 185 lines

In view of the fact that length seems to have been demonstrated as a feature of structural analysis, these figures suggest that they may be a factor also in the structuring of larger blocks within a literary unit. Since this study began by demonstrating the correspondence in length between the two poems in 5:8–25 and 9:7–10:4, which form a circle around the *Denkschrift* material, it is further proposed that chaps. 2–4 may well match 10:5–12:6 in forming another, larger, concentric circle around Isa 5:1–10:4.

The Relationship of Isaiah 2–4 and the Rest of Isaiah 2–12

It is proposed that chaps. 2–4 may well be related, both structurally and thematically, to the material in 10:5–12:6, as these form major blocks, like a very large-scale inclusio, around the intervening material. I have already considered the relationship of 10:5–12:6 to this material (see above, pp. 184ff.). This hypothesis will be strengthened by any linkages that can be demonstrated between chaps. 2–4 and the intervening chapters.

Indeed, a very clear link is readily apparent, since the very motif that plays a role in the structure of 2:5–22, namely, the refrain found in 2:9a, 11ab, and 17ab, is also to be found within the major poem in 5:8–25, at 5:15. The interplay between the vocables שחח and שפל, between רום and גבה, and between איש and אדם (see above, p. 201) is certainly also significant in 5:15, where these six vocables all appear (see above, p. 55). In fact, the following verse, 5:16, continues the thought in asserting that, by way of contrast, "Yahweh will be exalted." This contrast is also asserted in the following line in 2:11 and 2:17 as well.

It will be recalled that 10:5–12:6 contained clear links to the complementary poems in 5:8–25 and 9:7–10:4. Noted specifically were the use of the הוי formula in 10:5, directed against Assyria, as well as the "return of anger" theme from the refrains in 5:25 and in 9:7–10:4, which appears a seventh time in 12:1. More than just a thematic or vocabulary link, the use of this refrain appears to be a "piece" from another unit carefully woven into the fabric of a different segment of the garment. It forms a connection between chap. 9 and chap. 12.

Likewise, the thematic thread dealing with the humbling of man's arrogance forms a connection between chap. 5 and chap. 2. This motif found in 5:15 is also woven into the structure of 2:5–22. Thus there are linkages by means of actual component parts not only between the complementary poems of 5:8–25 and 9:7–10:4, which have formed the basis and starting point of the hypothesis concerning macrostructure, but also between these two poems and the next level of inclusio. The poem in 5:8–25 has a clear tie to chaps. 2–4; the poem in 9:7–10:4 has a clear tie to 10:5–12:6.

Of course, it has already become apparent that there are other relationships between chaps. 2–4 and the material in chaps. 5ff., including the *Denkschrift*, which lies in the center of the whole literary unit (see above, pp. 117, 131, 238–39). Certainly the "remnant" theme, embodied in the name of Isaiah's son "Shear-yashub," is in mind in 4:3 (הנשאר). I have noted the use of "that day" as a major motif, but apart from the one occurrence in 5:30, it is found only in chaps. 2–4, 10:5–12:6, and in the *Denkschrift* itself.

Another striking vocabulary link is the use of the verb בער, which occurs only ten times in Isaiah 1–39 but six times in Isaiah 2–12. In 3:14, the leaders of Judah are castigated for having "burned" Yahweh's vineyard, and in 5:5, the vineyard itself is described as being לבער, a place where "briars and thorns" will grow.

This theme is picked up in 9:17, where "wickedness burns like a fire" and consumes "briars and thorns." In 10:17 the Light of Israel is described as that which will "burn" his "briars and thorns." Thus there is at least one use of the theme in connection with "briars and thorns" in 2–4, one use in 10:5–12:6, one use in the complementary poems in chaps. 5 and 9, and one use in the smaller, transitional piece in 5:1–7.

What is more, the specific use of the infinitive לבער, which is not frequent in the entire Hebrew Bible,[3] occurs only twice in Isaiah 1–39, in 5:5 and in 6:13. Within the autobiographical account of Isaiah's commissioning, which forms the introduction to the *Denkschrift*, the occurrence of this infinitive in chap. 6 is quite likely significant. It calls attention to a theme that can be tracked from the central section to the material in chap. 5 and finally to chaps. 2–4. Isaiah's message began with the under-

---

3. The infinitive form occurs only seven times in the Hebrew Bible, three of which are in the prophetic corpus. All three are in Isaiah, but only two in Isaiah 1–39 (the third is Isa 44:15).

standing that the land would be "for burning" (6:13). This is then a clear link to the "Song of the Vineyard" in 5:1–7, which makes the same point and includes the only other use of this rather unusual infinitive expression.

The one remaining use of the root בער in Isaiah 2–12 is, interestingly, in 4:4.[4] Here the "burning" is perceived as a positive, cleansing, and purifying fire, by which Adonay will wash and cleanse the daughters of Zion ברוח משפט and ברוח בער. Since it has been argued that the pericope of 4:2–6 is an integral part of the unity of chaps. 2–4, this connection also with a major motif in chaps. 5ff. indicates in yet another way the sense of unity to the whole of Isaiah 2–12.

If this is true, then the large subsection in chaps. 2–4 is to be understood both as an introduction to chaps. 2–12 (if heard in a linear way) and as part of the conclusion to chaps. 2–12 (if heard in a circular way, from the middle out). Indeed, the contents of chaps. 2–4 function on both levels. The section itself has both a linear and a chiastic structure, beginning and ending with oracles of hope and restoration, yet perceived as future manifestations of the "day of Yahweh," *after* the present realities described in the intervening material (2:5–4:1) have been judged and destroyed.

In the same way, chaps. 2–4 as a whole, introduce chaps. 2–12. They announce a future and a hope, but only after the present situation has been dealt with. The theme of future restoration is picked up again in the corresponding large section at the end of chaps. 2–12, in 10:5–12:6, but only after the present situation described in 5:1–10:4 has been dealt with. That these central chapters clearly—and structurally—surround the *Denkschrift* indicates the focus of the entire literary unit upon the present situation, namely, the fearful and faithless response of Ahaz to the Syro-Ephraimite threat.

---

4. Following the reading in MT. See above, p. 224, translation note to 4:4e.

Chapter 7
Conclusion

The focus of this study has been twofold: first, to establish a method for poetic analysis that seeks to consider the variety of factors that too often become specialized and restricted categories for defining and describing poetry (see the concluding evaluation in pp. 9–10); second, to test this method by applying it to the prophetic rhetoric found in Isaiah 2–12, to determine if any new and helpful light might be shed on the structural issues and understanding of this literary unit (see pp. 18ff.).

Poetic Issues

Lineation

In the introductory discussion of the definitions and descriptions of Hebrew poetry (p. 1ff.), I noted that the two basic factors outlined by the watershed work of Robert Lowth have formed the foundation even for contemporary debate. Although his two categories have been challenged, denied, refined, or affirmed, they remain fundamental to the vexing issue of lineation. In my attempt to deal constructively with this problem, which, in my opinion, is often either ignored or decided arbitrarily, I have come to recognize the role of both parallelism and meter as complementary, at times conflicting, but nevertheless mutually controlling factors.

I have consistently lineated along the traditional lines of parallelism and syntax, recognizing, though not necessarily agreeing with, the observations of Kugel (1981), O'Connor (1980), and Cloete (1989a) concerning basic colon boundaries. However, as I have pointed out (see pp. 27–28), there are many cases where these categories fail, or at least fail to be conclusive, and even Cloete recognized the need for the addition of a metric (stress, or rhythmic) constraint. Furthermore, as Berlin (1985) has suggested, poetic expression includes "terseness." As I have suggested, terseness begs for clearer definition (p. 4).

Thus this study has taken seriously the factor of meter, broadly defined in recognition of the difficulty of definition and description. Stress accents, which really measure rhythm, do give some guide to the larger patterns of meter, although many problems must be acknowledged due to uncertainties about both the phonetics of Biblical Hebrew and the way original accentual systems may actually have functioned. In the introductory survey, various counting systems were noted (pp. 4ff.), with evaluations of the strengths and weaknesses of each. Although I do count stresses, I have argued for the primacy of syllable counting as a reasonable and more precise measurement of length.

The methodology discussed on pp. 28ff., which was put into practice with specific reference to the poems in Isa 5:8–25 and 9:7–10:4 (pp. 42ff. and 73ff. above), sought, first of all, to lineate according to parallelism and syntactical boundaries in all cases where line divisions were clear. On the basis of these lines, the plurality of the 8-syllable (and 3-stress) colon was observed. According to the hypothesis presented in the introduction, this line length has been demonstrated as normative elsewhere (Freedman 1972a, 1986). Once established as the dominant pattern, this 8-syllable colon was then used as a guide in cases where lineation was not clear. What was discovered was a large diversity in line lengths combined with a sense of balance and symmetry that controlled even larger poetic units around the norm of 8 syllables and 3 stresses per line. This basic colon length proved to be the average overall (see below, p. 247).

In the more detailed analysis in chapters 2 and 3, this hypothesis was tested on the level of bicola (pp. 46ff. and 77ff.), and it was confirmed by the fact that the average bicolon had 16 syllables and 6 stresses. Moreover, bicola themselves displayed a sense of balance, even when the individual lines were of different lengths. For example, the bicolon in Isa 5:19ab has lines of 13 + 4 syllables and 4 + 2 stresses, but the total for the bicolon is 17 syllables and 6 stresses. Likewise, Isa 5:8cd shows 2 lines of 4 + 12 syllables and 2 + 4 stresses, but the total is 16 syllables and 6 stresses. Even more striking is Isa 5:19cd, with 14 + 4 (= 18) syllables and 5 + 1 (= 6!) stresses. Further, bicola in which the initial (A) line was longer were generally matched by a similar number of bicola in which the second (B) line was longer.

These data suggest that lineation was controlled by a powerful sense of balance, which I have sought to describe by the simple factor of length. In fact, it is theoretically possible, as has been shown with reference to the two major poems in 5:8–25 and 9:7–10:4 in appendixes 1C and 2C, to demonstrate a lineation based entirely on the 8-syllable line, ignoring parallelism and syntactic boundaries, if necessary.

Nevertheless, it appears that both "parallelism" and "meter" function concurrently, and that, while enjambment remains a difficult question at the heart of the issue, lineation generally respects syntactic borders. Indeed, the argument for the inclusion of metric considerations is strengthened by the fact that I have lineated along traditional lines of parallelism and syntax and still have found that the average line length, even over the entire corpus of 588 lines, is 8 syllables and 3 stresses per line (see below, pp. 247, 249).

What has been shown, then, is that a metric constraint operates as a factor in lineation, although it seems to have functioned in the background, as an invisible grid against which and upon which the poet constructed his work. Exactly how the poet worked his craft may never be known, as any original graphic representation of what was likely an oral presentation has been lost to a manuscript tradition that, in the case of the prophetic literature, is not written stichometrically.

What is clear is that parallelism (semantic and syntactic) and meter functioned in a complementary way, but at different levels and sometimes at cross-purposes. Syntax serves the meaning; meter serves the structure. Each functions with its own system of signs (see p. 9 n. 8), but both are operative in the production of the text. At times they might work in tension with each other, pulling the hearer/reader/analyst in contrary directions, but in so doing, they enrich and enhance the texture and artistry of the text.

Syllable Counts

Syllable counting has proved to be a helpful measurement of length, both on the level of the line (and as such a factor in lineation) and on the level of larger structural relationships. This is true both among various corresponding parts of individual poems and between larger unit pairs within the macrostructure of a literary whole such as Isaiah 2–12.

The usefulness of syllable counting to the question of lineation is clear. To be sure, there exists a mutual, if not circular, relationship between the determination of the number of lines and the fixing of a specific number of syllables within a given range of possibilities, especially within a larger piece with a greater number of variables. Nevertheless, I have been aware of this concern and worked carefully within a range of syllables both to lineate and to suggest an actual number of syllables for each line whenever a variable exists.

Admittedly, I recognize a certain flexibility, both on the part of my analysis and, more significantly, on the part of the poet, to elide the prefixed conjunction, for example, in order to achieve a syllable count consistent with a metric pattern. There are, no doubt, other possible ways of fixing syllable counts for each line, but in any case, this method works within a clearly defined range. In general, I have worked toward the center of that range for each unit or poem.

The ranges and fixed numbers for each unit discussed are summarized in appendix 4. The MT counts have also been tracked and tabulated for the purpose of comparison. In general, the MT counts are higher and do not present the overall sense of balance in terms of structural concerns. While a degree of hypothetical reconstruction of the vocalization of the biblical period is admitted (see p. 24), the syllable counts present a greater accuracy than other systems of measurement. They are, therefore, a very helpful and reliable measure of length.[1]

While each individual unit within the entire corpus has been analyzed as a self-contained section, and while decisions concerning syllable counts have been made without attention to or consideration of the larger structure, the overall tabulation of the entire corpus of 588 lines shows exactly the kind of symmetry and balance around the 8-syllable norm that was suggested by the initial hypothesis:

3-syllable lines:	4 (0.7%)	9-syllable lines:	103 (17.5%)
4-syllable lines:	16 (2.7%)	10-syllable lines:	66 (11.2%)
5-syllable lines:	34 (5.8%)	11-syllable lines:	27 (4.6%)
6-syllable lines:	70 (11.9%)	12-syllable lines:	14 (2.4%)
7-syllable lines:	115 (19.6%)	13-syllable lines:	10 (1.7%)
8-syllable lines:	126 (21.4%)	14-syllable lines:	3 (0.5%)

Of the 588 lines,
   21.4% have 8 syllables,
   58.5% (344 lines) have 7–9 syllables,
   81.6% (480 lines) have 6–10 syllables.

The most common line length is 8 syllables.
The median line length is 8 syllables.
The average line length is 7.998 syllables per line.

Overall, this corpus has yielded a variety of line lengths from 3 to 14 syllables. Although only slightly more than 20% of the lines have 8 syllables, the 8-syllable line represents the most common line length. In spite of the diversity of line lengths, nearly 60% of the lines fall into the range of 7–9 syllables, and over 80% have 6–10 syllables.

1. Again, Freedman's comments (1987a: 20) are apt, "I count syllables because there are a lot of them, and hence a disagreement about a few of them will not make much difference." See again pp. 23ff. above for a detailed response to the criticism of syllable counting.

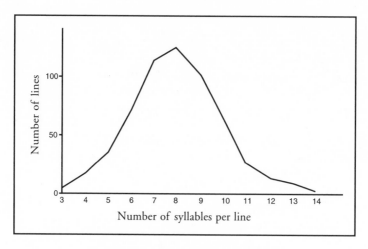

Fig. 7.1.   Distribution of line lengths in syllables:
Isa 2:1–5:30 and 8:19–12:6 (588 lines)

These data confirm the dominance of the 8-syllable line, while at the same time showing a great diversity around and away from it. The flexibility that allows such variations is, however, controlled by the norm. Represented graphically, the data form a bell-shaped curve, focused on the 8-syllable line (fig. 7.1).

There are 239 lines with less than 8 syllables and 223 with more than 8, making the graph slightly lopsided. There is also an additional category above the norm, that is, the 3-syllable lines are *five* less than 8, but the 14-syllable lines are *six* more, which also distorts the picture. However, if one adds up the total deviation from the 8-syllable norm, multiplying each number of lines by the difference from 8, one sees again the remarkable balance:

4 lines @ (−5) = 20	3 lines @ (+6) = 18
16 lines @ (−4) = 64	10 lines @ (+5) = 50
34 lines @ (−3) = 102	14 lines @ (+4) = 56
70 lines @ (−2) = 140	27 lines @ (+3) = 81
115 lines @ (−1) = 115	66 lines @ (+2) = 132
	103 lines @ (+1) = 103

Total: deviation below 8: *441*   deviation above 8: *440*

Stress Counts

Along with syllables, stress accents have been counted throughout. Again, there are variables and uncertainties, and in fact, stresses prove to be a less exact measurement of length. Nevertheless, the accentual system clearly has a role in defining and describing line length.

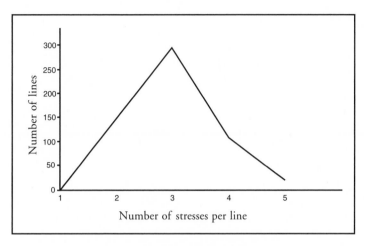

Fig. 7.2.   Distribution of line lengths in stresses:
Isa 2:1–5:30 and 8:19–12:6 (588 lines)

The MT accents have been logged for comparison, and here a closer correspondence has appeared between my counts and the MT text, due, in large measure, to the smaller number of total stresses as well as a smaller number of variables. The ranges and fixed numbers for each unit are shown in Appendix 4. The table below tabulates all the individual lines that have been discussed in detail:

1-stress lines:	3	(0.5%)
2-stress lines:	149	(25.3%)
3-stress lines:	299	(50.9%)
4-stress lines:	112	(19.0%)
5-stress lines:	25	(4.3%)

Of the 588 lines,
  50.9% have 3 stresses,
  95.2% (560 lines) have 2–4 stresses

The most common number of stresses per line is 3.
The median number of stresses is 3.
The average number of stresses is 3.012 per line.

While there is a variety in stresses per line from one to 5, the dominance of the 3-stress line is clearly demonstrated. Not only is it the most common line, but it also accounts for over 50% of all the lines. Furthermore, over 95% of the lines have 2–4 stresses, with a relatively equal number of 2-stress lines and 4-stress lines. These data confirm the normative function of the 3-stress line, not only as the dominant line length but also as a control on the lines that deviate from it. Represented graphically, the data illustrate this conclusion (fig. 7.2).

Prose Particle Counts

One of the stated objectives was to test the theory that prose particle
percentages are a helpful, if purely mechanical, measure of the poetic or
prosaic nature of a text. According to the hypothesis (see p. 26), pure,
classical poetry measures under 5% and narrative prose over 15%.

What has been found is a diversity in prose particle counts for each
unit analyzed, ranging from a low of 3% in 5:26–30 to a high of just
over 15% in 8:19–23a. Only three of the thirteen units show a count
under 5%. Six fall into the 5–10% range; three fall between 10–15%. In
all of the texts there appears to be a careful and deliberate use of the
prose particles for emphasis. They are often indicators of the structural
pattern.

Since the majority of the material under study falls between 5% and
15%, the general category of prophetic rhetoric as a *tertium quid* (see
p. 26) appears to be confirmed. In fact, it is quite likely that this middle
ground could be divided into two subgroups; one in the 5–10% range,
such as the three units in Isa 10:5–12:6, which could be generally characterized as prosaic poetry; and another in the 10–15% range, such as
Isa 8:19–9:6, which could be generally characterized as poetic prose.

The total overall prose particle count for the corpus of 2002 words,
with 175 prose particles, is 8.74%. The units are summarized here for the
sake of reference, grouped in the order in which they were discussed:

5:8–25:	10 particles,	218 words =	4.6%
9:7–10:4:	19 particles,	222 words =	8.6%
5:1–7:	4 particles,	100 words =	4.0%
5:26–30:	2 particles,	66 words =	3.0%
8:19–23a:	9 particles,	59 words =	15.3%
8:23b–9:6:	15 particles,	108 words =	13.9%
10:5–34:	24 particles,	357 words =	6.7%
11:1–16:	17 particles,	219 words =	7.8%
12:1–6:	4 particles,	62 words =	6.5%
2:1–4:	6 particles,	70 words =	8.6%
2:5–22:	25 particles,	183 words =	13.7%
3:1–4:1:	33 particles,	267 words =	12.3%
4:2–6:	7 particles,	71 words =	9.9%

Interestingly, the combined prose particle percentage of all the sections before
the *Denkschrift* is very close to the combined percentage of all the sections after the *Denkschrift*. This suggests that, in spite of a certain amount of diversity

at the level of individual units, there is a sense of balance and uniformity to the texture of the larger blocks of material as prophetic rhetoric:

> 2:1–5:30:   87 particles,   975 words = 8.9%
> 8:19–12:6:   88 particles, 1027 words = 8.6%

Rhetorical-Critical Issues

Verse, Strophe, and Gross Structure

As the discussion turned to the structuring of individual lines into verses, and of verses into strophes and stanzas, the insights of poetic analysis joined forces with those of so-called rhetorical criticism as a method of literary analysis (for example, Muilenburg; see pp. 10ff.).

At the level of verse structure, I have discovered and described careful and even intricate working of the poetic lines into an almost endless variety of interrelationships, involving both semantic and syntactic parallelism, wordplay, sound play, and both linear and chiastic structuring. While it is not my intention to catalog or systematize these observations, the work of A. Berlin (1985), for example, is clearly confirmed, and I would heartily affirm her expansions of the various categories of parallelism to include a wide range of possibilities, often with different structuring patterns within the same verse, such as a chiastic and linear arrangement in tension with one another.

At the level of strophes and stanzas within an individual unit, the attention to stylistic markers, such as inclusio and word repetition, have clearly played a major role, as Muilenburg suggested (see p. 10). Regarding his concern for the demarcation of units, I have also given attention to the paragraph notations in the MT, indicated by the *petuchah* and *setumah* breaks in the two major manuscripts (CL and CA), as well as the more complicated scheme in the Dead Sea Scrolls (see Oesch 1979). In general, these markers have proven to be helpful, though not infallible, guides to structural divisions both within individual pericopes and between the larger units.

I would further add to the list of stylistic markers noted by Muilenburg and cataloged by Alonso-Schökel (1988) and Watson (1986) the simple factor of length. It has been consistently shown that the measurement of length—as indicated especially by syllable counts as well as by the number of stresses and, at the larger levels, even by the number of words—is a helpful and virtually controlling factor in the relationship of subunits to one another within a literary piece. Indeed, it is this feature of length that has led to the discovery of the unifying macrostructure of Isaiah 2–12.

Form and Meaning

Moreover, attention to such structural features has enhanced the understanding of the texts under study. On the one hand, there is a possible
divergence and even tension between formal, stylistic features and the syn-
tactical/semantic features that convey the meaning of a text, analogous to
the different functions that syntax and meter serve on the level of lines and
bicola (see above, p. 246). On the other hand, it is to be assumed, and it
has been shown, that form and meaning often complement one another,
so that the method of structural analysis that has been modeled will contribute to the understanding of the meaning of the text.

For example, the structural interrelationship of the two major poems
in 5:8–25 and 9:7–10:4 indicates that each should be understood in the
light of the other. As a case in point, I suggested that the suspension of
the "seventh woe" from 5:23 to 10:1 created the rhetorical effect of
holding the hearer/reader's attention until the final stanza of the entire
unit. This would also help relate the meaning of both poems to the
material that lies in between. Likewise, the anticipation in 5:25 of the
refrain used in 9:7ff. would link the message of 5:8ff., directed primarily
against Judah, to the fate of Israel, which appears to be the major theme
in 9:7ff. And clearly the internecine tension between Israel and Judah
presented by the Syro-Ephraimite crisis lies at the heart of the intervening material.

Other examples are given throughout the study, especially under the
headings of "thought progression," although I have often tried to call attention to the relationship of structure to meaning at the smaller levels of
strophes and stanzas as well. For example, the intricate, chiastic structuring
of the middle of the seven "woes," in 5:19, is thematically and structurally
at the heart of the issue addressed by the whole poem. Further, it was
discovered that the speech of Yahweh in 10:24b–25 is approximately half as
long as the arrogant (and, by comparison, prolix) speeches of Assyria in
10:8b–11 and 13b–14. Further, the careful crafting and positioning of the
"lists" in 2:12–16, 3:1–3, and 3:18–23 suggested a connection among
these texts, as they catalog in an exhaustive, and exhausting, manner the
reasons and the ways and the means for Yahweh's exasperation and impending judgment.

On the larger levels, it was proposed, for example, that the so-called
Song of the Vineyard in 5:1–7 should be understood in relationship to the
messianic oracle or hymn in 8:23b–9:6. It was observed that 2:2–4 and
4:2–6 form an inclusio around 2:5–4:1, in which the "day of Yahweh"
forms a major motif. I have also noted the sevenfold use of the "day" theme
in 10:5–12:6 and argued that 12:1 may be the seventh use of the "anger

returns" vocabulary that forms an integral part of the relationship between the two poems in 5:8–25 and 9:7–10:4.

In sum, it has been shown that thematic and stylistic markers, such as repetitions of vocabulary, chiastic structures to call attention to individual verses, and even the placement and number of occurrences of divine names, contribute not only to the structural integrity but also to the meaning of the text as a whole.

The Macrostructure of Isaiah 2–12

Finally, it has been discovered that the factor of length, which produces a sense of balance and symmetry at the level of the single line and bicolon and which functions as a determining control over lineation, also functions in a similar way to produce a sense of balance and symmetry at the larger structural levels.

I began this study by applying a method of poetic analysis to the difficult question of the relationship of the material in Isa 5:8–30 and Isa 9:7–10:4 (and beyond), in light of recent research that suggests a more deliberate structuring of these units (L'Heureux 1984, Sheppard 1985, Anderson 1988, but contra Brown 1990; see pp. 20ff. and 96ff. for the basic problems and issues). This structural analysis has provided significant insights that are new to the discussion. First, I have established that the boundaries of the two poems are clearly 5:8–25 and 9:7–10:4. Further, each poem has been shown to have a unified structure of its own, independent of the other, so that the poetic units that form a link to the other poem cannot be explained as the result of accidental displacement or haphazard redactional activity. Third, I have argued that the links between the poems suggest that they are to be read or heard with the other in mind. Finally, I have confirmed the interrelationship of the two poems by demonstrating that they are exactly the same length: 496 syllables and 62 lines.

Building on this relationship, I suggested that the two complementary poems are intentionally placed around the intervening material, tradition-ally termed the Isaianic *Denkschrift*, 6:1–8:18. A structural outline for the *Denkschrift* itself was proposed, focusing on the Syro-Ephraimite conflict described in chaps. 7–8 and the sign of Immanuel in 7:10–17. Smaller, transitional pieces were found to surround the *Denkschrift* in 5:26–30 and 8:19–23a; and two additional units, precisely matched in length at 240 syllables and 30 lines (5:1–7 and 8:23b–9:6) filled out the remainder of the large section from Isa 5:1 to 10:4.

A significant number of thematic and vocabulary connections were de-scribed, binding these chapters together under the unified theme of the

Syro-Ephraimite crisis. It was also noted that the large sections that immediately surround the *Denkshrift*, determined as 5:1–30 and 8:19–10:4,
are approximately, but not exactly, equal in length. The first unit is slightly
longer than the second (by 15 syllables and 2 lines):

> 5:1–30:   887 syllables, 347 stresses, 384 words, 111 lines
> 8:19–10:4:   872 syllables, 325 stresses, 389 words, 109 lines

Attention was then turned to the larger units in Isa 10:5–12:6 (chapter 5) and in Isaiah 2–4 (chapter 6). Correspondences between these chapters suggested that they may function as a concentric circle around both
the *Denkshrift* and the first circle contained in Isa 5:1–10:4. Numerous
links of thematic material and vocabulary, especially the motif of the "day
of Yahweh" (also described as "that day"), supported the hypothesis that
these sections were connected. I also observed that these sections are approximately, but not exactly, equal in length. The first unit is slightly
shorter than the second (by 16 syllables and 2 lines):

> 2:1–4:6:   1464 syllables, 542 stresses, 591 words, 183 lines
> 10:5–12:6:   1480 syllables, 557 stresses, 638 words, 185 lines

Nevertheless, although very close, the correspondence in length is not
quite as exact as the correspondence discovered between the two poems in
5:8–25 and 9:7–10:4, although some degree of variance could be argued
between units of so many additional syllables and stresses. However, when
the material in Isaiah 2–4 is combined with the material in Isaiah 5 as one
large block before the *Denkshrift* (Isaiah 2–5), and it is compared with the
combination of the material after the *Denkshrift* (Isa 8:19–10:4 plus
10:5–12:6), one discovers a startling and striking balance and symmetry:

> 2:1–5:30:   2351 syllables, 889 stresses,   975 words, 294 lines
> 8:19–12:6:   2352 syllables, 882 stresses, 1027 words, 294 lines

Both of these large literary units are 294 lines in length, and the difference between them is merely one syllable. One could certainly suppose that
this extremely small discrepancy is possibly due to the variables of counting
rather than to the design of the poet/prophet. The difference in stresses is
only 7, which is remarkably close, considering the additional difficulties in
determining accent counts. In fact, the MT accents are, in this regard,
even closer: 900 for 2:1–5:30 and 905 for 6:19–12:6, although both MT
figures are slightly higher than the 882 to be expected from 294 lines
($294 \times 3 = 882$).

The number of words shows the greatest divergence, yet even the difference of 52 (a deviation of 2.6%) indicates that simply counting words may
be a helpful measure of length, though certainly less precise than syllables
and stresses.

In light of the dominance of the 8-syllable line, which has been verified as normative throughout this entire literary unit, the total figure of 2352 syllables corresponds exactly to the 294 lines that make up each of the large pieces surrounding the *Denkschrift.*

This correspondence is all the more striking in consideration of the fact that every decision for each individual line count was made at the basic level of the line itself, in relationship to the individual poem or pericope under study. No adjustments were made in relationship to the figures reached at the level of macrostructure, where no doubt the number of syllables could be adjusted within the ranges for each line and pericope and thus shown to be exactly equal for the larger units. Rather, my method has sought to fix a number of syllables and stresses at the smallest levels and thus to demonstrate this remarkable symmetry by building upward from part to whole.

Finally, I now return to the *Denkschrift* material itself, which has not been analyzed in the same detail but for which I have provided syllable counts (see appendix 3). I show a range of 1673–1712 syllables for the entire unit, Isa 6:1–8:18. Based again on the dominance of the 8-syllable line, one recognizes very near the midpoint of the syllable range the exact figure of 1696 syllables, which would be the equivalent of an additional 212 lines of prophetic verse (1696/8 = 212). Added to the 294 lines on either side of the *Denkschrift,* one reaches a grand total of exactly 800 8-syllable lines (294 + 294 + 212), or 6400 syllables, which I propose as the possible—and likely—intended total figure for the entire piece, which can be summarized as follows:

> A Isa 2:1–5:30:   2352 syllables (actual range: 2329–2365)
> B Isa 6:1–8:18:   1696 syllables (actual range: 1673–1712)
> A′ Isa 8:19–12:6: 2352 syllables (actual range: 2328–2377)

Ideally, one might suggest the numbers should be 2400 + 1600 + 2400 syllables, so that the number of lines might form a perfect 3:2:3 ratio (300 + 200 + 300 lines). But my stress counts also correspond to the selection of 294 as the number of lines, instead of the "ideal" number of 300. The figures reveal that even at this large level of "macrostructure," the prophet/poet has demonstrated the ability and freedom to deviate from the expected pattern while, at the same time, maintaining it as a norm.

Although the literary structuring of Isaiah 2–12 is indeed very complex, incorporating a number of smaller units that in themselves display a sense of thematic and structural unity, the overall, basic structure of the whole is exceedingly simple and sublime: an ABA chiasm, with both A sections exactly the same length.

Yet the length of the B section is perfectly complementary to the other two. The grand total of all three sections is grand indeed, for the total of

6400 syllables is itself determined by the dominant pattern of the single line: 8 syllables, multiplied by 8 × 100 lines.

That the Isaianic *Denkschrift*, sometimes called the Book of Immanuel, lies at the heart of this literary unit is no doubt central to the message of the whole. And if one would probe the very heart of this central unit, it would be discovered that its middle, according to the range of syllable counts, lies at the very end of Isa 7:14, and, according to the word count, comes after the word שְׁמוֹ in 7:14. There are 377 words before and 377 words after the four-word unit that concludes 7:14, and it can be calculated that there are 844 syllables before and 844 after this line (7:14b):

וְקָרָאת שְׁמוֹ עִמָּנוּ אֵל

If one might press—and thus test—the usefulness and accuracy of syllable counting to an extreme, it will be remembered that the actual syllable count for all of Isaiah 2–5 was determined to be 2351, one short of the total for the corresponding part in 8:19–12:6, which has 2352 syllables. If one speculates that such counts could, in fact, be that precise, the perfect chiasm would be one syllable off, and the actual remaining figure for the exact number of syllables in the *Denkschrift* would be 1697 (not 1696). Since the middle line of the *Denkschrift* has been determined as 7:14b, with 844 syllables and 377 words both before and after this line, it is striking that this colon has 9 syllables, not 8 .

As it turns out, this 9-syllable line divides into two units of 5 + 4 syllables, providing at the very center the additional syllable to even out the side with Isaiah 2–5. The break between וקראת שמו and עמנו אל divides chaps. 2–12 into equal halves of 3200 syllables.

Thus, not only does the Isaianic *Denkschrift* form the center of the completely balanced literary unit of Isaiah 2–12, this Book of Immanuel itself, along with the entire larger unit, turns on the name of this child. Whether the "word" that Isaiah ben Amoz "saw" (2:1) was in fact delivered in the wake of the Syro-Ephraimite conflict cannot be determined conclusively, but the literary framework into which the words of this word have been placed would suggest that they revolve around both the thematic—and the literary—center, the crisis of faith and trust brought about by this threat to Ahaz and to Judah. Regarding this situation Isaiah spoke words of both destruction and hope, and he offered a sign of God's presence to bring about judgment and justice, punishment and peace.

Appendix 1A

Isaiah 5:8–25

		Syllable Count		Stress Count	
			MT		MT
5:8a	הֹוי מַגִּיעֵי בַיִת בְּבַיִת	7	9	4	4
b	שָׂדֶה בְשָׂדֶה יַקְרִיבוּ	8	8	3	3
c	עַד אֶפֶס מָקֹום	4	5	2	3
d*	וְהוּשַׁבְתֶּם לְבַדְּכֶם	8	8	2	2
e	בְּקֶרֶב הָאָרֶץ:	4	6	2	2
9a	בְּאָזְנָי יְהוָה צְבָאֹות	8	8	3	3
b	אִם־לֹא בָּתִּים רַבִּים	6	6	3	3
c	לְשַׁמָּה יִהְיוּ	5	5	2	2
d	גְּדֹלִים וְטֹובִים	6	6	2	2
e	מֵאֵין יֹושֵׁב:	4	4	2	2
10a	כִּי עֲשֶׂרֶת צִמְדֵּי־כֶרֶם	6	8	2/(3)	3
b*	יַעֲשׂוּ בַּת אֶחָת	5	6	2	3
c	וְזֶרַע חֹמֶר	3	5	2	2
d*	יַעֲשֶׂה אֵיפָה:	4	5	2	2
11a	הֹוי מַשְׁכִּימֵי בַבֹּקֶר	6	7	3	3
b	שֵׁכָר יִרְדֹּפוּ	5	5	2	2
c	מְאַחֲרֵי בַנֶּשֶׁף	6	7	2	2
d	יַיִן יַדְלִיקֵם:	4	5	2	2
12a	וְהָיָה כִנֹּור וָנֶבֶל	7	8	3	3
b	תֹּף וְחָלִיל וָיַיִן מִשְׁתֵּיהֶם	9	10	4	4
c	וְאֵת פֹּעַל יְהוָה	5	6	2	3
d*	לֹא יַבִּיטוּ	4	4	1/(2)	2

Author's note: Appendix 1A has been lineated on the basis of syntax and parallelism, using shortest possible lines (compare with pp. 33ff.).

*See below, notes on lineation, for explanation of specific decisions regarding line divisions.

257

e	וּמַעֲשֵׂה יָדָיו	5	6	2	2
f*	לֹא רָאוּ:	3	3	1/(2)	2
13a	לָכֵן גָּלָה עַמִּי	6	6	3	3
b*	מִבְּלִי־דָעַת	4	5	1	1
c	וּכְבוֹדוֹ מְתֵי רָעָב	(7)/8	8	3	3
d	וַהֲמוֹנוֹ צִחֵה צָמָא:	7/(8)	7	3	3
14a	לָכֵן הִרְחִיבָה שְּׁאוֹל נַפְשָׁהּ	9	9	4	4
b	וּפָעֲרָה פִיהָ לִבְלִי־חֹק	8/(9)	9	3	3
c	וְיָרַד הֲדָרָהּ וַהֲמוֹנָהּ	9/(10)	9	3	3
d	וּשְׁאוֹנָהּ וְעָלֵז בָּהּ:	(7)/8	8	3	3
15a	וַיִּשַּׁח אָדָם וַיִּשְׁפַּל־אִישׁ	9	9	3	3
b	וְעֵינֵי גְבֹהִים תִּשְׁפַּלְנָה:	9	9	3	3
16a	וַיִּגְבַּהּ יְהוָה צְבָאוֹת בַּמִּשְׁפָּט	11	11	4	4
b	וְהָאֵל הַקָּדוֹשׁ נִקְדָּשׁ בִּצְדָקָה:	11	11	4	4
17a	וְרָעוּ כְבָשִׂים כְּדָבְרָם	9	9	3	3
b	וְחָרְבוֹת מֵחִים גָּרִים יֹאכֵלוּ:	10	10	4	4
18a	הוֹי מֹשְׁכֵי הֶעָוֹן	7	7	3	3
b*	בְּחַבְלֵי הַשָּׁוְא	5	6	2	2
c	וְכַעֲבוֹת הָעֲגָלָה חַטָּאָה:	10	11	3	3
19a	הָאֹמְרִים יְמַהֵר	7	7	2	2
b*	יָחִישָׁה מַעֲשֵׂהוּ	6	7	2	2
c	לְמַעַן נִרְאֶה	4	5	2	2
d	וְתִקְרַב וְתָבוֹאָה:	7	7	2	2
e*	עֲצַת קְדוֹשׁ יִשְׂרָאֵל וְנֵדָעָה:	11	11	4	4
20a	הוֹי הָאֹמְרִים לָרַע טוֹב	8	8	4	4
b	וְלַטּוֹב רָע	4	4	2	2
c	שָׂמִים חֹשֶׁךְ לְאוֹר	5	6	3	3
d	וְאוֹר לְחֹשֶׁךְ	4	5	2	2
e	שָׂמִים מַר לְמָתוֹק	6	6	3	3
f	וּמָתוֹק לְמָר:	5	5	2	2
21a	הוֹי חֲכָמִים בְּעֵינֵיהֶם	8	8	3	3
b	וְנֶגֶד פְּנֵיהֶם נְבֹנִים:	8	9	3	3
22a	הוֹי גִּבּוֹרִים לִשְׁתּוֹת יָיִן	7	8	4	4
b	וְאַנְשֵׁי־חַיִל לִמְסֹךְ שֵׁכָר:	8	9	4	3
23a	מַצְדִּיקֵי רָשָׁע עֵקֶב שֹׁחַד	7	9	4	4
b	וְצִדְקַת צַדִּיקִים יָסִירוּ מִמֶּנּוּ:	12	12	4	4

24a	לָכֵן כֶּאֱכֹל קַשׁ לְשׁוֹן אֵשׁ	8	9	5	5
b	וַחֲשַׁשׁ לֶהָבָה יִרְפֶּה	7/(8)	7	3	3
c	שָׁרְשָׁם כַּמָּק יִהְיֶה	6	6	3	3
d	וּפִרְחָם כָּאָבָק יַעֲלֶה	8	9	3	3
e	כִּי מָאֲסוּ	4	4	1	2
f*	אֵת תּוֹרַת יְהוָה צְבָאוֹת	8	8	3	4
g*	וְאֵת אִמְרַת קְדוֹשׁ־יִשְׂרָאֵל נִאֵצוּ׃	12	12	4	4
25a	עַל־כֵּן חָרָה אַף־יְהוָה בְּעַמּוֹ	10	10	4	4
b	וַיֵּט יָדוֹ עָלָיו וַיַּכֵּהוּ	10	10	4	4
c	וַיִּרְגְּזוּ הֶהָרִים	7	7	2	2
d	וַתְּהִי נִבְלָתָם כַּסּוּחָה	9	9	3	3
e	בְּקֶרֶב חוּצוֹת	4	5	2	2
f	בְּכָל־זֹאת לֹא־שָׁב אַפּוֹ	7	7	3	3
g	וְעוֹד יָדוֹ נְטוּיָה׃	7	7	3	3

Notes on Lineation

5:8de.   No clear parallelism; one could divide into 8 + 4 or 4 + 8.

5:10bd.   Parallelism of v. 10 could be either 2 or 4 lines, but if 2 lines, then v. 10a is too long for O'Connor/Cloete contraints.

5:12df.   Parallelism of 12cdef could be either 2 or 4 lines.

5:13b.   Awkward phrase; could well be added to 13a. On the basis of a similar construction in 14b, it probably should be, but it could go either way. Shortest possible lines are shown.

5:18b.   No real parallelism; v. 18 is the right length for a tricolon, which is arbitarily divided.

5:19b.   Could attach to either previous or following line, forming a bicolon. I show a tricolon to maintain short lines by way of example.

5:19e.   Very difficult to divide. The last word should parallel 19c, but one-word lines are ruled out of order by O'Connor/Cloete. Lines 19de must be a bicolon, and this is the best place for a break.

5:24f.   As parallel to line 24g, this line should be attached to the previous line (24e), making two very long lines with 12 syllables and 4/5 stresses. This is possible, but a division should fall at least between lines e and f.

5:24g.   Very long as one line, but no way to divide on the basis of syntax.

Summary

Leaving 24f and 13b as questionable, we have 72 (70) lines. Using the counts as determined in chap. 2 (see pp. 34ff. and 45), tabulation is as follows:

3-syllable lines:	2	8-syllable lines:	13
4-syllable lines:	12	9-syllable lines:	7
5-syllable lines:	8	10-syllable lines:	4
6-syllable lines:	9	11-syllable lines:	3
7-syllable lines:	12	12-syllable lines:	2

Of the 72 lines,
    18.1% (13 lines) have 8 syllables,
    44.4% (32 lines) have 7–9 syllables,
    62.5% (45 lines) have 6–10 syllables.

The most common line length is 8 syllables.
The median line length is 6 syllables.
The average line length is 6.89 syllables per line.

Appendix 1B

Isaiah 5:8–25

		Syllable Count	MT	Stress Count	MT
5:8a	הֹוי מַגִּיעֵי בַיִת בְּבַ֫יִת	7	9	4	4
b	שָׂדֶה בְשָׂדֶה יַקְרִיבוּ	8	8	3	3
c	עַד אֶפֶס מָקֹום	4	5	2	3
d	וְהוּשַׁבְתֶּם לְבַדְּכֶם בְּקֶרֶב הָאָֽרֶץ׃	12	14	4	4
9a	בְּאָזְנָי יְהוָה צְבָאֹות	8	8	3	3
b*	אִם־לֹא בָּתִּים רַבִּים לְשַׁמָּה יִהְיוּ	11	11	5	5
c*	גְּדֹלִים וְטֹובִים מֵאֵין יֹושֵֽׁב׃	10	10	4	4
10a	כִּי עֲשֶׂרֶת צִמְדֵּי־כֶרֶם יַעֲשׂוּ בַּת אֶחָת	11	14	4/(5)	6
b	וְזֶרַע חֹמֶר יַעֲשֶׂה אֵיפָֽה׃	7	10	4	4
11a*	הֹוי מַשְׁכִּימֵי בַבֹּקֶר שֵׁכָר יִרְדֹּפוּ	11	12	4	5
b*	מְאַחֲרֵי בַנֶּשֶׁף יַיִן יַדְלִיקֵֽם׃	10	12	4	4
12a	וְהָיָה כִנֹּור וָנֶבֶל	7	8	3	3
b	תֹּף וְחָלִיל וָיַיִן מִשְׁתֵּיהֶם	9	10	4	4
c	וְאֵת פֹּעַל יְהוָה לֹא יַבִּיטוּ	9	10	3/(4)	5
d	וּמַעֲשֵׂה יָדָיו לֹא רָאֽוּ׃	8	9	3/(4)	5
13a	לָכֵן גָּלָה עַמִּי מִבְּלִי־דָעַת	10	11	4	4
b	וּכְבֹודֹו מְתֵי רָעָב	(7)/8	8	3	3
c	וַהֲמֹונֹו צִחֵה צָמָֽא׃	7/(8)	7	3	3
14a	לָכֵן הִרְחִיבָה שְּׁאֹול נַפְשָׁהּ	9	9	4	4
b	וּפָעֲרָה פִיהָ לִבְלִי־חֹק	8/(9)	9	3	3
c	וְיָרַד הֲדָרָהּ וַהֲמֹונָהּ	(9)/10	9	3	3
d	וּשְׁאֹונָהּ וְעָלֵז בָּֽהּ׃	(7)/8	8	3	3
15a	וַיִּשַּׁח אָדָם וַיִּשְׁפַּל־אִישׁ	9	9	3	3
b	וְעֵינֵי גְבֹהִים תִּשְׁפַּֽלְנָה׃	9	9	3	3

Author's note: Appendix 1B has been lineated on the basis of syntax and parallelism, using shortest possible lines (compare with pp. 33ff.).

*See below, notes on lineation, for explanation of specific decisions regarding line divisions.

16a	וַיִּגְבַּה יְהוָה צְבָאוֹת בַּמִּשְׁפָּט	11	11	4	4
b	וְהָאֵל הַקָּדוֹשׁ נִקְדָּשׁ בִּצְדָקָה:	11	11	4	4
17a	וְרָעוּ כְבָשִׂים כְּדָבְרָם	9	9	3	3
b	וְחָרְבוֹת מֵחִים גָּרִים יֹאכֵלוּ:	10	10	4	4
18a	הוֹי מֹשְׁכֵי הֶעָוֹן בְּחַבְלֵי הַשָּׁוְא	12	13	5	5
b	וְכַעֲבוֹת הָעֲגָלָה חַטָּאָה:	10	11	3	3
19a	הָאֹמְרִים יְמַהֵר ǀ יָחִישָׁה מַעֲשֵׂהוּ	13	14	4	4
b	לְמַעַן נִרְאֶה	4	5	2	2
c	וְתִקְרַב וְתָבוֹאָה	7	7	2	2
d	עֲצַת קְדוֹשׁ יִשְׂרָאֵל וְנֵדָעָה:	11	11	4	4
20a*	הוֹי הָאֹמְרִים לָרַע טוֹב	8	8	4	4
b*	וְלַטּוֹב רָע	4	4	2	2
c*	שָׂמִים חֹשֶׁךְ לְאוֹר	5	6	3	3
d*	וְאוֹר לְחֹשֶׁךְ	4	5	2	2
e*	שָׂמִים מַר לְמָתוֹק	6	6	3	3
f*	וּמָתוֹק לְמָר:	5	5	2	2
21a	הוֹי חֲכָמִים בְּעֵינֵיהֶם	8	8	3	3
b	וְנֶגֶד פְּנֵיהֶם נְבֹנִים:	8	9	3	3
22a	הוֹי גִּבּוֹרִים לִשְׁתּוֹת יָיִן	7	8	4	4
b	וְאַנְשֵׁי־חַיִל לִמְסֹךְ שֵׁכָר:	8	9	4	3
23a	מַצְדִּיקֵי רָשָׁע עֵקֶב שֹׁחַד	7	9	4	4
b	וְצִדְקַת צַדִּיקִים יָסִירוּ מִמֶּנּוּ:	12	12	4	4
24a	לָכֵן כֶּאֱכֹל קַשׁ לְשׁוֹן אֵשׁ	8	9	5	5
b	וַחֲשַׁשׁ לֶהָבָה יִרְפֶּה	7/(8)	7	3	3
c	שָׁרְשָׁם כַּמָּק יִהְיֶה	6	6	3	3
d	וּפִרְחָם כָּאָבָק יַעֲלֶה	8	9	3	3
e	כִּי מָאֲסוּ אֵת תּוֹרַת יְהוָה צְבָאוֹת	12	12	4	6
f	וְאֵת אִמְרַת קְדוֹשׁ־יִשְׂרָאֵל נִאֵצוּ:	12	12	4	4
25a	עַל־כֵּן חָרָה אַף־יְהוָה בְּעַמּוֹ	10	10	4	4
b	וַיֵּט יָדוֹ עָלָיו וַיַּכֵּהוּ	10	10	4	4
c	וַיִּרְגְּזוּ הֶהָרִים	7	7	2	2
d	וַתְּהִי נִבְלָתָם כַּסּוּחָה בְּקֶרֶב חוּצוֹת	13	14	5	5
e	בְּכָל־זֹאת לֹא־שָׁב אַפּוֹ	7	7	3	3
f	וְעוֹד יָדוֹ נְטוּיָה:	7	7	3	3

Notes on Lineation

5:9bc. Could be 2 or 4 lines on basis of parallelism; long lines are indicated for the sake of example.

5:11ab. Could be 2 or 4 lines; longer lines shown here.

5:20. These lines are left somehwat short, but to combine them into three bicola (on the basis of syllables) makes them too long for O'Connor or Cloete's system.

Summary

58 lines. Using the counts as determined in chap. 2 (see pp. 34ff. and 45), tabulation is as follows:

4-syllable lines:	4	9-syllable lines:	7
5-syllable lines:	2	10-syllable lines:	7
6-syllable lines:	2	11-syllable lines:	6
7-syllable lines:	11	12-syllable lines:	5
8-syllable lines:	12	13-syllable lines:	2

Of the 58 lines,
    20.7% (12 lines) have 8 syllables,
    51.7% (30 lines) have 7–9 syllables,
    67.2% (39 lines) have 6–10 syllables.

The most common line length is 8 syllables.
The median line length is 8 syllables.
The average line length is 8.55 syllables.

Appendix 1C

Isaiah 5:8–25

		Syllable Count	MT	Stress Count	MT
5:8a	הֹוי מַגִּיעֵי בַיִת בְּבַיִת	7	9	4	4
b	שָׂדֶה בְשָׂדֶה יַקְרִיבוּ	8	8	3	3
c*	עַד אֶפֶס מָקֹום וְהוּשַׁבְתֶּם	8	9	3	4
d*	לְבַדְכֶם בְּקֶרֶב הָאָרֶץ׃	8	10	3	3
9a	בְּאָזְנָי יְהוָה צְבָאֹות	8	8	3	3
b*	אִם־לֹא בָּתִּים רַבִּים	6	6	3	3
c*	לְשַׁמָּה יִהְיוּ גְּדֹלִים	8	8	3	3
d*	וְטֹובִים מֵאֵין יֹושֵׁב׃	7	7	3	3
10a*	כִּי עֲשֶׂרֶת צִמְדֵּי־כֶרֶם יַעֲשׂוּ בַּת	9	12	4/(5)	5
b*	אֶחָת וְזֶרַע חֹמֶר יַעֲשֶׂה אֵיפָה׃	9	12	4	5
11a*	הֹוי מַשְׁכִּימֵי בַבֹּקֶר שֵׁכָר	8	9	4	4
b*	יִרְדֹּפוּ מְאַחֲרֵי	7	7	2	2
c*	בַנֶּשֶׁף יַיִן יַדְלִיקֵם׃	6	8	3	3
12a	וְהָיָה כִנֹּור וָנֶבֶל	7	8	3	3
b	תֹּף וְחָלִיל וָיַיִן מִשְׁתֵּיהֶם	9	10	4	4
c	וְאֵת פֹּעַל יְהוָה לֹא יַבִּיטוּ	9	10	3/(4)	5
d	וּמַעֲשֵׂה יָדָיו לֹא רָאוּ׃	8	9	3/(4)	4
13a	לָכֵן גָּלָה עַמִּי מִבְּלִי־דָעַת	10	11	4	4
b	וּכְבֹודֹו מְתֵי רָעָב	(7)/8	8	3	3
c	וַהֲמֹונֹו צִחֵה צָמָא׃	7/(8)	7	3	3
14a	לָכֵן הִרְחִיבָה שְּׁאֹול נַפְשָׁהּ	9	9	4	4
b	וּפָעֲרָה פִיהָ לִבְלִי־חֹק	8/(9)	9	3	3
c	וְיָרַד הֲדָרָהּ וַהֲמֹונָהּ	9/(10)	9	3	3
d	וּשְׁאֹונָהּ וְעָלֵז בָּהּ׃	(7)/8	8	3	3
15a	וַיִּשַּׁח אָדָם וַיִּשְׁפַּל־אִישׁ	9	9	3	3
b	וְעֵינֵי גְבֹהִים תִּשְׁפַּלְנָה׃	9	9	3	3

Author's note: Appendix 1C has been lineated on the basis of line length alone (62 lines) (compare with pp. 33ff.).

*See below, notes on lineation, for explanation of specific decisions regarding line divisions.

16a*	וַיִּגְבַּה יְהוָה צְבָאוֹת	8	8	3	3
b*	בַּמִּשְׁפָּט וְהָאֵל	6	6	2	2
c*	הַקָּדוֹשׁ נִקְדָּשׁ בִּצְדָקָה:	8	8	3	3
17a	וְרָעוּ כְבָשִׂים כְּדָבְרָם	9	9	3	3
b	וְחָרְבוֹת מֵחִים גָּרִים יֹאכֵלוּ:	10	10	4	4
18a*	הוֹי מֹשְׁכֵי הֶעָוֹן	7	7	3	3
b*	בְּחַבְלֵי הַשָּׁוְא וְכַעֲבוֹת	8	9	3	3
c*	הָעֲגָלָה חַטָּאָה:	7	7	2	2
19a*	הָאֹמְרִים יְמַהֵר	7	7	2	2
b*	יָחִישָׁה מַעֲשֵׂהוּ לְמַעַן נִרְאֶה	10	12	4	4
c*	וְתִקְרַב וְתָבוֹאָה עֲצַת	9	9	3	3
d*	קְדוֹשׁ יִשְׂרָאֵל וְנֵדָעָה:	9	9	3	3
20a	הוֹי הָאֹמְרִים לָרַע טוֹב	8	8	4	4
b	וְלַטּוֹב רַע שָׂמִים חֹשֶׁךְ	7	8	4	4
c	לְאוֹר וְאוֹר לְחֹשֶׁךְ שָׂמִים	8	9	4	4
d	מַר לְמָתוֹק וּמָתוֹק לְמָר:	9	9	4	4
21a	הוֹי חֲכָמִים בְּעֵינֵיהֶם	8	8	3	3
b	וְנֶגֶד פְּנֵיהֶם נְבֹנִים:	8	9	3	3
22a	הוֹי גִּבּוֹרִים לִשְׁתּוֹת יָיִן	7	8	4	4
b	וְאַנְשֵׁי־חַיִל לִמְסֹךְ שֵׁכָר:	8	9	4	3
23a	מַצְדִּיקֵי רָשָׁע עֵקֶב שֹׁחַד	7	9	4	4
b	וְצִדְקַת צַדִּיקִים יָסִירוּ מִמֶּנּוּ:	12	12	4	4
24a	לָכֵן כֶּאֱכֹל קַשׁ לְשׁוֹן אֵשׁ	8	9	5	5
b	וַחֲשַׁשׁ לֶהָבָה יִרְפֶּה	7/(8)	7	3	3
c	שָׁרְשָׁם כַּמָּק יִהְיֶה	6	6	3	3
d	וּפִרְחָם כָּאָבָק יַעֲלֶה	8	9	3	3
e*	כִּי מָאֲסוּ אֵת תּוֹרַת יְהוָה	9	9	3	5
f*	צְבָאוֹת וְאֵת אִמְרַת	7	7	3	3
g*	קְדוֹשׁ־יִשְׂרָאֵל נִאֵצוּ:	8	8	3	3
25a*	עַל־כֵּן חָרָה אַף־יְהוָה	7	7	3	3
b*	בְּעַמּוֹ וַיֵּט יָדוֹ עָלָיו	9	9	4	4
c*	וַיַּכֵּהוּ וַיִּרְגְּזוּ	8	8	2	2
d*	הֶהָרִים וַתְּהִי נִבְלָתָם	9	9	3	3
e*	כַּסּוּחָה בְּקֶרֶב חוּצוֹת	7	8	3	3
f	בְּכָל־זֹאת לֹא־שָׁב אַפּוֹ	7	7	3	3
g	וְעוֹד יָדוֹ נְטוּיָה:	7	7	3	3

Notes on Lineation

5:8cd. וְהוּשַׁבְתֶּם is moved to line 8c, creating enjambment but balancing 8cd at 8 syllables and 3 stresses each.

5:9bcd. Syntactically, these lines divide into 2 or 4 lines. The total length is equivalent to a tricolon.

5:10. Retained as a bicolon, but the moving of אֶחָת to the second line creates a balance of 9 syllables per line.

5:11. Similar to 9bcd; what are syntactically either 2 or 4 lines are, in terms of overall length, equivalent to a slightly short tricolon.

5:16. What is clearly a bicolon in parallelistic structure is, in terms of length, equivalent to a tricolon.

5:18. Again, the long bicolon (22 syllables, 8 stresses) is represented as a tricolon.

5:19. The double bicolon is retained as a 4-line unit, but emjambment allows the length of each line to become more balanced.

5:24efg. The long bicolon of 24 syllables and 9 stresses is shown as a well-balanced tricolon.

5:25a–e. Four lines totalling 40 syllables and 15 stresses are shown as 5 lines, averaging 8 syllables and 3 stresses.

Summary

62 lines. Using the counts as determined in chap. 2 (see pp. 34ff. and 45), we tabulate as follows:

6-syllable lines:	4	10-syllable lines:	3
7-syllable lines:	17	11-syllable lines:	0
8-syllable lines:	22	12-syllable lines:	1
9-syllable lines:	15		

Of the 62 lines,
35.5% (22 lines) have 8 syllables,
87.1% (54 lines) have 7–9 syllables,
98.4% (61 lines) have 6–10 syllables.

The most common line length is 8 syllables.
The median line length is 8 syllables.
The average line length is 8 syllables per line.

Appendix 2A

Isaiah 9:7–10:4

		Syllable Count		Stress Count	
			MT		MT
9:7a	דָּבָר שָׁלַח אֲדֹנָי בְּיַעֲקֹב	10	11	4	4
b	וְנָפַל בְּיִשְׂרָאֵל:	7	7	2	2
8a	וְיָדְעוּ הָעָם כֻּלּוֹ	8	8	3	3
b	אֶפְרַיִם וְיוֹשֵׁב שֹׁמְרוֹן	8	9	3	3
c	בְּגַאֲוָה וּבְגֹדֶל לֵבָב לֵאמֹר:	9/(10)	12	4	4
9a	לְבֵנִים נָפָלוּ	6	6	2	2
b	וְגָזִית נִבְנֶה	5	5	2	2
c	שִׁקְמִים גֻּדָּעוּ	5	5	2	2
d	וַאֲרָזִים נַחֲלִיף:	(5)/6	7	2	2
10a	וַיְשַׂגֵּב יְהוָה אֶת־צָרֵי רְצִין עָלָיו	12	12	5	5
b	וְאֶת־אֹיְבָיו יְסַכְסֵךְ:	8	8	2	2
11a	אֲרָם מִקֶּדֶם	4	5	2	2
b*	וּפְלִשְׁתִּים מֵאָחוֹר	6/(7)	7	2	2
c	וַיֹּאכְלוּ אֶת־יִשְׂרָאֵל בְּכָל־פֶּה	11	11	3	3
d	בְּכָל־זֹאת לֹא־שָׁב אַפּוֹ	7	7	3	3
e	וְעוֹד יָדוֹ נְטוּיָה:	7	7	3	3
12a	וְהָעָם לֹא־שָׁב עַד־הַמַּכֵּהוּ	10	10	3	3
b	וְאֶת־יְהוָה צְבָאוֹת לֹא דָרָשׁוּ:	11	11	3	4
13a	וַיַּכְרֵת יְהוָה מִיִּשְׂרָאֵל	9	9	3	3
b	רֹאשׁ וְזָנָב	4	4	2	2
c*	כִּפָּה וְאַגְמוֹן	5	5	2	2
d	יוֹם אֶחָד:	3	3	2	2
14a	זָקֵן וּנְשׂוּא־פָנִים	(6)/7	7	2	2
b*	הוּא הָרֹאשׁ	3	3	2	2
c	וְנָבִיא מוֹרֶה־שֶּׁקֶר	6	7	2	2
d*	הוּא הַזָּנָב:	4	4	2	2
15a	וַיִּהְיוּ מְאַשְּׁרֵי הָעָם־הַזֶּה מַתְעִים	13	13	5	5
b	וּמְאֻשָּׁרָיו מְבֻלָּעִים:	8/(9)	9	2	2

Author's note: Appendix 2A has been lineated on the basis of syntax and parallelism, using shortest possible lines (compare with pp. 73ff.).

*See below, notes on lineation, for explanation of specific decisions regarding line divisions.

16a	עַל־כֵּן עַל־בַּחוּרָיו	6	6	2	2
b	לֹא־יִשְׂמַח ׀ אֲדֹנָי	6	6	2	2
c	וְאֶת־יְתֹמָיו וְאֶת־אַלְמְנֹתָיו	11	11	2	2
d	לֹא יְרַחֵם	4	4	2	2
e	כִּי כֻלּוֹ חָנֵף וּמֵרַע	8	8	3	4
f	וְכָל־פֶּה דֹּבֵר נְבָלָה	8	8	3	3
g	בְּכָל־זֹאת לֹא־שָׁב אַפּוֹ	7	7	3	3
h	וְעוֹד יָדוֹ נְטוּיָה׃	7	7	3	3
17a	כִּי־בָעֲרָה כָאֵשׁ רִשְׁעָה	8	8	3	3
b	שָׁמִיר וָשַׁיִת תֹּאכֵל	6	7	3	3
c	וַתִּצַּת בְּסִבְכֵי הַיַּעַר	8	9	3	3
d	וַיִּתְאַבְּכוּ גֵּאוּת עָשָׁן׃	9	9	3	3
18a	בְּעֶבְרַת יְהוָה צְבָאוֹת	8	8	3	3
b	נֶעְתַּם אָרֶץ	3	4	2	2
c	וַיְהִי הָעָם כְּמַאֲכֹלֶת אֵשׁ	8	10	4	4
d	אִישׁ אֶל־אָחִיו לֹא יַחְמֹלוּ׃	8	8	3	3
19a	וַיִּגְזֹר עַל־יָמִין וְרָעֵב	9	9	3	3
b	וַיֹּאכַל עַל־שְׂמֹאול וְלֹא שָׂבֵעוּ	11	11	3	3
c	אִישׁ בְּשַׂר־זְרֹעוֹ יֹאכֵלוּ׃	9	9	4	4
20a	מְנַשֶּׁה אֶת־אֶפְרַיִם	6	7	2	2
b	וְאֶפְרַיִם אֶת־מְנַשֶּׁה	7	8	2	2
c	יַחְדָּו הֵמָּה עַל־יְהוּדָה	8	8	3	3
d	בְּכָל־זֹאת לֹא־שָׁב אַפּוֹ	7	7	3	3
e	וְעוֹד יָדוֹ נְטוּיָה׃	7	7	3	3
10:1a	הוֹי הַחֹקְקִים חִקְקֵי־אָוֶן	9	10	4	3
b	וּמְכַתְּבִים עָמָל כִּתֵּבוּ׃	9/(10)	10	3	3
2a	לְהַטּוֹת מִדִּין דַּלִּים	7	7	3	3
b	וְלִגְזֹל מִשְׁפַּט עֲנִיֵּי עַמִּי	10	10	4	4
c	לִהְיוֹת אַלְמָנוֹת שְׁלָלָם	8	8	4	4
d	וְאֶת־יְתוֹמִים יָבֹזּוּ׃	8	8	2	2
3a	וּמַה־תַּעֲשׂוּ לְיוֹם פְּקֻדָּה	9	10	3	3
b	וּלְשׁוֹאָה מִמֶּרְחָק תָּבוֹא	8/(9)	9	3	3
c	עַל־מִי תָּנוּסוּ לְעֶזְרָה	8	8	3	3
d	וְאָנָה תַעַזְבוּ כְּבוֹדְכֶם׃	10	10	3	3
4a	בִּלְתִּי כָרַע תַּחַת אַסִּיר	7	8	3	3
b	וְתַחַת הֲרוּגִים יִפֹּלוּ	8	9	3	3
c	בְּכָל־זֹאת לֹא־שָׁב אַפּוֹ	7	7	3	3
d	וְעוֹד יָדוֹ נְטוּיָה׃	7	7	3	3

Notes on Lineation

9:11b. The line could be retained as one longer line, but the parallelism allows it to be divided easily.

9:13c. Again, the parallelism with the previous line is clear, and the division is natural. Actually, the 2 shorter lines match well the following line in 13d.

9:14, d. As a bicolon, 20 syllables (10 + 10) are not unusual, though slightly long. On the other hand, 4 short lines are also possible.

Summary

66 lines. Based on the counts determined in chap. 3 (see pp. 66ff. and p. 76), tabulation is as follows:

3-syllable lines:	3	9-syllable lines:	8
4-syllable lines:	4	10-syllable lines:	4
5-syllable lines:	3	11-syllable lines:	4
6-syllable lines:	8	12-syllable lines:	1
7-syllable lines:	13	13-syllable lines:	1
8-syllable lines:	17		

Of the 66 lines,
    25.8% (17 lines) have 8 syllables,
    57.6% (38 lines) have 7–9 syllables,
    75.8% (50 lines) have 6–10 syllables.

The most common line length is 8 syllables.
The median line length is 8 syllables.
The average line length is 7.51 syllables per line.

Appendix 2B

Isaiah 9:7–10:4

		Syllable Count		Stress Count	
			MT		MT
9:7a	דָּבָר שָׁלַח אֲדֹנָי בְּיַעֲקֹב	10	11	4	4
b	וְנָפַל בְּיִשְׂרָאֵל׃	7	7	2	2
8a	וְיָדְעוּ הָעָם כֻּלּוֹ	8	8	3	3
b	אֶפְרַיִם וְיוֹשֵׁב שֹׁמְרוֹן	8	9	3	3
c	בְּגַאֲוָה וּבְגֹדֶל לֵבָב לֵאמֹר׃	9/(10)	12	4	4
9a*	לְבֵנִים נָפָלוּ וְגָזִית נִבְנֶה	11	11	4	4
b*	שִׁקְמִים גֻּדָּעוּ וַאֲרָזִים נַחֲלִיף׃	(10)/11	12	4	4
10a	וַיְשַׂגֵּב יְהוָה אֶת־צָרֵי רְצִין עָלָיו	12	12	5	5
b	וְאֶת־אֹיְבָיו יְסַכְסֵךְ׃	8	8	2	2
11a	אֲרָם מִקֶּדֶם וּפְלִשְׁתִּים מֵאָחוֹר	10/(11)	12	4	4
b	וַיֹּאכְלוּ אֶת־יִשְׂרָאֵל בְּכָל־פֶּה	11	11	3	3
c	בְּכָל־זֹאת לֹא־שָׁב אַפּוֹ	7	7	3	3
d	וְעוֹד יָדוֹ נְטוּיָה׃	7	7	3	3
12a	וְהָעָם לֹא־שָׁב עַד־הַמַּכֵּהוּ	10	10	3	3
b	וְאֶת־יְהוָה צְבָאוֹת לֹא דָרָשׁוּ׃	11	11	3	4
13a	וַיַּכְרֵת יְהוָה מִיִּשְׂרָאֵל רֹאשׁ וְזָנָב	13	13	5	5
b*	כִּפָּה וְאַגְמוֹן יוֹם אֶחָד׃	8	8	4	4
14a	זָקֵן וּנְשׂוּא־פָנִים הוּא הָרֹאשׁ	(9)/10	10	4	4
b	וְנָבִיא מוֹרֶה־שֶּׁקֶר הוּא הַזָּנָב׃	10	11	4	4
15a	וַיִּהְיוּ מְאַשְּׁרֵי הָעָם־הַזֶּה מַתְעִים	13	13	5	5
b	וּמְאֻשָּׁרָיו מְבֻלָּעִים׃	8/(9)	9	2	2
16a*	עַל־כֵּן עַל־בַּחוּרָיו לֹא־יִשְׂמַח | אֲדֹנָי	12	12	4	4
b*	וְאֶת־יְתֹמָיו וְאֶת־אַלְמְנֹתָיו לֹא יְרַחֵם	15	15	4	4
c	כִּי כֻלּוֹ חָנֵף וּמֵרַע	8	8	4	4
d	וְכָל־פֶּה דֹּבֵר נְבָלָה	8	8	3	3
e	בְּכָל־זֹאת לֹא־שָׁב אַפּוֹ	7	7	3	3
f	וְעוֹד יָדוֹ נְטוּיָה׃	7	7	3	3

Author's note: Appendix 2B has been lineated on the basis of syntax and parallelism, using longest possible lines (compare with pp. 73ff.).

*See below, notes on lineation, for explanation of specific decisions regarding line divisions.

17a	כִּי־בָעֲרָה כָאֵשׁ רִשְׁעָה	8	8	3	3
b	שָׁמִיר וָשַׁיִת תֹּאכֵל	6	7	3	3
c	וַתִּצַּת בְּסִבְכֵי הַיַּעַר	8	9	3	3
d	וַיִּתְאַבְּכוּ גֵּאוּת עָשָׁן	9	9	3	3
18a*	בְּעֶבְרַת יְהוָה צְבָאוֹת נֶעְתַּם אָרֶץ	11	12	5	5
b	וַיְהִי הָעָם כְּמַאֲכֹלֶת אֵשׁ	8	10	4	4
c	אִישׁ אֶל־אָחִיו לֹא יַחְמֹלוּ׃	8	8	3	3
19a	וַיִּגְזֹר עַל־יָמִין וְרָעֵב	9	9	3	3
b	וַיֹּאכַל עַל־שְׂמֹאול וְלֹא שָׂבֵעוּ	11	11	3	3
c	אִישׁ בְּשַׂר־זְרֹעוֹ יֹאכֵלוּ׃	9	9	4	4
20a	מְנַשֶּׁה אֶת־אֶפְרַיִם	6	7	2	2
b	וְאֶפְרַיִם אֶת־מְנַשֶּׁה	7	8	2	2
c	יַחְדָּו הֵמָּה עַל־יְהוּדָה	8	8	3	3
d	בְּכָל־זֹאת לֹא־שָׁב אַפּוֹ	7	7	3	3
e	וְעוֹד יָדוֹ נְטוּיָה׃	7	7	3	3
10:1a	הוֹי הַחֹקְקִים חִקְקֵי־אָוֶן	9	10	4	3
b	וּמְכַתְּבִים עָמָל כִּתֵּבוּ׃	9/(10)	10	3	3
2a	לְהַטּוֹת מִדִּין דַּלִּים	7	7	3	3
b	וְלִגְזֹל מִשְׁפַּט עֲנִיֵּי עַמִּי	10	10	4	4
c	לִהְיוֹת אַלְמָנוֹת שְׁלָלָם	8	8	4	4
d	וְאֶת־יְתוֹמִים יָבֹזּוּ׃	8	8	2	2
3a	וּמַה־תַּעֲשׂוּ לְיוֹם פְּקֻדָּה	9	10	3	3
b	וּלְשׁוֹאָה מִמֶּרְחָק תָּבוֹא	8/(9)	9	3	3
c	עַל־מִי תָּנוּסוּ לְעֶזְרָה	8	8	3	3
d	וְאָנָה תַעַזְבוּ כְּבוֹדְכֶם׃	10	10	3	3
4a	בִּלְתִּי כָרַע תַּחַת אַסִּיר	7	8	3	3
b	וְתַחַת הֲרוּגִים יִפֹּלוּ	8	9	3	3
c	בְּכָל־זֹאת לֹא־שָׁב אַפּוֹ	7	7	3	3
d	וְעוֹד יָדוֹ נְטוּיָה׃	7	7	3	3

Notes on Lineation

7:9ab. Verse 9 is either a long bicolon (at 21/22 syllables) or a short quatrain. Here longer lines are preferred.

9:13b. The division of v. 13 is difficult. The break shown here follows a syntactic division and forms a rather long bicolon (13 + 8 = 21).

9:16ab. The parallelism is clear. Again, there seems to be either a 2- or a 4-line unit.

9:18a. The unit נֶעְתַּם אָרֶץ is short as a single line. Here it is added to the previous line.

Summary

56 lines. Using the syllable counts determined in chap. 3 (see pp. 66ff. and 76), tabulation is as follows:

6-syllable lines:	2	11-syllable lines:	6
7-syllable lines:	12	12-syllable lines:	2
8-syllable lines:	17	13-syllable lines:	2
9-syllable lines:	7	14-syllable lines:	0
10-syllable lines:	7	15-syllable lines:	1

Of the 56 lines,
   30.4% (17 lines) have 8 syllables,
   64.3% (36 lines) have 7–9 syllables,
   80.4% (45 lines) have 6–10 syllables.

The most common line length is 8 syllables.
The median line length is 8 syllables.
The average line length is 8.82 syllables per line.

Appendix 2C

Isaiah 9:7–10:4

		Syllable Count	MT	Stress Count	MT
9:7a	דְּבָר שָׁלַח אֲדֹנָי בְּיַעֲקֹב	10	11	4	4
b	וְנָפַל בְּיִשְׂרָאֵל׃	7	7	2	2
8a	וְיָדְעוּ הָעָם כֻּלּוֹ	8	8	3	3
b	אֶפְרַיִם וְיוֹשֵׁב שֹׁמְרוֹן	8	9	3	3
c	בְּגַאֲוָה וּבְגֹדֶל לֵבָב לֵאמֹר׃	9/(10)	12	4	4
9a*	לְבֵנִים נָפָלוּ	6	6	2	2
b*	וְגָזִית נִבְנֶה שִׁקְמִים	7	7	3	3
c*	גֻּדָּעוּ וַאֲרָזִים נַחֲלִיף׃	(8)/9	10	3	3
10a*	וַיְשַׂגֵּב יְהוָה אֶת־צָרֵי רְצִין	10	10	5	5
b*	עָלָיו וְאֶת־אֹיְבָיו יְסַכְסֵךְ׃	10	10	2	2
11a*	אֲרָם מִקֶּדֶם וּפְלִשְׁתִּים	7/(8)	9	3	3
b*	מֵאָחוֹר וַיֹּאכְלוּ	7	7	2	2
c*	אֶת־יִשְׂרָאֵל בְּכָל־פֶּה	7	7	2	2
d	בְּכָל־זֹאת לֹא־שָׁב אַפּוֹ	7	7	3	3
e	וְעוֹד יָדוֹ נְטוּיָה׃	7	7	3	3
12a*	וְהָעָם לֹא־שָׁב עַד־	6	6	2	2
b*	הַמַּכֵּהוּ וְאֶת־יְהוָה	8	8	2	2
c*	צְבָאוֹת לֹא דָרָשׁוּ׃	7	7	2	3
13a*	וַיַּכְרֵת יְהוָה	5	5	2	2
b*	מִיִּשְׂרָאֵל רֹאשׁ וְזָנָב	8	8	3	3
c*	כִּפָּה וְאַגְמוֹן יוֹם אֶחָד׃	8	8	4	4
14a	זָקֵן וּנְשׂוּא־פָנִים הוּא הָרֹאשׁ	(9)/10	10	4	4
b	וְנָבִיא מוֹרֶה־שֶּׁקֶר הוּא הַזָּנָב׃	10	11	4	4
15a*	וַיִּהְיוּ מְאַשְּׁרֵי	7	7	2	2
b*	הָעָם־הַזֶּה מַתְעִים	6	6	3	3
c*	וּמְאֻשָּׁרָיו מְבֻלָּעִים׃	8/(9)	9	2	2

Author's note: Appendix 2C has been lineated on the basis of line length alone (62 lines) (compare with pp. 73ff.).

*See below, notes on lineation, for explanation of specific decisions regarding line divisions.

273

16a*	עַל־כֵּן עַל־בַּחוּרָיו לֹא־יִשְׂמַח	9	9	3	3
b*	אֲדֹנָי וְאֶת־יְתֹמָיו	8	8	2	2
c*	וְאֶת־אַלְמְנֹתָיו לֹא יְרַחֵם	10	10	2/(3)	3
d	כִּי כֻלּוֹ חָנֵף וּמֵרַע	8	8	3	4
e	וְכָל־פֶּה דֹּבֵר נְבָלָה	8	8	3	3
f	בְּכָל־זֹאת לֹא־שָׁב אַפּוֹ	7	7	3	3
g	וְעוֹד יָדוֹ נְטוּיָה׃	7	7	3	3
17a	כִּי־בָעֲרָה כָאֵשׁ רִשְׁעָה	8	8	3	3
b	שָׁמִיר וָשַׁיִת תֹּאכֵל	6	7	3	3
c	וַתִּצַּת בְּסִבְכֵי הַיַּעַר	8	9	3	3
d	וַיִּתְאַבְּכוּ גֵּאוּת עָשָׁן׃	9	9	3	3
18a*	בְּעֶבְרַת יְהוָה צְבָאוֹת נֶעְתַּם	10	10	4	4
b*	אֶרֶץ וַיְהִי הָעָם כְּמַאֲכֹלֶת אֵשׁ	9	12	5	5
c	אִישׁ אֶל־אָחִיו לֹא יַחְמֹלוּ׃	8	8	3	4
19a	וַיִּגְזֹר עַל־יָמִין וְרָעֵב	9	9	3	3
b	וַיֹּאכַל עַל־שְׂמֹאול וְלֹא שָׂבֵעוּ	11	11	3	4
c	אִישׁ בְּשַׂר־זְרֹעוֹ יֹאכֵלוּ׃	9	9	4	3
2 a	מְנַשֶּׁה אֶת־אֶפְרַיִם	6	7	2	2
b	וְאֶפְרַיִם אֶת־מְנַשֶּׁה	7	8	2	2
c	יַחְדָּו הֵמָּה עַל־יְהוּדָה	8	8	3	3
d	בְּכָל־זֹאת לֹא־שָׁב אַפּוֹ	7	7	3	3
e	וְעוֹד יָדוֹ נְטוּיָה׃	7	7	3	3
10:1a	הוֹי הַחֹקְקִים חִקְקֵי־אָוֶן	9	10	4	3
b	וּמְכַתְּבִים עָמָל כִּתֵּבוּ׃	9/(10)	10	3	3
2a	לְהַטּוֹת מִדִּין דַּלִּים	7	7	3	3
b	וְלִגְזֹל מִשְׁפַּט עֲנִיֵּי עַמִּי	10	10	4	4
c	לִהְיוֹת אַלְמָנוֹת שְׁלָלָם	8	8	4	4
d	וְאֶת־יְתוֹמִים יָבֹזּוּ׃	8	8	2	2
3a	וּמַה־תַּעֲשׂוּ לְיוֹם פְּקֻדָּה	9	10	3	3
b	וּלְשׁוֹאָה מִמֶּרְחָק תָּבוֹא	8/(9)	9	3	3
c	עַל־מִי תָּנוּסוּ לְעֶזְרָה	8	8	3	3
d	וְאָנָה תַעַזְבוּ כְּבוֹדְכֶם׃	10	10	3	3
4a	בִּלְתִּי כָרַע תַּחַת אַסִּיר	7	8	3	3
b	וְתַחַת הֲרוּגִים יִפֹּלוּ	8	9	3	3
c	בְּכָל־זֹאות לֹא־שָׁב אַפּוֹ	7	7	3	3
d	וְעוֹד יָדוֹ נְטוּיָה׃	7	7	3	3

Notes on Lineation

9:9.   Divided by syntax or parallelism, v. 9 is either 2 or 4 lines. Here we divide the 22 syllables into a tricolon.

9:10.   Retained as a bicolon, but עָלָיו is moved to the following line to create better balance, against even the MT *athnah*.

9:11abc.   This longer bicolon (21 syllables) is divided into a tricolon of 7 syllables per line.

9:12.   What has to remain a bicolon in all other lineations is here divided as a tricolon of 21 syllables.

9:13.   Three lines are retained, but they are arranged as more evenly balanced.

9:15.   A long bicolon (21 syllables) is divided as a tricolon.

9:16abc.   What seems to be a quatrain of shorter and uneven lines is here shown as a more evenly balanced, if slightly long, tricolon (27 syllables).

9:18ab.   Awkward as either a bicolon or a tricolon, these lines are arranged as a rather balanced bicolon, with enjambment.

Summary

62 lines. Using the counts determined in chap 3 (see pp. 66ff. and 76), tabulation is as follows:

5-syllable lines:	1	9-syllable lines:	10
6-syllable lines:	5	10-syllable lines:	9
7-syllable lines:	18	11-syllable lines:	1
8-syllable lines:	18		

29.0% (18 lines) have 8 syllables,
74.2% (46 lines) have 7–9 syllables,
96.8% (60 lines) have 6–10 syllables.

The most common line lengths are 7 and 8 syllables.
The median line length is 8 syllables.
The average line length is 8.00 syllables per line.

Appendix 3

Syllable and Word Counts
for Isaiah 6:1–8:18

			Syllables	Words
Chapter 6	v.	1	35	16
	v.	2	41	17
	v.	3	28	14
	v.	4	22	8
	v.	5	45/46	23
	v.	6	28/29	11
	v.	7	29/32	13
	v.	8	29	14
	v.	9	29/31	13
	v.	10	39/41	18
	v.	11	42	18
	v.	12	20	8
	v.	13	37	15
Total Chapter 6			424–433 syllables	188 words
Chapter 7	v.	1	54/56	25
	v.	2	35/36	17
	v.	3	46/48	21
	v.	4	49/51	20
	v.	5	19/20	10
	v.	6	28/30	11
	v.	7	15	8
	v.	8	27/28	14
	v.	9	28	13
Total 7:1–9			301–312 syllables	139 words
	v.	10	12	6
	v.	11	22/24	11
	v.	12	16	8
	v.	13	26	14
	v.	14	31	15
	v.	15	18/19	8

	v. 16	35/36	16
	v. 17	37/40	20
	v. 18	34	14
	v. 19	34/36	11
	v. 20	41	18
	v. 21	19	9
	v. 22	27/29	14
	v. 23	30	16
	v. 24	20	10
	v. 25	36/37	16

Total 7:10–25	438–450 syllables	206 words

Chapter 8	v. 1	29/31	15
	v. 2	29	11
	v. 3	32	15
	v. 4	32	17

Total 8:1–4	122–124 syllables	58 words

	v. 5	12	6
	v. 6	31	15
	v. 7	52	24
	v. 8	34/35	15

Total 8:5–8	129–130 syllables	60 words

	v. 9	30	11
	v. 10	21	10

Total 8:9–10	51 syllables	21 words

	v. 11	28	13
	v. 12	30	15
	v. 13	21	9
	v. 14	32/35	13
	v. 15	23	7
	v. 16	12	5
	v. 17	21	8
	v. 18	41/42	16

Total 8:11–18	208–212 syllables	86 words

Total 6:1–8:18	1673–1712 syllables	758 words

Appendix 4

Summary of Syllable and Stress Counts

	Pericope	Syllable Counts Range	Total	(MT)	Stress Counts Range	Total	(MT)	Words	Lines
	2:1–4	173–176 = 176		(181)	62–64 = 64		(59)	70	22
	2:5–22	438–440 = 440		(455)	162–165 = 165		(168)	183	55
	3:1–4:1	672–685 = 680		(713)	248–251 = 251		(250)	267	85
	4:2–6	166–172 = 168		(177)	61–62 = 62		(62)	71	21
Subtotal	2:1–4:6	1449–1473 = 1464		(1526)	533–542 = 542		(539)	591	183
	5:1–7	236–241 = 240		(255)	89–91 = 90		(93)	100	30
	5:8–25	494–500 = 496		(532)	200–203 = 200		(207)	218	62
	5:26–30	150–151 = 151		(157)	55–57 = 57		(61)	66	19
Subtotal	5:1–30	880–892 = 887		(944)	344–351 = 347		(361)	384	111
Total	2:1–5:30	2329–2365 = 2351		(2470)	877–893 = 889		(900)	975	294
	8:19–23a	135–137 = 136		(142)	48–50 = 50		(50)	59	17
	8:23b–9:6	239–243 = 240		(258)	90–92 = 90		(92)	108	30
	9:7–10:4	494–501 = 496		(517)	185–185 = 185		(187)	222	62
Subtotal	8:19–10:4	868–881 = 872		(917)	323–327 = 325		(329)	389	109
	10:5–34	818–836 = 824		(876)	310–321 = 310		(321)	357	103
	11:1–16	505–512 = 512		(548)	193–196 = 193		(198)	219	64
	12:1–6	137–148 = 144		(151)	54–55 = 54		(57)	62	18
Subtotal	10:5–12:6	1460–1496 = 1480		(1575)	557–572 = 557		(576)	638	185
Total	8:19–12:6	2328–2377 = 2352		(2492)	880–899 = 882		(905)	1027	294
Grand Total		4657–4742 = 4703		(4962)	1757–1792 = 1771		(1805)	2002	588
Average per line ($\frac{x}{588}$)		7.998		(8.439)	3.012		(3.070)		

Bibliography

Ackroyd, P.
1963   A Note on Isaiah 2:1. *Zeitschrift für die alttestamentliche Wissenschaft* 75: 320.
1978   Isaiah I–XII: Presentation of a Prophet. Pp. 16–48 in *Congress Volume, Göttingen 1977*. Vetus Testamentum Supplements 29. Leiden: Brill.

Alonso–Schökel, L.
1963   *Estudios de poética hebrea*. Barcelona: Juan Flors. = *Das Alte Testament als literarisches Kunstwerk*. Translated by K. Bergner. Köln: Backem, 1971.
1988   *A Manual of Hebrew Poetics*. Rome: Pontifical Biblical Institute.

Alter, R.
1981   *The Art of Biblical Narrative*. New York: Basic Books.
1985   *The Art of Biblical Poetry*. New York: Basic Books.

Andersen, F. I., and Forbes, A. D.
1983   "Prose Particle" Counts of the Hebrew Bible. Pp. 165–83 *The Word of the Lord Shall Go Forth: Essays in Honor of David Noel Freedman in Celebration of His Sixtieth Birthday*, edited by C. Meyers and M. O'Connor. Winona Lake, Indiana: Eisenbrauns.

Andersen, F. I., and Freedman, D. N.
1980   *Hosea*. Anchor Bible 24. Garden City, New York: Doubleday.
1989   *Amos*. Anchor Bible 26. Garden City, New York: Doubleday.

Anderson, B.
1988   "God with Us"—In Judgment and in Mercy: The Editorial Structure of Isaiah 5–10(11). Pp. 230–45 in *Canon, Theology, and Old Testament Interpretation: Essays in Honor of Brevard S. Childs*, edited by G. Tucker, D. Petersen, and R. Wilson. Philadelphia: Fortress.

Avishur, Y.
1984   *Stylistic Studies of Word-Pairs in Biblical and Ancient Semitic Literatures*. Neukirchen-Vluyn: Neukirchener Verlag.

Ball, I.
1987   The Rhetorical Shape of Zephaniah. Pp. 155–65 in *Perspectives on Language and Text: Essays and Poems in Honor of Francis I. Andersen's Sixtieth Birthday, July 28, 1985*, edited by E. Conrad and E. Newing. Winona Lake, Indiana: Eisenbrauns.

Barr, J.
1961   *The Semantics of Biblical Logic*. Oxford: Oxford University Press.

Barth, H.
1977   *Die Jesaja-Worte in der Josiazeit*. Neukirchen-Vluyn: Neukirchener Verlag.

Berlin, A.
1979   Grammatical Aspects of Biblical Parallelism. *Hebrew Union College Annual* 50: 17–43.
1985   *The Dynamics of Biblical Parallelism.* Bloomington: Indiana University Press.
Brinkman, J.
1964   *A Political History of Post-Kassite Babylonia.* Rome: Pontifical Biblical Institute.
1984   *Prelude to Empire.* Occasional Publications of the Babylonian Fund 7. Philadelphia: University Museum of the University of Pennsylvania.
Brownlee, W.
1964   *The Meaning of the Qumran Scrolls for the Bible.* Oxford: Oxford University Press.
Brown, W.
1990   The So-Called Refrain in Isaiah 5:25–30 and 9:7–10:4. *Catholic Biblical Quarterly* 52: 432–43.
Budde, K.
1882   Das hebräische Klagelied. *Zeitschrift für die alttestamentliche Wissenschaft* 2: 1–52.
1922   *Der Segen Moses.* Tübingen: Mohr.
Carr, D.
1993   Reaching for Unity in Isaiah. *Journal for the Study of the Old Testament* 57: 61–80.
Ceresko, A.
1978   The Function of Chiasmus in Hebrew Poetry. *Catholic Biblical Quarterly* 40: 1–10.
Childs, B.
1979   *Introduction to the Old Testament as Scripture.* Philadelphia: Fortress.
Christensen, D.
1984   Two Stanzas of a Hymn in Deuteronomy 33. *Biblica* 65: 382–89.
1985a Prose and Poetry in the Bible: The Narrative Poetics of Deuteronomy 1, 9–18. *Zeitschrift für die alttestamentliche Wissenschaft* 97: 179–89.
1985b The Song of Jonah: A Metrical Analysis. *Journal of Biblical Literature* 104: 217–31.
1991   *Deuteronomy 1–11.* Dallas: Word.
Clements, R.
1980a *Isaiah and the Deliverance of Jerusalem: A Study in the Interpretation of Prophecy in the Old Testament.* Journal for the Study of the Old Testament Supplement Series 13. Sheffield: JSOT Press.
1980b *Isaiah 1–39.* New Century Bible. Grand Rapids, Michigan: Eerdmans.
Clifford, R.
1966   The Use of HOY in the Prophets. *Catholic Biblical Quarterly* 28: 458–64.
Cloete, W. T. W.
1989a *Versification and Syntax in Jeremiah 2–25.* Atlanta: Scholars Press.
1989b The Concept of Meter in Old Testament Studies. *Tydskrif vir Semitistiek* 1: 39–53.
Collins, T.
1978   *Line-Forms in Hebrew Poetry.* Rome: Pontifical Biblical Institute.

Conrad, E.
 1991   *Reading Isaiah.* Minneapolis: Fortress.
Cooper, A.
 1976   *Biblical Poetics: A Linguistic Approach.* Ph.D. Dissertation, Yale University.
Cross, F. M.
 1983   Studies in the Structure of Hebrew Verse: The Prosody of Lamentations 1:1–22. Pp. 129–55 in *The Word of the Lord Shall Go Forth: Essays in Honor of David Noel Freedman in Celebration of His Sixtieth Birthday,* edited by C. L. Meyers and M. O'Connor. Winona Lake, Indiana: Eisenbrauns.
Cross, F. M., and Freedman, D. N.
 1950   *Studies in Ancient Yahwistic Poetry.* Baltimore: Johns Hopkins University Press. = Missoula: Scholars Press, 1975.
Cross, F. M., Freedman, D. N., and Sanders, J. A. (eds.)
 1972   *Scrolls from Qumrân Cave I: The Great Isaiah Scroll, the Order of the Community, the Pesher to Habakkuk, from Photographs by J. C. Trever.* Jerusalem: The Albright Institute of Archaeological Research / Shrine of the Book.
Dahood, M.
 1965   *Psalms I.* Anchor Bible 16. Garden City, New York: Doubleday.
 1968   *Psalms II.* Anchor Bible 17. Garden City, New York: Doubleday.
 1970   *Psalms III.* Anchor Bible 18. Garden City, New York: Doubleday.
Darr, K. P.
 1994   Isaiah's Vision and the Rhetoric of Rebellion. Pp. 847–82 in *Society of Biblical Literature 1994 Seminar Papers.* Society of Biblical Literature Seminar Papers. 33. Atlanta: Scholars Press.
Duhm. B.
 1922   *Das Buch Jesaia.* Göttingen: Vandenhoeck & Ruprecht.
Eichrodt, W.
 1960   *Der Heilige in Israel: Jesaja 1–12.* Die Botschaft des Alten Testaments. Stuttgart: Calwer.
Follis, E. (ed.)
 1987   *Directions in Biblical Hebrew Poetry.* Journal for the Study of the Old Testament Supplement Series 40. Sheffield: Sheffield Academic Press.
Franke, C.
 1994   *Isaiah 46, 47, and 48: A New Literary-Critical Reading.* Biblical and Judaic Studies from the University of California, San Diego 3. Winona Lake, Indiana: Eisenbrauns.
Freedman, D. N.
 1960   Archaic Forms in Early Hebrew Poetry. *Zeitschrift für die alttestamentliche Wissenschaft* 72: 101–7.
 1972a   Acrostics and Metrics in Hebrew Poetry. *Harvard Theological Review* 65: 367–92 (= 1980, pp. 51–76).
 1972b   The Broken Construct Chain. *Biblica* 53:534–36.
 1972c   Prolegomenon. Pp. vii–lvi in G. B. Gray, *The Forms of Hebrew Poetry Considered with Special Reference to the Criticism and Interpretation of the Old Testament.* The Library of Biblical Studies (Reprint of 1915 Edition). New York: Ktav (= 1980, pp. 23–50).

1974   Strophe and Meter in Exodus 15. Pp. 163–203 in *A Light unto My Path: Old Testament Studies in Honor of Jacob M. Myers*, edited by H. N. Bream, R. D. Heim, and C. A. Moore. Gettysburg Theological Studies 4. Pittsburgh: Temple University Press (= 1980 pp. 187–227).

1977   Pottery, Poetry, and Prophecy: An Essay on Biblical Poetry. *Journal of Biblical Literature* 96: 5–26. (= 1980, pp. 1–22)

1980   *Pottery, Poetry, and Prophecy: Studies in Early Hebrew Poetry.* Winona Lake, Indiana: Eisenbrauns.

1983   Discourse on Prophetic Discourse. Pp. 141–58 in *The Quest for the Kingdom of God: Studies in Honor of George E. Mendenhall*, edited by H. Huffmon, F. Spina, and A. Green. Winona Lake, Indiana: Eisenbrauns.

1986   Acrostic Poems in the Hebrew Bible: Alphabetic and Otherwise. *Catholic Biblical Quarterly* 48: 408–31.

1987a   Another Look at Biblical Hebrew Poetry. Pp. 11–28 in *Directions in Biblical Hebrew Poetry*, edited by E. R. Follis, Journal for the Study of the Old Testament Supplement Series 40. Sheffield: JSOT Press.

1987b   Headings in the Books of the Eighth-Century Prophets. *Andrews University Seminary Studies* 25: 9–26.

1987c   The Structure of Isaiah 40:1–11. Pp. 167–93 in *Perspectives on Languages and Text: Essays and Poems in Honor of Francis I. Andersen's Sixtieth Birthday, July 28, 1985*, edited by E. Conrad and E. Newing. Winona Lake, Indiana: Eisenbrauns.

Friedlaender, M. (trans.)

1873   *The Commentary of Ibn Ezra on Isaiah.* New York: Feldheim.

Geller, S.

1979   *Parallelism in Early Biblical Poetry.* Missoula, Montana. Scholars Press.

1982   Theory and Method in the Study of Biblical Poetry. *Jewish Quarterly Review* 73: 65–77.

Gerstenberger, E.

1962   The Woe-Oracles of the Prophets. *Journal of Biblical Literature* 81: 249–63.

Gibson, A.

1981   *Biblical Semantic Logic: A Preliminary Analysis.* Oxford: Blackwell.

Gileadi, A.

1981   *A Holistic Structure of the Book of Isaiah.* Ph.D. Dissertation, Brigham Young University.

Gitay, Y.

1980   A Study of Amos' Art of Speech: A Rhetorical Analysis of Amos 3:1–15. *Catholic Biblical Quarterly* 42: 293–309.

1981   *Prophecy and Persuasion: A Study of Isaiah 40–48.* Bonn: Linguistica Biblica.

1983   Reflections on the Study of the Prophetic Discourse: The Question of Is. 1:2–20. *Vetus Testamentum* 33: 207–21.

1991   *Isaiah and His Audience.* Assen: Van Gorcum.

Goshen-Gottstein, M.

1975   *The Book of Isaiah.* Jerusalem: Magnes.

Gottwald, N.

1962   Hebrew Poetry. Pp. 835–36 in volume 3 of *Interpreter's Dictionary of the Bible.*

Gray, G. B.
   1912   *A Critical and Exegetical Commentary on the Book of Isaiah I–XXVI.* International Critical Commentary. Edinburgh: T. & T. Clark.
   1915   *The Forms of Hebrew Poetry.* New York: Ktav. Reprint, 1972.
Greenstein, E.
   1982   How Does Parallelism Mean? Pp. 41–70 in *A Sense of Text: The Art of Language in the Study of Biblical Literature.* Jewish Quarterly Review Supplement. Philadelphia: Dropsie College.
Hagstrom, D.
   1988   *The Coherence of the Book of Micah: A Literary Analysis.* Atlanta: Scholars Press.
Hayes, J., and Irvine, S.
   1987   *Isaiah, the Eighth-Century Prophet: His Times and His Preaching.* Nashville: Abingdon.
Hillers, D.
   1983   *Hôy* and *Hôy*-Oracles: A Neglected Syntactic Aspect. Pp. 185–88 in *The Word of the Lord Shall Go Forth: Essays in Honor of David Noel Freedman in Celebration of His Sixtieth Birthday,* edited by C. L. Meyers and M. O'Connor. Winona Lake, Indiana: Eisenbrauns.
Holladay, W.
   1976   *The Architecture of Jeremiah 1–20.* Lewisburg, Pennsylvania: Bucknell University Press.
   1978   *Isaiah, Scroll of a Prophetic Heritage.* Grand Rapids, Michigan: Eerdmans.
Hummel, H.
   1957   Enclitic *Mem* in Early Northwest Semitic, Especially Hebrew. *Journal of Biblical Literature* 76: 85–107.
Janzen, W.
   1972   *Mourning Cry and Woe Oracle.* Beihefte zur Zeitschrift für die Alttestamentliche Wissenschaft 125. Berlin: de Gruyter.
Kaiser, O.
   1963   *Der Prophet Jesaja.* Das Alte Testament Deutsch. Göttingen: Vandenhoeck & Ruprecht, 1963, English translation by R. A. Wilson. Old Testament Library. Philadelphia: Westminster, 1972.
   1979   *Der Prophet Jesaja.* Revised Edition. Das Alte Testament Deutsch. Göttingen: Vandenhoeck & Ruprecht. English translation by J. Bowden. Philadelphia: Westminster, 1983.
Kosmala, H.
   1964   Form and Structure in Ancient Hebrew Poetry: A New Approach. *Vetus Testamentum* 14: 423–45.
   1966   Form and Structure in Ancient Hebrew Poetry: A New Approach. *Vetus Testamentum* 16: 152–80.
Kselman, J.
   1977   Semantic-Sonant Chiasm in Biblical Poetry. *Biblica* 58: 219–23.
Kugel, J.
   1981   *The Idea of Biblical Poetry.* New Haven: Yale University Press.
Kurylowicz, J.
   1972   *Studies in Semitic Grammar and Metrics.* Prace Jezykoznaze 67. Wroclaw: Polska Akademia Nauk.

1975   *Metrick und Sprachgeschichte.* Wroclaw: Polska Akademia Nauk.

Lack, R.

1973   *La symbolique du livre d'Isaïe.* Rome: Pontifical Biblical Institute.

Ley, J.

1875   *Grundzüge des Rhythmus, des Vers- und Strophen-baues in der hebräischen Poesie.* Halle.

1886   *Die metrischen Formen der hebräischen Poesie.* Leipzig.

L'Heureux, C.

1984   The Redactional History of Isaiah 5.1–10.4. Pp. 99–119 in *In the Shelter of Elyon: Essays on Ancient Palestinian Life and Literature in Honor of G. W. Ahlström,* edited by W. Boyd Barrick and John R. Spencer. Journal for the Study of the Old Testament Supplement Series 31. Sheffield: JSOT Press.

Liebreich, L.

1956   The Compilation of the Book of Isaiah. *Jewish Quarterly Review* 56: 259–77; 57: 114–38.

Longman, T.

1982   A Critique of Two Recent Metrical Systems. *Biblica* 63: 230–54.

Louw, J.

1982   *Semantics of New Testament Greek.* The Society of Biblical Literature Semeia Studies. Philadelphia: Fortress / Chico, California: Scholars Press.

Lowth, R.

1753   *De sacra poesi Hebraeorum.* Translated by G. Gregory, *Lectures on the Sacred Poetry of the Hebrews.* London: Tegg, 1835.

1778   *Isaiah: A New Translation with a Preliminary Dissertation, and Notes, Critical, Philological, and Explanatory.* Tenth Edition, Boston: Hilliard, 1834, has been used.

Lundbom, J.

1975   *Jeremiah: A Study in Ancient Hebrew Rhetoric.* Society of Biblical Literature Dissertation Series 18. Missoula, Montana: Scholars Press.

Machinist, P.

1983   Assyria and Its Image in the First Isaiah. *Journal of the American Oriental Society* 103: 719–37.

Marshall, R. J.

1962   The Structure of Isaiah 1–12. *Biblical Research* 7: 19–32.

Marti, K.

1900   *Das Buch Isaiah erklärt.* Kurzer Handcommentar zum Alten Testament 10. Tübingen: Mohr.

Melugin, R.

1976   *The Formation of Isaiah 40–55.* Beihefte zur Zeitschrift für die alttestamentliche Wissenschaft 141. Berlin: de Gruyter.

Meyers, C., and O'Connor, M. (eds.)

1983   *The Word of the Lord Shall Go Forth: Essays in Honor of David Noel Freedman in Celebration of His Sixtieth Birthday.* Winona Lake, Indiana: Eisenbrauns.

Moran, W.

1950   The Putative Root ʿtm in Is. 9:18. *Catholic Biblical Quarterly* 12: 153–54.

Muilenburg, J.
    1956   The Book of Isaiah, Chapters 40–66. Pp. 381–773 in volume 5 of *The Interpreter's Bible*. New York: Abingdon.
    1969   Form Criticism and Beyond. *Journal of Biblical Literature* 88: 1–18.
Muraoka, T.
    1985   *Emphatic Words and Structures in Biblical Hebrew*. Leiden: Brill.
O'Connor, M.
    1980   *Hebrew Verse Structure*. Winona Lake, Indiana: Eisenbrauns.
Oesch, J.
    1979   *Petucha und Setuma*. Göttingen: Vandenhoeck & Ruprecht.
Orlin, L., et al.
    1976   *Michigan Oriental Studies in Honor of George G. Cameron*. Ann Arbor: Department of Near Eastern Studies, The University of Michigan.
Oswalt, J.
    1986   *The Book of Isaiah, Chapters 1–39*. Grand Rapids, Michigan: Eerdmans.
Pardee, D.
    1981   Ugaritic and Hebrew Metrics. Pp. 113–30 in *Ugaritic in Retrospect: Fifty Years of Ugarit and Ugaritic*, ed. G. D. Young. Winona Lake, Indiana: Eisenbrauns.
    1988   *Ugaritic and Hebrew Poetic Parallelism*. Leiden: Brill.
Parunak, H.
    1978   *Structural Studies in Ezekiel*. Ph.D. Dissertation, Harvard University.
Polzin, R.
    1977   *Biblical Structuralism: Method and Subjectivity in the Study of Ancient Texts*. Philadelphia: Fortress.
Raabe, P.
    1990   *Psalm-Structures: A Study of Psalms with Refrains*. Sheffield: JSOT Press.
Rendtorff, R.
    1984   Zur Komposition des Buches Jesaja. *Vetus Testamentum* 34: 295–320.
    1989   Jesaja 6 im Rahmen der Komposition des Jesajabuches. Pp. 73–82 in *The Book of Isaiah*, edited by Jacques Vermeylen. Bibliotheca ephemeridum theologicarum lovaniensium 81. Louvain: Louvain University Press.
    1991   The Book of Isaiah: A Complex Unity—Synchronic and Diachronic Reading. Pp. 8–20 in *Society of Biblical Literature 1991 Seminar Papers*. Society of Biblical Literature Seminar Papers 30. Atlanta: Scholars Press.
Schramm, G.
    1976   Poetic Patterning in Biblical Hebrew. Pp. 167–91 in *Michigan Oriental Studies in Honor of George G. Cameron*, edited by L. Orlin et al. Ann Arbor: University of Michigan.
Scott, R. B. Y.
    1956   The Book of Isaiah, Chapters 1–39. Pp. 149–381 in volume 5 of *The Interpreter's Bible*. New York: Abingdon.
    1957   The Literary Structure of Isaiah's Oracles. Pp. 175–86 in *Studies in Old Testament Prophecy*, edited by H. H. Rowley. Edinburgh: T. & T. Clark.
Seeligmann, I.
    1948   *The Septuagint Version of Isaiah: A Discussion of Its Problems*. Leiden: Brill.

Sheppard, G.
  1985   The Anti-Assyrian Redaction and the Canonical Context of Isaiah 1–39. *Journal of Biblical Literature* 104: 193–216.
Seitz, C. R.
  1991   *Zion's Final Destiny*: Minneapolis: Fortress Press.
  1993   *Isaiah 1–39*. Louisville: John Knox Press.
Sievers, E.
  1901   *Metrische Studien*. Volume 1 in *Studien zur hebräischen Metrik*. Leipzig.
  1904   *Metrische Studien*. Volume 2 in *Die hebräischen Genesis*. Leipzig.
Stansell, G.
  1988   *Micah and Isaiah: A Form and Tradition Historical Comparison*. Atlanta: Scholars Press.
Stenning, J. (ed.)
  1949   *The Targum of Isaiah*. Oxford: Clarendon.
Stuart, D.
  1976   *Studies in Early Hebrew Meter*. Missoula, Montana: Scholars Press.
Sweeney, M.
  1988   *Isaiah 1–4 and the Post-Exilic Understanding of the Isaianic Tradition*. Berlin: de Gruyter.
Vermeylen, J.
  1977   *Du prophète Isaïe à l'apocalyptique*. Paris: Gabalda.
Waltke, B., and O'Connor, M.
  1990   *An Introduction to Biblical Hebrew Syntax*. Winona Lake, Indiana: Eisenbrauns.
Wanke, G.
  1966   *ʾwy* und *hwy*. *Zeitschrift für die Alttestamentliche Wissenschaft* 78: 15–18.
Watson, W. G. E.
  1986   *Classical Hebrew Poetry: A Guide to Its Techniques*. Sheffield: JSOT Press.
Watts, J.
  1985   *Isaiah 1–33*. Waco, Texas: Word.
  1987   *Isaiah 34–66*. Waco, Texas: Word.
Westermann, C.
  1960   *Grundformen prophetischer Rede*. Munich: Kaiser.
Wiklander, B.
  1984   *Prophecy as Literature: A Text-Linguistic and Rhetorical Approach to Isaiah 2–4*. Uppsala: Gleerup.
Wildberger, H.
  1972   *Jesaja, 1–12*. Biblischer Kommentar: Altes Testament. Neukirchen-Vluyn: Neukirchener Verlag. English translation by Thomas H. Trapp. *Isaiah 1–12*. Minneapolis: Fortress, 1991.
  1978   *Jesaja, 13–27*. Biblischer Kommentar: Altes Testament. Neukirchen-Vluyn: Neukirchener Verlag.
  1982   *Jesaja, 28–39*. Biblischer Kommentar: Altes Testament. Neukirchen-Vluyn: Neukirchener Verlag.
Willis, J. T.
  1969   The Structure of Micah 3–5 and the Function of Micah 5:9–14. *Zeitschrift für die alttestamentliche Wissenschaft* 81: 191–214.

Wuellner, W.
    1987   Where Is Rhetorical Criticism Taking Us? *Catholic Biblical Quarterly* 49: 448–63.
    1989   *Hermeneutics and Rhetorics.* Scriptura S 3. Stellenbosch: Centre for Hermeneutical Studies.